SUPERVISORY MANAGEMENT

4E

The Art of Empowering and Developing People

DONALD C. MOSLEY, PH.D.
University of South Alabama

LEON C. MEGGINSON, PH.D.
University of Mobile

PAUL H. PIETRI, D.B.A.
University of South Alabama

SOUTH-WESTERN College Publishing

An International Thomson Publishing Company

Editor-in-Chief: Valerie A. Ashton
Acquisitions Editor: Randy G. Haubner
Developmental Editor: Alice C. Denny
Production Editor: Shelley Brewer
Production House: Litten Editing and Production with Shepard Poorman Communications
Cover and Internal Designer: Craig LaGesse Ramsdell
Cover Photograph: © Charles M. Murray/Westlight
Photo Research/Internal Photos: Ferrett Research/Mary Goljenboom
Photo Research/Chapter Opener Photos: Alix Roughen
Cartoon Illustrations: Boston Graphics, Inc.
Marketing Manager: Stephen E. Momper

Library of Congress Cataloging-in-Publication Data:

Mosley, Donald C.
    Supervisory management : the art of empowering and developing
people / Donald C. Mosley, Leon C. Megginson, Paul H. Pietri, Jr.—
4th ed.
        p.   cm.
    Includes bibliographical references and index.
    ISBN 0-538-85560-6 (hc : alk. paper)
    1. Personnel management.   2. Supervision of employees.
I. Megginson, Leon C.   II. Pietri, Paul H.   III. Title.
HF5549.M667   1997
658.3'02—dc20   96-24986
                                                            CIP

1 2 3 4 5 6 7 8 9 PR 4 3 2 1 0 9 8 7 6
Printed in the United States of America

I(T)P

International Thomson Publishing
South-Western College Publishing is an ITP Company.
The ITP trademark is used under license.

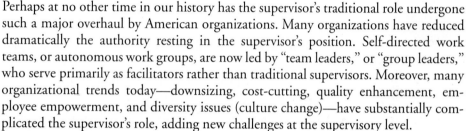

Perhaps at no other time in our history has the supervisor's traditional role undergone such a major overhaul by American organizations. Many organizations have reduced dramatically the authority resting in the supervisor's position. Self-directed work teams, or autonomous work groups, are now led by "team leaders," or "group leaders," who serve primarily as facilitators rather than traditional supervisors. Moreover, many organizational trends today—downsizing, cost-cutting, quality enhancement, employee empowerment, and diversity issues (culture change)—have substantially complicated the supervisor's role, adding new challenges at the supervisory level.

As one CEO told us, supervisors function where "the rubber meets the road." It is direct interface with operating employees that captures the essence of supervisory management, whether it be within the culture of a self-managing work team environment or a more traditional one. Supervisory management is working through people to develop and empower them. That is the theme of this fourth edition.

To ensure that this fourth edition meets your changing needs as a supervision instructor, we asked you, through an extensive market research study, to identify the key competencies that produce exceptional supervisors. Thanks to an overwhelming response, we learned, among other competencies, that students need practical supervisory skills to help them manage complex situations. As you will see from the outline for this new edition, we have addressed your concerns by providing the most relevant supervision product available today.

This new edition of *Supervisory Management: The Art of Empowering and Developing People* focuses on the contemporary issues of today's workplace. We have added more practical skill-building features to enhance the development of better supervisors. Particular attention has been given to providing activities to meet the SCANS requirements.

WHAT'S NEW IN THE FOURTH EDITION?

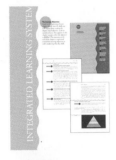

A number of changes have been made to keep the fourth edition a fast-paced, relevant, skill-based text. New pedagogical features and overall text improvements that more accurately reflect supervisory management in today's business world are introduced.

- **Integrated Teaching/Learning System.** The text and supplements are organized around the learning objectives presented at the beginning of each chapter. Numbered icons identify the objectives and appear next to the material throughout the text and Instructor's Manual where each objective is fulfilled. When students need further review to meet a certain objective, they can quickly identify the relevant material by simply looking for the icon. This integrated structure creates a comprehensive teaching and testing system.

- **Skill-Development Scenario Videos** consist of good and poor supervisory situations to serve as skill-based examples for your students. Scenarios are offered for ten of the eighteen chapters.

- **BusinessLink Video Case Studies** highlight real companies with real supervisory issues to provoke student discussion and encourage critical thinking. These professional-quality videos, produced by instructors, bring the real world into your classroom.

- **New Four-Color format.** The fourth edition has a new full-color layout with more photos and illustrations to capture your students' attention. This easy-to-follow format will improve student comprehension.

- **Three new chapters,** Quest for Quality and Empowerment (Chapter 2), Coaching for Higher Performance (Chapter 13), and Facilitation Skills, Managing Conflict and Stress (Chapter 15), place the text at the cutting edge of today's trends.

- **New coverage** has been added on contemporary topics, such as self-managing work teams; transformational and transactional leadership; the concept of partnering; newer organizational forms such as the wagon wheel, inverted pyramid and network; motivating a diverse work force; dealing with ineffective employees; facilitation skills; and human resource issues involving sexual harassment, drug testing, comparable worth (or pay equity), and affirmative action.

- **Updated coverage** throughout the text reflects current trends and developments, such as downsizing, employee diversity, AIDS and substance abuse, and the role of the computer.

- **Ten new chapter opening cases** represent a cross-section of organizational contexts in manufacturing, service, governmental, and small entrepreneurial organizations.

- **End-of-chapter activities** consist of cases and Skill-Builder experiential exercises, 23 of which are new to this edition. In capturing the spirit of the team concept in organizations, each chapter contains a new learning exercise which can serve as a student group activity. These activities are highlighted by a special icon.

MEETING THE SCANS REQUIREMENTS

In 1992, the U.S. Department of Labor published the report of the Secretary's Commission on Achieving Necessary Skills (SCANS). The commission was formed to encourage a high-performance economy characterized by high-skills, high-wage employment. To help achieve this goal, the commission report identifies five workplace competencies and a three-part foundation of skills and personal qualities needed for job performance. These eight requirements are essential preparation for all students, those moving directly into the work force and those planning further education. The competencies identified by the SCANS study are applicable from the shop floor to the executive suite, in large and small organizations, and in service and goods-producing environments.

According to SCANS, the competencies and the foundation skills should be taught and understood in an integrated fashion that reflects the workplace contexts in which they are applied. The new edition of *Supervisory Management* fosters that integrated approach and provides information, cases, and skill-builder exercises aimed at satisfying, directly or indirectly, many of the stated requirements.

FEATURES OF THE BOOK

Designed to facilitate understanding and retention of the material presented, each chapter contains the following:

- Each chapter begins with a statement of **Learning Objectives**. Icons for identifying the learning objectives appear throughout the text material. The Chapter Review is also organized by the learning objectives.
- An **Opening Case** example illustrates a major topic to be covered in the chapter.

empowerment Granting authority to employees to make key decisions within their areas of responsibility.

- **Key terms and phrases** highlight the management vocabulary introduced in each chapter. Definitions are also highlighted in notes that appear in the margin. Key terms are also listed at the end of the chapter, and appear in the glossary at the end of the text.

- **Self-Check** questions allow students to check their understanding of concepts and improve their study routines. They also act as a simplified self-study guide, covering all supervisory topics within the text.

Workplace Competencies Effective Workers Can Productively Use:	Examples	Areas of Detailed Coverage
Resources	Allocating time, money, materials, space, and staff.	Skill Builders 8-1, 8-2, and 16-1
Interpersonal Skills	Working on teams, teaching others, serving others, serving customers, leading, negotiating and working well with people from culturally diverse backgrounds.	Chapters 14 & 15 and Skill Builders 8-4, 9-1, 10-2, 11-2, 11-3, 12-1, 13-1, 13-2, 14-1, 14-2, 15-1, 15-2, and 18-1
Information	Acquiring and evaluating data, organizing and maintaining files, interpreting and communicating, using computers to process information.	Chapter 12 and Skill Builder 12-2
Systems	Understanding social, organizational, and technological systems, monitoring and correcting performance, and designing or improving systems.	Chapter 12 and Skill Builders 3-2, 8-1, 11-1, 11-2, 11-3, 12-2, 12-3, 13-1, 13-3, 14-3, and 17-1
Technology	Selecting equipment and tools, applying technology to specific tasks, and maintaining and trouble-shooting technologies.	Since the text is directed to managerial skill development, direct skill-based activities are not included.

Foundation Skills Competent Workers in a High-Performance Workplace Need:	Examples	Areas of Detailed Coverage
Basic Skills	Reading, writing, arithmetic and mathematics, speaking and listening.	Chapters 7 and 12, productivity measurements, and Chapter 13 and Skill Builders 7-1, 8-3, and 13-2
Thinking Skills	Thinking creatively, making decisions, solving problems, seeing things in the mind's eye, knowing how to learn, and reasoning.	End-of-chapter cases 1-1, 2-1, 3-1, 8-1, 9-1, 10-1, 11-1, 12-1, 15-1, 16-1, 17-1, 17-2, 18-1 and Skill Builders 1-1, 2-1, 2-2, 8-4, 9-2, 10-2, 15-1, 16-1, and 18-1
Personal Qualities	Individual responsibility, self-esteem, sociability, self-management, and integrity.	Skill Builders 1-2, 3-1, 3-2, 15-3, 15-4, 16-2, 17-1, and 18-2

- **Questions for Review and Discussion** at the end of each chapter assist learning by encouraging the reader to review and reflect on the chapter objectives.

- **Skill Builder exercises** appear at the end of each chapter; many of them relate to the SCANS requirements followed by many schools. A special icon designates exercises that involve teams or collaborative activities.

- **Cases** also located at the end of each chapter can be used to synthesize the chapter concepts and simulate the practice of supervision.

ORGANIZATION OF THE TEXT

The text retains the traditional functional (supervisory) management framework while emphasizing the skills which supervisors need in order to succeed in today's organizations.

Part I, Overview, consists of two chapters that set the stage for the rest of the book. Chapter 1 begins with the role that supervisors play and addresses some of the significant trends affecting supervision. Chapter 2, a new chapter to this edition, focuses on the newer processes of empowerment and quality that drive many organizational processes today.

Part II, Planning, focuses on the fundamentals of planning, time management, and decision-making/problem-solving processes.

Part III, Organizing, deals with the fundamentals of organizing and delegating authority.

Part IV, Leading, is the book's longest part, addressing communicating with and motivating employees and providing leadership. New to this part is a chapter on team building and managing change.

Part V, Controlling, zeros in on the controlling process and the supervisor's role in controlling productivity, quality, and safety.

Part VI, Skill Development, targets critical supervisory skills required for success in the environment of the late 90s: coaching for higher performance, managing group dynamics and conducting meetings, facilitating, and managing conflict and stress.

Finally, Part VII, Managing Human Resources and Diversity, discusses selecting, training and compensating employees, appraising and disciplining employees, and labor relations.

INSTRUCTIONAL RESOURCES

Instructor's Manual

Supervisory Management
The Art of Empowering and Developing People

Mosley, Megginson, Pietri   4e

Supervisory Management is accompanied by comprehensive instructional support materials.

Instructor's Manual. The instructor's manual (ISBN: 0538-85563-0) provides resources to increase the teaching and learning value of *Supervisory Management.* The manual was prepared by M. Jane Byrd, Donna J. Counselman, and Janet M. Wharton under the guidance of text author Leon C. Megginson. For each text chapter, the manual provides an outline and lecture notes, answers to the end-of-chapter questions and Skill-Builders, responses to case questions, and notes for the video materials. The manual also includes the transparency masters noted in the lecture outline. The test bank portion contains multiple choice questions, true/false questions, and essay questions for each chapter. There is also a chart that shows how questions are coordinated with the chapter learning objectives.

Computerized Test Package. The examinations presented in the manual are also available on disk with the test generator program, MicroExam 4.0 (ISBN: 0538-85565-7). This versatile software package allows instructors to create new questions and edit and delete existing questions from the test bank.

Videos. There are two videos that accompany the new edition of the text. One video (ISBN: 0538-85566-5) contains ten skill-development scenarios. The relevant text chapters contain discussion questions that will allow the instructor to incorporate the scenarios in classroom discussions.

The second video (ISBN: 0538-86754-X) contains BusinessLink video case studies. These interactive videos, professionally developed by instructors, involve real companies and contain critical thinking questions that will provide an excellent forum for classroom analysis. These videos are the first of their kind offered for the supervision course. Written cases will accompany the videos; they can be ordered free as a supplement to the text.

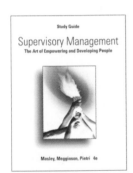

Study Guide. The study guide (ISBN: 0538-85561-4) that accompanies the fourth edition of *Supervisory Management* will be a real asset for your students. It is designed to ensure that they understand and retain important supervision skills. For each text chapter, the study guide includes an overview, the objectives, an expanded study outline, and review questions and activities. The study guide was prepared by M. Jane Byrd and Suzanne S. Barnhill to carefully augment the text.

ACKNOWLEDGMENTS

A number of people played key roles in making the important changes in this new edition. The following reviewers contributed greatly:

Daniel Bialas
Muskegon Community College

Michael Cicero
Highline Community College

Linda Clark
Maple Woods Community College

Sam Dunbar
Delgado Community College

Tommy Gilbreath
The University of Texas at Tyler

Kenneth L. Lehmann
Forsyth Technical College

Michael McClymonds
College of Southern Idaho

Lloyd R. McLachlan
Ivy Tech

A. Ally Mishal
Stark Technical College

Lee Munson
Santa Rosa Junior College

Deniz S. Ones
University of Houston

Robert Redick
Lincoln Land Community College

Michael D. Rogers
Albany State College

H. Giles Schmid
Winona State University

Charles C. Quinn
Austin Community College

Rosemary Fittje was our unifying agent interfacing directly with the editor, putting our material into printed manuscript form, and keeping us on schedule. Her contributions, including securing permissions, were critical to completion of this project. Additional typing support was provided by Jo Megginson, Kay Emanuel, and Suzanne Barnhill.

We appreciate the efforts of the Marketing/Management Team at South-Western College Publishing who helped to develop and produce this text. They include Randy Haubner, Acquisitions Editor; Alice Denny, Developmental Editor; Shelley Brewer, Production Editor; Pamela Person, Associate Marketing Manager. Others who contributed include Mike Stratton, Designer at South-Western; Jennifer Mayhall, Photo Manager; and at Litten Editing and Production, Malvine Litten, Project Manager.

We also acknowledge our colleagues and administrators, especially Carl Moore, Dean of the College of Business and Management Studies, and Dr. Edward Harrison, Chair of the Department of Management, at the University of South Alabama. We also wish to thank Dr. Michael Magnoli, President, Dr. Audrey Eubanks, Academic Vice President, and Dr. Anne Lowery, Interim Dean of the School of Business, University of Mobile. Our families were patient and encouraging throughout.

As with our other three editions, the fourth edition of *Supervisory Management: The Art of Empowering and Developing People* is dedicated to the thousands of supervisors and managers we've worked with through the years from manufacturing companies, hospitals, banks, public service companies, governmental organizations, and other groups requiring supervision. Their comments and feedback continue to keep us in touch with the real challenges of supervisory life.

Donald C. Mosley
Leon C. Megginson
Paul H. Pietri, Jrsa.

The Learning Objectives

listed at the beginning of every chapter briefly state the skills you will acquire from reading the chapter. Each objective, with its numbered icon, then appears in the chapter margin where the objective is fulfilled. The summary at the end of the chapter is organized around the learning objectives as well, reinforcing these key skills.

Case 8

The Demotivating Environment

A new president of a large, public utility firm in a southern state was concerned because his firm was not performing anywhere near its potential effectiveness. The new president believed one of the problems was that the management system was under a traditional command-and-control approach and needed to shift to a more participative, team approach. Accordingly, he contacted a management consulting firm that had an excellent reputation in facilitating an organization's culture to change toward a participative team approach.

The consulting firm's plan was to conduct a research diagnosis phase by surveying a large sample of employees and customers through questionnaires and interviews. Once the diagnosis phase was completed, the plan called for a series of training programs during which managers, supervisors, and key employees were trained in participative management concepts such as team building, leadership, coaching, and empowerment.

After the training programs were completed, the plan called for the formation of ad hoc teams to develop solutions to priority issues and problems identified in the research and diagnosis phase.

Shortly after the consulting firm started to work, it informed the president that the pay and reward system now in effect was in opposition to the planned participative team approach. They discovered that seven years prior, the former president had brought in another consulting firm to study their compensation program. This firm recommended a pay system whereby each employee was evaluated by his supervisor and placed in a normal distribution of all employees of the firm. Each year, money available for raises was distributed based on one's placement in the normal distribution ranking. The recommended pay system was implemented, and the percentage in each category is shown graphically in Exhibit 8–1.

At the meeting with the new president the just-hired consulting firm indicated the pay and reward system was causing serious morale problems. During the interviews, many employees, including a number ranked in the top fifty percent, perceived the system as unfair and creating an environment of dysfunctional competition rather than a climate of cooperation and teamwork. Moreover, the way the system worked, the top management of the firm evaluated and placed ... normal distribution first. Invariably they placed their ...tegories of the distribution, and lower levels were ...g placements.

...ly agreed with the consultants that the pay system and ...company culture were incompatible. It was decided that ... research/diagnosis and training phase, an ad hoc task ...consultants and provide recommendations to the president ... pay and reward system.

215

LEARNING OBJECTIVES
After reading and studying this chapter, you should be able to:

1 Understand and explain Maslow's hierarchy of needs theory.

2 Understand and explain Herzberg's theory of motivation.

3 Explain the supervisor's role in helping employees achieve satisfaction of their needs.

4 State the relationship among money, motivation, and the expectancy theory.

5 Define and explain other theories of motivation, such as equity, positive reinforcement, and goal-setting theories.

6 Explain motivational practices in the best-managed companies.

---

236   **Part 4   Leading**

Chapter Review

Learning Objective 1
Understand and explain Maslow's hierarchy of needs theory.
The principles underlying Maslow's theory of a hierarchy of needs are that needs are arranged in a hierarchy of importance and that, once a need has been satisfied, it is no longer a primary motivator. The lower-level needs include physiological, security, and social needs, and the higher-level needs are esteem and self-fulfillment.

Learning Objective 2
Understand and explain Herzberg's theory of motivation.
Herzberg's research discovered that motivators are those factors that have an uplifting effect on attitudes or performance, whereas hygiene factors are those factors that prevent serious dissatisfaction but do not motivate by themselves. The motivators are achievement, recognition, the work itself, responsibility, and advancement. The hygiene factors are company policy and administration, supervision, relationship with the supervisor, working conditions, and pay. The motivators relate to the two highest levels of the Maslow hierarchy, self-fulfillment and esteem. Hygiene factors relate to lower-level needs, especially the security needs. Although pay is listed as a hygiene factor, it becomes a motivator when it is directly related to achievement and/or recognition.

Learning Objective 3
Explain the supervisor's role in helping employees achieve satisfaction of their needs.
The supervisor plays a major role in whether or not an employee's needs are met. Our opening quote by Sydney Harris highlights this fact. If ... finding environment, there is a climate of demotivation ... security and self-esteem needs: a climate of positive recogni... provides a motivating climate. If there is a climate in which ... to achieve agreed-upon goals and are rewarded according... ees' needs and expectancies are met.

Learning Objective 4
State the relationship among money, motivation, and expect...
An example of money becoming a motivator is gainsharin... related to achievement, increased responsibility, and effe...

The expectancy theory of motivation states that wor... resulting in effective performance, to be followed by a re... not met, employees can be demotivated. Equity theory ... acknowledges that employees will consider how their o... rewarded as compared to other employees'. If, for examp... men are making more for comparable work and perform... demotivating—and even lead to a lawsuit.

Learning Objective 5
Define and explain other theories of motivation, such as equ... and goal-setting theories.
The positive reinforcement theory of motivation is base... supervisor provides praise and perhaps positive salary ... performance, this will tend to encourage continued good ...

Goal-setting theory undergirds the other motivational... ting of difficult but attainable goals. The ideal cause-and-... vating employees is found in Exhibit 8–13.

Chapter 8   Motivation   **217**

most people behave irrationally and unpredictably. They would argue that, if more people understood the *why* of human behavior, other people's behavior would seem more rational and predictable.

Since the 1960s, much research has been done on the behavior of people at work. Some significant theories have been developed that are important to anyone in a position of leadership who wants to avoid unnecessary friction arising from human relationships in the organization. We will discuss some of these theories of motivation and see how they relate to supervision.

Some students do not enjoy studying theory because they believe it is abstract and unrelated to the real world. Actually, whatever the discipline, a sound theory provides a basis for understanding, explaining, and predicting what will happen in the real world. Kurt Lewin, famous for his work in the study of groups, once said that nothing is more *practical* than good theory.[1] For a person of action, such as a supervisor who has to work with and through people, an understanding of motivation theory is essential.

MASLOW'S HIERARCHY OF NEEDS THEORY

Learning Objective 1
Understand and explain Maslow's hierarchy of needs theory

One theory that is particularly significant and practical was developed by psychologist Abraham H. Maslow.[2] This theory is known as the hierarchy of needs. Of all motivation theories, it is probably the one best known by managers.

Principles Underlying the Theory

hierarchy of needs
Arrangement of people's needs in a hierarchy, or ranking of importance.

The two principles underlying Maslow's **hierarchy of needs** theory are that (1) people's needs may be arranged in a hierarchy, or ranking of importance, and (2) once a need has been satisfied, it no longer serves as a primary motivator of behavior. To understand the significance of these principles to Maslow's theory, let us examine the hierarchy of needs shown in Exhibit 8–2.

Exhibit 8–2
Maslow's Hierarchy of Needs

Self-Fulfillment or Self-Actualization

Ego or Esteem

Social or Belonging

Safety or Security

Physiological or Biological

The authors are firmly convinced that nothing is so practical as good theory. We are also convinced that the leading contributors to good management theory are professors whose laboratories are the real world of organizations and people. We were greatly influenced by role models, including Professor/Consultants Dr. Douglas McGregor and Dr. Rensis Likert.

While we cannot hope to make the contributions of these giants, we think our active involvement in the real world as consultants/facilitators/change agents has been a primary reason our book is one of the leaders in the supervisory field and is now entering its fourth edition.

Donald C. Mosley. At the present time, Donald C. Mosley is professor of management at the University of South Alabama and also the founder and president of the Synergistic Consulting Group. Don and the Synergistic Group have been pioneers in the area of partnering, having designed and developed the original "partnering model" in the first formalized partnering workshop in the public sector. This model has been adopted throughout the United States and used internationally as well.

In the 1960s, as a young professor/consultant, Mosley developed his skills by being instrumental in helping a financially plagued chemical plant become the most profitable plant in the company's division within one year. During this period he was one of the first to utilize 360-degree evaluations by peers, work team members, and bosses as a basis for providing feedback and coaching for key managers.

Paul H. Pietri. Paul Pietri brings a wealth of knowledge of the supervisory field based on his over 25 years' experience as a trainer/consultant to private and public sector organizations. He has developed and conducted training designs in over 35 states for well over 5,000 supervisors from organizations such as International Paper Company, U.S. Department of Agriculture, Dupont, and others. Because of his extensive background in supervisory training, Pietri was chosen as one of seven U.S. team members to attend a Sao Paulo, Brazil, conference aimed at assisting Brazil's development of first- and mid-level managers. "Supervisors need and want answers to everyday, practical problems," Pietri feels. "A supervisory management textbook should employ, where possible, a strong hands-on approach that addresses real world issues and situations. I believe also that a good text emphasizes the practical, skills-oriented side of supervision throughout the entire text, not just in special applications tossed in at the end of a chapter."

Since 1986 Pietri has been actively involved in course design and training for Bowater Carolina, helping the company shift from a traditional, authority-based organizational culture towards one that emphasizes empowerment, teamwork, and quality. "Supervisors are especially strained and play a pivotal role in such change," he states. "The new culture entails a dramatic turnaround from the traditional way of managing that these supervisors practiced and were encouraged to practice in the past. These challenges—learning the new skills of empowering, facilitating, coaching, and managing conflict, to name a few—are being made to supervisors from all types of organizations throughout the country."

Leon Megginson. Leon Megginson has over ten years of managerial experience in the world of academics, practicing many of the skills found in our book. He served two years as associate dean of the business school at LSU and was chairman and dean of the school of business at the University of Mobile for eight years. He also served as operations officer of a squadron of over 100 pilots and airmen in the 25th Bomb Squad, U.S. Air Force, during WW II. He was a Fulbright Research Scholar in Spain during the 1960s and was a Ford Foundation Advisor in Pakistan, assisting the Pakistani in the area of management development.

BRIEF CONTENTS

CONTENTS

PART 2
PLANNING

PART 4
LEADING

PART 7
MANAGING HUMAN RESOURCES AND DIVERSITY

UNION PRINCIPLES, OBJECTIVES, AND
METHODS OF ATTAINING OBJECTIVES   515

LIVING WITH THE AGREEMENT   525

Chapter 1
Supervisory Management Roles and Challenges

Case 1

James Medlin: New-Style Supervisor

Supervisor James (Jamie) Medlin has worked at Bowater Inc.'s Carolina Division in Catawba, South Carolina, for 16 years. He became a full-time employee of the company, a leading paper manufacturer, after completing his liberal arts studies at nearby Winthrop College. His entry position was utility worker in the maintenance department, which entailed cleaning the shop area and equipment and doing odds and ends. He had previously worked in the same position during summer breaks from college.

Medlin held various utility and helper positions for six years. Then, in 1984, he served a stint as a temporary supervisor during one of the company's major equipment rebuilds. Shortly thereafter, he was chosen to receive special training in the use of Honeywell equipment. Then it was back to maintenance work! Several months later, he worked on the addition of a new paper mill, pulp mill, and woodyard, where he was a liaison between the company and the contractor. In 1986, he was made responsible for the plantwide upkeep of the Honeywell system. His next promotion came in June 1990, when he became foreman of an instrumentation crew of 12 mechanics and apprentices, charged with providing maintenance of electrical equipment and instruments used in the power and pulp mill departments.

Medlin's latest promotion was in July 1993, when he was made responsible for overseeing instrument and distribution control system maintenance millwide. The relationship of Medlin's unit to the organization is shown in Exhibit 1–1.

Medlin's workday actually begins near the end of the workday for production employees. He reviews the work that has been done that day and notes the progress made. He knows what work has been scheduled for the next day and leaves work with an idea of how to assign his employees to do it.

He arrives the next morning at 6:45 and strolls through the pulp area—chatting with incoming pulp supervisors, taking note of their needs. He then phones the powerhouse (which is too far away to reach quickly on foot) and discusses any emergency or pressing needs not already scheduled. Next, he makes out his schedule for the day and plans for his morning crew meeting.

At 7:30 a.m., his crew arrives. During the morning's meeting, Medlin listens to their reports on the previous day's work and progress, talks about safety, and outlines the day's job assignments.

Medlin's duties encompass a wide range of activities, including daily job planning and assignment, monitoring work progress through daily visits, and responding to emergency requests that demand immediate attention. He purchases equipment and tools, completes cost reports, and is heavily involved in safety, including publishing the department's safety newsletter. He also completes the department's monthly cost report and serves on several company committees.

Medlin's job requires him to interact with many people, especially his crew and his "customers"—the managers in the pulp and power departments whose equipment the crew services. He also spends time with his boss—the assistant superintendent—and with outside vendors: "It's a way to keep up with what's new in my area," he says. Occasionally, when a disciplinary problem crops up, he deals

LEARNING OBJECTIVES
After reading and studying this chapter, you should be able to:

1 Explain why management is needed in all organizations.

2 Describe the different levels of management.

3 Discuss what managers do.

4 Explain the basic skills required for effective management.

5 Discuss the improving position of supervisory managers.

6 Clarify the different relationships supervisory managers have with others.

7 Discuss some trends challenging supervisors.

with the union representative. He is increasingly spending more time seeing suppliers and performing administrative functions.

Bowater's management has moved strongly toward a team-oriented atmosphere in which hourly personnel assume greater responsibility for their own work. As part of the plant's Carolina Quality II Process, all employees will eventually be trained in the team approach and assigned to a continuous quality improvement team. Medlin's views of his supervisory role seem to fit well with this process:

> **I view my role as a supervisor as being a resource to my crew. My people can make or break me, so I'm not going to smother them by looking over their shoulders and trying to detail everything they do. They are highly trained and have better technical expertise than I do in the instrumentation area. I like to hand them a project and let them go out and perform. But I want them to let me know when they run into a problem or get stumped. I'm there to help. I'll get some help from another department, or I'll dig out a reference manual or call the manufacturer; I'll get some action.**

Medlin feels that college helped him prepare for his career in many ways.

> **Regardless of your major, you learn about resources, where to look for—and how to find—answers. When I had a problem and no answers, there were resources, including my instructors and the library. I'd come up with a plan to get some answers. This kind of thinking is exactly what's involved in being a supervisor. I certainly don't have all the answers to problems, but there are resources around me that I can use. A supervisor can't be paralyzed by not having answers—he's got to come up with plans to get them.**

Medlin continues to advance his own knowledge and skills. He is presently taking evening classes toward a second degree—this time in business administration. He aspires to higher-level management positions and believes the business studies will help him prepare for them.

Bowater is fortunate to have supervisory managers like James Medlin. Such supervisors are largely responsible for making the company one of the world's leading paper manufacturers.

Source: Reprinted with permission of Bowater Inc.

Supervisors are linking pins who are members of, and link or lock together, independent groups within an organization.

Rensis Likert

This case illustrates how the supervisor's role has substantially changed in recent years. In the past, supervisors were expected to be the technical experts who knew all the answers to production and distribution problems. Now, they are coaches who lead and empower team members. The case also describes some of the fundamental aspects of the supervisory manager's job and some of the changes and challenges supervisors now face.

Although technical knowledge is increasingly important, members of a current work crew may know far more than the supervisor about some subjects, as James Medlin would readily admit. Now, though, more than ever, the concern of supervisors is to assist their people—to help them perform their jobs more effectively. Today's

Exhibit 1–1
Partial Organization Chart of Bowater Inc.'s Carolina Division

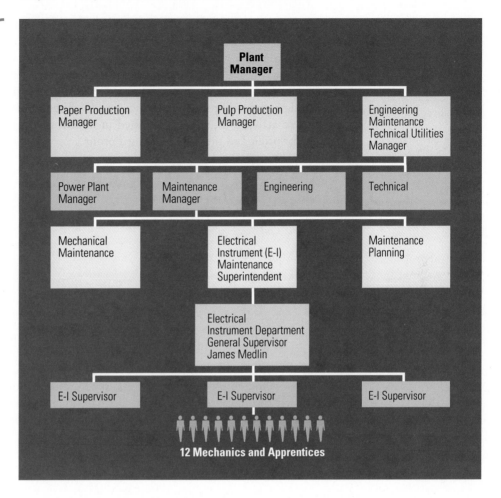

supervisors are generalists rather than specialists, and they need even greater abilities, training, and experience.

The case also indicates some of the roles played—and functions performed—by supervisors and suggests some of the relationships that supervisors have with others. Supervisors also use many skills in dealing with a diverse work force, technological developments, and economic changes.

Finally, the case indicates some of the challenges facing supervisors as they try to cope with a rapidly changing environment. Bowater's move to teams, for example, demonstrates the kind of widespread change happening in organizations across the country. There is a great need for capable supervisors to fulfill the challenging job of being part of supervisory management.

THE NEED FOR MANAGEMENT

Learning Objective 1

Explain why management is needed in all organizations.

Whenever a group of people work together in a structured situation to achieve a common objective, they form an **organization.** That organization may be a student group, a business firm, a religious group, a governmental institution, a military unit, a sports team, or a similar group. The main objective of such organizations is to

organization A group of people working together in a structured situation for a common objective.

operations Producing an organization's product or service.

distribution Marketing and distributing an organization's product or service.

financing Providing or using funds to produce and distribute an organization's product or service.

produce a product or provide a service. Other organizational objectives may be to provide satisfaction to members, employment and benefits to workers, a product to the public, and/or a return to the owners of the business (usually in the form of a profit). To reach these objectives, management must perform three basic organizational activities. These are (1) **operations,** or producing the product, (2) **distribution,** or marketing and distributing the product, and (3) **financing,** or providing and using funds. These activities must be performed in almost all organizations—both those operating for profit and those not seeking a profit.

What Is Management?

Organizations are the means by which people get things done. People form organizations simply because they can accomplish more working together than they can achieve alone. But to combine and coordinate the efforts of the members of the organization, the process of management is required. Without management, people in the group would go off on their own and try to reach the organization's objectives independently of other group members. If small organizations lacked management, the members' efforts would be wasted. If management were absent in the larger, more complex organizations, objectives would not be reached and chaos would result. In summary, *managers are found everywhere.*

Management is the process of working with people, the human resources of an organization, to make decisions and achieve objectives.

SELF-CHECK
What managers have you come in contact with during the past week—either in person or on the phone, TV, or radio? What were their titles? At what level in their organization were they? What were some of their job responsibilities?

management Working with people to achieve objectives by effective decision making and coordination of available resources.

human resources The people an organization requires for operatons.

physical resources Items an organization requires for operations.

financial resources The money, capital, and credit an organization requires for operations.

Management can be defined as the process of working with and through people to achieve objectives by means of effective decision making and coordination of available resources. The basic resources of any organization are **human resources,** which are the people involved; **physical resources,** which include buildings, furnishings, machinery, equipment, tools, materials, and supplies; and **financial resources,** such as money, capital, and credit.

The term *management* is also used to describe the people within the organization who are responsible for making decisions and coordinating available resources and activities. In this sense, *management* and *managers* mean the same thing. Exhibit 1–2 shows *the vital task of management: combining resources and activities into a productive system to attain organizational objectives.*

Exhibit 1–2
How Management Combines the Organization's Resources Into a Productive System

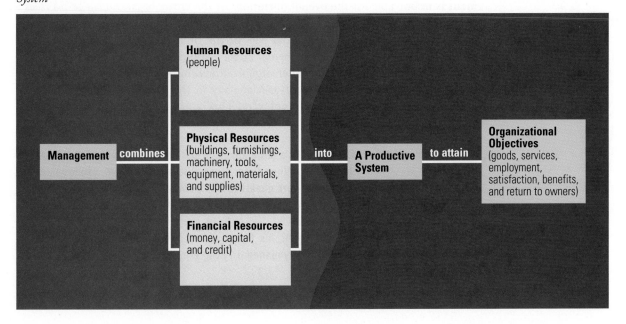

Levels of Management

Learning Objective 2

Describe the different levels of management.

authority The right to tell others how to act to reach objectives.

responsibility The obligation of an employee to accept a manager's delegated authority.

Except in very small organizations, there are usually different levels of management based on the amount of responsibility and authority required to perform the job. Individuals at higher levels of the organization have more authority and responsibility than those at lower levels. **Authority** is the right to tell others to act or not act in order to reach objectives. **Responsibility** is the obligation that is created when an employee accepts a manager's delegated authority.

Large organizations usually have at least three levels of management, plus a level of operative employees. These levels are generally referred to as (1) *top management,* (2) *middle management,* and (3) *supervisory management.* In a very large organization, there may be many more levels.

SELF-CHECK

In Case 1, for example, how many levels of management exist at the Bowater plant?

top management Responsible for a major segment of the organization.

middle management Responsible for a substantial part of the organization.

supervisory management Controls operations of smaller organizational units.

Exhibit 1–3 shows that authority and responsibility increase as one moves from the nonmanagerial level into the managerial ranks and then into the higher managerial levels. The titles and designations listed are only a few of those actually used in organizations.

Although the duties and responsibilities of the various management levels vary from one organization to another, they may be summarized as follows. **Top management** is responsible for the overall operations of the entire organization or oversees a major segment of the organization or a basic organizational activity. **Middle management** is responsible for a substantial part of the organization (perhaps a program, project, division, plant, or department). Finally, **supervisory management** has control over the operations of a smaller organizational unit (such as a production line, operating unit, office, or laboratory). Managers in this last group are in charge of nonmanagerial, or rank-and-file, employees. They are the managers with whom most employees interact, as illustrated in the following example.

> **Bob Malone, the administrator of a large hospital, had remained close friends with college classmate Peter Chen. When Peter's son Billy enrolled at a college near Bob's hospital, Peter and Billy were guests in Bob's home for a couple of days. Billy then moved into a dormitory and got a part-time job at the hospital. His supervisor was Joan Davies, the head nurse.**
>
> **During Billy's first visit home, his father asked, "How's Bob Malone?" Billy replied, "I never see him. The only manager I ever see is Joan Davies."**

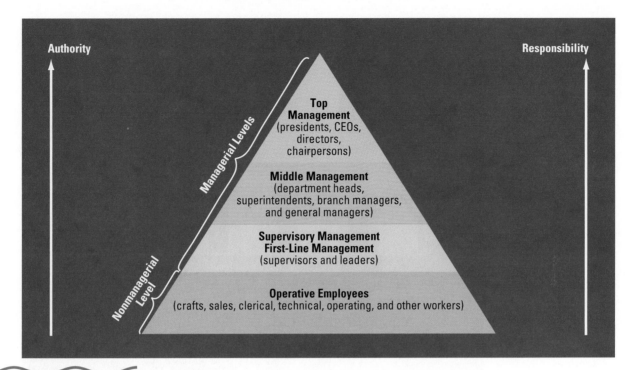

Authority

Responsibility

Managerial Levels

Top Management
(presidents, CEOs, directors, chairpersons)

Middle Management
(department heads, superintendents, branch managers, and general managers)

Supervisory Management First-Line Management
(supervisors and leaders)

Nonmanagerial Level

Operative Employees
(crafts, sales, clerical, technical, operating, and other workers)

Exhibit 1–3
How Management Authority and Responsibility Increase at Higher Levels

Another difference among managers at different levels is the amount of time they spend carrying out various activities. Exhibit 1–4 shows how managers of one electrical appliance manufacturer spend their time. The terms and titles are different from those used in this text, but the exhibit illustrates how the importance of particular activities differs according to managerial level.

This book deals primarily with the first level of managers, who may be called *supervisory managers* or simply *supervisors*.

SELF-CHECK

Did you notice in Exhibit 1–4 that the president and group executives spend the greatest percentage of their time "thinking ahead" and "doing work that cannot be delegated," whereas "working with people on lower levels" takes most of the time of supervisory managers? Do you think this allocation of time is logical and reasonable? Why or why not?

Exhibit 1–4
*How Managers Spend
Their Time*

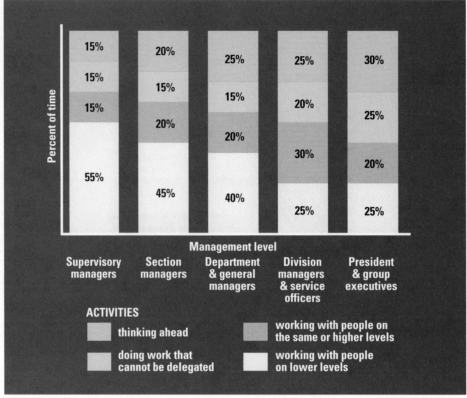

Source: Based on a study of managers of a company that asked to remain anonymous.

WHAT DO MANAGERS DO?

Learning Objective 3
Discuss what
managers do.

It is now time to see what managers do that makes them so needed. First we will examine the functions managers perform. Then we will look at some roles managers play. It should be noted at this point that not all managers spend the same amount of time performing each management function or playing each role.

Functions Performed by Managers

managerial functions
The acts expected of a
manager in a given
situation.

Managerial functions are the acts or operations expected of a manager in a given situation. There is no single generally accepted classification of these functions, but we believe that there are at least five separate, but interrelated, basic functions that must be performed by any manager at any level in any organization. Successful managers perform these functions effectively; unsuccessful ones do not. The functions are:

1. Planning
2. Organizing
3. Staffing

4. Leading
5. Controlling

PLANNING. Planning means more than just thinking ahead; it involves selecting future courses of action for the organization as a whole and for each of its subunits and deciding how to achieve the desired results. It also encompasses gathering and analyzing information in order to make these decisions. Through planning, the manager establishes goals and objectives and determines methods of attaining them. All other basic managerial functions depend on planning, because it is unlikely that they will be successfully carried out without sound and continuous planning. Chapters 3 and 4 are devoted to some of the more important aspects of planning.

planning Selecting future courses of action for the organization and deciding how to achieve the desired results.

> **Note that Jamie Medlin ends each day with a tentative game plan for the next day and modifies it each morning before making his daily work assignments. This is an example of the planning function.**

SELF-CHECK

What happens to managers' need to plan as they move up in an organization, as illustrated in Exhibit 1–4? Why does this happen?

ORGANIZING. Deciding what activities are needed to reach goals and objectives, dividing human resources into work groups, and assigning each group to a manager are tasks that make up the **organizing** function. Another aspect of organizing is bringing together the physical, financial, and human resources needed to achieve the organization's objectives. More will be said about the organizing function in Chapters 5 and 6.

organizing Deciding what activities are needed to reach goals and dividing human resources into work groups to achieve them.

STAFFING. The process of recruiting, selecting, developing, promoting, and paying and rewarding people to do the organization's work is called **staffing.** This basic function is sometimes regarded as a part of the organizing function, but we think it is important enough to be considered separately. Chapters 16 and 18 will elaborate on this function.

staffing Recruiting, training, promoting, and rewarding people to do the organization's work.

LEADING. The **leading** function involves conducting, guiding, enhancing, and supervising employees in the performance of their duties and responsibilities. It consists of coaching and empowering employees; facilitating their activities; communicating ideas and instructions; and motivating employees to perform their work efficiently. As shown in Exhibit 1–4, middle managers and supervisory managers are more heavily involved in leading—that is, "working with people"—than are top managers. Chapters 7 through 10 provide more details about this function.

leading Coaching and empowering employees and communicating ideas and instructions.

CONTROLLING. The **controlling** function involves comparing actual performance with planned standards and taking corrective action, if needed, to ensure that objectives are achieved. Control can be achieved only by setting up standards of performance, checking to see whether they have been achieved, and then doing what is necessary to bring actual performance in line with planned performance. This function must be executed successfully in

controlling Comparing actual performance with planned and taking corrective action if needed.

order to make certain that the other management functions are effectively performed. Chapters 11 and 12 deal with various aspects of this function.

Note that Medlin made rounds daily to monitor how his crew members were progressing on their job assignments.

HOW THE FUNCTIONS ARE RELATED. Although the five management functions must be performed by managers in all types of organizations and at all management levels, they may be performed in different ways and given different emphases by various managers. One or more functions may be stressed over the others at a particular level. For example, planning is done most often by top management, leading is more common among supervisory managers, and controlling seems to be chiefly the job of middle managers. Yet the functions are interrelated, interactive, and interdependent, as shown in Exhibit 1–5. Although they may be performed in any order, they tend to be performed in the sequence indicated by the numbers in the exhibit.

Exhibit 1–5
*How the Management
Functions Are Related*

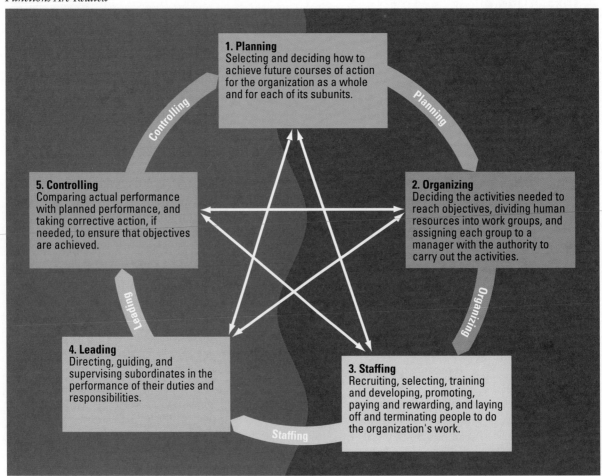

1. Planning
Selecting and deciding how to achieve future courses of action for the organization as a whole and for each of its subunits.

2. Organizing
Deciding the activities needed to reach objectives, dividing human resources into work groups, and assigning each group to a manager with the authority to carry out the activities.

3. Staffing
Recruiting, selecting, training and developing, promoting, paying and rewarding, and laying off and terminating people to do the organization's work.

4. Leading
Directing, guiding, and supervising subordinates in the performance of their duties and responsibilities.

5. Controlling
Comparing actual performance with planned performance, and taking corrective action, if needed, to ensure that objectives are achieved.

Roles Played by Managers

Another way to explain what management is and why it is so important is to explore the different roles played by managers in performing the management functions. The discussion of these functions might lead you to believe that the manager's job is orderly, well-organized, systematic, and harmonious. But this is just not so. In performing these functions, managers engage in a great many varied, disorganized, fragmented, and often unrelated activities. These activities may last for only a very short time or may extend over a long period.

In carrying out these activities, managers play **roles** as if they were actors, and these roles change rapidly and frequently. Ten managerial roles have been identified, grouped as follows: (1) interpersonal roles, (2) informational roles, and (3) decision-making roles. Exhibit 1–6 shows how the roles are grouped, describes what each one involves, and gives an example of each.

Like managerial functions, these roles are given varying degrees of emphasis by managers in different organizations and at different levels in the same organization. Managers vary in how they interpret the roles, the time they devote to them, and the importance they assign to them, but the roles must be played, as the following example shows.[1]

roles Parts played by managers in the performance of their functions.

> **AT&T, one of the nation's largest companies before its breakup into smaller, independent companies in 1984, spent several years studying the principal duties performed by its managers. These duties and the frequency with which first-line supervisors performed them are listed in Exhibit 1–7. As shown, the supervisors spent 15 percent of their time performing the control function, which included monitoring work progress, inspecting results, obtaining progress reports, and making modifications or adjustments to the work being done. Other duties are listed in rank order, according to the length of time devoted to each. Note that the duties shown combine the functions of management and the roles that managers play.**

The list appears overwhelming, doesn't it? Yet, with training and experience, supervisors can learn to perform these duties effectively.

SKILLS REQUIRED FOR EFFECTIVE MANAGEMENT

Learning Objective 4

Explain the basic skills required for effective management.

You may be wondering at this point what basic skills managers need in order to perform the managerial functions and play the managerial roles most effectively. Although many skills are needed, a few of the most common ones are:

1. Conceptual skills
2. Human relations skills
3. Administrative skills
4. Technical skills

The relative importance of these skills varies according to the type of industry in which the managers work, the organization to which they belong, their level in the managerial ranks, the job being performed, and the employees being managed.

Exhibit 1–6
*Roles Played by
Managers*

Role	What Is Involved	Examples
Interpersonal Roles		
Figurehead	Representing the organization or unit as its symbolic head.	Serving on public boards; attending public ceremonies.
Leader	Helping personnel achieve organizational and personal goals.	Leading, guiding, empowering, motivating, and enhancing employees.
Liaison	Maintaining relationships between the unit and outsiders.	Attending conferences and business-related meetings.
Informational Roles		
Monitor	Seeking information about and for the organization that is especially relevant to developing trends, ideas, and government actions.	Reading trade journals and related publications; taking trips; meeting outsiders such as suppliers or customers.
Disseminator	Providing pertinent information to appropriate organization members.	Routing articles, reports, and periodicals; sending letters and memos to employees.
Spokesperson	Representing employees to supervisors and vice versa; representing the organization to outsiders and groups.	Speaking to professional and trade groups; representing the unit in competing for resources and promotions.
Decision-Making Roles		
Entrepreneur	Conceiving and initiating new opportunities and introducing systematic change into the organization—especially for growth.	Introducing new equipment or processes; encouraging innovation; encouraging others to take calculated risks.
Disturbance Handler	Solving or resolving interorganizational or interpersonal conflicts or destructive competition.	Helping resolve employee complaints or grievances; trying to resolve personality conflicts among personnel.
Resource Allocator	Allocating the organization's scarce resources and setting priorities.	Helping prepare budgets; deciding which machines and equipment to replace; prioritizing job assignments.
Negotiator	Representing the organization in negotiations with individuals and groups.	Helping negotiate contracts; bargaining for favorable terms with other departments or suppliers.

Source: "Roles Played by Managers," adapted from *The Nature of Managerial Work,* by Henry Mintzberg. Copyright © 1973 by Henry Mintzberg. Reprinted by permission of HarperCollins Publishers.

Rank Order	Duty	Percentage of Supervisor's Time	Performance Frequency
1	Controlling (work activities)	15	Daily
2	Solving problems	12	Daily
3	Planning (work activities)	11	Daily
4	Communicating informally and orally	11	Daily
5	Communicating with superiors	11	Daily
6	Providing performance feedback to employees	10	Daily
7	Coaching employees	10	Daily
8	Writing letters and memos	6	Daily
9	Creating and maintaining a motivating atmosphere	5	Daily
10	Managing time	3	Daily
11	Attending meetings	3	Twice monthly
12	Reading and other self-development activities	1	Weekly
13	Career counseling with an employee	1	Bimonthly
14	Representing the company	1	Monthly

Source: Adapted from C. McDonald, *Performance Based Supervisory Development.* Copyright 1982, HRD Press. Reprinted by permission of HRD Press, 22 Amherst Rd., Amherst, MA 01002, 1-800-822-2801.

Exhibit 1–7
Supervisors' Duties

Exhibit 1–8 shows an estimate of the relative importance of these skills at different management levels.

Conceptual Skills

conceptual skills The ability to acquire and interpret information logically.

Conceptual skills involve the ability to acquire, analyze, and interpret information in a logical manner. All managers need to understand the environments in which they operate, as well as the effects of changes in those environments on their organization. In other words, managers should be able to "see the big picture." Top managers particularly need strong conceptual skills, because changes affecting the organization tend to be more important at their level than at other managerial levels. Around a third of their time is spent using conceptual skills.

Human Relations Skills

human relations skills Understanding other people and interacting effectively.

Human relations skills consist of the ability to understand other people and to interact effectively with them. These skills are most needed in performing the leading function because they involve communicating with, motivating, leading, coaching, empowering, and facilitating employees, as well as relating to other people. These

Exhibit 1–8
The Relative Importance of Managerial Skills at Different Managerial Levels

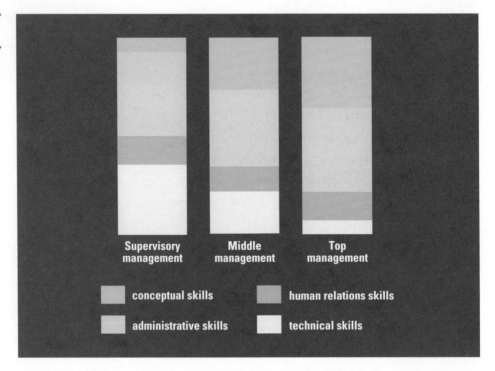

Supervisory management | Middle management | Top management

conceptual skills   human relations skills

administrative skills   technical skills

skills are important in dealing not only with individuals, but also with people in groups and even with relationships among groups. These skills are important to managers at all levels, but especially to supervisory managers, who spend almost one-half of their time using human relations skills.

Administrative Skills

administrative skills
Establishing and following procedures to process paperwork in an orderly manner.

Administrative skills are the skills that permit managers to use their other skills effectively in performing the managerial functions. These skills include the ability to establish and follow policies and procedures and to process paperwork in an orderly manner. By lending *coordination, order,* and *movement* to tasks, administrative skills underlie the ability some people have to "make things happen" and "get things done." These are similar to those of good students, who are well organized and get things done efficiently.

Technical Skills

technical skills Understanding and being able to supervise effectively specific processes required.

Technical skills include understanding and being able to supervise effectively the specific processes, practices, or techniques required to perform specific duties. While other managers should possess sufficient technical skills to keep their organization competitive, supervisory managers should have enough of these skills to see that day-to-day operations are performed effectively. Technical skills are more important for supervisors than for top managers, since supervisors are closer to the actual work being performed. They must often tell—or even show—employees how to perform a job,

Supervisors need to gather the technical skills necessary to keep on top of day-to-day operations and judge the performance and effectiveness of the operations.

as well as know when it is done properly. About a third of supervisors' time is devoted to activities involving technical skills, such as computer and information management skills.

A head nurse in a hospital, for example, must have some degree of technical understanding of proper equipment use, nursing procedures, medication, chart maintenance, and other important aspects of a nurse's job. We are not saying that the head nurse, or any other supervisor, must be a technical expert, but merely that a supervisor needs a basic understanding of the work being done in order to perform the managerial functions and roles effectively.

A word of caution is needed here. Do not assume that an operative employee who is highly skilled and who has been able to perform technical jobs also has the characteristics required to become an effective supervisor or manager. A *good producer is not necessarily a good supervisor or executive.*

In summary, effective supervisory management requires all of the skills—conceptual, human relations, administrative, and technical. The appropriate mix, however, depends on the level of management and the circumstances surrounding the managerial situation.

SELF-CHECK   To what extent do you think James Medlin needs and uses each of the four kinds of managerial skills?

THE IMPROVING POSITION OF SUPERVISORY MANAGERS

Learning Objective 5

Discuss the improving position of supervisory managers.

Now let us concentrate on the supervisor's place in management and see how the role of supervisors has changed. At one time, supervisors had autocratic power over employees. Employees either produced efficiently or were fired (Exhibit 1–9). The new concept today is one of leading or coaching a team or work group, rather than driving subservient workers. In essence, the supervisor must find a compromise between exercising too much authority and being a "rubber stamp" for higher managers.

Experts agree that the role of supervisory management is now in the process of drastically changing—but improving. For example, Barry Stein, president of a consulting firm, said that supervisors are not going to control people any more. Instead, they will have to "coach them, help do the planning, approve organizational direction, and make sure the directions are clear. It will be an enabling function rather than a control function."[2] *Our view, though, is that supervisors must both enable and control if they are to be effective.*

intermediaries Go-betweens who act as mediators.

Supervisors are now viewed as **intermediaries,** or go-betweens, acting as mediators between their employees and higher levels of management. According to this concept, supervisors stand between and among groups and have a sense of both belonging and not belonging to those groups. Thus, supervisors are caught between having to report to their managers and being representatives of management in relations with employees. Supervisors are transmitters of decisions made by their managers, but they also have authority for making recommendations to those managers. In other words, they are the "persons-in-the-middle" between the workers and higher-level managers. Supervisors also serve as buffers to keep them apart.

SELF-CHECK

To what extent does this description of the supervisor as an intermediary fit Jamie Medlin in relation to his employees?

No matter what type of role supervisors play, their goal is the same—getting out production, maintaining quality, holding down costs, maintaining high morale, and otherwise serving as management's representative, as well as acting as a spokesperson for employees. Although the knowledge required to perform most jobs has greatly increased and the methods used are different, the central objective has remained the same—obtaining quality and quantity production while maintaining good human relationships.

A study of supervisors in two plants of the same company illustrates this point.[3] One plant followed traditional organizing practices: the supervisor had authority to supervise, to determine working conditions, to plan the work and schedule it, and to

Exhibit 1–9
Supervisors Once Had Autocratic Power

control it. In the other plant, "team advisors" were used instead of supervisors, with the focus on facilitation rather than traditional direction of the work teams. As it turned out, "exceptional" and "average" supervisors at both plants, whether they were called supervisors or team advisors, exhibited characteristic behaviors.

"Exceptional" supervisors:

1. Were competent, caring, and committed both to getting the job done and to their employees.
2. Pushed for high quality, provided clear direction, and motivated employees with timely, accurate feedback.
3. Willingly shared information with personnel, even if the system didn't require it.
4. Were committed to teamwork and employee participation in the department's decisions.
5. Shared skills and knowledge willingly and saw their role as one of coach rather than driver.
6. Understood what was involved beyond their own units, from the broader perspectives of the plant.
7. Took the initiative in implementing changes and new approaches.

Supervisors considered only "average" in the two differently organized plants also exhibited similar behaviors. These supervisors:

1. Set narrowly defined goals and had more specific performance standards.
2. Were less attuned to the plant's overall goals and focused more narrowly on their own unit.
3. Provided less information or feedback about performance to their work groups.
4. Were less flexible, less innovative, and less willing to change.
5. Maintained tighter controls and were uncomfortable practicing participative management.

SUPERVISORY RELATIONSHIPS

Learning Objective 6

Clarify the different relationships supervisory managers have with others.

If we are to understand the role of supervisory managers in organizations, we must look at some of the relationships they have with different groups. Any study of the supervisory position must take into account the different sets of interactions and interrelationships that must be handled differently. For example, supervisors are legally a part of management and interact upward with other members of management. But they are often not accepted as peers by those managers, who usually have more education, come from outside the organization, and have higher social status and position. Before their promotion, supervisors typically worked as peers with those whom they now supervise.

There are three major types of relationships that require supervisors to play different and demanding roles, as shown in Exhibit 1–10. These are personal relationships, organizational relationships, and external relationships.

Personal Relationships

At one time it was believed that managers and employees left their personal problems at home when they entered the workplace. We now recognize that people bring their problems—as well as their pleasures—to their jobs. Supervisors' relationships with

Exhibit 1–10
The Supervisor's Relationships

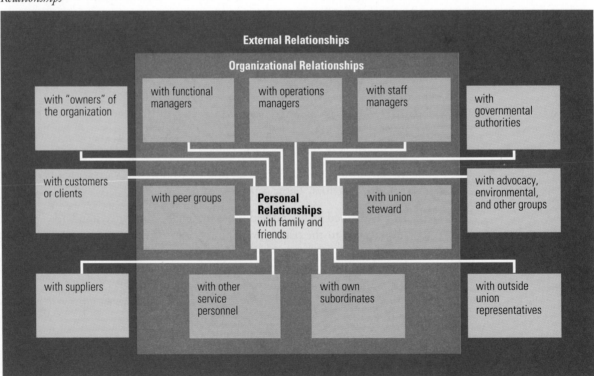

their families and their friends determine their attitudes and frame of mind as they perform managerial duties. Their attitudes, in turn, influence the relationships they have with other people, both inside and outside the organization.

Organizational Relationships

Within the organization, supervisory managers have varied and often conflicting relationships. These relationships flow in three directions: from manager to employee, with peers or managers on same level, and from employee to manager, as shown in Exhibit 1–11.

MANAGER-TO-EMPLOYEE RELATIONSHIPS. Supervisory managers must relate to their own employees and to people from other units who perform some type of service for them. As Exhibit 1–11 illustrates, a manager-to-employee relationship exists where the supervisor facilitates and directs nonmanagerial personnel. It gives the supervisor a sense of importance.

RELATIONSHIPS WITH PEERS OR OTHER MANAGERS. There are essentially two sets of horizontal relationships: those with other supervisory managers and those with the union steward or other representative(s) of the employees. Supervisors need the feeling of support and reinforcement that comes from associating with other supervisors who are considered their equals or peers. Yet the relationship can result in competition or even conflict if they seek to be promoted to the same job at the next higher level.

> **Note that Jamie Medlin indicated how important it was that he maintain relationships with managers from the production departments serviced by his work group—his maintenance "customers."**

union steward A union member elected by other members to represent their interests to management.

In a unionized organization, employees select a **union steward** to represent them in their dealings with management. Although the steward is a supervisor's peer—legally, if not organizationally—he or she does represent the supervisor's employees. Therefore, the association between the supervisor and the union steward may be competitive or even combative. This association provides supervisors with a challenge

Exhibit 1–11
Supervising Relationships

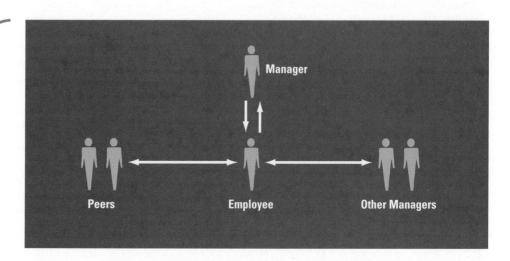

but can also be frustrating. For example, a supervisor will probably attempt to motivate employees to improve productivity, whereas a union steward may encourage them to maintain the status quo for fear that their jobs will be eliminated.

SUPERVISOR-TO-MANAGER RELATIONSHIPS. Supervisors have a *reverse* manager-to-employee relationship with managers at higher levels. As a result of downsizing, reengineering, empowering, and similar new managerial approaches, though, this relationship is being upgraded. Staff executives in other departments, such as legal and research, may also tell supervisors what to do. Functional executives, such as the controller and the human resource director, direct supervisors in handling certain activities. In this association, supervisors are the employees who must support and reinforce their managers.

External Relationships

Supervisory managers must also deal with people outside the organization. Some of the people who must be served or catered to are the owners of the business, customers or clients, suppliers, higher-level union representatives, governmental authorities, and leaders of environmental and advocacy groups. These relationships can be quite difficult and frustrating for supervisors, who represent their organizations but usually do not have the authority to make decisions and enforce them.

SOME CURRENT TRENDS CHALLENGING SUPERVISORS

Learning Objective 7
Discuss some trends challenging supervisors.

As shown earlier, today's supervisors must be prepared to adjust to the many current trends that will challenge their best performance. Among the more significant of these trends are (1) dealing with a more diverse work force, (2) emphasizing team performance, (3) coping with exploding technology, (4) adjusting to occupational and industry shifts, (5) improving quality and productivity, (6) meeting global challenges, and (7) improving ethical and social behavior.

Dealing With a More Diverse Work Force

As the share of women, African American, Hispanic, and Asian and Native American workers rises dramatically, from 46, 11, 9, and 3 percent, respectively, to 48, 12, 11, and 4 percent,[4] the future work force will be more diverse than at any time in our history.

While men and women are entering the work force at about the same rate, men—who have been in the work force longer—are retiring at a faster rate. Thus, like racial and ethnic minorities, women will assume an even greater role in supervisory management.

The work force is also aging, along with the rest of the U.S. population. For example, while those from 35 to 54 years of age made up 40 percent of the work force in 1990, the group will comprise about 50 percent of the work force by the year 2000. Providing equal opportunities for these groups, along with women, will be a challenge to future supervisors.

Michele Luna, President of Atlas Headwear, estimates that 94 percent of her employees are Asian and Hispanic and that at least 80 percent are women.

glass ceiling Invisible barriers that limit women from advancing in an organization.

Providing opportunities for women is particularly challenging, as there appears to be a **"glass ceiling,"** in many organizations. These ceilings are considered invisible barriers that limit the advancement of women into higher levels of the organization. Thus, supervisors will be expected to design programs to attract and to develop women and minority employees and to provide them with a full range of opportunities for growth and development, the same as they do for all other employees.

Emphasizing Team Performance

empowerment Equipping employees to function on their own and with less direct supervision.

team advisors Share responsibility with team for cost, quality, and prompt delivery of products.

As organizations seek to equip their employees to function on their own, less direct supervision is required. This **empowerment** results in supervisors increasingly working with work groups or teams. These teams make suggestions for improvements in activities to make things run smoothly and accomplish goals effectively.[5]

When supervisors work with these teams, their roles are changed. No longer are they "bosses," but they become leaders, facilitators, or **team advisors,** who share responsibility with the team for maintaining cost, quality, and prompt and effective delivery of products. Therefore, supervisors must provide further training to their teams in order to manage the production process more effectively.

Coping With Exploding Technology

Most working Americans now earn their living through some form of creating, processing, utilizing, and distributing information. As innovations in computer and other communications technology have displaced thousands of workers who used different skills, new opportunities are opening up for those who have the needed education, training, and temperament. Conversely, employees with the older skills are being replaced in the workplace.

The primary effect of exploding technology on supervisors will be the need to improve training and overcome resistance to change. Therefore, supervisors must keep up to date on the latest developments so that they can effectively train their people. (See Exhibit 1–12.) As change brings with it uncertainty and as most people resist that which is uncertain, overcoming resistance to change becomes an increasing part of the supervisor's training activities.

An example of exploding technology is the system used by Dillard's Department Stores, which has a near-fanatical focus on computer technology and freeing supervisors and employees from many manual activities. Their Quick Response program orders basic items from the vendor each week—electronically, without human intervention—on the basis of the previous week's sales.[6]

Adjusting to Occupational and Industry Shifts

The previously mentioned technological advancements, along with cultural and marketing changes, have resulted in shifts in occupation and industry mixes. First, there is a declining emphasis on the traditional industries, with a concurrent shift toward more people-related activities such as services and marketing.

reinvention Recasting something old into a different form.

Along with these shifts, there has been a **reinvention** of many organizations, especially a reduction in the size and markets for businesses. Many of the large companies have also been **reengineering** their activities by wiping the slate clean as far as current operations are concerned and asking: "If we blew this place up and started over, what would we do differently? What should we eliminate entirely? What can we

reengineering Revamping the organization.

Exhibit 1–12

Source: *The Rotarian,* May 1995, p. 10.

do that would make things easier for our customers?"[7] Not only are manufacturing companies reengineering, but so are many service companies.

downsizing Eliminating unnecessary levels of management.

These, and other, activities resulted in another trend, called **downsizing,** in which an organization strives to become leaner and more efficient by reducing work force and consolidating departments and work groups.

Some of the best-known companies, such as American Express, Taco Bell, General Motors, IBM, and Sears, have been reinvented, or reengineered. The results usually have included the elimination of 10 to 20 percent of a company's jobs, especially at the management level.[8] In fact, something like 23,000 managerial jobs are disappearing each month, which means that front-line workers—and their supervisors—must handle more diverse tasks, think more creatively, and assume more responsibility. On the downside, though, those same people must work harder and be under more pressure.[9]

> **For example, a survey of a dozen big employers showed that two-thirds of their workers were stretched so thin that they could not take advantage of flexible work schedules, personal leave, or other benefits.[10]**

Meeting Global Challenges

As business activities are becoming more global, those interested in supervisory management need to understand that they may have to operate in a one-world market. In fact, we estimate that up to one-half of all college graduates will work in some type of international activities in the future. U.S. exports of services are not exempt from this trend, since they are growing even faster than product exports.[11]

> **An example of exporting services is AT&T. In 1993, the company went through a massive top-level reorganization in order to "accelerate AT&T's globalization and move into multimedia products and communications services world-wide."[12]**

A result of the global challenge is the large number of U.S. businesses—such as Magnavox, Sylvania, and Quasar—that are foreign-owned. This changing ownership may lead to differing cultures and management styles, especially at the supervisory level.

Another aspect of global challenge is that many U.S. production facilities may be moved to Asia, Africa, Mexico, South America, Korea, or other areas where low wages and high productivity lead to a competitive advantage. When supervisors move to those areas to supervise the local workers, or when a foreign company acquires a domestic company, supervisors must learn to adjust and adapt to cultural differences and find ways to adjust to nontraditional styles.

Improving Quality and Productivity

One result of global competition has been a search for improved quality and productivity in U.S. businesses. There are two ways supervisors can achieve improved performance, namely, (1) let employees know what level of performance is expected of them and then (2) involve the workers in achieving that performance level.

quality A product's
features that improve
its ability to satisfy
the customers.

Although the term means different things to different people, we use the term **quality** to mean the features and characteristics of a product that improve its ability to satisfy the requirements of customers. In more progressive organizations, supervisors emphasize the right way to achieve a high level of quality from the beginning of their training and orientation of employees.

A second way of achieving high performance is by involving workers in the process. One factor leading to increased productivity is harnessing the creative potential of employees through employee involvement. This trend has also been found in many other foreign organizations.

> **A study by _Fortune_ magazine highlighted several products known for their high quality. For example, any worker at Baccarat Crystal in France who sees a flaw immediately smashes the goblet: There's no such thing as a "second" at Baccarat. At Dunhill Pipes in London, a pipemaker may turn as many as 50 bowls in an effort to produce a single perfect one, and it takes up to a month to make and "season" each pipe.[13]**

productivity A measure
of efficiency of inputs to
outputs.

Equally as important as achieving better quality is achieving improved **productivity,** which is a measurement of the amount of input needed to generate a given amount of output. As it is the basic measurement of the efficiency of people and processes in an organization, it becomes a challenge for supervisors to improve productivity.

Improving Ethical and Social Behavior

ethical dilemmas Situations where a person is
unsure of the correct
behavior.

Today's supervisors are facing increased **ethical dilemmas,** which are situations where the supervisor is not certain what is the correct behavior expected. Thus, they will have to define "right and wrong" conduct for themselves and their employees. As will be shown in Chapter 4, these ethical problems are becoming increasingly difficult in decision making and problem solving. Also, companies are under pressure from the government, media, and society to act in more socially acceptable ways. For example, Xerox has a Social Service Leave Program that pays employees a full year's salary while they are performing public service.[14]

Chapter Review

 **Explain why management is needed in all organizations.**
Management is needed whenever people form organizations. An organization is a group of people in a structured situation with a common purpose. People form organizations because they realize that they can achieve more working together than they can alone.

Management is the process of working through people to achieve objectives by making effective decisions and by coordinating the development and use of scarce human, financial, and physical resources.

 **Describe the different levels of management.**
Large organizations usually have at least three levels of management. Top management oversees the overall operations—or a major segment of the organization or one of the

basic organizational activities; middle management is responsible for a smaller part, such as a division or department; and supervisory management controls a smaller organizational unit.

Discuss what managers do.

Managers at all levels do essentially the same things, but to different degrees. First, they perform the same functions—namely, planning, organizing, staffing, leading, and controlling. In performing these functions, managers engage in many varied and often unrelated activities that require them to play different roles. In playing interpersonal roles, a manager may act as a figurehead, a leader, or as a liaison between different groups. Informational roles include acting as a monitor, disseminator, and/or spokesperson. Finally, decision-making roles require the manager to be an entrepreneur, disturbance handler, resource allocator, and/or negotiator.

Explain the basic skills required for effective management.

Effective managers need various skills in order to perform their functions and play their roles. Conceptual skills are needed in acquiring, interpreting, and analyzing information in a logical manner. Human relations skills involve understanding other people and interacting effectively with them. Administrative skills provide the ability to get things done by using other skills effectively. Technical skills consist of understanding and being able to supervise the processes, practices, or techniques required for specific jobs in the organization.

Discuss the improving position of supervisory managers.

The role of supervisory managers has drastically changed during the last century. No longer are they the foremen wielding autocratic power over subordinates, but they are supervisors leading people to be more productive. Until about 100 years ago, supervisors were essentially subcontractors, who tended to understand and relate to workers. Then, with growing organizational size and power, supervisors gained almost complete authority over their units. Now they are considered linking pins, or intermediaries between their employees and higher levels of management.

Clarify the different relationships supervisory managers have with others.

Supervisory managers are involved in at least three sets of relationships. First, they have personal relationships with their families and their friends. Second, they have sometimes conflicting organizational relationships with lower-level employees, fellow supervisors, and higher levels of management. Third, they have external relationships with outsiders such as business owners, customers or clients, suppliers, union representatives, governmental authorities, and leaders of environmental and advocacy groups.

Discuss some trends challenging supervisors.

As the supervisory position is growing in importance, it is also becoming more complex because of many trends that are challenging supervisors' abilities to perform their jobs. The more important trends challenge supervisors to: (1) deal with a more diverse work force, (2) emphasize team performance, (3) cope with exploding technology,

(4) adjust to occupational and industry shifts, (5) meet global challenges, (6) improve quality and productivity, and (7) improve ethical and social behavior.

Important Terms

administrative skills *pg. 14*   human resources *5*   quality *24*
authority *6*   intermediaries *16*   reengineering *22*
conceptual skills *13*   leading *9*   reinvention *22*
controlling *9*   management *5*   responsibility *6*
distribution *4*   managerial functions *8*   roles *11*
downsizing *23*   middle management *6*   staffing *9*
empowerment *21*   operations *4*   supervisory
ethical dilemmas *24*   organization *3*   management *6*
financial resources *5*   organizing *9*   team advisors *21*
financing *4*   physical resources *5*   technical skills *14*
glass ceiling *21*   planning *9*   top management *6*
human relations skills *13*   productivity *24*   union steward *19*

Questions for Review and Discussion

1. Why do people form organizations?
2. Why is management needed in organizations?
3. How would you define these terms?
   a. organization
   b. management
   c. supervisory management
   d. planning
   e. organizing
   f. staffing
   g. leading
   h. controlling
   i. conceptual skills
   j. human relations skills
   k. administrative skills
   l. technical skills
4. What are the three levels of management found in most large organizations? Describe each, giving its responsibilities.
5. What are some of the roles that managers play?
6. What skills do managers need? Describe each.
7. Trace the changing concepts of supervision. Why did these changes occur?
8. What are the three types of supervisory relationships? Explain.
9. Take each of the seven trends discussed in the chapter and explain—very briefly—how you would cope with each.

Skill Builder 1–1
Effective and Ineffective Supervisors

Join together with two or three of your classmates. Think of all the supervisors for whom you've worked—part-time or full-time. If any of you have not worked for a supervisor, try to observe a few in action in some organization, or consider some of your teachers. Then, try to choose two supervisors: one who was most effective and one who was least effective. Then list the reasons each supervisor was effective or ineffective, and list the qualities that led to the effective or ineffective performance.

Skill Builder 1–2
Identifying Your Supervisory Strengths and Weaknesses

Examine the duties in Exhibit 1–7. Identify the two or three duties with which you would feel *most* comfortable if you were a supervisor. Identify the two or three with which you would feel *least* comfortable.

1. What might account for your confidence—or lack of confidence—in your ability to perform the duties you selected?
2. How could you be trained or prepared to better perform those duties about which you feel less comfortable?
3. Compare your answers to questions 1 and 2 with answers given by other students, and discuss the similarities and differences.

CASE 1–1

The Weak Supervisor

Henry Osmond was a participant in a supervisory training course conducted by one of the authors for a large clock manufacturing firm. He was in his mid-thirties, tall, quiet, and reserved—somewhat meek in appearance. He contributed little during the first two days of the course and during breaks didn't mingle with his 15 colleagues, all of whom, like himself, were first-line supervisors for the company. During one of the breaks, the instructor asked one of the participants about Henry.

"Well," said the participant, "don't blame yourself or the course for Henry's not getting involved. That's just Henry. He's a most interesting case. He's like that in the plant, too. It's a shame what's happened to him, really. Believe it or not, Henry is one of the top clockworks men in the country. His dad worked in this plant and had the same outstanding reputation—better, in fact, than Henry's. Henry Senior's retired now, but he makes more money running a clock repair operation than he ever did here. He's even had private planes land here, pick him up, and carry him to Europe to repair expensive collectors' or museum clocks. Well, Henry has the same skill. He picked up everything from his dad. The guy can look at a clock movement and immediately spot a problem that'd take someone else several hours to track down. I know—I've worked for three different firms in this industry—the guy has a special talent.

"Well, here's what happened. About nine months ago, the company moved Henry up to movement supervisor—this is the department that reworks, makes adjustments, or tries to correct any problems in the movements before we ship a clock to a retailer. The department also handles any defective movements that a retailer returns.

"Now our union contract doesn't allow supervisors to do actual 'hands-on' work, but ole Henry will generally bird-dog the best jobs—I mean, you'll see him looking over the shoulder of one of his people, giving step-by-step detailed instructions on what to do. He drives his technicians absolutely batty, interjecting himself into the most challenging jobs and oversupervising. Not only is he resented, but he's our weakest supervisor—very shy and timid, won't discipline, and doesn't get the paperwork done. He's a failure as a supervisor—and he knows it. Never should have been offered the job and never should have taken it. It'd be a real loss of face now for him to be 'demoted' back to movement technician—at least in his eyes. I guess when they promoted him to supervisor, they didn't realize that they were taking away his tool box. And Henry just doesn't have much else to offer. What a waste!"

Answer the following questions:

1. What did the supervisor mean when he said that the company "took away Henry's tool box"?
2. What criteria besides technical skills could the company have used to determine whether Henry had supervisor potential?
3. Many companies automatically promote the top technical person in a department to fill a vacant supervisory position. What are the pros and cons of this practice?
4. Suppose that you were Henry's manager. What would you do about the situation, assuming the remarks about his performance were true?

Chapter 2
Quest for Quality and Empowerment

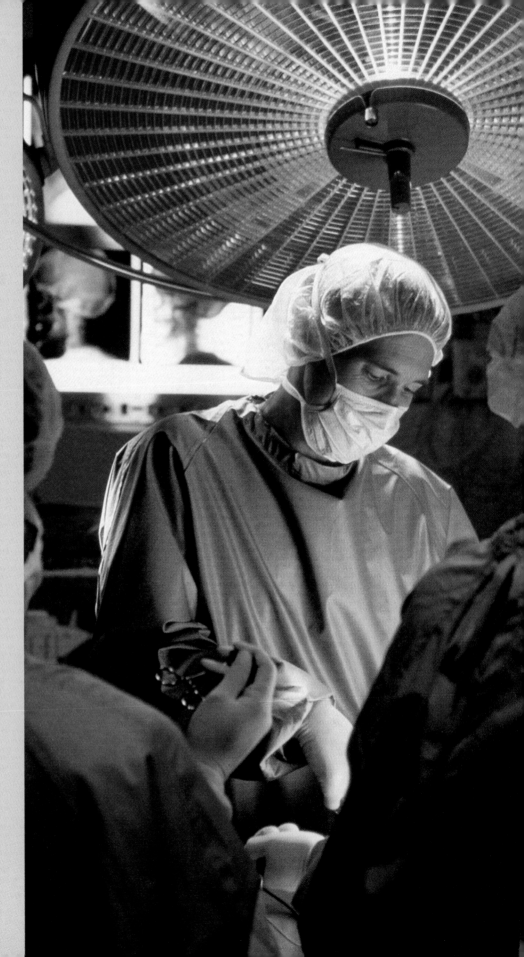

Case 2

City Hospital

In recent years City Hospital, a large 1,200-bed hospital in a major metropolitan area, faced many pressures. These included increased competition from other general hospitals, specialized orthopedic centers, women's and children's hospitals, and other health-care providers, such as outpatient surgery centers. Furthermore, all hospitals were coming under increasingly strong cost control pressure from private insurers as well as government. Two years ago a new administrator from outside the hospital was appointed, and within three months the hospital announced a "Total Quality Initiative (TQI)" that would "dramatically change the way the hospital was managed."

Under "TQI," all areas of the hospital's operations, ranging from bedside care of patients to processing of patients' records to inventory control, would be targeted for continuous measurement and improvement. Employees at all levels, be they salaried or hourly, would be given greater responsibility for their own work. Numerous cross-functional, problem-solving teams would address major issues in the hospital in an attempt to unleash a wave of creativity and commitment.

A TQI task force was named, consisting of 20 persons representing all levels of the hospital. The task force's role was to chart out the hospital's strategy in planning and implementing the new process. Task force members visited the country's outstanding hospitals to observe firsthand their programs. They also visited Federal Express, Xerox, and other non-health-care firms that had won awards for quality excellence. A series of three-day training courses in problem solving, statistics, and group dynamics was initiated to help employees function in the new environment. Cross-functional TQI teams were formed to address high-priority hospital problems.

Several programs were initiated to spur greater involvement and commitment by employees. Monthly "peak performers" were selected for providing outstanding patient service. Communication between upper management and other levels opened considerably; the hospital administrator met regularly with employees from different departments, encouraging them to speak their minds. Supervisors were encouraged to delegate greater responsibility to their employees and to allow employees greater latitude in performing their work. A 360-degree feedback system was implemented in which managers were given performance feedback by peers and employees as well as managers.

Two years into the initiative the hospital's human resources director talked about the changes:

We've definitely made progress. Getting employees and supervisors to buy into the process has been difficult, though. Some of the more entrenched, longer-term managers and professionals felt that nothing would really change. When they saw changes actually taking place in how we began operating, a number felt threatened by the potential loss of power or the feeling that they lacked the needed skills to effectively handle the new requirements. Under our new system, we're saying that the old ways of managing—intimidation and

LEARNING OBJECTIVES
After reading and studying this chapter, you should be able to:

1

Define empowerment and give an example.

2

Identify and differentiate among the four levels of empowerment.

3

Describe how the recent U.S. quality resurgence began.

4

Identify the four approaches to managing quality.

5

Understand the three components of total quality management.

6

Explain how the supervisor's job is affected by empowerment and quality programs.

fear—are now out the window. That's been a hard pill for many old-line managers to swallow.

Most expected our TQI to be a lot of window dressing—all talk, no substance. However, our administrator means business. Recently a relatively young professional catapulted past two levels to be named one of our assistant administrators. That got everybody's attention, especially the more senior, old-line, management-style types who were vaulted over. Our nursing administrator, a 30-year vet, was as entrenched as they come and openly refused to change. She opted for early retirement, as did our rehab director. But people are buying on every week. We've had some terrific results already with some of our task force teams and we've empowered people. My own department is a good example. Each year the hospital has an annual management meeting where about 50 of our top managers assemble for two days at a retreat site in a nearby resort. One day is for work, the other play. My training director and I usually put together the "whole show"—selecting a theme, developing the agenda, making the arrangements—the entire works. This year, given our team and involvement atmosphere, we selected a task force of managers to take on the assignment—the complete retreat planning and coordination—and we had the best retreat ever. We have run into some resistance at the salaried and hourly levels. Some employees, professionals included, would much rather have managers calling all the shots rather than having to stick their own necks out. "Why take on the added responsibility?" they ask. We hope they will realize that they must stick out their necks for this hospital to be its best. That may sound trite, but it's the only way we can be a quality, successful operation. They're beginning to realize that by learning a broader range of jobs, their value increases. And, if we downsize here, they will be more employable at a competitor or elsewhere in the industry.

Quality begins with education and ends with education.

Kaoru Ishikowa

The quality movement . . . is in fact the first wave in building learning organizations—organizations that continually expand their ability to shape their future.

Peter Senge

Peter Drucker, world-renowned management consultant, author, and academic, predicted in 1983 that tremendous organizational changes would impact the job of supervisory managers in organizations such as City Hospital.[1] One of the organizational changes would be brought about by the "quality" movement. In an effort to continuously search for improved quality of products, services, and processes, Drucker noted that top management would of necessity conclude that the rank-and-file employees, not supervisors, would be in the best position to lead the charge. The second change, Drucker said, would be to give greater authority to rank-and-file employees to do what was necessary to perform their jobs more effectively. This would include such things as planning, determining the resources to perform their jobs best, and interfacing directly with personnel who impact their job, such as customers, suppliers, service department personnel, and others. In combination, the quality goal and greater employee authority would directly affront the power and status of traditional supervisors and would require quite different supervisory roles. In the thirteen years since Drucker wrote the article, much has changed in American organizations such as City Hospital. Drucker proved to be "on target." The two affronts to traditional supervisory status and power have become trends that are presently steamrolling organizations of all types, large and small, profit and not-for-profit, manufacturing, service, and governmental. Today these changes are characterized as "total quality" and "empowerment."

EMPOWERMENT

Learning Objective 1

Define empowerment and give an example.

empowerment Granting authority to employees to make key decisions within responsibility.

Empowerment is part of the sweeping movement occurring in organizations today. One reason for the increasing use of empowerment is the reduction in employee numbers in recent years. "Downsizing" eliminated over 3.4 million jobs in America's largest firms (the Fortune 500) from 1982 to 1991. In 1993 alone, the broader index of firms (the Fortune 1000) cut back another 4 million jobs.[2] The result—fewer corporate staff, fewer layers of management, and fewer operating-level employees—has resulted in leaner, trimmer organizations. The employees remaining share more power as they perform their daily tasks. But even in organizations that have grown rather than downsized, worker empowerment has become an increasingly important vehicle for improved organizational performance.

Empowerment means many things, but essentially it is the granting of authority to employees to make key decisions within their areas of responsibility. The driving idea of empowerment is that the individuals closest to the work and to customers should make the decisions. Rather than being constricted by rigid rules and controls or the need for approval from their supervisors, the best use of employees' skills and talents is to give them the latitude, and the resources, to make relevant decisions. Empowerment also may include authority to "bend the rules" as appropriate, given the employee's judgment of the circumstances. Note the consistent theme in the empowerment examples shown in Exhibit 2–1. In each case, employees are granted authority to impact their jobs in a meaningful way.

Perhaps the most publicized empowerment story is the GM Saturn Plant in Spring Hill, Tennessee. Built in response to U.S. auto makers' loss of market share to Japanese imports in the 1980s, Saturn was planned with the premise that its workers would function far differently from a traditional U.S. auto plant. They were to be formed in about 150 teams of 15 or so each. Each worker was to be able to perform a wide range of jobs. Moreover, teams were to be empowered to make decisions traditionally reserved for their managers (recall Drucker's forecast), such as work scheduling, selection of team members, and greater control of their own work quality. In one 1995 television commercial, a Saturn production worker tells of team members' pride in their work and points to the cord that runs over his work area. One pull of the cord, he states, is all it takes to shut down the line when he or his team members discover a quality problem. Then the race begins to track down its origin. In traditional auto plants, managers rather than workers make these decisions. Many aspects of the Saturn story have been a success, but because of its uniqueness—new physical plant, newly hired employees, a technology designed to encourage empowerment, and management/union cooperation—GM has not been able to fully generalize it to other plants.

The following examples of empowerment reflect power sharing in various organizations.

AT&T Universal Card Services
When a cardmember calls in for help, telephone associates at the second largest card-service in the industry (behind the Discover Card) are empowered to do what it takes, even if it includes bending the rules. One desperate caller from Paris was stranded when an ATM "ate" his AT&T card on a Saturday afternoon. The cardholder had no cash and was scheduled to leave Paris the next day. With the cardmember on hold, an empowered associate contacted the American Embassy and arranged for a limo to take the traveler to the only bank open in Paris where an authorized emergency cash advance had been arranged.

Midas Mufflers
At most Midas Muffler shops, a mechanic's job is narrowly defined . . . lift the car on the rack, determine what's needed, get a go-ahead from the service manager, and repair the vehicle as directed. But at some Midas shops, mechanics are empowered to do much, much more. A mechanic may handle phone customers, greet walk-in customers, inspect a vehicle, write up an estimate and discuss it with the customer, perform the repairs, test the car (as needed), explain and offer to sell an extended warranty, collect payment, and even adjust customers' bills when they are dissatisfied. "It's good business," said one Midas manager. "My mechanics have much more pride in their work and better understand our total operation. Also, we have customers who have identified with their service representative and only want to talk with that person."

The Ritz-Carlton
At the Ritz, top management has empowered its employees to assume ownership of customer problems. So when a customer comes to you with a problem, it's *your* problem. Employees can spend up to $2,000 to handle customer problems, ranging from mailing items left in a room by a checked-out guest to arranging for free accommodations or complimentary meals to remedy an error.

Motorola
Empowered employees work in teams and have authority to carry out a wide range of functions. They create their own production schedules, develop and manage budgets, schedule their training, select new team members, and choose their own leaders. As you will read later in the chapter, Motorola is considered a leading company in applying empowerment and quality principles.

Exhibit 2–1
*Empowerment Through
Job Involvement*

Levels of Empowerment

Learning Objective 2

Identify and differentiate among the four levels of empowerment.

You can better understand the range of empowerment by thinking of it along a continuum as shown in Exhibit 2–2. In the lower lefthand corner, under traditional management, minimal empowerment exists. Major decision-making authority rests outside the control of employees, in the hands of managers or a system such as the traditional production line approach. The traditional production line breaks work down into a series of specialized, programmed activities of limited scope, dictates the speed of work, and so on. The worker's task is to complete the job as required; he or she can do little to influence the outcome. Even service work often employs traditional production line principles. The job of a McDonald's server, just like an assembly line worker, is carefully programmed. The server gives a standard greeting, secures the order and places it on the tray in prescribed format (cold drinks are put on the tray

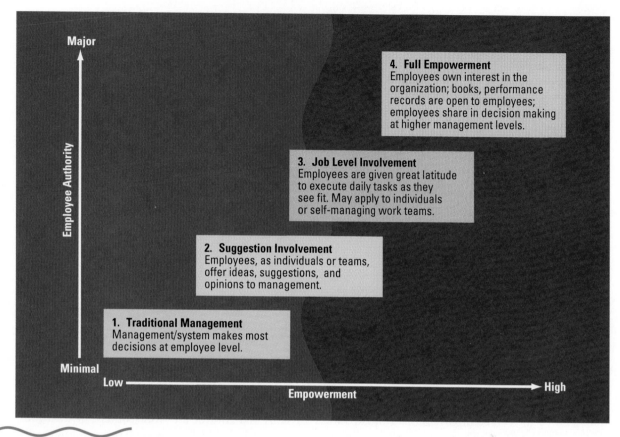

Exhibit 2–2
Levels of Empowerment

first, then hot, etc.), follows a set procedure in collecting payment, and gives a closing farewell to the customer. A Disney Theme Park operator gives a standardized talk and closely follows established procedures; even many so-called "ad lib" comments are often carefully programmed. Thus, much work in production and service industries alike requires such consistent job behavior that little opportunity for employee empowerment exists.

The second empowerment level is that of **suggestion involvement.** At this level, employees are actively encouraged to make suggestions to improve aspects of their work or to determine their opinion about tentative changes in the way work is conducted. This level of "involvement" doesn't change the fact that management or the "system," rather than employees, exercises true control over the primary work decisions that determine *what* is to be done and *how* to do it. The narrow job duties may remain, but *some* empowerment occurs through the suggestion process. McDonald's, for example, listens closely to its front-line employees. The Big Mac, Egg McMuffin, and McDLT all were invented by McDonald's employees, as was the system of wrapping burgers that avoids leaving a thumbprint in the bun.[3] The suggestion level of empowerment frequently utilizes employee teams designed specifically to address job or work environment problems and to make suggestions for resolving them. This is true of many "quality teams" or "problem-solving teams."

suggestion involvement
Employees are actively encouraged to make suggestions to improve aspects of their work.

Though employees at a Florida Motorola plant were at first wary of company empowerment programs, most now enjoy their new "take-charge" attitude.

job involvement Employees use a broad variety of skills and control the work content of their jobs.

The third level is job involvement. In **job involvement,** jobs are defined so that employees use a broad variety of skills and control the work content of their jobs. There are several conditions necessary for individuals to become truly empowered at the job involvement level. These include the following:

1. Having self-confidence to perform the job well. To be empowered, employees must feel that they have the skills and abilities to successfully perform their work.
2. Being able to make work choices. A condition of empowerment is that employees have significant latitude in determining how their work is performed. Often these choices include decisions about what, how, and when the work is done, as well as how work problems are handled.
3. Believing the work is meaningful. Empowered employees feel that their work has purpose and value—be it in the product or the service they produce. They feel that their extra effort and initiative contributes in an important rather than trivial way.
4. Feeling that individual effort can "make a difference." Truly empowered employees feel that they can personally impact job outcomes. The decisions that they make about their jobs largely determine whether the job results are a success or failure.
5. Knowing there is management support. Since empowered employees take risks in assuming responsibility, they must trust their own supervisors and higher managers to back them up.

Examples of job involvement given earlier from Saturn, AT&T Card Services, Midas Muffler, and The Ritz-Carlton reflect empowerment at the job level. Employees are generally highly trained to be able to perform at this level. Saturn, for example, trained employees over 700 hours prior to startup of the company, despite the fact that most of its work force consisted of veteran GM employees. Recall that the examples of Motorola and Saturn reflected empowered work "teams." Sometimes called self-managed or autonomous work teams, these teams exercise a strong influence over the work content of their jobs. The employee teams, rather than supervisors or managers, control many aspects of their work, such as scheduling, assigning tasks, budgeting, selection of new team members, and evaluation of their own performance. This degree of empowerment is significantly broader than that given to the part-time, problem-solving teams found at the suggestion level of empowerment. At the job involvement level of empowerment, supervisors need to be reoriented toward supporting their people rather than closely directing them.

full empowerment The total organization is involved.

The fourth level is **full empowerment.** In a full empowerment organization the total organization is involved. The organization's performance information is openly shared and made available to all employees. Employees are highly skilled in teamwork and problem-solving techniques and actively participate in work unit and higher-level management decisions. Some form of ownership is held by all employees through profit sharing and stock ownership. Because full empowerment represents such dramatic change from the traditional and even the suggestion and job involvement levels of empowerment, relatively few organizations incorporate *all* aspects of full empowerment.

SELF-CHECK   What level of empowerment is found in City Hospital? Explain.

QUALITY

This section addresses the major impact that the search for ever-increasing achievement of high-quality products and services is having upon organizations. Just as was the situation with City Hospital, employee empowerment plays an important role in the quest for high quality.

"Quality Is Job 1"

Maytag commercials show the lonely repairman who never gets called. British Airways claims, "We take more care of you." Pepsi and Coke wage huge advertising battles over which product tastes best. A small hometown diner advertises it has "the best burgers in town." Articles in *Business Week, Fortune, Industry Week, Forbes, The Wall Street Journal,* and others highlight quality as the hot current topic that it is. For the 1992–1995 period, almost 2,000 articles on quality are listed by "INFOTRAC," a database of business periodicals. The governmental sector has also gotten into the act—a national survey showed that by 1995 over 40 states had adopted some form of "quality initiative" within state government; New York, Texas, Missouri, and Maryland have established annual quality awards. Training courses in "quality" management are regular offerings by consultants and training firms. Business schools at numerous universities have introduced courses in quality. Companies have allocated large budgets for quality training and created quality control departments, frequently headed by managers with high corporate visibility, such as vice-presidents. Despite the quality emphasis, however, we can all point to frequent experiences with poor-quality products and services (see Exhibit 2–3).

SELF-CHECK   Think of a poor "quality" experience that you have had lately, be it with a product or service. What quality issue(s) shown in Exhibit 2–3 was involved? Do you believe that your poor experience with the product or service was an exception? Why?

Exhibit 2–3
Quality Issues in Manufacturing and Service

Manufacturing
1. Performance: a product's primary operating characteristics.
2. Features: the "bells and whistles" of a product.
3. Reliability: whether the product works consistently as specified.
4. Conformance: the extent to which physical and performance characteristics match pre-established standards.
5. Durability: how long the product lasts.
6. Serviceability: ease and costs of a product's repair.
7. Aesthetics: how a product looks, feels, sounds, tastes, and smells.
8. Perceived quality: subjective assessment resulting from image, advertising, brand names.

Service
1. Time: how long a customer must wait.
2. Timeliness: whether a service is performed when promised.
3. Completeness: the extent to which all items or services are performed.
4. Courtesy: the extent to which employees are polite, friendly, and accommodating.
5. Accessibility and convenience: the ease of obtaining service.
6. Accuracy: the extent to which the service is performed correctly the first time.
7. Responsiveness: whether service personnel react quickly and resolve unexpected problems.

Reasons for the Recent Quality Revolution

A number of reasons exist for the increased quality consciousness of organizations today, as discussed in the following sections.

First is the exceptionally high quality of many foreign parts. In today's global economy, access to products and services of foreign-owned firms has become relatively easy. Think of the highest-quality auto tire, auto, or CD player that you can. Did names of foreign makers such as Michelin or Bridgestone, Toyota, Honda, or Mercedes, and Sony or Panasonic come to mind? We are all familiar with Japanese dominance of our auto and electronic markets. The ease of access of high-quality foreign makers to the U.S. market and the openness of the global market to U.S.-based firms mean that those firms with the best-quality products/services globally will set the standard. No longer does a U.S. manufacturer have to beat out only its U.S. competitors; it must beat out foreign competitors as well. As Jack Welch, General Electric's CEO notes, in the last decade the performance bar has been raised much higher for organizations to remain competitive, much less retain a market leadership.

Second is the enormous cost associated with poor quality. Some experts estimate that U.S. manufacturers spend two cents of every sales dollar just to rework poor-quality parts. This figure does not even include the costs of items that have to be scrapped as unusable.

A third reason is the increase in policing of quality by external groups. The network of quality information has increased dramatically in recent years. Groups such as the Consumer Product Safety Commission and other consumer organizations have begun to police quality through public opinion, boycotts, adverse publicity, and legal action. Auto manufacturers eagerly (or perhaps dreadfully) await the annual results of auto quality ratings by J.D. Power and Associates, the independent rating agency, or automobile safety ratings assigned by other groups. Restaurants and hotels await ratings of their services by AAA, Mobil, and other travel-related rating services. All types of manufacturers await the ratings of groups such as *Consumer Reports*. The publication *Successful Meetings* annually lists the resorts with the best meeting facilities and service. Many other industry publications do the same for firms operating in their industry.

ISO 9000 Registration certifying that a company meets certain quality standards.

A fourth reason for increased quality emphasis is the global certification requirement. With the opening of markets to global firms, some form of standardization is needed. **ISO 9000** registration certifies that a company meets certain quality standards in such areas as product design and development, manufacturing processes, testing, final inspection, installation, and service. For example, in the design and development of products, a company must have in place a system that enables it to understand customer needs, verify and control its design process, provide employees with correct documentation, assume responsibility for supplier and internal quality, maintain traceability throughout the assembly process, and maintain appropriate records and documentation. Companies whose systems are certified to comply with all standards achieve "registration." The rigorous documentation and standards required for ISO 9000 certification help many companies discover problems with their processes and take steps to get their house in order prior to visitation by the third-party auditor.

Evolution of the Quality Explosion in the United States

Learning Objective 3

Describe how the recent U.S. quality resurgence began.

Deming's 85–15 rule

Assumes that when things go wrong, 85 percent of the time the cause is from elements controlled by management.

The background of today's surging quality movement in the United States traces to Japan. Following World War II, the words "Made in Japan" connoted cheap, inferior quality. As part of General MacArthur's program to help rebuild the country, 50-year-old W. Edwards Deming, a U.S. statistical quality control advocate, was brought to Japan to teach statistical quality control concepts. Deming addressed 21 top Japanese executives who were eager to learn and who represented the industrial leaders of the country. His theories formed the basis of **Deming's 85–15 rule.** This rule assumes that when things go wrong, 85 percent of the time the cause is attributed to elements controlled by management, such as machinery, materials, or processes, while only about 15 percent of the time are employees at fault. Thus, Deming believes that management rather than employees is to blame for most poor quality. The Japanese embraced Deming's message and transformed their industries by using his techniques. His "fourteen points for quality," as shown in Exhibit 2–4, are the actions he believed necessary for an organization to successfully make the quality "transformation."

Deming's contributions were recognized early by the Japanese. In 1951 the Deming Application Prize was instituted by the Union of Japanese Scientists and Engineers, and Deming was awarded the nation's highest honor, the Royal Order of the Sacred Treasure, from the Emperor of Japan. By the mid-1970s the quality of Japan's products

Exhibit 2–4
Deming's Fourteen Points for Quality

1. Top management should establish and publish a statement of the organization's purpose and commitment to quality products and services and continuous improvement.
2. Everyone throughout the organization should learn the new philosophy.
3. Dependence on "inspecting" quality into products should be shifted to an attitude of "expecting" quality by having it built into the system.
4. There must be a systematic way to select quality suppliers, rather than simply on the basis of cost.
5. The organization must be devoted to continuous improvement.
6. All employees should be trained in the most modern quality and problem-solving techniques.
7. Leadership techniques consistent with getting the most commitment from employees should be practiced throughout the entire organization.
8. Fear should be eliminated from the work environment.
9. Teams and work groups must work smoothly together; barriers between functional departments must be eliminated.
10. Exhortations, posters, and slogans asking for new levels of workforce productivity must be backed by providing the methods to achieve these.
11. Numerical production quotas should be eliminated. Constant improvement should be sought instead.
12. Barriers that deprive employees from pride in their work must be removed.
13. A vigorous program of education, retraining, and self-improvement for all employees must be instituted.
14. A structure in top management that will push the thirteen points above to achieve the transformation must be created.

Source: Reprinted by permission of The Putnam Publishing Group from *Deming Management at Work* by Mary Walton. Copyright © 1990 by Mary Walton.

Dr. W. Edwards Deming (1900–1993) was a visionary whose work is credited with creating the quality revolution. Deming continued lecturing on quality, even at the ripe old age of 93.

exceeded that of Western manufacturers, and Japanese companies made significant U.S. and global market penetration.

In 1980 U.S. automakers commanded a 71 percent share of the U.S. market; by 1991 this had fallen to 62 percent. U.S.-made computers dropped from 94 percent of the U.S. market in 1979 to 66 percent in 1989. Similar losses occurred in the machine tool, electronics, steel, motorcycle, and other industries. Harley-Davidson, the revered 90-year-old motorcycle manufacturer, saw its market share drop from 40 percent to 23 percent over a four-year period in the 1980s. Xerox, which invented the copier, fell from 90 percent to 15 percent market share as Japanese copiers gobbled up competition. American business was being threatened as never before.

In the early '80s, David Garvin of the Harvard Business School spent several years in Japan and the United States studying air conditioning manufacturers. He found that Japanese companies were far superior. The failure rate in such key components as compressors, coils, and thermostats of the worst Japanese manufacturer was less than half that of the best U.S. manufacturer! Yet he found that manufacturing techniques were basically the same. The difference was in management. At Japanese plants, supervisors said quality was their major goal; at U.S. plants, supervisors said meeting production quotas was the major goal. At Japanese plants, meetings were held daily to discuss failure; at American plants, the range was anything from 10 meetings monthly in the best plants to just 4 a month in the worst plants. All Japanese companies had goals for quality, such as the percent of defects allowable, against which their managers and workers were measured; only one-half of U.S. plants had quality goals. In Japanese plants, the top quality manager reported to a higher-level manager than in most American plants. New hires in Japanese plants received much broader training and for considerably longer time periods than their U.S. counterparts. Little wonder that "Made in the U.S.A." had become no match for Japan's higher-quality products in many industries.[4]

The United States' quality problem was first highlighted in 1980 when NBC aired a program entitled, "If Japan Can . . . Why Can't We?" The program introduced the then 80-year-old Deming who, although an American, was virtually unknown in this country. This program ignited a spark that awakened American executives and helped fuel a quality turnaround. Major companies, especially those which were threatened, embarked on extensive programs to improve quality. Ford Motors was among the first to invite Deming to help transform its operations. Within a few years, Ford's results improved dramatically; its profits became the highest for any company in automotive history, and by 1992 its Ford Taurus unseated the Honda Accord as the best-selling domestic model.

Malcolm Baldrige Quality Award A symbol of America's best in quality.

In 1987 Congress established the **Malcolm Baldrige National Quality Award** (see Exhibit 2–5), which generated a remarkable interest in quality by American business.

Dr. Joseph Juran, who, like Deming, was one of the premier leaders in the quality movement both in Japan and the United States, observed

> I have become optimistic for the first time since the quality crisis descended upon the United States. I now believe that during the 1990s the number of U.S. companies that have achieved stunning results will increase by orders of great magnitude. I also believe that during the 1990s the United States will make great strides toward making "made in the U.S.A." a symbol of world-class quality.[5]

Approaches to Managing Quality

Learning Objective 4

Identify the four approaches to managing quality.

Organizations may seek to manage quality in one of several ways. These approaches are (1) traditional, (2) problem solving, (3) proactive, and (4) total quality.

TRADITIONAL APPROACH. The **traditional quality approach** to managing quality emphasizes quality assurance, quality control, or statistical quality control techniques based on random sampling. This approach focuses on inspection as the basis for ensuring that products or services meet the company's standards. The emphasis is not so much on error *prevention* as it is on error *detection*.

traditional approach Emphasizes quality assurance, quality control, or statistical quality control techniques based on random sampling.

PROBLEM-SOLVING APPROACH. The **problem-solving quality approach** emphasizes identification of defects through the traditional approach while rigorously seeking remedies to these problems through team problem-solving techniques such as quality teams. Training team members in problem solving and group dynamics is an important part of this approach.

problem-solving approach Emphasizes identifying defects while seeking remedy to these problems through quality teams.

PROACTIVE APPROACH. The **proactive quality approach** is a more aggressive quality approach, focusing on building quality into the process in advance rather than on "inspecting it into" the system. It emphasizes error *prevention* through training of employees, design of systems, selection of suppliers, and so on.

proactive approach Building quality into the process in advance rather than "inspecting it into" the system.

Exhibit 2–5

*The Malcolm Baldrige
National Quality Award*

The prize is only a gold-plated medal encased in a crystal column 14 inches tall. But since 1987, when the U.S. Congress created the Malcolm Baldrige National Quality Award at the urging of business leaders, it has symbolized America's best in quality. Named for the much-admired former U.S. Secretary of Commerce, Malcolm Baldrige, who died in 1987, the award is administered by the National Institute of Standards and Technology, with endowments covering costs of administration and judging of applicants.

Applications are scored by examination teams drawn from senior ranks of business, consultants, and academics. The highest scoring applicants move on to stage two—a site visit by four to six examiners who verify the facts in the application and probe more deeply into organizational processes. They report back to a nine-judge panel, which recommends winners to the Secretary of Commerce. The White House makes the formal announcements.

Winning a Baldrige has proved tough. In 1988, the first year of eligibility, only 3 of 66 applicants were winners; in 1989, only 2 of 40.

There are eight essentials that organizations must observe in order to win:

1. Establish a plan to seek improvement continuously in all phases of operations—not just manufacturing but purchasing, sales, human relations, and other areas.
2. Put in place a system that accurately tracks and measures performance in those areas.
3. Establish a long-term strategic plan based on performance targets that compare with the world's best in that particular industry.
4. Link closely in a partnership with suppliers and customers in a way that provides needed feedback for continuous improvement.
5. Demonstrate a deep understanding of customers in order to convert their wants into products.
6. Establish and maintain long-lasting customer relationships, going beyond product manufacture and delivery to include sales, service, and ease of maintenance.
7. Focus on preventing mistakes instead of developing efficient ways to correct them; that is, feedforward control is a must.
8. Perhaps most difficult, but imperative, is to make a commitment to quality improvement throughout all levels of the organization, including top, middle, and bottom.

Past winners since its inception in 1988 are shown below:

1995	Manufacturing	Corning Telecommunications Products	1991	Manufacturing	Solectron Corp. Zytec Corp.
		Armstrong World Industries		Small Business	Marlow Industries
1994	Service	AT&T Consumer Communication	1990	Manufacturing	Cadillac Motor Car Co.
		GTE Directories			IBM Rochester
	Small Business	Wainwright Industries		Service	Federal Express Corp.
1993	Manufacturing	Eastern Chemical Company		Small Business	Wallace Co.
	Small Business	American Rubber Company	1989	Manufacturing	Miliken & Co.
1992	Manufacturing	AT&T Network Systems Group/Transmission Systems			Xerox Business Products & Systems
		Texas Instruments Defense Systems and Electronic Group, Dallas, TX	1988	Manufacturing	Motorola, Inc. Westinghouse Commercial Nuclear Fuel Division
	Service	AT&T Universal Card Services, The Ritz-Carlton Hotel, Co.		Small Business	Globe Metallurgical, Inc.
	Small Business	Granite Rock Co.			

TOTAL QUALITY APPROACH. Also known as total quality management (TQM), the **total quality approach** reflects a major reorganization that strives to achieve customer satisfaction through continuous improvement of the organization's products and/or services and processes. It goes beyond the three approaches above; the term "total" reflects the fact that it is an overall organizational strategy initiated and committed to by top management and reflected at all organizational levels, including all employees, customers, and suppliers. The premise of the total quality approach is that a chain of events occurs when an organization's "quality" improves. Increased quality leads to increased market share, which increases profitability, as shown in Exhibit 2–6.

TQM Reflects a major reorganization to achieve customer satisfaction through continuous improvement of products or services.

Exhibit 2–6
*The Total
Quality Chain*

A diagram showing three boxes connected by arrows: "Improved Products/Services" → "Increased Market Share" → "Increased Profitability"

Total Quality Management (TQM)

Learning Objective 5

Understand the three components of total quality management.

A major criticism of management is its attempt to grab onto any perceived solution—any hot new buzzword of the decade—and attempt to incorporate it. TQM, unfortunately, has been victimized in this same way as many organizations have adopted catchy slogans when, in fact, most U.S. firms have not come anywhere near the commitment required to adopt a total quality management process fully.

As one expert puts it, very few companies have considered adequately how they transform "the show"—the quality banners, slogans, and pep rallies—into a basic way of organizational life, i.e., "the way we do things around here."[6] Approaches to total quality management vary greatly among organizations not only because of differing commitment levels, but also because each organization must fit the framework best into its own unique environment.

Whatever the abbreviation (such as City Hospital's TQI), the key to recognizing an organization's true commitment to quality is that it will enlist most of Deming's fourteen points.

A true quality process has three fundamental bases, as shown by the three-legged stool in Exhibit 2–7. These are (1) customer focus, (2) continuous improvement, and (3) employee involvement. Note how these are reflected in Motorola's overall statement of its fundamental objective, beliefs, goals, and initiatives (Exhibit 2–8).

CUSTOMER FOCUS. In the book *In Search of Excellence*, Peters and Waterman identified what they considered the excellent U.S. companies and what made them so.[7] One of the common characteristics of these companies was their excellent service to customers. They made a point of understanding and keeping up with their customers' problems and complaints and in maintaining a feedback system as to how they could be more effectively served. Under TQM the entire organization commits itself to the concept of customer satisfaction.

While external customers are the most obvious, each organization has many internal customer links. Maintenance personnel serve operating departments. The information provided by accounting departments serves operating managers who use the

Exhibit 2–7
Three Bases of Total Quality Management

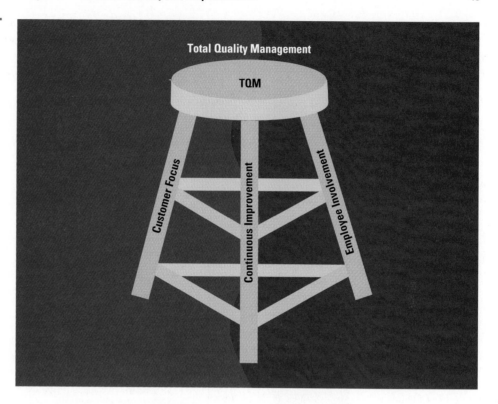

information to make decisions. Materials, products, and services contracted by purchasing specialists serve those internal customers for whom they are ordered. Even a manufacturing system can be viewed as a set of interrelated services: manufacturing is a customer of product design; assembly is a customer of manufacturing; sales is a customer of packaging and distribution. Thus, the concept of "total quality" can be viewed as the umbrella under which everyone in the organization strives to create customer satisfaction.

Central to "customer orientation" is the new way of viewing customers, quite unlike the incident shown below, as described by a quality consultant:

> **Several years ago I applied for a teaching job at a university out on the West Coast. At the time of the job interview, I entered the dean's outer office where his secretary was working at her desk. After seeming to ignore my presence for several minutes, she looked up. With a strong sense of impatience she snapped, "What do you want?".... I responded that I was there for a scheduled job interview with the dean. Upon hearing this, she smiled broadly and said, "Oh, I'm so sorry; I thought you were a student."[8]**

One important aspect of service is complaint resolution. Research has shown that about 80 to 95 percent of unhappy customers *will* do business with a company again if their complaint is resolved quickly. This drops to 20 to 45 percent if complaints are not resolved. Of unhappy customers who do *not* complain, only about 10 to 40 percent will become repeat customers.[9]

> **At Coca-Cola 60 employees in the Industry and Consumer Affairs Department are responsible for handling consumer inquiries as well as complaints. While most of**

Exhibit 2–8
Motorola's Fundamental Objective and Key Beliefs, Goals, and Initiatives Reflect Commitment to Quality

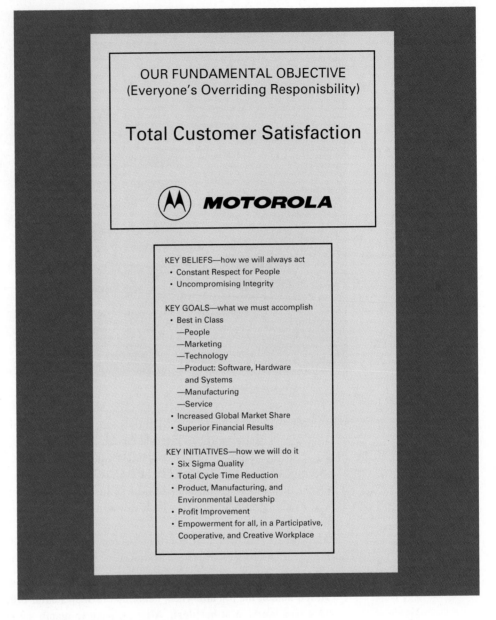

the 500,000 yearly contacts are inquiries about the product, when a customer calls with a problem, Coca-Cola sends a letter of apology, as well as coupons that allow replacement of the product. The customer also receives a "Service Quality Survey" asking the customer to rate the quality of Coke's response, including such factors as the professionalism and courtesy of the employee responding to the problem and whether the customer will continue to purchase Coca-Cola products. About 90 percent of customers express satisfactory handling of their complaint, but the company strives for perfection—100 percent satisfaction.[10]

CONTINUOUS IMPROVEMENT. A second important element of a total quality process is continuous improvement, or "kaizen," the Japanese term for it. Cummins Engine provides a five-day employee training program that targets continuous improvement. The company's "Just Do It" principles give you a good idea of what continuous improvement entails:

1. Discard conventional, fixed ideas about doing work.
2. Think about how to do it, rather than why it cannot be done.
3. Start by questioning current practices.
4. Begin to make improvements even if only 50 percent of them can be completed.
5. Correct mistakes immediately.[11]

Note that the approach not only emphasizes correction of errors, but complete rethinking of current practices.

Often, improvements are stimulated by having employees work on special problem-solving teams. Teams receive training in statistics, problem-solving skills, and team decision making to help them work effectively in solving problems and in generating improvement. As shown in Exhibit 2–9, all types of organizations employ such teams effectively.

Rick Pitino, head basketball coach of the University of Kentucky Wildcats, uses the following remarks to demonstrate the need for continuous improvement in coaching. At his coaching clinics he asks coaches in attendance to silently name the following:

1. The NFL football dynasty in 1960.
2. The NBA basketball dynasty of the '60s.
3. The Major League Baseball dynasty of the '60s.
4. The best-known American growth company of the '60s.

He usually gets as answers (depending somewhat upon the age of the coaches!) the Green Bay Packers, Boston Celtics, New York Yankees, and IBM. Then he asks, "Where are these today?" In each case, he notes, in the middle of the pack, or worse. He then talks about IBM's smugness with itself, and the premise, "If it's not broke, don't worry about fixing it." Pitino's theme to coaches reflects his continuous improvement theme, "If it's not broke," he states, "then break it."

Earlier you read about Deming's fourteen points. Point number eleven urges elimination of numerical production quotas. Deming feels that the emphasis on quantitative goals isn't conducive to the concept of continuous long-term improvement. Employees and managers obsessed with "making short-term quota" do it at the expense of "quality." Managers may defer maintenance or allow lower-quality work so as to meet production quotas. Additionally, Deming feels that quotas imply a type of finality. For example, a cost-cutting program is thought of as a one-time event with a start and an end . . . the cost-cutting goal is reached, and therefore, additional cost cutting requires a new program. Under a quality process, the continual, ongoing, cost-cutting effort would become built into the organization's continuous improvement culture.

Perhaps one reason that Western management tends to be complacent about methods, processes, and results is because at one time it did things the best way. Frederick W. Taylor and his associates in Scientific Management in the early 1900s asserted that the one best way to accomplish any job or work can be determined through systematic study. These best ways are carefully mapped out by industrial engineers, taught to workers, and monitored by supervisors to ensure that workers

Exhibit 2–9
*Continuous
Improvement Teams
Work in All Sectors*

Manufacturing

A team at Motorola's Americas Parts Division in Schaumburg, Ill., simplified the way its operation handled customer-service calls. The changes slashed the percentage of customers who got a busy signal or hung up in frustration from 43% to 2% and saved the business at least $238,000 a year. The regulatory streamlining team at circuit-board maker Solectron in Milpitas, Calif., worked with local government officials to cut red tape involved in getting a commercial building permit—a key problem in the computer business where companies can't afford delays. The suggestions made it possible for 95% of permits—including many complicated permits involving companies that produce hazardous waste—to be processed in one day, most of the rest within a week. Previously, the process often would take weeks.

Service

"The Uptimers" team at Chase Manhattan dramatically reduced the time that Chase's automated teller machines were inaccessible to customers—an area where Chase lagged its banking competitors. The team found that the machines were running out of audit tape and that employees were shutting the ATMs down too often for servicing. Their suggestions—which included better training—cut ATM downtime more than 90%. The guaranteed access providers team at Pacific Bell in California worked with supplier Northern Telecom to reduce phone-service outages, 85% of which were caused by technician error. The team beefed up training for technicians and standardized operating procedures. Result: Outages fell 57%, saving Pacific Bell $9 million.

Government

The "Innovators" team at the Tennessee Valley Authority's John Sevier Fossil Plant in Rogersville, Tenn., developed procedures to prevent water pumps from failing and causing power outages. After the changes, the average time between the failures rose to 731 days from 206 earlier, saving TVA up to $24,000 a year and giving customers a more reliable source of power. A five-member team at U.S. Defense Plant Representative Office Sikorsky cut the number of oil leaks in the General Electric T700 engines that power Sikorsky Black Hawks and other military helicopters, a problem that had caused the aircraft to need unscheduled maintenance. The team revised GE's engine assembly procedures and improved training. The cost of maintenance fell to $4,000 a month last year from $20,000 a month in 1991.

Not for Profit

A team at the Swedish-American Health System in Rockford, Ill., found that only 47% of chronic lung-disease patients were using their inhalers properly two to three weeks after being discharged from the hospital. The team produced an instructional video and improved the hospital's instruction booklet, using large print, pictures, and simple language. The percentage of recently discharged patients using inhalers properly shot to 90%. A team at the Anderson Area Medical Center in Anderson, S.C., revamped the hospital's record-keeping system. The changes sharply reduced the number of duplicate records, giving doctors more complete and accurate information about patients.

Small Organization

A six-member team at Madison Paper Industries in Madison, Maine, reduced the amount of waste generated by Madison's paper plant by 60%—enough paper to roll out a 5-foot-wide sheet from Portland, Maine, to Los Angeles 16 times. The waste reduction saved the company at least $3.25 million a year. The 13-member adipic acid packaging team at Hi-Port, a packager and distributor of specialty chemicals in Highlands, Texas, improved inventory control and communications internally and with corporate customers. Shipments of adipic acid went from a 93% error-free rate in early 1993 to a 100% error-free rate last year.

perform as taught. Taylor's philosophy is strongly pervasive today among U.S. managers. Times change, however, and today's "best way" will not likely last. A total quality culture encourages continual change, a constant search for improvement. As shown below, there is no smugness at Motorola, the first Baldrige Award winner in 1988.

> **Perhaps the best-known and most ambitious continuous improvement goal is by Motorola. In 1987 Chairman Robert Galvin committed the company to a quality goal of 10 times improvement by 1989, 100 times improvement by 1991, and Six Sigma capability by 1992. Note that while it was quantitative, it was also continuous! To give you an idea of how much improvement this would be, "Six Sigma" reflects a defect rate of only 3.4 parts per million in each of the company's processes, whether manufacturing or administrative. On average, Motorola operations fell slightly short of Six Sigma (5.4) in 1992, a phenomenal result in and of itself. Its leaders have recommitted to going beyond Six Sigma, planning to change its measures from parts per million to parts per billion and to pursue a goal of 10 times defect reductions every two years. It also has established a reduction goal in new product development cycle time of 10 times improvement over a 5-year period.[12]**

Organizations have numerous tools/processes that can help them in their quest for continuous improvement. Two important concepts with which you should be familiar are benchmarking and reengineering.

BENCHMARKING. Benchmarking is the process of comparing company practices and methods against the practices of firms who are world-class performers. Benchmarking gives you a lofty standard to reach for, but it helps you improve. As shown below, a number of benchmarks, rather than only one, may be appropriate. IBM's Rochester, New York, division, in creating a new minicomputer, the AS 400, benchmarked top-notch internal IBM divisions as well as successful outside firms. Outside firms visited included: (1) Xerox, the first U.S. firm to utilize benchmarking in the late 1970s and world-class in benchmarking processes; (2) Motorola, world-class for reducing quality defects; (3) 3M, which provided information for resource manufacturing planning capability; (4) Hewlett-Packard, which provided insights into the effective use of service representatives; and (5) Japanese firms, in the area of just-in-time inventory. IBM Rochester was able to produce from start to finish a minicomputer that exceeded all expectations.

benchmarking Comparing company practices against those of world-class performers.

SELF-CHECK

Assume that you are director of nursing at City Hospital. How would you apply the principle of benchmarking to continually improve "quality" in the nursing department?

REENGINEERING. Reengineering is a fundamental rethinking and redesign process to achieve improvements in a critical area of performance, such as cost, quality, service, or speed. Rather than modifying current work procedures, reengineering begins with a clean slate and replans the job from beginning to end. Thus, inefficiencies can be eliminated and productivity increased.

reengineering A redesign process for improving critical areas of performance.

Hewlett-Packard successfully reengineered a process to enable it to produce significant and measurable improvements in customer satisfaction—in less than nine months.

A good example of reengineering is the case of Wal-Mart and Procter & Gamble. The two worked together to reengineer the inventory system for Pampers Diapers, which were stored at Wal-Mart distribution centers. When distribution centers ran low, the order would be placed to Procter & Gamble, which shipped to the distribution centers, which then shipped to the stores. The reengineered system provides information on each store's inventory to Procter & Gamble, who now has authority to ship directly to Wal-Mart stores. This saves Wal-Mart the costs of ordering, storage, and distribution and allows Procter & Gamble to develop a closer link with its direct customers, the individual Wal-Mart stores. Both companies have benefited from this reengineering.[13]

EMPLOYEE INVOLVEMENT. The third major component of total quality management is the active involvement of employees in the process. Already you have learned about this topic in the section on employee empowerment, so our remarks here serve primarily as reinforcement. As the spirit of a total quality philosophy is to unleash the creativity and capture the commitment of those workers most closely linked to the organization's services and products, it is essential that *all* employees, not just a select few managers or professionals, actively participate in the total quality process.

Note that at City Hospital, numerous cross-functional teams throughout the hospital were "involved" in solving problems within the hospital.

Employee involvement is the key vehicle used in achieving customer satisfaction and continuous improvement, the two other legs of the total quality stool.

At Bowater Carolina, for example, to increase employees' awareness and identification with the "entire company operations," external users of the company's products are frequently brought in to discuss what they require of good quality paper, special needs they may have, and the quality of Bowater's paper as compared to competitors. Bowater has also arranged for employees to visit end-users of their products, such as the *Charlotte Observer,* to observe the products they've created being put to use. They also interface with *Observer* employees. The result is that Bowater employees identify more with their own company, its products, and their customers.

Employee involvement also helps achieve continuous improvement through participation in special problem-solving teams, natural work teams, or as individuals empowered to make their own job improvements.

In understanding total quality, organizations seem to underrate the commitment level needed to practice employee involvement. Major commitments to training in job skills, problem solving, and group dynamics require large commitments of money and time. Because management styles and attitudes are often inconsistent with the notion of "empowered" employees, some programs never fully leave the ground. Top management must not only lend support to the shift to employee involvement practices, they must visibly lead the way.

ROLE OF THE SUPERVISOR IN EMPOWERMENT AND TOTAL QUALITY

As you have seen throughout this chapter, the trends toward greater empowerment and the increasing emphasis on quality have their largest impacts upon the way operating-level personnel perform their work. But the jobs of managers at all levels, and especially the first-line supervisory level, also require significantly changed roles.

Major Impact at the Supervisory Management Level

Learning Objective 6

Explain how the supervisor's job is affected by empowerment and quality programs.

Since first-line supervisors work directly with operating-level employees, their own jobs are significantly modified under empowerment and total quality initiatives. Consider the major changes sought at the operation level: increased commitment, greater use of employee involvement, continuous improvement, increased pride in work, highly trained employees capable of solving their own job problems, design of jobs to allow employees greater responsibility, and the elimination of fear from the work environment. These factors, if they are actively sought by upper management, have a profound impact upon the way supervisors perform their jobs.

Empowerment and total quality efforts require much top management commitment and even structural changes. But the fact remains: the employee level is where the "rubber meets the road." The first-line supervisor then becomes the agent of change in helping overcome numerous resistances. For example, employees may resist additional responsibility, may distrust management's commitment to the changes, or may feel threatened by having to learn new skills. They may resist empowerment because they fear taking risks. The supervisor's challenge becomes one of attempting to overcome these obstacles. As shown in City Hospital, managers and supervisors may also harbor many of the same, if not more, doubts as employees and also resist empowerment and total quality initiatives.

The Emerging Supervisor: Teacher, Leader, Coach

Some ways in which the supervisor's job in a traditional organization tends to differ from one in an empowered or total quality organization are discussed below and shown in Exhibit 2–10.

1. The traditional view focuses on the supervisor as the key to effectiveness. The supervisor plans, schedules, organizes, has the most responsibility for problem solving, and so on. In the empowered/quality view, work teams are the primary players. They often perform, plan, schedule, and provide much of their own work direction.
2. Traditionally the supervisor has the dominant work-unit role and is actively involved in all major elements of the work. Under an empowered/quality approach, employees assume more responsibility for their own work. Thus, the supervisor plays a supportive role.
3. In traditional systems supervisors are required to possess strong technical skills; often they are as technically competent, if not more so, than their work group members. This is less the case in empowered/total quality organizations. The supportive role played by supervisors requires primary skills in facilitation, such as helping, encouraging, and supporting.
4. The traditional supervisor's job may be seen as seeking stability, maintaining a consistent performance level, and managing the status quo. Supervisors of empowered/total quality groups seek constant improvement, encouraging change and departure from the status quo.
5. Because they were technically expert and the focal point of departmental decisions, traditional supervisors rely on their ability to inform, explain, and persuade. Supervisors of empowered and total quality organizations rely more on effective listening . . . to employees' needs, concerns, and ideas.
6. Under the traditional system supervisors bear primary responsibility for their work unit's results, be they good or bad. Supervisors of empowered groups share responsibility for results with employees, since employees strongly influence their own performance.
7. In the traditional system supervisors are expected to resolve most performance problems. In empowerment and total quality organizations supervisors are more likely to involve employees in problem solving. Or, as is the case in self-managed teams, teams themselves are expected to solve their own problems.

Exhibit 2–10
Changing Views of the Supervisor's Job

View of Supervisor's Job in Traditional Organization	View of Supervisor's Job in Empowered/Total Quality Organization
Supervisor-focused work unit	Team-focused work unit
Dominant role	Supportive role
Technical skills emphasis	Facilitation skills emphasis
Seeking stability	Encouraging change
Telling, selling skills	Listening skills
Personal responsibility for results	Shared responsibility for results
Personal problem solving	Team problem solving
Narrow, vertical communication	Broader, horizontal, external communication
Fear, pressure used to motivate employees	Pride, recognition, growth used to motivate employees
Autocratic decision style	Participative decision style

8. Traditional supervisors' primary interactions are vertical—with their own supervisor and their immediate work group. Supervisors or empowered employees interact with a broader constituency—peers, suppliers, service departments, and customers, as well as their immediate work group.

9. In the traditional system fear, pressure, and close supervision are common supervisory approaches. These are less appropriate in an empowered high-quality work culture, which values trust, recognition, pride, and employee involvement.

10. Because traditional supervisors are often the most knowledgeable about work processes in their department, they often use an autocratic approach; they make decisions and run the show. Today's empowerment/total quality culture invests heavily in trained, highly competent employees; supervisors are expected to use approaches that involve employees in decision making.

You might think of the supervisor's job in a high empowerment/total quality organization as being summarized by the two roles of leader and coach. As a *leader* the supervisor provides vision and ensures that members understand, accept, and are committed to the unit's goals. As a *coach* the supervisor trains, shows, explains, provides performance feedback, and helps members increase their levels of job performance.

As you recall, the title of this book is *Supervisory Management: The Art of Empowering and Developing People.* Also note that much of this text deals with topics that can be closely tied to the teacher-leader-coach roles: communication (Ch. 7); motivation (Ch. 8); leadership (Ch. 9); team building and managing change (Ch. 10); coaching for higher performance (Ch. 13); facilitation skills, managing conflict and stress

(Ch. 15); selecting, training, and compensating employees (Ch. 16); and appraising and disciplining employees (Ch. 17).

We feel that empowerment and the three underlying components of the total quality movement—customer focus, continuous improvement, and employee involvement—will continue to become increasingly critical approaches to organizations in the future. And with it will come increasingly important challenges for employees, managers, and supervisors.

Chapter Review

Learning Objective 1

Define empowerment and give an example.

Two important trends currently impacting organizations of all types are empowerment and total quality. Empowerment is the granting of authority to employees to make key decisions within their area of responsibility. Empowerment exists along a continuum, ranging from traditional management to full empowerment.

Learning Objective 2

Identify and differentiate among the four levels of empowerment.

In traditional management most decisions are made above the employee level and little empowerment exists. At the suggestion level of involvement, employees are empowered to participate in suggestion system programs, or as part of problem-solving teams to make recommendations to resolve problems. Decision-making authority, though, rests with management. At the job involvement level of empowerment, employees are given much latitude to run their own jobs, making the major decisions involved. Finally, at full empowerment: (1) employees are involved to the highest extent on their own jobs, through profit sharing and ownership and/or stock awards; (2) company performance records are open to all employees; and (3) employees participate in making decisions beyond their own jobs and at the highest level of the organization.

A second recent trend is the quality movement. Quality of products and services has become increasingly important today because of (1) the major costs associated with poor quality, (2) the high-level quality of global conception, (3) activities of higher-profile groups that police quality, such as governmental bodies, consumer groups, and industrial and service quality rating agencies, and (4) the increasing use of certification requirements for firms that export. An example of the latter is ISO 9000, a registration process that certifies that a supplier meets certain standards of quality.

Learning Objective 3

Describe how the recent U.S. quality resurgence began.

The history of the current emphasis on quality traces to Dr. W. Edwards Deming, who, following World War II, helped Japanese firms greatly increase their levels of quality and capture large market shares in key U.S. industries. It was not until the early 1980s that the U.S. quality movement gained momentum and Deming's work became popular. His "Fourteen Points for Quality" reflect his formula for improved quality. In 1987 Congress established the Malcolm Baldrige National Quality Award, given to U.S. firms who meet the highest standards of quality performance.

 **Identify the four approaches to managing quality.**

Organizations generally follow one of several approaches to managing quality. The traditional approach uses such processes as quality control and statistical sampling and essentially emphasizes error detection. The problem-solving approach emphasizes identification of defects while rigorously pursuing improvements through the use of quality teams. In a proactive approach, organizations use employee training and careful choice of suppliers and other processes to "do it right the first time." In the total quality (TQM) approach, the organization embraces a comprehensive systemwide effort that entails continuous improvement, customer focus, and employee involvement as its major parts.

Learning Objective 5 **Understand the three components of total quality management.**

The total quality approach is based on the "quality chain" where higher-quality products and services lead to increased market share, which in turn leads to increased profitability. The customer focus of total quality includes internal as well as external customers.

Two important continuous improvement methods are benchmarking and reengineering. In benchmarking, a company compares its practices and methods to the practices of "world-class" performers as a basis for measuring its own progress. In reengineering, a company looks to create totally new approaches to how processes and activities can be performed effectively.

Learning Objective 6 **Explain how the supervisor's job is affected by empowerment and quality programs.**

Since empowerment and total quality have their largest impact at the operating level, the first-line supervisor's job is greatly affected. The supervisor must overcome many program obstacles such as employee resistance to change and lack of trust in higher management and lack of willingness to take on additional responsibility for effective performance. Whereas traditional supervisors may be directive and autocratic, the supervisor's role when total quality and empowerment programs are employed can be thought of more in terms of leader and coach.

Important Terms

benchmarking *pg. 49*
Deming's 85–15 rule *40*
empowerment *33*
full empowerment *37*
ISO 9000 *39*
job involvement *36*
Malcolm Baldrige
  National Quality
  Award *42*

proactive quality
  approach *42*
problem-solving quality
  approach *42*
reengineering *49*
suggestion
  involvement *35*

total quality approach
  (TQM) *44*
traditional quality
  approach *42*

Questions for Review and Discussion

1. What is meant by empowerment?
2. What are the four levels of empowerment?
3. What factors have caused the current quality emphasis in today's organizations?
4. What are the four different approaches to managing quality?
5. What are the three components of TQM?
6. In what ways is the supervisor's job affected by empowerment and total quality?

Skill Builder 2–1
Applying Empowerment

In Exhibit 2–3 you read about some actual examples of companies that practice "job involvement." These included specifics about employees at The Ritz-Carlton, Midas Muffler, AT&T, and Motorola.

Shown below are some positions with which you are likely to be familiar. To test your understanding of empowerment, give examples of how *job involvement* might be applied to empower individuals who hold these positions.

a. Waiter/waitress position in a casual dining restaurant chain such as Chili's or Applebees.
b. Clothing department salesperson position for a national department store chain such as Sears, Penneys, or Dillards.
c. Administrative assistant to the department head of a college or junior college.

Your instructor may want you to discuss your answers as part of a small group.

GROUP ACTIVITY

Skill Builder 2–2
The Quality Assignment

Assume that you are Medical Records Director of City Hospital, referred to in the opening case of the chapter. The major activities of your 65 department employees include the following:

a. Maintaining archives for medical records of all hospital patients.
b. Ensuring that charts of all discharged patients have been received from the various departments of the hospital that provided the major service to the patient.
c. Providing data to upper management on such items as bed occupancy rates, length of stay, diagnosis at admission, and so on.
d. Examining the records received from servicing departments to ensure completion. This includes such items as diagnosis, test reports, medications given, attending physician's notes, discharge summary, signatures, etc.
e. Providing record copies to requesting hospitals, physicians, and other health-care providers.
f. Providing information for legal or insurance purposes to third parties such as attorneys, governmental agencies, and insurers.

Assume that you were on board at the hospital when the new administrator indicated to all department heads that the hospital would be embarking on a total quality approach. Shortly thereafter, you and other department heads attended a three-day course designed to teach the overall total quality approach. At the end of the day one instructor concluded with, "You all have a good grasp now of what is involved in total quality. Accordingly, I have an assignment for you to bring to our next class. Be prepared to discuss your answers with your colleagues." The following questions were on the sheet given to you:

- Make a list of your department's key customers, both internal and external.
- List the important quality requirements that your department's customers have.
- Do they all have the same requirements or do some differ?
- List the suppliers that your department depends upon to meet your customers' quality requirements.
- Take one major activity of your department, and show how "continuous improvement" principles could be used.

Instructions:

1. Using the information presented in the six major activities of the medical records department as your basis, prepare your answers; respond to the instructor's assignment.
2. Meet in groups of 3–5 students and discuss.
3. Select a spokesperson who will present to the overall class a summary of your team's answers and discussion.

CASE 2–1

Hillshire Farm/Kahn's[14]

In 1988 Hillshire Farm merged with Kahn's to gain economies of scale and buying power in the smoked sausage market. Milton Schloss, president of Kahn's at the time of the merger, wanted to produce smoked sausage products that were equal to or superior to the market leader, Eckridge.

As president of Hillshire Farm and Kahn's, Schloss was a firm believer in "managing by walking around." He made a habit of making a daily tour of the plant and asking employees, "What's new?" One day an employee asked him if he really meant it. This surprised Schloss, and he arranged to meet privately with the employee early the next morning. The employee arrived with a balsa wood model of a new plant layout he had been working on at home. Recognizing the superiority of his ideas, Schloss asked him why he had not come forward sooner. The employee said that nobody had ever asked him. The design was implemented, and portions are still in place at Hillshire Farm in Cincinnati. This event was a catalyst for further quality efforts.

Drawing from a similar program at Procter & Gamble, Hillshire Farm developed a system called Deliberate Methods Change (DMC) to seek ways for continually improving processes. Using DMC, semivoluntary groups of salaried employees met to improve current processes. By emphasizing the positive aspects of improvement and refusing to place blame on workers for process design flaws, these groups built trust among the workforce.

Schloss was a firm believer in quality within the meat industry, and especially at Hillshire Farm. He used customer complaints—or more accurately, what customers found unacceptable—as the basis for defining quality. Schloss personally answered all customer complaints promptly, something that was unheard of at the time. Frequently customers were so surprised to hear from the company president that they apologized for their complaints. However, Schloss listened carefully to understand the nature of the complaint so that he could improve product quality. Also, he believed that a phone call from the company president would allow Hillshire Farm to keep the customer for life.

Schloss took a variety of steps to show his commitment and improve quality. He kept the plant grounds free of litter, freshly painted all the walls, and kept the grass and shrubbery neatly trimmed. In this way he communicated to employees the attitude they should adopt when they entered the building. Schloss also required that all telephone calls be answered after two rings and that the caller not be kept on hold for long.

The company defined four dimensions of quality—taste, particle definition, color, and packaging—and kept all employees continually informed of the company's quality standards. The accounting and finance departments judged quality according to how promptly and accurately they could make invoices and payments. Marketing and sales were responsible for identifying the features of the product that the customer perceived as most valuable and differentiable and for convincing the customer of Hillshire Farm's leadership in these features.

Schloss personally saw to it that these activities were performed throughout the company. He believed that management must act immediately on new ideas and suggestions. Getting commitment from supervisors was the most difficult task. Management had to explain the "hows and whys" behind the changes, motivate the workers, and recognize the top performers.

Instructions:
1. As described above, to what extent is Hillshire Farm/Kahn's incorporating each of the three components of total quality:
    a. customer focus
    b. continuous improvement
    c. employee involvement
2. What similarities/differences do you note between the quality/empowerment approaches taken by City Hospital (opening case) and Hillshire Farm/Kahn's?

BusinessLink
Quality: Wainwright Industries, Inc.

Wainwright Industries, a family-owned supplier to the automotive and aerospace industries, decided to upgrade its quality to remain competitive. To move the company forward, top management used the Baldrige Award criteria as guides to quality improvement. Wainwright emphasized training and empowering employees, customer satisfaction, and continuous improvement based on employee input and involvement. Team rewards replaced individual rewards. The company first focused on employee satisfaction. Satisfied employees would then be better able to respond to customer needs. Key results from quality improvement included lower costs, better safety, and higher profits. Through its efforts, Wainwright won the Baldrige Quality Award in the Small Business classification.

Chapter 3
Fundamentals of Planning and Time Management

Case 3

Changes at Dixon

Harold Marshall, newly promoted general manager of the Dixon Division of Computronix, Inc., was addressing a meeting of Dixon's 35 department heads, superintendents, and supervisors. The Dixon Division was one of the oldest in the Computronix system and one of the least cost-effective. In fact, there were rumors that it would gradually be phased out of operation.

Most people at the meeting were seeing Marshall for the first time, although his reputation had preceded him. At age 32, he had gained widespread exposure as manager of the company's "experimental" plant in Fresno, California. That plant utilized totally new technology and many radically innovative management techniques.

Marshall began:

> Ladies and gentlemen, it's good to meet many of you for the first time. We are faced with an important challenge—to increase the efficiency of this plant—and it's going to take dedication and commitment. I've promised Mr. Alexander [the vice-president] that I'll give it my all, and together we can show progress that will make top management commit itself to capital spending that will again make our division a top producer in the company.
>
> If we're going to improve, our management system must change drastically. At Dixon, we have been practicing "defensive" management. That is, we react to problems when or after they occur. We've been good at doing that. But to be effective today, we must become far better at planning our future—setting goals and objectives, developing ways to reach them, and making sure we get there. Our industry cannot fly by the seat of its pants as we've done in the past. Each and every one of us is going to have to become adept at planning—for the division, for each department, and for each work unit. This is especially true of our supervisory level, for that is where the rubber meets the road, so to speak. In the past, top management has done most of your planning for you—in fact, we're the ones responsible for your becoming "fire fighters." Things will have to change.
>
> Under the new unit planning system that we will establish, each of you will be required to commit to writing a unit plan to be signed by you and your manager, with copies sent to the next higher level. The plan will contain five major objectives of your unit for the next six months. Each objective will be specific and include actual figures, such as "to reduce labor costs in my unit by 12 percent in the next six months." These objectives should cover the most critical areas of your operation and, of course, will require your own manager's approval.

LEARNING OBJECTIVES
After reading and studying this chapter, you should be able to:

1 Explain the steps involved in planning.

2 Explain how planning differs at top, middle, and supervisory management levels.

3 Explain how the hierarchy of objectives works.

4 Discuss important guidelines in setting performance objectives.

5 Identify the steps in management by objectives (MBO).

6 Differentiate the various kinds of standing and single-use plans.

7 Draw a simple PERT chart.

8 Discuss some ways to effectively manage time.

Additionally, your unit plan will include the steps you'll take to achieve each objective, along with a timetable and names of employees responsible for each step. It should also identify the major potential impediments to reaching each objective, as well as your contingency plans for addressing these potential impediments. Finally, the plan should identify the process you'll use to monitor progress toward achieving the objectives.

Those of you who know me know that I am a firm believer in effective planning at all levels. I'm confident that implementing such a planning system—along with good follow-through—can help us make Dixon the most profitable division in the Computronix system.

Marshall continued to speak for about 15 minutes on such topics as the need to involve employees in the planning system, the importance of delegation, and the need for effective teamwork. He closed with an announcement that workshops would be held for all managers and supervisors to acquaint them with specific details of the new unit planning system.

If you don't know where you're going, any road will get you there.

Author Unknown

Nothing is more terrible than activity without insight.

Thomas Carlyle

We wish Marshall well in his attempt to turn Dixon around. Note the emphasis he places on effective planning. He is correct in his assessment of the role of supervisory management. Many managers see themselves as being strictly "fire fighters"—handling first this problem, then another, and then another. He is also correct in his view that supervisors at all levels must become more proficient at planning—perhaps the most neglected function of management.

This chapter builds on the ideas presented in Chapters 1 and 2. In Chapter 1 we discussed what management is, the managerial functions performed by managers, and the changing role of supervisory management. We now focus on one of the management functions—planning. As you learned in Chapter 2, much planning must precede effective empowerment of employees and achievement of improved quality.

SOME IMPORTANT POINTS ABOUT PLANNING

Suppose that you and a group of friends decide to take a weekend camping trip. Effective planning requires answers to the following kinds of questions. What constraints impact the group, such as the distance you can travel or the funds you have available? What activities most interest the group, such as hiking, boating, fishing, or mountain biking? What camping sites are available to choose from, and which activities are offered at each? What supplies and equipment will be needed, and does the group have the means to obtain them? Only after questions such as these are answered can the plan develop. Your group can then decide when and where to go, what time to leave, who will bring what, and perhaps even schedule your planned activities. Your plan should also anticipate future contingencies such as weather and occupancy of sites. Should rain be forecast, might you postpone the trip to a later date? If not, might you bring rain gear or have games available for indoor use? Might you reserve a site in advance or, if not, have a nearby backup site in mind?

Obviously, the trip's effectiveness greatly depends upon the quality of planning that you and your group put into it. Supervisory planning works much the same way. Supervisors perform planning—both routine and more detailed—as an ongoing part of their jobs. These may include plans for scheduling work, developing and living within budgets, making job assignments, and so on. They must also plan for major events that may happen infrequently, such as when a department manager of a major department store plans for an annual inventory count or when a pizza store manager knows a week in advance that he must deliver 300 freshly baked pizzas to a convention of 600 people.

A major planning activity for maintenance supervisor Jamie Medlin of Bowater (Case 1) involves a planned shutdown of a major piece of equipment, such as a paper machine. Medlin must determine the major tasks involved, ensure that the resources needed are on hand, and assign his team of mechanics to various maintenance tasks best suited to their abilities. He must also make contingency plans to address special problems encountered and have on hand backup personnel to support other departments' maintenance needs. Since a paper machine loses thousands of dollars for every hour it is nonoperational, it is imperative that the seven-hour shutdown run smoothly as scheduled.

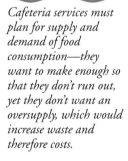

Cafeteria services must plan for supply and demand of food consumption—they want to make enough so that they don't run out, yet they don't want an oversupply, which would increase waste and therefore costs.

Basic Steps in Planning

As stated in Chapter 1, planning means deciding what will be done in the future. It is forward-looking. A manager must have a lot of discipline to set aside the time needed to solve present problems and to plan for the future. Moreover, much planning is intellectual; it is a "between the ears" activity that is hard work. Do you recall the discussion in Chapter 1 of the conceptual, human relations, administrative, and technical skills used by managers? Planning is normally an example of a conceptual skill. But it also requires other skills, especially to get the plans adopted and implemented.

Planning covers a wide variety of activities, from simple to complex, and from short- to long-term. But in all such cases, the three basic planning steps listed below exist. These are shown in Exhibit 3–1.

1. Setting an objective, or goal
2. Identifying and assessing present and future conditions affecting the objective
3. Developing a systematic approach by which to achieve the objective (the *plan*)

Three additional steps must also be taken in order to achieve the objective or goal established in step 1, though they are not exactly planning steps. These include

4. Implementing the plan. (Organizing, Leading, Staffing)
5. Monitoring the plan's implementation. (Controlling)
6. Evaluating the plan's effectiveness. (Controlling)

These last three steps illustrate how closely related planning is to the other managerial functions, especially controlling.

The first step in planning—setting objectives or goals—addresses the issue of what one hopes to achieve. In the opening case, note that Marshall's new planning system would require each manager to develop a plan that addresses five major objectives that their unit seeks to achieve. We shall discuss the important process of objective setting later in the chapter.

The second planning step—identifying and assessing present and future conditions affecting objectives—recognizes important variables that may influence objectives. In our camping trip example given earlier, these would include factors such as equipment needed, weather, site availability, and so on. Since planning involves the future, certain assumptions about the future must be made. Medlin, when planning his paper machine maintenance job, makes assumptions about length of time to complete certain parts of the job, about key personnel showing up on time, about necessary parts being on hand, and so on.

The third step of planning is the developing of a systematic approach to achieve the objective. This third step becomes the *Plan*. It addresses such issues as the what,

Exhibit 3–1
*The Three
Planning Steps*

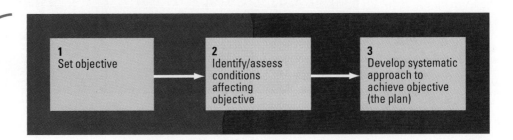

when, who, where, and how of the plan. The plan's complexity and importance is a major factor in determining how formal and detailed this final step must be. The plan to build a new 200-bed wing expansion for City Hospital (Case 2) will be much more formal and detailed than Supervisor Medlin's plan for the paper machine scheduled shutdown. Many daily plans are routine, however, and are carried about in supervisors' heads rather than being committed to paper.

Planning Is Most Closely Related to Controlling

Of the managerial functions, planning is probably most closely related to controlling. As you will see in more detail in Chapter 11, the steps in controlling are

1. Setting performance goals, or norms.
2. Measuring performance.
3. Comparing performance with goals.
4. Analyzing results.
5. Taking corrective action as needed.

"Siamese twins" of management Planning and controlling.

Note carefully the first step in the above list. It involves planning! Because planning is such an integral part of controlling, these two functions are sometimes called the **"Siamese twins" of management.**

Managers Tend to Neglect Planning

Poor planning results in disorganized and uncoordinated activities, thus wasting time, labor, and money. Since thinking is often more difficult than doing, many managers, including supervisors, tend to slight planning. It is very tempting to forgo thinking about the future in order to get busy performing a task or solving present work problems. The result is frequently unsatisfactory, as shown in Exhibit 3–2.

Exhibit 3–2
Lack of Planning

As Harold Marshall, the new Dixon general manager in Case 3, pointed out, it's not unusual for a supervisor to spend his or her day fighting one "fire" after another—seemingly never catching up. Consider the following example:

> **Hank Green, a supervisor, had a hectic schedule and was about to be driven up a wall. He said: "Today I had three no-shows because of the weather, and my department is absolutely swamped. I'm pitching in myself, but I've also got to conduct a tour for some of our home office staff personnel after lunch. I'm supposed to meet with our industrial relations people on a case that goes to arbitration next week. To cap it off, Barbara Brown is asking for a transfer out of the department and wants to talk about it today. She and two of the other workers can't get along. This afternoon, I've got to have figures ready for the cost accounting department. On top of all this, I'm supposed to supervise my 19 people, three of whom are new hires and being broken in. What a day! But they all seem to be like this."**

Is it any wonder that this supervisor forgoes planning when his typical daily schedule is so demanding? But, ironically, many of the short-run crises that confront supervisors could be greatly eased by proper planning. As shown in Exhibit 3–3, when a supervisor devotes too little time to planning, short-run problems are likely to result, including impossible deadlines, unforeseen obstacles, crises, and crash programs. These problems preoccupy the supervisor, leaving little time to devote to planning—and the cycle goes on.

Contingency Planning Anticipates Problems

contingency planning
Thinking in advance about possible problems or changes that might arise.

It is important for a supervisor to build in flexibility by preparing contingency plans. **Contingency planning** means thinking in advance about problems or changes that may arise so that we are prepared to deal with them smoothly when they do arise. Consider the following example:

> **When the x-ray unit in the radiology department went down, Nurse Ratchett knew exactly whom to contact and how to divert patients to the x-ray machine in the hospital's emergency room.**

Exhibit 3–3
The Nonplanner's Cycle

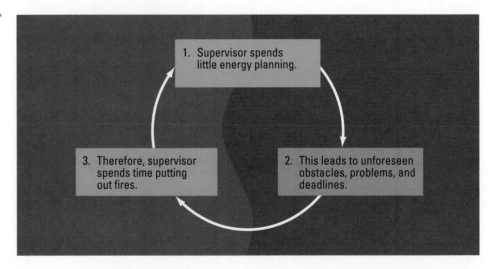

In earthquake-prone areas like California and Japan, companies must plan for the possibility that they or their suppliers will be shut down. Toyota, for instance, must make contingency plans for communications, supplies, and distribution in the event that a damaging quake occurs, like the recent one that hit Kobe, Japan.

Three weeks earlier, Charlie Fay had been relieved of his regular duties for a few days so that he could be trained as a backup forklift operator. Although not as expert as Willie Burns, Fay performed smoothly on the forklift when Burns was absent twice in one week.

You might think of contingency planning as the responses to the "what if . . . ?" questions that describe serious cast scenarios or events.

Contingency planning separates effective managers from ineffective ones. Proper anticipation of a crisis may prevent it from happening. If you are to be a good contingency planner, you will need to ask yourself the following questions and find answers to them.

1. What might happen that could cause problems within my area of responsibility?
2. What can I do to prevent these events from happening?
3. If these events do occur, what can I do to minimize their effect?
4. Have similar situations occurred in the past? If so, how were they handled?

PLANNING AT DIFFERENT MANAGEMENT LEVELS

Learning Objective 2

Explain how planning differs at top, middle, and supervisory management levels.

Management planning differs according to the level of management occupied, as shown in Exhibit 3–4. Top managers are more involved in **strategic planning,** which has longer time horizons, affects the entire organization, and deals with the organization's interface with its external environment. Strategic plans include:

1. The **mission,** which defines the fundamental purpose the organization attempts to serve and identifies its services, products, and customers.

Exhibit 3–4
Planning at Three Management Levels

Level	Planning Periods	What Is Planned
Top managers	Strategic long-term and intermediate-range plans of 1 to 5 or more years	Growth rate Competitive strategies New products Capital investments
Middle managers	Intermediate- and short-range plans of 1 month to 1 year	How to improve scheduling and coordination How to exercise better control at lower levels
Supervisors	Short-range plans of 1 day, 1 week, 1 to 6 months	How to accomplish performance objectives How to implement new policies, work methods, and work assignments How to increase efficiency (in costs, quality, etc.)

strategic planning Has longer time horizons, affects the entire organization, and deals with its interface to its external environment.

mission Defines the purpose the organization serves and identifies its services, products, and customers.

operational planning Consists of intermediate and short-term planning.

2. The overall objectives that drive the organization, such as profitability, customer satisfaction, employee relationships, environmental protection, or other critically important ends to be sought.
3. Strategies, the overall general activities that help the organization adapt to the important factors that comprise its external operating environment, including consumers, customers, suppliers, competitors, and social, political, economic, and technological conditions.

Middle and supervisory level managers are more concerned with operational planning. **Operational planning** consists of intermediate and short-term planning that facilitates achievement of the long-term strategic plans set at higher levels. As shown in Exhibit 3–4, these plans "operationalize" the plans made at higher levels and are much narrower in scope and much shorter-term than those planned for at higher levels. As one first-line manager related:

> Planning? Sure, I spend time planning. But most of my department's goals, objectives, and schedules are handed down to me from others. My planning is more along the lines of: How can I get better performance from my work group members? How can I cut down turnover and absenteeism? Given my group's workload for the week, or for the day, what's the best way to attack it? Whom should I assign to various jobs? Take last week for example. Four of my people were out—two sick and two on vacation—and I had a lot of planning to do figuring who'd work where and when. Things seemed to go a lot more smoothly because I'd put in some time anticipating the problems. I've learned to plan on having a few people out "sick" on the opening day of hunting season!

As you can see, all managers need to plan, regardless of their position in the hierarchy. Although planning at the supervisor level generally is less complex and involves less uncertainty than planning at higher levels, it is still crucial that such planning be done effectively.

SELF-CHECK What are other examples of events that supervisory managers must plan for?

IMPORTANCE OF SETTING OBJECTIVES

Objectives are crucial to effective planning. As the opening quotation in this chapter implied, only if you first know where you are heading can you effectively plan to get there.

What Are Objectives?

objectives or goals
Where the organization is going or what it wants to accomplish.

Objectives (goals) tell you where you are going or what you want to do. They answer the question "What do I want to accomplish?" Plans are aimed at achieving objectives.

Is there a difference between an *objective* and a *goal*? Management experts disagree on this matter. Some say that goals are broad and nonspecific, whereas objectives are narrow and specific. Others reverse the distinction just given. Still others do not distinguish between the two. Since the terms *goal* and *objective* are often used interchangeably, we will treat them as synonyms in this book.

Objectives as a Stimulus for Motivation and Effort

If you follow organized sports, you know that athletes frequently have objectives. Baseball players strive to hit .300; basketball players, to average 20 points; and football quarterbacks, to average 50 percent pass completions. A weekend golfer steps up to the first tee with an 85 in mind. A Friday-night league bowler shoots for an average of 150. Just as athletes are motivated by goals or objectives, so are people in the world of work.

> **Ann Casey really felt good. In her second week as a sales rep for Dover Apparel, she had sold over $12,000 worth of merchandise to retail stores in her southern Illinois territory. Her boss, too, was quite pleased. "We had set a goal for Casey of $15,000 for the entire month. She's likely to pass that next week, the way she's going. Casey's doing a great job."**

Objectives provide a stimulus for effort; they give people something to strive for. If Casey had no set goal—if she simply planned to go out and sell—she'd have no benchmark for telling whether she was doing well or poorly.

> **Lou Holtz, the now-famous coach from Notre Dame, is a firm believer in objective setting, as he tells in his video, *Do Right*. Fired from his first job as an assistant coach even before he reported to work (the coach who had hired him was fired, as were all his assistants), Holtz, with no contract, no job, and no money, became despondent and moped around the house.**

His wife bought him David Schwartz's *The Magic of Thinking Big.* Holtz stayed up all night reading it. One exercise required him to list 100 things he wanted to achieve in life. Enthusiastically, he showed the list to his wife. It included such aspirations as skydiving, meeting the Pope, and going into a submarine.

Before reading the book, Holtz had been unsure he wanted to be a football coach. But there, included in his list of 100 things he wanted to do in life, were two important items: to be head coach at Notre Dame and to win a national football championship!

Holtz credits Schwartz's book with turning his life around by making him focus on his objectives—what he wanted to achieve in life. He continues to stress the importance of objective setting among his coaches and players—not just in football but in academic performance and their personal lives as well.

Hierarchy of Objectives

Learning Objective 3

Explain how the hierarchy of objectives works.

hierarchy of objectives
A network with broad goals at the top level of the organization and narrower goals for individual divisions, departments, or employees.

In any organization, objectives are first needed at the top-management level. Once top management has determined broad objectives or goals, other levels of the organization, including supervisory management, reflect these in objectives or goals of their own, thus creating a **hierarchy of objectives.** Exhibit 3–5 presents a hypothetical hierarchy of objectives for Computronix, the firm described in Case 3.

Computronix's overall organizational objectives are increased profits, improved market share, new product introductions, and cost effectiveness, as well as others not mentioned. Note how one of these, the cost-effectiveness objective, is reflected at progressively lower organizational levels. At the division level, Dixon's objectives address cost effectiveness through objectives that seek a 5 percent reduction in production costs and the implementation of a new inventory control system. The Dixon maintenance department reflects the plant's 5 percent production cost reduction through the objectives of reduction of equipment downtime and upgrading the training of maintenance technicians. The preventive maintenance supervisor's objectives reflect the maintenance department head's objectives, and so on down the line. This diagram, though simplified, shows how the individual worker can be linked to top corporate levels through objective setting.

Unified Planning Through Objectives

unified planning Coordinating departments to ensure harmony rather than conflict or competition.

A major advantage of organizational objectives is that they give managers at lower levels guidance in developing their own tactical plans and coordinating their own activities. Ideally, top management's objectives should give tactical plans at lower levels unity of purpose. **Unified planning** means ensuring that plans at all organizational levels are in harmony, rather than at cross-purposes, with one another. Unified planning is especially important where coordination is required among departments or work units. Many supervisors are extremely dependent on other departments in accomplishing their own objectives. As shown in the example below, lack of unified planning at Computronix's Dixon Division has led to difficulties!

"This is ridiculous! Those @#$%&* are trying to cut me down," stormed Juan Fernandez, supervisor of the processing department at the Dixon Division. The division was under the gun to reach its monthly production quota, and Fernandez's

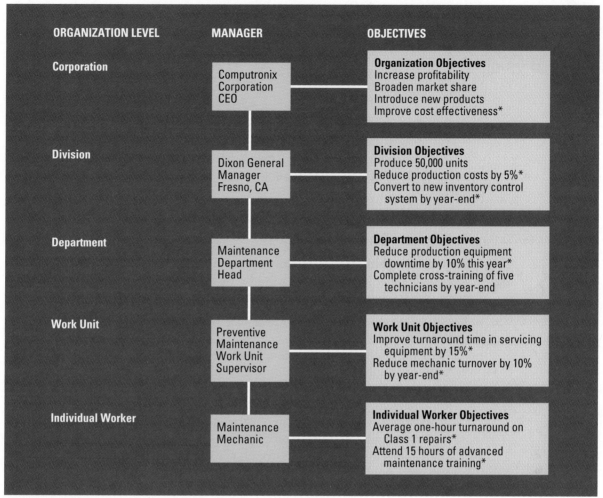

ORGANIZATION LEVEL	MANAGER	OBJECTIVES
Corporation	Computronix Corporation CEO	**Organization Objectives** Increase profitability Broaden market share Introduce new products Improve cost effectiveness*
Division	Dixon General Manager Fresno, CA	**Division Objectives** Produce 50,000 units Reduce production costs by 5%* Convert to new inventory control system by year-end*
Department	Maintenance Department Head	**Department Objectives** Reduce production equipment downtime by 10% this year* Complete cross-training of five technicians by year-end
Work Unit	Preventive Maintenance Work Unit Supervisor	**Work Unit Objectives** Improve turnaround time in servicing equipment by 15%* Reduce mechanic turnover by 10% by year-end*
Individual Worker	Maintenance Mechanic	**Individual Worker Objectives** Average one-hour turnaround on Class 1 repairs* Attend 15 hours of advanced maintenance training*

*Objectives directly linked to improved cost effectiveness.

Exhibit 3–5
*Hierarchy of Objectives
for Computronix*

department absorbed a lot of the pressure. Fernandez continued: "If *we* don't process quota, the division doesn't make quota. It's as simple as that. But those jerks in maintenance are killing me. Last week, they were supposed to shut me down for PM [preventive maintenance]. But what happened? Absolutely nothing! They couldn't get to me because they were caught shorthanded. You tell me why they had to send three of their technicians to a training school last week. I built my whole departmental schedule around last week's being slack. They knew I was scheduled for PM last week. There's no way they're shutting me down for even one minute during the next three weeks."

Dixon has a problem here! Fernandez doesn't want to shut down for maintenance, but he risks some downtime later if his equipment doesn't receive the proper preventive maintenance. The lack of unified planning at lower levels may cost Dixon its objectives. It has already strained the relationships among personnel in the plant.

What action would you take now if you were Juan Fernandez? What should be done to prevent this type of situation in the future?

As you will see shortly, other types of plans may also be established to aid in unified planning at lower levels. These other types of plans—policies, procedures, and rules—are more specific than objectives and spell out the methods used at lower levels.

Guidelines for Setting Performance Objectives

Learning Objective 4

Discuss important guidelines in setting performance objectives.

performance objectives
Tell employees what is acceptable.

Performance objectives tell employees what they must do to make their performance acceptable. Since all supervisors should set performance objectives in their departments, the following guidelines should prove helpful to managers at all levels.

1. *Select key performance areas for objectives.* Since objectives focus attention and effort, the more important areas will suffer if there are too many objectives. Instead of having 15 objectives, select four or five key areas of performance, such as quality, quantity, customer relations, and cost controls, that really count!
2. *Be specific, if possible.* The objective "to have good quality" probably means different things to you and to an employee. "To produce parts with a 99 percent acceptance rate by the inspection department" is more specific, and it gives the worker a tangible measure of progress.
3. *Set challenging objectives.* Objectives should not be set so low that they can be met through "average" effort. They should require some stretching, but they should not be so difficult to achieve that an employee is discouraged from committing to them.
4. *Keep objective area in balance.* Effort expended in one performance area frequently affects another. The quality of work required influences the quantity of work, and the quantity of work may affect employee safety. Objectives may be needed in each of these areas so as to balance them properly.
5. *Involve employees in setting objectives.* What do employees consider the key performance areas of their job? What do they think is a challenging but fair objective in a given area? When possible, ask these questions. There are times, however, especially during periods of financial difficulties and other crises, when it is not feasible or desirable to involve employees in objective setting.
6. *Follow up.* Once objectives have been set, supervisors tend to let up. Frequently only the supervisor knows the results of a worker's performance. Discuss progress

Note the quality objective in guideline 2: "to produce parts with a 99 percent acceptance rate by the inspection department." Do you see any problems with making this the only objective? Explain.

with employees. Sharing results and discussing employees' progress will improve their commitment and demonstrate your own.

THE SUPERVISOR AND MBO

management by objectives Managers and employees jointly establish objectives and develop a systematic approach for monitoring results.

Management by objectives (MBO) is a system whereby managers and their employees jointly establish objectives and develop a systematic approach for monitoring results. MBO is also called *management by results, joint target setting,* and *key performance area management,* among other terms. Its popularity has grown greatly since its introduction in the 1950s, especially in large organizations.

Do you recall the hierarchy of objectives mentioned earlier? Usually, MBO refers to an organizational system that ties together all levels of the organization's hierarchy. However, even a first-line manager may establish an MBO approach within his or her own unit. That's why the principles of MBO can be important to you as a supervisor, even if MBO is not used in your organization as a whole. The following example shows how MBO can work.

> **Ann Phillips, sales supervisor for a large cosmetics firm, said: "My boss doesn't believe in joint target setting or MBO or anything like that. She tells me what my group's goal is for the next year, and I have very little, if any, input into what the figure is. Once that's established, though, I meet with my salespeople. Then we come up with individual objectives for each of them as to sales volume, number of new accounts, timeliness in filing sales reports, average number of calls a day, and so on. I find that when I involve my people, they push themselves more. MBO has been very helpful to me."**

Steps in MBO

 **Learning Objective 5**

Identify the steps in management by objectives (MBO).

Although the approaches to MBO vary in detail, they usually involve five distinct steps, shown in Exhibit 3–6. As you will see later, the broken arrows labeled "6" can have several meanings. But first, let us explain each of the five steps.

STEP 1: DISCUSS THE SUPERVISOR'S RESPONSIBILITIES AND OBJECTIVES. The first step in MBO attempts to ensure effective communication and understanding between the supervisor and the employees. To illustrate the importance of this step, we invite you to take a simple test. Rank these items in order of importance for *your job*, with 1 being most important and 7 least important.

___ Safety of employees
___ Quality of output
___ Quantity of output
___ Cost control
___ High employee morale
___ Reduction of equipment downtime
___ Good housekeeping (clean work environment)

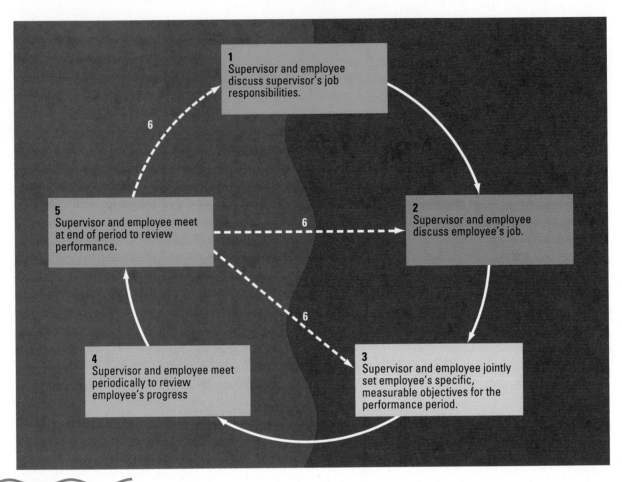

Exhibit 3–6
*Steps in the
MBO Process*

Now consider what priority *your boss* would say you should give to each of these items. The extent to which you and your boss agree reflects the degree of understanding between you. If the two of you rank these items similarly, you are directing your energy and efforts in the right direction (at least from your boss's viewpoint). But is there always such a clear understanding?

At a recent seminar, 17 supervisors were asked by the trainer to rank the objectives on the preceding list. The 17 supervisors ranked quantity of output, quality of output, and cost control as the three most important areas. The plant manager, present as an observer at the back of the room, was astounded by their response. Why? Because the plant had the poorest safety record of any of the six plants in the company system. In the industry, this plant ranked third from the bottom in safety among 60 plants in the Southwest. For the past four months, at weekly meetings with his department heads, the plant manager had been emphasizing safety as the primary objective in the plant. Obviously, the supervisors hadn't gotten the message. They were, in effect, working on the wrong priorities.

If you were the plant manager, what action would you take to ensure that the supervisors "got the message"? What might explain the difference in the way the plant manager and his 17 supervisors ranked safety?

The first step of MBO, properly taken, would have cleared up the misunderstanding in the preceding example. By discussing your own responsibilities and objectives with your employees, you allow them to understand where their own jobs fit into the bigger picture.

STEP 2: DISCUSS THE EMPLOYEE'S JOB. This step is an eye-opener for many supervisors. As the plant manager in the preceding example learned, employees' priorities may be quite different from those of their supervisor. Sometimes workers take on responsibilities outside the normal job description or spend time on duties that, from the supervisor's viewpoint, are not important. Step 2 of the MBO cycle permits clear communication and agreement as to just what the employees' jobs should entail.

STEP 3: SET OBJECTIVES JOINTLY. The joint selection of key performance objectives is the heart of MBO. Exhibit 3–7 illustrates some statements of specific, measurable objectives.

Note that we said that the specific performance targets should be set jointly. Does this mean that you have to accept anything employees come up with? Certainly not! It is crucial that the employees' ideas be reflected; however, as supervisor, *you* have the final say. Any big disagreements must be reconciled in a way acceptable to both parties. Remember, employees are more highly committed to objectives that they have helped to set. Our experience shows that most employees set their own objectives higher than their supervisors would set them!

Exhibit 3–7

Examples of Statements of Specific, Measurable Objectives in the MBO Process

Performance Area	Specific and Measurable Objective
Customer satisfaction	Number of formal complaints by clients about quality or speed of service
Quantity of work	Number of clients processed, units produced, sales
Safety	Number of safety warnings issued by safety inspector to employee
Quality of work	Acceptance/rework ratio of parts produced by employee, as determined by quality control department
Cost of scrap	Weight, bulk, or cost of scrapped material
Work flow	Minutes lost by coordinating departments in waiting for completed work-in-process by employee
Attendance	Days employee is absent from job
Training and development	Number of hours of training completed

If you are presently a supervisor, what measurable performance areas would be appropriate for your work group? Explain.

STEP 4: REVIEW PROGRESS PERIODICALLY. It is important that, as supervisor, you meet periodically with employees to discuss the progress being made toward achieving objectives. Weekly or monthly meetings may be appropriate. If meetings are held too frequently (unless the worker is new), you'll defeat the purpose of allowing employees to manage their own work and make their own decisions. You should, however, make known your support and availability to discuss major problems at any time.

During a discussion of progress with an employee, if performance is below par, play the role of a helper rather than a critic. Ask yourself these questions: Why is performance deficient? What are the employee's ideas? What can be done to get back on track? Are there factors beyond the employee's control, such as deficient parts or machine breakdowns, that have caused substandard performance? If so, perhaps you need to modify the original objective. Periodic reviews are important because you can learn about unanticipated problems that have developed.

STEP 5: REVIEW END-OF-PERIOD PERFORMANCE. At the end of the performance period, both the employee and the supervisor generally know whether the employee's objectives have been reached. It is important for the supervisor to again play the role of helper in reviewing overall performance during the period. What accounted for success or failure in reaching objectives? What was learned? What might be done to better prepare the employee for improved performance? What might the supervisor have done to provide more help?

Now refer back to Exhibit 3–6. The broken arrow (6) connecting Step 5 to Step 3 means that the MBO process for a particular period has been successfully completed, and a new MBO cycle for another period can now be established. The broken arrows connecting Step 5 to Step 1 and Step 2 mean that some circumstances have changed during the performance period in question. Perhaps Step 1 or Step 2—or both— should be repeated so as to permit better understanding of the supervisor's and employee's jobs before the next cycle is begun.

Advantages of MBO

Among the advantages of MBO are the following:

1. *MBO improves communication between supervisor and employees.* MBO requires goal-oriented communication that might not otherwise occur.
2. *MBO increases employee morale.* Since employees play an active part in goal setting and can measure their own progress, they feel greater ownership of their jobs and higher commitment to results.
3. *MBO encourages individuality.* Employees don't all have equal talents. Under MBO, the goals and objectives set for one person may cover aspects of that person's job that are unlike another's. Moreover, performance targets may be set to reflect each individual's talents.

4. *MBO allows supervisors to assume a helper's role.* Since employees know whether or not they are on target, criticism is built into the system. In the traditional system, the supervisor rather than the system plays the role of critic. MBO frees the supervisor to be a helper or coach instead of a critic.

5. *MBO targets key performance areas.* Whereas in the traditional system every aspect of an employee's job is weighed equally, in MBO key objectives channel effort toward narrower goals. If a worker's attendance has been poor, for example, establishing an objective based on attendance will focus the employee's attention on that behavior for the performance period.

Disadvantages of MBO

Perhaps we have given you the impression that MBO is a perfect system. If that were the case, all organizations and managers would use it. MBO has many disadvantages, however, including the following:

1. *MBO is time-consuming.* Going through the MBO process takes a lot of the supervisor's time. The greater the number of employees, the greater the time commitment required.

2. *MBO dilutes supervisory authority.* When you ask employees to help set their own objectives, you are sharing some authority that you previously held alone. For this reason, some supervisors see MBO as a threat. In the traditional system, a supervisor could presumably say, "Here's what I expect from you." In the MBO system, the supervisor says, "Let's determine together what to expect from you."

3. *MBO makes it difficult to tie results to rewards.* Since MBO reflects performance, it is normally tied to rewards. MBO doesn't replace the need for judgment, however. Suppose that Worker A is more talented than Worker B and sets higher goals than B but doesn't reach them. Worker B, less talented, sets lower goals but reaches them. Who should receive what reward? The supervisor must still use judgment to determine a reward system.

4. *MBO requires greater supervisory skill.* Supervisors who practice MBO must use a number of skills. Conceptual skills are required to find specific, measurable performance areas and a way to provide feedback to the employee. This can be very challenging. In addition, the human relations skills of empathy, listening, and counseling are crucial in conducting the one-to-one meetings required in the system.

5. *MBO doesn't suit all jobs.* Because of the need for measurable, verifiable performance objectives, MBO is not easy to use for all types of jobs. Some jobs are much easier to quantify and verify than others.

SELF-CHECK   Can you think of some types of jobs that are difficult to quantify and verify? Explain.

Should you use MBO? We cannot answer that question for you. Perhaps your organization is already committed to it and you are required to use it. Even if your own manager does not use it, however, you may want to consider implementing it among your own employees.

TYPES OF PLANS

Differentiate the various kinds of standing and single-use plans.

Once objectives have been set to determine *what* needs to be accomplished, plans can be developed to outline *how* the objectives can be attained. Basically, these plans fall into two categories: standing plans and single-use plans.

Standing Plans

standing plans or repeat-use plans Used repeatedly over time.

Standing plans, or **repeat-use plans,** are those that are used repeatedly over a period of time. Three types of standing plans are policies, rules, and procedures.

POLICIES. A **policy** is a guide to decision making—a sort of boundary. It's a way to provide consistency among decision makers. For example, suppose that an *objective* of Computronix (recall Case 3) is "to operate our divisions so as to achieve high safety." Note that this objective tells the "what." A *policy* for achieving this objective at the various divisions could be that "All flammable substances will be stored and handled in a manner consistent with federal, state, and local regulations." Another policy might be "Each division shall emphasize safety performance of employees through a well-designed promotional campaign."

policy Provides consistency among decision makers.

Within the Dixon Division of Computronix, an overall policy established by Marshall might be "Each operating department shall hold regular safety meetings to encourage adherence to rules and solicit employee safety suggestions." Other examples of policies are shown in Exhibit 3–8.

Exhibit 3–8
Examples of Policies

Compensation policy: "This company shall establish and maintain wages on a level comparable to those paid for comparable positions in other firms in the community."

Overtime policy: "Supervisors shall offer overtime opportunities first to the most senior employees in the department."

Grievance policy: "Each employee shall have an opportunity for due process in all disciplinary matters."

Purchasing policy: "Where feasible, several sources of supply shall be utilized so as not to be solely dependent on one supplier."

Supervisory policy: "Managers shall periodically hold group meetings with employees for the purposes of discussing objectives, explaining new developments that may affect employees, responding to questions, and, in general, encouraging more effective and accurate communications within the organization."

Supervisory managers fit into the policy picture in two key ways. First, they play an important part in implementing organizational policies that have been established by higher management. Second, they create policies within their departments as guides for their own work groups. Here are some examples:

1. *Absence notification.* "Employees who will be absent should notify me in advance, assuming this is feasible."
2. *Decision making.* "You are encouraged to make decisions on your own within the realm of your job description."

SELF-CHECK   What are some other examples of supervisory policies? Can you think of any examples of policies established by the teacher of this course?

Policies established by upper-level managers should be put into writing, since they must be enforced at operating levels by supervisors. Supervisory policies like the ones mentioned above, however, may be communicated orally. Some policies may be unwritten, implied, or based on past practices because "that's the way things actually happen."

> **It was Mary Hicks's first week on the job. Her supervisor, Clara Sanchez, had been very helpful in showing her the ropes. Each day, Mary had shown up for work a few minutes before starting time—just to make sure she was on time. She noticed, however, that at least a third of the employees drifted in five to ten minutes late. This was true not only in her department, but also in others throughout the building. On asking one of her co-workers about this, she was told, "Yeah, they don't get really upset about five or ten minutes, just so it's not the same person all the time."**

The above example describes a practice that has become so widespread that supervisors may treat it as a policy. Supervisors must keep in mind that action or even inaction may come to be thought of as policy by employees and serve as a guide to their behavior.

Policies are relatively permanent but should not be set in stone. Circumstances change, and management must from time to time reexamine the appropriateness of its policies.

RULES. Like policies, rules provide guidance. But a **rule** is stronger than a policy in that the guidance given by a rule is final and definite. Rules are inflexible and *must* be obeyed, under threat of punishment. If you work in a plant that has the rule "No smoking on the premises," you cannot smoke, and that is that. Note the difference between a policy and a rule as shown in the following examples:

rule A policy that is invariably enforced.

1. *Policy.* "Employees who violate the no-smoking rule are *subject to discharge.*"
2. *Rule.* "Employees who violate the no-smoking rule are *automatically discharged.*"

Why distinguish between rules and policies, especially when the distinction is sometimes a fine one? First, as a supervisor, you must know when you do not have flexibility. Second, too many rules can result in overmanagement. Taking too much discretion away from the employees leads them to say, "Well, let me look in the rule book and see what I'm supposed to do."

SELF-CHECK   What are some examples of rules that you can think of? Can a supervisor establish his or her own rules? Give an example.

Although rules have an important place in organizations, their overuse can lead to problems. When there are too many rules, supervisors lose their individualism and may use the rules as crutches. Or they may offer weak, apologetic reasons when they enforce the rules. For example, consider the following dialogue:

> **"Catherine, I'm sorry to have to write you up for punching in three minutes late."**
>
> **"But you know I was actually here ten minutes early and just forgot to punch in. I was at my desk all the time. I can't afford to get laid off half a day for being written up."**
>
> **"Sorry, Catherine. It doesn't seem fair to me, either, but I've got to stick by the rule book. A rule's a rule."**

PROCEDURES. The need for procedures arises when an organization or department requires a high degree of consistency in activities that occur frequently. Procedures are established to avoid "reinventing the wheel" and ensure that an effective sequence is followed. A **procedure** outlines the steps to be performed when a particular course of action is taken. Organizations have procedures for obtaining leaves of absence, ordering parts through central purchasing, taking weekly inventory, processing an employee's grievance, and so on.

procedure Steps to be performed when a particular course of action is taken.

SELF-CHECK   Can you think of a procedure for a regular activity that takes place in each of the following organizations: airline, hospital, retail store, high school?

Single-Use Plans

single-use plans Developed to accomplish a specific purpose and then discarded after use.

Single-use plans are developed to accomplish a specific purpose and are then discarded. Unlike policies, rules, and procedures, single-use plans detail courses of action that won't be performed on a repetitive basis. Examples of single-use plans are programs, projects, and budgets.

Like business programs, the space program must consider the time, money, and human resources required to complete its objectives.

PROGRAMS. We hear and read about programs daily—the U.S. space program, your city's pollution control program, a voter registration program, and so on. A **program** is a large-scale plan that involves a mix of objectives, policies, rules, and smaller projects. A program outlines the specific steps to be taken to achieve its objectives and the time, money, and human resources required to complete it. It is essentially a set of single-use plans carried out over a period of time. Other examples of programs are:

program A large-scale plan composed of a mix of objectives, policies, rules, and projects.

1. A tourism marketing program undertaken by the state of Alabama.
2. A research program undertaken by drug producer Pfizer to develop vaccines for major diseases, such as AIDS and Parkinson's.
3. An upscaling program by Kmart to modernize the appearance of their stores.

PROJECTS. A **project** is a distinct, smaller part of a program. For example, Alabama's tourism program involves many projects, such as selection of a tourism committee, benchmarking several states with outstanding tourism programs, promoting eight new Robert Trent Jones public golf courses, and upgrading of the welcome centers that greet transit visitors on its interstate highways. Each project has its own objectives and becomes the responsibility of personnel assigned to oversee it.

project A distinct part of a program.

BUDGETS. Every individual, family, or organization uses some form of budgeting. A well-planned budget serves as both a planning and a controlling tool. Simply stated, a **budget** is a forecast of expected financial performance over a period of time. A departmental budget covers such items as supplies, equipment, scrap, overtime, and personnel payroll. We will discuss budgets in more detail in Chapter 11.

budget A forecast of expected financial performance over time.

SCHEDULES. A **schedule** is a plan showing activities to be performed and their timing. Scheduling techniques range from a simple note or appointment book used to schedule your day to sophisticated schedules for such major challenges as building a new plant or launching a space shuttle. Two scheduling approaches with which you should be familiar are the Gantt chart and PERT Network.

schedule A plan of activities to be performed and their timing.

The **Gantt chart** is a visual progress report that identifies work stages or activities on a vertical axis and scheduled completion dates horizontally. It is named after its developer, Henry Gantt, a management consultant who introduced the basic idea in the early 1900s. Since then, Gantt charts have been used extensively as a planning tool. Exhibit 3–9 illustrates a simplified Gantt chart. Note the specific activities that proceed from contract negotiation to job start-up and the scheduled times for each. Also note that one activity, long lead purchasing, can be carried on simultaneously with development of a manufacturing schedule. In actual practice, Gantt charts may include movable strips of plastic to represent bars, with different colors to indicate scheduled and actual progress. At a glance, a manager or supervisor can see whether a project is on time, ahead of schedule, or behind. While the Gantt chart is helpful as a planning tool, it does not show directly how the various activities involved in a job depend on one another. It is in showing such dependencies of activities that PERT Network analysis can be helpful.

Exhibit 3–9
Example of Gantt Chart Showing Activities Needed in Production Start-up

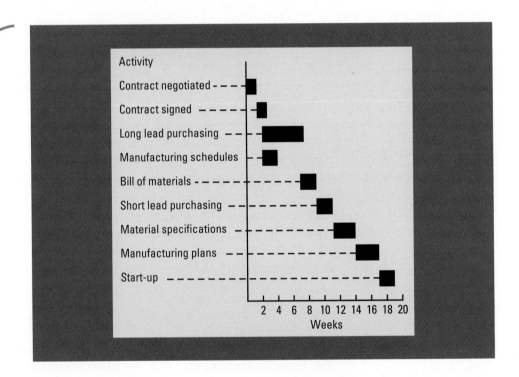

Program Evaluation and Review Technique (PERT) is a management scheduling tool which shows relationships among a network of activities and events to determine the completion time of a project. Typically, PERT is used on highly complex, one-time projects, such as building a skyscraper or completing the prototype of a new jet aircraft, and requires the use of a computer. However, its principles are relevant for many supervisors, especially in planning and scheduling various aspects of their jobs.

Let's examine a PERT chart that can be applied at the supervisory level. Suppose that you are a maintenance supervisor and your department has to overhaul an important machine. You have determined that the following activities must be done to complete the job:

A. Remove the machine from its foundation.
B. Haul the machine to the repair shop.
C. Dismantle the machine.
D. Order and receive new replacement parts from the manufacturer.
E. Repair the machine.
F. Test-run the machine.
G. Build a new machine foundation.
H. Move the repaired machine to the factory floor.
I.   Secure the machine to the new foundation.

Now, assume that you are asked to estimate when the machine can be ready for use again. The PERT network of events and activities involved in your analysis is shown in Exhibit 3–10. The numbered squares represent events at which the different activities to complete the job *begin* and are *completed*. For example, Event 2 marks the completion of Activity A and the beginning of Activities B and G. The lines represent the activities to be performed. The hours represent your estimate as to how long each activity will take to complete based on your experience or on information supplied by others.

Note that the estimated completion time for the job is 62 hours. This total time is obtained by adding the hours necessary to complete the series of activities that comprise the *longest* route, in terms of time, to complete the job. This route is called the **critical path.** The series of activities on the critical path include A, B, C, D, E, F, H, and I. These are the activities that determine the completion time for the job. Activity G is not a critical step in the network because it can be begun and completed independently of activities B through I and is not included on the critical path.

A major advantage of PERT networks, even for simple problems, is that they graphically display the dependent parts of a total job. The supervisor thus has a better grasp of the total job to be completed.

critical path The series of activities in a PERT network that comprise the longest route, in terms of time, to complete the job.

Exhibit 3–10
PERT Network for Completing Machine Overhaul

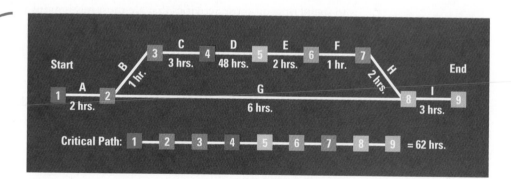

SELF-CHECK

Suppose that it takes you four hours rather than the two hours estimated to repair the machine (activity E) as shown in Exhibit 3–10. Will this cause your project to be completed later than planned?

MANAGING YOUR TIME

In Chapter 1 we said that an organization's three types of resources are human, physical, and financial resources. Some management experts would include *time* as a fourth resource. Make no mistake about it, time is one of the greatest resources a supervisor has. **Time management** is the ability to use one's time to get things done *when* they should be done. Another definition, which reflects planning and prioritizing, is "arranging to accomplish the things you choose to get done within the time available." Without this ability, all your other management skills are for naught. Even if you have excellent human relations skills, poor time management can leave you too easily distracted to effectively listen to an employee's problems. Or pressures can keep you from thinking clearly enough to use your conceptual skills fully. You may not even be able to take the time to display your technical skills by showing a new employee the ropes. To be effective as a supervisor, then, you must make effective use of your time.

time management
Ability to use one's time to get things done *when* they should be done.

The Time Log: Where Your Time Goes

Time management experts say that the first step in making effective use of your time is to determine where your time is currently going. Conscientiously filling in a time log like the one shown in Exhibit 3–11 is an excellent way to see how your time is spent.

Setting Priorities: A "Must"

Once you know where your time is going, you can analyze whether it is going in the proper direction. Not everyone can do all that he or she wants to do. The secret, then, is to spend time on those activities that are most meaningful and that contribute most significantly to your doing a top-notch job.

Hoi Mon Sol, whose time log is shown in Exhibit 3–11, said that he could not find enough time to do everything he wanted to do because he was so busy. Yet, when he got home, he looked back at his day and called his activities "wheel spinning." He didn't feel good about what he had accomplished. Sol, like many supervisors, typically spent his day handling many low-priority activities rather than the high-priority ones!

Let's establish a rating system for classifying the priority of activities to be performed in a given day:

1. "A" activities are the most important—they are critical to your job.
2. "B" activities are of medium priority—important, but less so than "A's."
3. "C" activities are of low priority—routine and/or relatively unimportant.

The more efficient supervisor will spend a greater percentage of his or her time performing "A" activities. Note how well this approach worked for Charles Schwab, former president of Bethlehem Steel.

In his best-selling book *The Time Trap*, R. Alec Mackenzie, a noted management consultant, tells an interesting story about how time management worked for

DAILY TIME LOG

Name _____ *Hoi Mon Sol* _____

Date _____ *March 1, 199—* _____

On this log record each activity that you performed during the workday. Make sure that you include every activity performed such as telephone calls, conversations, rest breaks, reading, and so on. Do this for a period of time long enough to reflect normal "workdays." A week should normally be sufficient.

From – To	Minutes	Type of Activity	People Involved	Priority A	B	C
8:00 – 8:05	5	Talked in hall	Dan, Patsy			
8:05 – 8:15	10	Read status report on work progress				
8:15 – 8:20	5	Checked progress on slow job	Ronald			
8:20 – 8:30	10	Prepared for supt. meeting				
8:30 – 9:30	60	Attended supt. meeting	Dept. heads & Supt.			
9:30 – 9:45	15	Coffee	Al, Peter, Karen			
9:45 – 9:50	5	Tried to return two phone calls -- no luck				
9:50 – 10:02	12	Completed questionnaire from Personnel Dept				
10:02 – 10:06	4	Went for mail				
10:06 – 10:20	14	Opened & read mail				
10:20 – 10:23	3	Called Purchasing Dept. to check status of order	Kawahara			
10:23 – 10:50	27	Discussion with Supt. about objectives for Dept.	McWilliams			
10:50 – 11:00	10	Visited Personnel office to check status of applicants	Alice			
11:00 – 11:55	55	Met with United Way Committee	too many!			
11:55 – 12:10	15	Began work on dept. budget proposal				
12:10 – 12:50	40	Lunch	Dan, Patsy, Al			
—						
—						

Exhibit 3–11
Daily Time Log

Charles Schwab, then president of Bethlehem Steel. Schwab presented Ivy Lee, a management consultant, with the unusual challenge of showing Schwab how to get more done with his time. Lee asked Schwab for a sheet of paper and asked him to write down the most important tasks he had to perform the next day, then to number them in the order of their importance. She then told Schwab that, on getting to work in the morning, he should begin task Number 1 and stick with it until he finished it. Then he was to recheck his priority list and start on item Number 2. The important thing was to keep working on the most important task until it was done.

"If this system works for you," Lee said, "have your other people also use it. Try it as long as you like. Then send me your check for what you think it's worth." Some weeks later, Lee received a check from Schwab for $25,000, along with the message that the lesson was the most profitable he had ever learned!"

Many of the "brush fires" to which supervisors devote a large percentage of their time are "B" or perhaps even "C" priority items. In the next section, we hope to help you learn to spend more of your time on your "A's"!

SELF-CHECK   Examine the list of activities shown in Exhibit 3–11. Identify an "A" activity and a "C" activity. On what types of activities did Sol spend most of his time?

Handling the Common Time Wasters

Many activities that you carry out during a typical day are time wasters—inefficient uses of your time (see Exhibit 3–12). These may include doing routine work that someone else could handle, excessive socializing, or fighting a losing battle against paperwork.

- Distractions and interruptions
- Failure to set priorities
- Procrastination
- Nonessential phone conversations
- Ineffective meetings

- Indecision
- Drop-in visitors
- Personal disorganization
- Poor delegation
- Excessive paperwork

Exhibit 3–12
*Ten Common
Supervisory
Time Wasters*

Learning Objective 8

Discuss some ways
to effectively
manage time.

Supervisory jobs vary a great deal in terms of the demands on the supervisor's time. That's why maintaining a time log is an important first step in diagnosing your time management habits. Following is a broad list of "do's," which may help you to use your time more effectively:

1. *Set priorities.*
   a. Establish "A," "B," and "C" priorities.
   b. Determine daily priorities.
   c. Focus effort on high-priority items.
2. *Do not procrastinate.*
   a. Break big jobs into smaller parts.
   b. Get started, even if on a minor part of a job.
   c. Do the more unpleasant parts of a job first.
   d. Reward yourself for doing things on schedule.
3. *Manage the telephone effectively.*
   a. Have someone else take your calls and handle them if possible.
   b. Handle all return calls at set times of day.
4. *Make your meetings effective.*
   a. Prepare an agenda.
   b. Announce the agenda in advance.
   c. Begin meetings on time.
   d. Stick to the topics on the agenda.
   e. Make decisions or come to conclusions.
5. *Learn to delegate.*
   a. Delegate details that are time-consuming.
   b. Delegate jobs that will help employees to develop.
   c. Delegate low-priority responsibilities.
   d. Delegate jobs that employees can perform better than you.
6. *Handle people who drop in.*
   a. Close your door for periods of time.
   b. Keep books or materials on extra chairs to prevent visitors from sitting down and "locking in."
   c. Stand up and remain standing until the visitor leaves.
   d. Meet long-winded persons at their work area, so that you can leave when you are ready.
   e. Train your boss and work group to respect your time.
7. *Be decisive.*
   a. Set a personal deadline for making a decision.
   b. Once you have the facts, make the decision.
8. *Get organized.*
   a. Use a daily planner.
   b. Implement a filing system.
   c. See 1b above.
9. *Stay on top of paperwork.*
   a. Handle papers only once!
   b. Handwrite short notes directly on original documents and forward them to the persons concerned.
   c. Have a secretary or assistant classify papers according to importance and route them for you.
10. *Avoid distractions and interruptions.*
    a. Keep a neat desk; work and papers piled on a desk are distracting.
    b. Try to set aside uninterrupted blocks of time.
    c. See 6a above.
    d. Face your desk away from the view of others.

Chapter Review

Learning Objective 1

Explain the steps involved in planning.

Planning is deciding what will be done in the future. The three planning steps are (1) setting an objective or goal, (2) identifying and assessing present and future conditions affecting the goal, and (3) developing a systematic approach to achieve the goal. Properly done, planning helps managers accomplish the four other management functions of organizing, leading, staffing, and controlling. Of these functions, planning is most closely linked to controlling.

Because it is a difficult and time-consuming process, many supervisors tend to neglect planning. Instead of planning, they scurry about solving one problem, then another, seemingly too busy to plan anything. Effective planning anticipates many problems so that they are more easily handled when they occur.

Learning Objective 2

Explain how planning differs at top, middle, and supervisory management levels.

Planning differs for top-, middle-, and first-level management. Top managers spend a greater proportion of their time developing strategic long-term and intermediate-range plans of one to five or more years. Strategic plans include the organization's mission, objectives, and strategies and interfacing with its external environment. Middle-level and supervisory managers perform operational planning—intermediate-range and short-range plans of one year to one day—that operationalize strategic plans.

Learning Objective 3

Explain how the hierarchy of objectives works.

Objectives are crucial to effective planning. Once established, objectives provide a stimulus for individual effort. The objectives set at one management level reflect the objectives of the next higher operational level. This network of objectives is called a hierarchy of objectives. Objectives permit unified planning and coordination at lower management levels.

Learning Objective 4

Discuss important guidelines in setting performance objectives.

Among the guidelines for setting performance objectives are (1) setting them in only selected, key performance areas; (2) making them specific; (3) making them challenging rather than easy; (4) balancing them properly, as may be the case with volume and quality; (5) involving employees in setting them; and (6) following up on results.

Learning Objective 5

Identify the steps in management by objectives (MBO).

Management by objectives (MBO), also commonly known as management by results and joint target setting, is a system whereby managers and employees jointly establish objectives and develop a systematic approach for achieving results. MBO typically involves five steps: (1) the supervisor and each employee discuss the supervisor's responsibilities and objectives; (2) the supervisor and the employee discuss the employee's job; (3) the supervisor and the employee jointly set specific, measurable objectives for a given performance period; (4) the supervisor and the employee meet periodically to review the employee's progress; and (5) the supervisor and the employee meet at the end of the period to review performance. The supervisor and the employee can then begin a new cycle.

Among the advantages of MBO are that it improves communication between a supervisor and employees, increases employee morale, encourages individuality, focuses effort on key performance areas, and allows the supervisor to be a coach or helper rather than a critic. The disadvantages of MBO are that it is time-consuming, requires the supervisor to share authority with employees, may be difficult to tie to a reward system, requires greater supervisory skill, and is difficult to apply to positions where performance cannot be easily measured.

Learning Objective 6

Differentiate the various kinds of standing and single-use plans.

After objectives have been established, plans can be developed throughout the organization. Standing, or repeat-use, plans direct action that deals with recurring situations. They include policies, rules, and procedures. A policy is a guide to individual decision making. Policies allow some flexibility, whereas rules are final and definite as to what action must be taken. A procedure outlines the steps that should be taken to complete a given action, such as applying for a vacation leave or processing a grievance. Single-use plans are one-time plans that are discarded upon completion. Examples of these are programs, projects, budgets, and schedules.

Learning Objective 7

Draw a simple PERT chart.

Two important types of schedules are Gantt charts and PERT charts, each of which provide a visual display of activities to be performed and the time frames involved.

Learning Objective 8

Discuss some ways to effectively manage time.

One of a supervisor's greatest planning resources is time. Maintaining a time log is a necessary first step toward becoming a more efficient time manager. Such a log enables a supervisor to see exactly where his or her time is being spent. More effective supervisors spend a greater proportion of their time on "A" priorities—activities that are ranked number one in terms of importance to the effective performance of their jobs. The following time-saving tips can help you to make better use of your time: (1) set priorities, (2) do not procrastinate, (3) manage the telephone effectively, (4) make meetings effective, (5) delegate to others, (6) handle people who drop in, (7) be decisive, (8) get organized, (9) stay on top of paperwork, and (10) avoid distractions and interruptions.

Important Terms

budget *pg. 81*

contingency planning *66*

critical path *82*

Gantt chart *83*

hierarchy of
  objectives *70*

management by objectives
  (MBO) *73*

mission *67*

objectives or goals *69*

operational planning *68*

performance
  objectives *72*

policy *78*

procedure *80*

program *81*

Program Evaluation and
  Review Technique
  (PERT) *82*

project *81*

rule *79*

schedule *81*

"Siamese twins" of
  management *65*

single-use plans *80*

standing plans or
  repeat-use plans *78*

strategic planning *67*

time management *84*

unified planning *70*

Questions for Review and Discussion

1. What are the three steps in planning? Why do supervisors tend to slight the planning function?
2. How does planning differ among top, intermediate, and supervisory management levels?
3. What are some guidelines for setting performance objectives?
4. What is meant by a hierarchy of objectives? Explain.
5. What is MBO, and what steps are involved?
6. What is the difference between a policy, a rule, and a procedure?
7. What is a Gantt chart? How does it differ from a PERT chart?
8. What actions can a manager take to effectively manage time?

Skill Builder 3–1
Testing Your Planning Skills

Harold Marshall, general manager at Computronix's Dixon Division, has just named you as chairperson of the first annual blood drive, to be conducted at the plant site. A strong believer in the company's participation in community affairs and himself a member of the local Red Cross board of directors, Marshall has committed the division's 500 employees to the blood drive. Your committee will set the exact dates for the drive, which is to be held in three or four months.

As chairperson, you have been assigned a team of four other company employees to plan and implement the project. All members are highly respected, competent people, representing a true cross-section of the employees: one is a production worker who is president of the local union; another, an engineer, represents the professional segment; the human resources manager represents the management group; and a payroll clerk represents the administrative office group.

Marshall was given your name by your boss, who expressed confidence in your ability to lead a successful donor campaign at the plant. At 27, you are the youngest person on the committee and anxious to do a good job. You have called the first committee meeting, which you have advertised as a "preliminary planning meeting," to identify key factors that must be planned for in order for the committee to meet its objective: having a successful blood drive at Computronix.

Instructions:
1. Make a list of what you consider the key planning issues that should be identified by the committee at this initial planning meeting.
2. Of the items on your list, which two or three do you believe are the most crucial? Why?
3. Identify major problems that could prevent accomplishment of your objective. What contingency planning could be done to avert them or minimize their impact?
4. To help in your preparation for the planning meeting, identify six to ten steps that you feel will be needed to achieve a successful blood drive. These steps might be such things as:

a. Determine a date.
b. Identify a location.
c. Secure commitment from Red Cross, etc.
   Draw a PERT chart that shows the sequence and relationship of the activities identified. (You need not be concerned with the length of time needed for each activity.)
5. Compare your responses to questions 1, 2, 3, and 4 with those of other students. To what extent do they agree with you?

GROUP ACTIVITY

Skill Builder 3–2
Determining Priorities

Assume that you are a high school principal. Organizationally, 12 teachers, 5 coaches, your secretary, and an assistant principal report to you. The assistant principal supervises another eight teachers, four clerical workers, a custodian, a librarian, a counselor, and the cafeteria dietitian.

Listed below are a number of activities you performed during the past week.

a. Preparing a 15-minute speech which you will deliver to your school's PTA.
b. Meeting a sales representative from a local computer company to discuss possible purchase of computer equipment.
c. Filling in as a substitute teacher for an eleventh-grade math teacher, who left school ill at lunchtime.
d. Meeting with the student homecoming committee to acquaint them with the guidelines for homecoming activities.
e. Preparing your list of yearly objectives and budget requests that must be submitted to the city superintendent's office.
f. Meeting with a group of four parents to discuss their complaints about unreasonably high demands by one of your teachers.
g. Listening to councilwoman Judith Johnson, who spoke to a civics class on "Your City Government."
h. Touring the school halls during changes in class periods.
i. Interviewing two final candidates for a woman's basketball and volleyball coaching position.
j. Discussing next week's homecoming game against a crosstown rival with the football coach.

Instructions:
1. Indicate how you would classify these in priority: MI (most important), RI (relatively important), or RU (relatively unimportant). Be prepared to defend your choices.
2. What additional information about the principal's activities may have helped you establish your priority listings? How would this information have helped?
3. Meet with groups of three-five other students to compare your choices of priorities. Discuss these and be prepared to report your results to the class.

Setting Performance Objectives

Jane Persons supervises the word processing center at Computronix, which consists of seven word processors. Work done by this section consists of word processing various reports and correspondence as required by other departments and handling all photocopying for the plant. Persons had just attended a meeting with the other section heads and heard Edna Strong, the administration department head, talk briefly about the new planning system in store for the Dixon Division. As Strong heard it from Marshall, the plant manager and all department heads and supervisors would be required to identify five key performance areas in their departments. These were supposed to be areas that had a significant impact on performance.

It was the meeting with Strong that puzzled Persons. Strong had asked her to come up with the five key performance objectives for her word processing section. Persons said: "I can understand how our sales group or production groups can have specific objectives. But I can't see how our section can have anything like that. What am I supposed to come up with? Something like 'We will process 9,500 pages in the next year' or 'At least 99.5 percent of our pages will be error-free'? This whole unit planning system seems like a lot of 'wheel spinning' to me. My people know their objectives without this planning stuff. Their objective is to do a good job at getting the required word processing done for these other departments as quickly as possible."

Answer the following questions:

1. Do you agree with Jane Persons' view that the new planning system is "wheel spinning"? Why or why not?
2. Are there some key performance areas that Persons could identify for her action? What are they?
3. To what extent does Persons' last sentence meet the criteria discussed in the text under "Guidelines for Setting Performance Objectives"?
4. Can you develop one or more statements of objective for Persons' department that will be consistent with the "specific" criteria as required in MBO?

Skill-Development Scenario
Planning and Time Management

Jane Farrell is Store Operations Supervisor for McElvey Department Stores' Ross Town Mall location. Despite her good intentions, Farrell is not a good planner and doesn't make good use of her time. In the first part of the video she seems to be continuously dealing with one minor crisis after another.

Answer the following questions:

1. What examples did you see of Farrell's ineffective planning and time management?
2. After viewing the second part of this video, discuss the methods Farrell employs to increase her productivity through better planning and time management.

Chapter 4
Decision Making and Problem Solving

Case 4

The Advancing Landscape Architect

Bobby Jones was hired as a landscape architect for Lane Corporation five years ago. His responsibilities include supervising a crew of 23 groundskeepers who are responsible for maintaining the corporate grounds. Because the work requires physical stamina and is performed mostly outdoors, the majority of the groundskeepers are men, although there are four women employed.

Brenda Lewis was hired by Jones six months ago. During her initial interview with Jones, she was told that she would be expected to perform the same duties as the male groundskeepers. However, once she was employed, she was assigned to work with a second female worker in the greenhouse. The two other female groundskeepers were assigned to caring for the indoor plants in the corporate offices. Brenda's duties consisted mainly of transplanting seedlings and watering plants. When she indicated to Jones that she would like to be given the opportunity to work outdoors with the rest of the crew, she was told that she was needed to work in the greenhouse because it was more suited for females and that she could not be expected to work like a man, mowing lawns and planting shrubs.

Jones frequently came by the greenhouse to see how the two female employees were doing. Although Lewis had been employed for six months and Maria Taylor had been there a year, Jones never called them by name. He always addressed them as "Babe" or "Honey." As he was giving them instructions, he had a habit of putting his arm around their shoulder or running his fingers through their hair. He always made a point to tell them his latest joke—usually one with sexual overtones.

On several occasions Jones insisted that Lewis help him deliver new plants to the grounds crew for planting. On these trips she rode with him in a golf cart. When the cart hit a bump or made a turn, Jones would put his hand on Lewis's leg to steady her. When she protested, he insisted he was just concerned for her safety.

In addition, Jones gave Lewis a book dealing with insecticides and told her that she would need to learn the information in order to work safely with the various chemicals stored near the greenhouse. He suggested that perhaps they should study the book together at her apartment after work.

At this point Lewis went to Jones' supervisor and filed a complaint of sexual harassment against Jones. She stated that she had never welcomed any of his "advances." When he put his arm around her shoulder, she pulled away. She did not laugh at his jokes, and she objected to his putting his hand on her leg. She also rejected his offer to study with him after work. She stated that she was afraid to tell him how she really felt because he was her supervisor, and she feared he would fire her.

Source: Prepared by James D. Powell, Professor of Management, University of North Texas, Denton, Texas, and adapted from Leon C. Megginson, Geralyn M. Franklin, and M. Jane Byrd, *Human Resource Management* (Houston, TX: Dame Publications, Inc., 1995), p. 605.

LEARNING OBJECTIVES
After reading and studying this chapter, you should be able to:

1
Explain the role of decision making in the supervisor's job.

2
Discuss why supervisors need to make so many decisions.

3
Define decision making and identify at least four elements involved.

4
Discuss how decisions are made.

5
Name some factors to keep in mind when making decisions.

6
Explain the role of ethics in the supervisor's decision making.

7
Decide when to use the individual approach or the group approach when making decisions.

8
Discuss some ways of improving decision making.

He who makes no mistakes makes no progress.

Theodore Roosevelt

There are few things as useless—if not as dangerous—as the right answer to the wrong question.

Peter F. Drucker

Bobby Jones' supervisor is certainly in a difficult position! This chapter deals with his task—decision making and problem solving. As Case 4 shows, supervisors must make effective, but often difficult, decisions if they are to be successful.

Chapter 3 covered the fundamentals of planning. Throughout this discussion, the need for decision making was implied. We now look at that subject in detail. Decisions must be made about people, about processes, and about priorities, to name just a few issues! Keep the supervisor's problem in mind, as we shall return to his situation throughout the chapter.

ROLE OF DECISION MAKING IN SUPERVISORY MANAGEMENT

Learning Objective 1

Explain the role of decision making in the supervisor's job.

Managers must make decisions whenever they perform any of the five management functions—planning, organizing, staffing, leading, and controlling—discussed in Chapter 1. Without decision making, the entire management system would cease to exist. For example, in planning, the supervisor must decide which objectives to seek, which policies to establish, and what rules and regulations to institute. In organizing, choices must be made as to who gets what authority and how duties and responsibilities are grouped. The function of leading entails deciding how best to communicate with and motivate employees. In staffing, decisions must be made concerning employee selection, placement, training and development, performance appraisal, compensation, and health and safety. In controlling, if actual performance does not conform to planned performance, decisions must be made about how best to bring them together.

The decisions that managers make often must be made quickly—and frequently with little information, or even conflicting information. Then, those decisions must be carried out in order to achieve the department's objectives!

Decision Making: The Heart of Supervisory Management

Decision making is central to the supervisor's job. Supervisors must continually decide what is to be done, who is to do it, and how, when, and where it is to be done (see Exhibit 4–1). As we will show throughout the chapter, although these decisions may be discussed separately, they are interrelated. One decision is affected by, and builds upon, previous ones. For example, what your department produces determines what types of production facilities are needed. Decisions about production, in turn, influence the types of employees needed and the training and compensation they should receive. All these decisions affect the amount of money budgeted for the department.

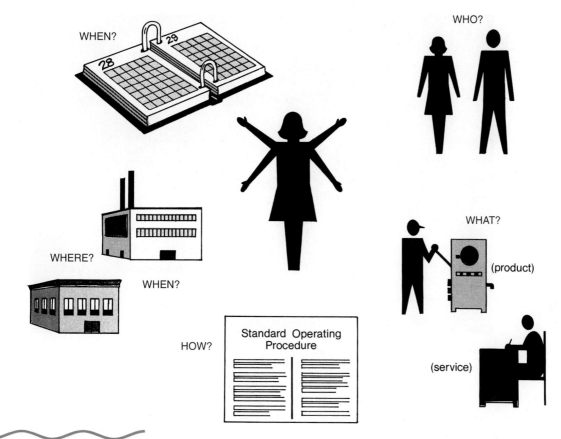

Exhibit 4–1
Decision Making Is the Heart of Supervisory Management

Why Supervisors Need to Make So Many Decisions

Learning Objective 2

Discuss why supervisors need to make so many decisions.

Supervisory managers—even more than managers at other levels—are involved in directing employees' behavior toward achieving the organization's goals, as well as those of the employees themselves. Supervisors must make more decisions more frequently—and often more quickly—than other managers, since they're operating on a day-by-day, person-to-person basis. These decisions involve a variety of activities, as the following example illustrates.

> **Wilma Malone, nursing supervisor at Alquippa Medical Center, had been at work for only three hours, but she had already made seven major decisions.**
>
> 1. **She signed up to attend a one-day course on time management, to be offered the following week.**
> 2. **She assigned performance ratings to five of her new nurses on their performance appraisal forms.**
> 3. **She approved vacation requests for two nurses in her department.**

In this GE Medical Systems factory, just one layer of management separates the shop floor worker from the boss.

4. She referred to the floor physician a patient's request to be taken off a prescribed medication.
5. She resolved a dispute between one of the nurses and a floor orderly.
6. She selected Jane Moore to serve as her replacement when she took her vacation in three weeks.
7. She requisitioned supplies needed by her department.

In addition, she made a handful of other minor decisions. The young trainee assigned to Malone said, "Are you always this busy, or is it just because it's Monday morning?" Malone replied, "It's all a normal part of a supervisor's job."

Employees look to their first-line supervisors for more direction, assistance, guidance, and protection than do subordinates of managers at higher levels. Also, in general, supervisors spend more time socializing with others in the organization since they have more employees than other managers. All these activities require decision making.

The lower the level of management, the greater the **span of management** or **span of control,** which is the number of immediate employees a manager can supervise effectively. Therefore, supervisors make decisions that affect not only their own behavior, but also that of many other people.

span of management
The number of immediate employees a manager can supervise effectively.

SELF-CHECK

What was Jones' span of management in Case 4? Do you think that span was too great, just right, or too little for this type of business? Explain.

WHAT IS DECISION MAKING?

Learning Objective ③

Define decision making and identify at least four elements involved.

Let us now define decision making, discuss its characteristics, look at some selected types of decisions, and consider some differences between decision making and problem solving.

Decision Making Defined

Have you known people who couldn't ever make up their minds? They might say, "I really don't know what to do. If I do this, such and such will happen. If I do that, then something else might happen." They just can't make decisions. The word *decide* comes from a Latin word meaning "to cut off." When you make a decision, you first consider a matter causing you some uncertainty, debate, or dispute and then make a choice or judgment that more or less results in a definite conclusion. You cut off further deliberation on the matter. Thus, **decision making** is the conscious consideration and selection of a course of action from among available alternatives in order to produce a desired result.

decision making Considering and selecting a course of action from among alternatives.

Elements Involved in Decision Making

There are several facts you should know about decision making. The most important ones are that (1) a decision may not be needed, (2) decisions involve the future, (3) the process is a conscious one, and (4) there must be more than one alternative solution.

A DECISION MAY NOT BE NEEDED. A wise decision maker begins by asking, "Is a decision needed?" It may seem strange to include this question in a discussion of decision making, but it's important. In many supervisory situations, no decision is needed, and decision making would be in vain. If a given event is inevitable or if higher management is going to act in a certain way regardless of the supervisor's wishes, then making a decision is a waste of time. Some things cannot be changed regardless of the supervisor's wishes or actions.

> "You really have guts, Will," said Carol Sheffield to Will Hauser, office supervisor for Gridtronics, Inc. "You didn't waste a lot of time with competing bids or even looking at what different word processors can do. Don't you feel uncomfortable getting the vice-president to approve the purchase of a $10,000 piece of equipment? What if he wants some evidence that you really shopped around?"
>
> "Well," said Hauser, "that's a good question, I suppose. But there's one thing you don't know. Getting competing bids and spending a lot of time evaluating different systems would have been a waste of my time. A 'decision' really wasn't needed. The guy I bought that piece of equipment from is the vice-president's son!"

DECISIONS INVOLVE THE FUTURE. Surely you have heard others say, "If only I had done this, then that wouldn't have happened." They assume that if they had made a different decision, it would have resulted in a happy marriage, a rapid promotion, or a killing in the stock market. It is said that hindsight is 20/20, but the supervisor's world is no place for Monday-morning quarterbacking. Rather, it's a place to prepare for today or tomorrow. Because a supervisor's decision making is future-oriented, it always contains an element of uncertainty.

DECISION MAKING IS A CONSCIOUS PROCESS. Decision making involves a conscious process of selection. No decisions are needed about breathing or digestion, because these are unconscious, reflexive actions. In making a decision, the individual consciously (1) becomes aware of a want that needs to be satisfied, (2) seeks relevant behavioral alternatives, and (3) evaluates them as a basis of choice, as shown in Exhibit 4–2.

DECISION MAKING INVOLVES MORE THAN ONE ALTERNATIVE. As indicated earlier, for a true decision to be made, there must be two or more available alternatives to choose from, including the possibility of doing nothing. Frequently, there are only two choices, as in a "yes or no" or "to do or not to do" situation. The decision to do nothing is sometimes the worst decision.

Most decision situations involve several alternatives with varying expected outcomes. You may not be aware of some of the alternatives and may not have decision authority over others. For other alternatives, you must estimate expected outcomes. You then evaluate each outcome in terms of its desirability. Sometimes there are no desirable alternatives. In such cases you have to decide between two undesirable ones.

SELF-CHECK

What are the possible alternatives that Jones' supervisor had in the situation in Case 4?

Types of Decisions to Be Made

Although there are many ways of classifying decisions, we will discuss only one at this point—namely, categorizing decisions as either programmed or unprogrammed.

Exhibit 4–2
The Decision-Making Process

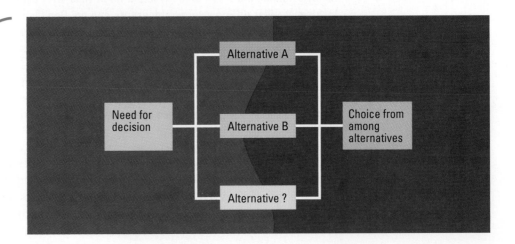

programmed decisions
Routine and repetitive decisions.

Programmed decisions are those that are routine and repetitive. Since such decisions tend to be similar and must be made frequently, supervisors usually establish a systematic way of handling them. Some examples of this type of decision are:

1. How to handle an employee who reports to work late or is absent without permission.
2. How to schedule work, shifts, vacations, and other time variations.
3. How to determine which employees need training and what type of training should be given to them.
4. How frequently to do maintenance servicing of machinery and equipment.

The supervisor handles these decisions in a systematic way and may even set up a decision framework, including guidelines such as policies, procedures, or rules (see Chapter 3) to be followed.

unprogrammed decisions Decisions that occur infrequently and require a separate response each time.

Unprogrammed decisions are those that occur infrequently. Because different variables are involved, requiring a separate and different response each time, it is difficult to establish a systematic way of dealing with such decisions. Some examples of unprogrammed supervisory decisions are:

1. Whether to buy an important piece of machinery or equipment, especially an expensive, complex one.
2. How to react to a union representative who says that a grievance will be filed if you give a written reprimand to a certain worker for a work-related violation of safety rules.
3. How to handle a severe accident or explosion.
4. Whom to promote to a supervisory position.

How Decision Making and Problem Solving Relate

opportunity A chance for development or advancement.

problem An existing unsatisfactory situation causing anxiety or distress.

In one of his educational films, Joe Batten, a well-known management consultant, has a manager say, "We have no problems here, just opportunities. Each problem should be considered an opportunity." Although we don't necessarily agree with that conclusion, it does give us a chance to show how decision making and problem solving are related. An **opportunity** is a set of circumstances that provide a chance to improve a situation or help reach a goal. A **problem** is an existing unsatisfactory situation causing anxiety or distress, which must be addressed.

Effective supervisors must be able to identify problems—and their cause(s)—to analyze complex and involved situations, and to solve problems by removing their cause(s). But placing too much emphasis on problems can prevent one from identifying opportunities. After all, solving a problem only eliminates or neutralizes a negative situation. Progress or advancement comes from seeking and identifying opportunities; recognizing the emotions, needs, and motivations of the people involved; and analyzing ways of satisfying them. Here are some examples of "opportunity" decision making at the supervisory level:

1. Replacing a piece of equipment that, while it is still functioning well, can be upgraded to increase efficiency.
2. Improving an already effective preventive maintenance system.
3. Cross-training employees to broaden their skills and raise morale.
4. Creating a new position for a highly skilled technician who has recently left the employ of a competitor.
5. Instituting the most innovative new processes and techniques.

SELF-CHECK   What other examples of "opportunity" decision making can you think of?

HOW TO MAKE DECISIONS

Learning Objective 4
Discuss how decisions are made.

Exhibit 4–3 shows that the decision-making process involves six basic steps. We have already mentioned most of them. We'll use Case 4, involving Jones' supervisor, to illustrate each step of this process.

Step 1: Define the Idea or Problem

As Peter Drucker stated in the opening quotation, a decision is only as good as the correct definition of the problem. In other words, the right cure for the wrong problem is just as bad as the wrong cure for the right problem. But it is not always easy to know what the problem is or what is the best opportunity to seek. When you have a fever, it is only a symptom of the true problem—an infection or other disorder. Likewise, as a supervisor, you should remember that low morale, high turnover, many complaints or grievances, waste, and declining sales are not the real problem. They are only symptoms of the real problem.

If the decision to be made involves solving a problem, its cause, or the factors that are creating it, must be determined. Without identifying the cause (or causes), it is difficult to solve the problem, for you may be treating its symptom rather than the root cause(s).

Exhibit 4–3
*Steps in
Decision Making*

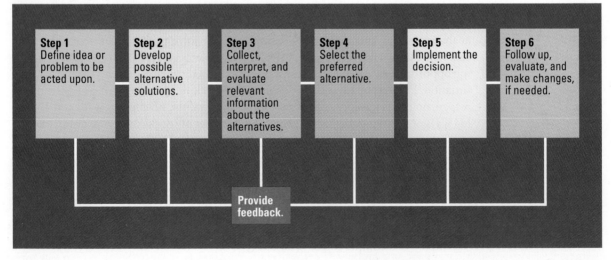

SELF-CHECK   What do you see as the real problem facing Jones' supervisor in Case 4? What was/were the cause(s) of the problem?

Step 2: Develop Alternatives

alternatives Possible courses of action that can satisfy a need or solve a problem.

The second step is to develop alternative ways of solving the problem or taking advantage of the opportunity. **Alternatives** are possible courses of action that can satisfy a need or solve a problem. Usually several choices are available if you are able to identify and develop them. It is easier to choose from a few alternatives than from many, so reduce the number to as few as is feasible. Also, be aware that, if choices are limited, they may include only undesirable ones.

This is the stage where you decide whether you should make the choice or channel it to the person who has the authority or expertise to make it. If you decide that it is your "call," one choice is to do nothing, hoping that the problem will go away or solve itself in time. You must be careful, though, that this doesn't become an excuse for not making a difficult choice. If it does, you may get a reputation for being indecisive—the "kiss of death" to many promising supervisory careers.

Step 3: Collect, Interpret, and Evaluate Information About Alternatives

Usually there are many sources from which to gather information affecting a decision. Sometimes standing orders, policies, procedures, rules, and regulations provide relevant information. In fact, these documents may have already made the decision for you—or at least may indicate how you should decide. Other sources of information include your own experience, company records and reports, discussion with the people directly and indirectly involved, and personal observations.

SELF-CHECK   In Case 4, where do you think Jones' supervisor can get the information he needs to make his decision? What additional information beyond that given in the case would be helpful to him in reaching the best decision?

Perhaps you've heard the saying "Tell me what you want to prove, and I'll get you the data to prove it." The effective evaluation of alternatives involves looking *objectively* at the pros and cons of each one. Choices can be evaluated in many ways. The information can be written down on a type of balance sheet, as shown in Exhibit 4–4, with the reasons for each alternative on one side and the reasons against it on the other. Or a process of elimination can be used in which the undesirable (or less desirable) choices are dropped.

Even as the first 1992 model-year Civics were hitting the road, Honda Motor Co. was putting together a 12-member team that would spend the next 18 months scouring its U.S. suppliers and its Ohio factory workers for ideas to make the next Civic cheaper to build.

Exhibit 4–4
Evaluating Alternatives

Step 4: Select the Preferred Alternative

Finally, you reach the point where you must make a choice. You look at your conclusions from Step 3 and then logically and rationally pick the alternative you think is most desirable for all concerned from an objective, ethical, and practical point of view. Selecting the preferred alternative involves cost/benefit analysis and risk analysis.

cost/benefit analysis
Estimating and comparing the costs and benefits of alternatives.

Using the technique of **cost/benefit analysis,** you estimate what each alternative will cost in terms of human, physical, and financial resources. Then you estimate the expected benefits. Finally, you compare the two estimates. You choose the one with the greatest payoff, where the ratio of benefits to cost is most favorable.

risk The possibility of defeat or injury.

Analysis of risk is inherent in decision making. **Risk** is the possibility of defeat, disadvantage, injury, or loss. Prudent decision makers try to minimize risk by effectively forecasting outcomes and considering all variables.

SELF-CHECK   From what is told in Case 4, what decision should the supervisor make? Why?

Step 5: Implement the Decision

Effective decision making doesn't stop when you choose from among alternatives. The decision must be put into operation. For example, you might need to obtain and allocate some equipment and supplies. Or you might need to develop methods and procedures. Or you might have to select, train, or even terminate some employees. This is a difficult part of decision making, because you must face and deal with people who may not like your choice. Many good supervisory decisions are ineffective because of the way they're implemented.

Step 6: Follow Up, Evaluate, and Make Changes—If Needed

This last step in the decision-making process involves exercising management's control function. It determines whether the implementation of the decision is proceeding smoothly and achieving the desired results. If not, and the decision can be changed or modified, it should be. If it can't be changed, then you "live with it" and try to make it succeed.

FACTORS TO KEEP IN MIND WHEN MAKING DECISIONS

Learning Objective 5

Name some factors
to keep in mind when
making decisions.

It is relatively easy to describe the general steps in decision making, but actually
making decisions is much more difficult because of several factors. The number and
variety of such factors is extensive; we'll discuss only the more important ones.

The Right Person Should Make the Decision

Although there is no hard-and-fast rule as to who should make a given decision, in
general, decisions are best made by the person in authority closest to the point of
action. The key consideration is that the decision maker have adequate knowledge
of the conditions and people involved as well as the authority needed to implement
the decision.

Decisions Should Contribute to Objectives

Relating each decision to the organization's objectives facilitates decision making and
helps the organization carry out its mission. It also helps in getting decisions accepted
and carried out. If a given decision doesn't help achieve objectives, it should be ques-
tioned. For example, suppose the manager of an agricultural cooperative decides to
buy fertilizer from a company owned by him, his wife, and his son. Although the
manager and his family will make a nice profit on their operations, the farmers who
buy the fertilizer will pay higher prices. You would expect the farmers to question this
decision.

There's Seldom Only One Acceptable Choice

Most organizational problems can be solved, or resolved, in more than one way. The
best choice depends on what factors you consider important, what weight you give to
each, and what you do about them. Even when the outcome of a decision turns out
to be not as expected, people tend to try to make it come out "right." For example, if
a supervisor hires a computer programmer over the objections of the human resource
manager, the supervisor will do everything possible to see that the new employee
succeeds, regardless of any weaknesses the employee exhibits.

Both Feeling and Thinking Should Be Used

Supervisory decisions affect people. Such decisions may involve who is assigned which
jobs, who receives overtime, how a new process will affect personnel, and so on.
Supervisors must certainly be sensitive and understanding regarding the effects of
their decisions on individuals. They must also, however, be willing to make decisions
that affect people negatively.

feeling decision process Giving great weight to the "people" side of a decision.

thinking decision process Focuses predominantly on analysis, logic, and objectivity to solve problems.

Two basic ways in which people make decisions are through feeling and thinking processes. Supervisors who are primarily feeling-oriented tend to use a **feeling decision process,** giving greater weight to the human issues—the "people" side of a decision. They essentially view many problems or inefficiencies as being explainable in human terms. They tend to focus on personal, human issues in decisions and give considerable weight to the effects their decisions will have on others.

Thinking-oriented supervisors, on the other hand, use a **thinking decision process,** focusing problem solving on analysis, logic, rationalization, and objectivity. Although the human factor may be relevant, it is not the dominant factor in the thinking decision process unless analysis and logic show it to be.

SELF-CHECK

Which process should Jones' supervisor use in solving the problem in Case 4? Explain.

There is, of course, no one best approach; therefore, a balance of the two is needed. Supervisors who are overly feeling-oriented may be considered too compassionate, too compromising, and wimpy. When carried to extremes, their sensitivity may cause them to fail to address issues or to make decisions that can have a negative effect on others (in disciplinary situations, for example). On the other hand, supervisors who are excessively thinking-oriented may be considered too cold, too inflexible, too unsympathetic and impersonal. Their failure to fully consider the human element may severely limit the effectiveness of their decisions. To be effective, supervisors must reflect a certain balance of dimensions in their decision making. The exercise in Exhibit 4–5 will give you some insight into your own style.

Effective Decision Making Takes Considerable Time and Effort

There is no such thing as a button-pushing, finger-snapping supervisor who spits out decisions with machine-gun rapidity. It takes quality time and effort—mental and often physical—to make effective decisions. Unfortunately, many choices are made simply on the basis of fatigue. After spending many hours evaluating various alternatives, the exhausted supervisor will subconsciously think, "I'll choose the next one, regardless of what it is, just to get it over with." Or, to save time, a supervisor will say, "That's not a bad choice. I can live with it if you can." Such decisions rarely turn out to be successful.

Decision Making Improves with Practice

People can't be taught to make effective decisions. They must learn by actually going through the process and living with the consequences. Like any learned skill, decision making improves the more you exercise it, assuming that you use it effectively.

Instructions: Circle the response that seems to best describe you. Remember, there are no "correct" answers. If two answers are an absolute toss-up, leave that question unanswered and move on.

1. Are you more careful about (a) people's rights or (b) how people feel?
2. Are you more likely to be impressed by (a) principles and standards or (b) emotions and feelings?
3. In making decisions, which is more important to you: (a) objectivity or (b) how people will feel?
4. Do people who know you see you as basically (a) strong-willed or (b) warm-hearted?
5. If another person says something that is incorrect, would you normally (a) point out the error or (b) ignore it?
6. Are you best described as making decisions based on (a) logical, step-by-step analysis or (b) how your decisions make you and others feel?
7. Which do you feel is the greater mistake: (a) being too merciful or (b) being too firm?
8. Are you best described as (a) a rational person or (b) a caring person?
9. Assuming that you could perform equally well, would you feel more comfortable with the role of (a) judge or (b) counselor?
10. Which describes you better: (a) firm or (b) sympathetic?

Scoring: Count the number of "a" and "b" answers you gave. Your "a" answers tend to represent a thinking orientation; your "b" answers a feeling orientation. If there is a strong imbalance, you may need to be especially conscious of the overlooked dimension in your decision making.

Exhibit 4–5
*Are You a Thinking-
or Feeling-Oriented
Decision Maker?*

A Decision May Not Please Everyone

Seldom does a decision please everyone concerned. The challenge facing the supervisor after the decision is made is to explain the decision and to win the individual's or group's cooperation.

An office manager was authorized to phase out 12 old computers over a period of a year, replacing three every four months. She assigned the first three new ones to the most efficient employees, only to hear complaints from those with the most seniority. She told them that, if their performance improved, they would get the next new ones.

A Decision Starts a Chain Reaction

Since all parts of an organization are interrelated, don't be surprised when a decision made in another department affects yours, or vice versa. A decision maker should be prepared to defend, change, or drop a decision in view of the chain of events it starts.

Julie Acree was perplexed. She had recently made a decision to allow Maria Montano, one of her top technicians, to attend a two-day seminar on some of the new developments in her field. The superintendent had agreed and approved payment of the $150 tab for tuition. Now, Acree had just come from the superintendent's office, where she'd been told that supervisors in a number of other departments had also

recommended their people for seminars. The decision to pay Montano's way was temporarily on hold until a policy could be worked out. "I can't afford to suddenly have 20 people attend seminars at the same time," the superintendent said.

Ethical Considerations Play a Part

Learning Objective 6

Explain the role of ethics in the supervisor's decision making.

ethics Standards used to judge "rightness" or "wrongness" of one's behavior toward others.

Supervisors must be particularly concerned with ethical considerations when making decisions and solving problems. They should have a true concern for the well-being of others, both inside and outside the organization. Therefore, supervisors should not only obey all laws and conform to the ethical code(s) of practice established by their employer and society, but they should have a personal set of ethical principles that guide their actions. The difficult question, however, is: What is and what isn't ethical?

Ethics are the standards used to judge the "rightness" or "wrongness" of one person's behavior toward others. As this concept of ethical behavior is the individual's personal *ethic,* it is the highest and most rigid level of behavior. The next highest level is adhering to professional and organization *codes of ethics,* which are statements of what is and isn't acceptable behavior. The lowest level is the *legal level,* where we are all expected to adhere to the "law of the land."

In essence, ethical behavior requires considerations of *fairness*—that is, fair treatment of people with regard to hiring, job placement, grievances, benefits, terminations, and other employment activities. For an organization or supervisor to be fair, priorities must be balanced: that is, as much concern must be given to people and their problems as is given to economic and financial considerations. For example, there is often a conflict between job demands and personal considerations.

Consider the dilemma of a supervisor in a software development company. An independent programmer has presented him with an exciting new software concept that would save his employer a considerable sum. It would also be an excellent new product for his wife's fledgling software development firm—if he doesn't refer the idea to his boss.[1]

In essence, to "be fair" means to balance your self-interest with the interests of others who are concerned with the problem. Thus, ethical supervisors know how and when to put aside selfish, personal needs and act favorably toward others.

SELF-CHECK   In Case 4 what are the ethical factors that the supervisor must consider?

While there are many guides to ethical behavior—most religions have them—there are two that we think deserve your attention. The first is Rotary International's "Four-Way Test." It requires that four simple questions be asked when considering an action.

1. Is it the truth?
2. Is it fair to all concerned?

Exhibit 4–8
*Advantages and
Disadvantages of
Group Decision Making*

Advantages	Disadvantages
• Provides the supervisor with a broader range of information on the problem, alternatives, and recommended solution.	• Holds the supervisor accountable for the group's decisions.
• Lends a more creative approach to solving problems, since ideas may be "piggybacked."	• Takes the work group's time away from other aspects of their jobs.
• Improves communication in the department because the work group becomes aware of issues facing the supervisor.	• May force the supervisor to choose sides and thus cause morale problems.
• Creates higher morale in the work group.	• Allows strong personalities to dominate the work group, in which case the decision may not reflect the entire group's opinion.
• Stresses a stronger commitment to the decision once it is made, since the work group helped to make it.	• Requires more supervisory skill in communicating and clarifying the group's role in a given decision.
	• Is difficult to use if the decision must be made quickly.

SELF-CHECK   Which of the three approaches mentioned in this section would you recommend to Jones' supervisor? Why?

IMPROVING DECISION MAKING

Learning Objective 8
Discuss some ways of improving decision making.

In order to improve decision making, a supervisor should understand the basis on which decisions are made and the techniques used to make them. The *basis* of a decision is the frame of reference in which it is made. The *technique* is the method used in the decision process.

Bases of Decision Making

Some of the most frequent bases of decision making are authority of position, experience, facts, intuition, and a "follow-the-leader" attitude. From a practical point of view, there is no one best basis. Supervisors should use the bases that best suit the circumstances.

AUTHORITY OF POSITION. The authority vested in the decision maker's position is probably the most frequently used basis. Decisions made on this basis tend to conform to the organization's strategies, policies, and procedures. For example, supervisory authority is the basis for decisions about job priorities, enforcement of company rules, and whom and when to discipline. Decisions made on the basis of authority of position also tend to provide continuity and permanence (since they are generally official), to be readily accepted, and to be considered authentic and legitimate. Yet these decisions may also reflect an unpopular company position, may be too routine, and may be made without due regard to the situation.

EXPERIENCE. We see and understand things in terms of concepts and ideas with which we are familiar. Experience provides us with meaningful guides for selecting alternatives. It gives us practical knowledge of what has been done in the past and of the outcomes of those decisions. It also provides "tried and true" knowledge that tends to be accepted by those who have shared the experience. Yet a decision maker's experience may be limited or unique, and the choice made may be based on outmoded or obsolete experience.

FACTS. Most discussions of decision making state that a decision should be based on "all the pertinent facts." If that ideal can be reached, well and good, for it gives the impression that the resulting choice is logical, sound, and proper. The pertinent facts may not be readily available, however, and if one waits to get them, no decision can be made. Also, getting the facts may be too costly or too time-consuming. Furthermore, "facts" may be misleading— or even wrong, as shown in Exhibit 4–9—and may be merely someone's opinion or belief. Thus, although a supervisor must use the facts available, these facts must be carefully classified, diagnosed, and interpreted to reveal their inadequacies and flaws.

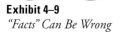

Exhibit 4–9
"Facts" Can Be Wrong

"Miss, I don't care what my check says. This is not my hat."

Source: 1963 © Saturday Review Magazine Co. Reprinted by permission.

GROUP
ACTIVITY

Skill Builder 4–1
Whom Do You Promote?

Your company recently developed a plan to identify and train top hourly employees for promotion to first-line supervision. As a part of this program, your boss has requested a ranking of the six hourly workers who report to you with respect to their promotion potential. Given their biographical data, rank them in the order in which you would select them for promotion to first-line supervisor; that is, the person ranked Number One would be first in line for promotion.

Biographical Data
1. *Sam Nelson*—Caucasian male, age 45, married, with four children. Sam has been with the company for five years, and his performance evaluations have been average to above average. He is well liked by the other employees in the department. He devotes his spare time to farming and plans to farm after retirement.
2. *Ruth Hornsby*—Caucasian female, age 32, married, with no children; her husband has a management-level job with the power company. Ruth has been with the company for two years and has received above-average performance evaluations. She is very quiet and keeps to herself at work. She says she is working to save for a down payment on a new house.
3. *Joe Washington*—African American male, age 26, single. Joe has been with the company for three years and has received high performance evaluations. He is always willing to take on new assignments and to work overtime. He is attending college in the evenings and someday wants to start his own business. He is well liked by the other employees in the department.
4. *Ronald Smith*—Caucasian male, age 35, recently divorced, with one child, age 4. Ronald has received excellent performance evaluations during his two years with the company. He seems to like his present job but has removed himself from the line of progression. He seems to have personality conflicts with some of the employees.
5. *Betty Norris*—African American female, age 44, married, with one grown child. Betty has been with the company for ten years and is well liked by fellow employees. Her performance evaluations have been average to below average, and her advancement has been limited by a lack of formal education. She has participated in a number of technical training programs conducted by the company.
6. *Roy Davis*—Caucasian male, age 36, married, with two teenage children. Roy has been with the company for ten years and received excellent performance evaluations until last year. His most recent evaluation was average. He is friendly and well liked by his fellow employees. One of his children has had a serious illness for over a year, resulting in a number of large medical expenses. Roy is working a second job on weekends to help with these expenses. He has expressed a serious interest in promotion to first-line supervisor.

Answer the following questions:
1. What factors did you consider in developing your rankings?
2. What was the most important factor you considered?

Continued

3. What information in the biographical data, if any, should not be considered in developing the rankings?

Source: This exercise was prepared for this book by Carl C. Moore, University of South Alabama.

Skill Builder 4–2
Personal Problems

An office manager was hired by a group of physicians in a small town in Kansas to head the employees at their private clinic. The office manager supervised a receptionist, two nurses, a lab technician, and a typist.

The receptionist was married and had three children. She was a long-term employee who was quite capable in her work and seemed to get along with everyone, including the patients. However, she began to receive many phone calls during work hours. Word got around that it was her husband who was calling her so often; everyone knew that he was an alcoholic. At times he kept her on the phone at great length, and she would ask the other employees to answer the other lines.

It eventually got to the point where the receptionist could not make appointments for patients or handle the incoming calls as she should. One day, when the receptionist had gone home early to handle a family problem, the office manager asked the other five employees to stay after work for a little while to discuss the problem.

Instructions:
Get together with four classmates and discuss what you would suggest to the office manager at the meeting.

The Overworked Maintenance People

The maintenance department of a midwestern manufacturing plant had seven maintenance employees. Two of them, Jay and Ricky, did much better work and were more dependable, cooperative, and obliging than the rest. For this reason, some of the other maintenance workers, and even the supervisor of the department, would take advantage of them. For example, when the supervisor made his rounds and found that there was a paint job or some repair work that hadn't been done properly, instead of mentioning this to the workers involved, he would send Jay and Ricky to do the job over. Other personnel, seeing this, began to do their work only halfway, knowing that Jay and Ricky would be sent to bail them out.

The supervisor hadn't realized that he wasn't being fair to Jay and Ricky and other conscientious workers. However, at a meeting with the plant manager to discuss the "poor maintenance problem," this was brought to his attention. The plant manager indicated that something had to be done about it, and in a hurry.

Answer the following questions:
1. If you were the supervisor, what would you do after the meeting was over?
2. How would you define the problem?
3. How would you solve the problem? Explain.
4. What type of follow-up would you maintain?

Skill-Development Scenario
Decision Making

Jane Farrell is Store Operations Supervisor for McElvey Department Stores' Ross Town Mall location. In the first part of the video Farrell is pressured to make some decision quickly.

Answer the following questions:
1. What examples did you see of the shortcomings in Farrell's decision-making process?
2. After viewing the second part of this video, review how Farrell used the six-step decision-making process to solve the furniture problem.

Chapter 5
Fundamentals of Organizing

Case 5

John Moody's Growing Organization

Stage 1: The One-Person Organization. Our story begins in 1980 in a small Midwestern city of 75,000. Our main character is John Moody, 26, who has been working in a large paper mill on the outskirts of the city since his graduation from high school. Although Moody still holds the same semiskilled job at the operative level that he started with, he is actually a motivated person. His basic satisfaction in life comes from the challenge of building and creating things in his garage workshop. Although he assumes that he will never get rich, he feels his take-home pay is sufficient to take care of the necessities of life and to support his hobbies. Even though his job at the mill is not very challenging, he gets all the challenge he needs from tinkering around in his workshop.

Unfortunately, in early 1980 the country begins to slide into an economic recession, which has an adverse effect on the paper industry. Several mill employees, including Moody, are laid off because of excessive inventory buildup. Moody signs up for unemployment compensation and decides to spend time building a new boat trailer in his garage. He puts a lot of thought and effort into the task. The result is an excellent trailer—such a fine one that it prompts several of his friends to talk him into building trailers for them for 20 percent more than his expenses. Even at this price, his boat trailers sell for less than those sold in local stores. Before long, so many requests are coming in that Moody finds himself spending all his time in his garage.

At this point, Moody decides to work full-time building boat trailers as long as he can make a living doing so.

Stage 2: The Organization with Assistants Added. After three months, so many orders are coming in that John Moody cannot fill them. In the past few years, the federal government has built a number of dams near Moody's town, creating four new lakes in the region. Fishing has been good, and there is a large demand for boats and boat trailers. Moody is now making more money per day than he did when he was with the mill. To keep pace with the orders, he hires Ray Martin, a former high school friend, to help build the trailers. For a small monthly salary, Moody also hires his wife, Nancy, to keep books and handle the financial details. Before the month is out, Martin has mastered his job so well that he and Moody are producing more boat trailers than they have orders for.

At this point, Moody and Martin start thinking about hiring someone as a salesperson. Martin's friend, Paul Cree, has just graduated from college with a major in marketing. After hearing about Moody's business from Moody and Martin, Cree decides that it has possibilities. With the assurance of an opportunity to buy into the business in the future, Cree starts to work for Moody as a salesperson.

Paul Cree proves to be an excellent salesperson, and the business continues to grow. To keep up with the increasing volume of orders, Moody hires additional people. Also, the business moves to a larger building. After two years Moody has 19 people working for him. His net income is such that Nancy Moody has quit working, but Moody finds himself so busy that he cannot enjoy his higher income. More important, he feels that he is losing control of the business; the increased costs per trailer support this belief.

In desperation, John Moody asks Martin and Cree for advice about his problem. Cree recalls that in one of his college courses, the instructor talked about the management principle of *span of control*. This principle holds that there is a limit to the number of people a manager can supervise effectively. In Cree's opinion, the solution is to select managers for the areas of finance, production, and sales.

Cree's solution seems so simple that John Moody wonders why he didn't think of it himself. He places Beth Fields—his best accountant—in charge of finance, Ray Martin in charge of production, and Paul Cree in charge of sales.

Stage 3: The Line Organization. As a result of the line organization and the capabilities of each manager, the unit cost of making each boat trailer is lowered. Under the leadership of sales manager Paul Cree, the business expands its sales territory to cover most of the states in the Midwest. As sales increase, production also increases. New people are added in both sales and production. The line organization develops to accommodate the increased growth. Keeping in mind the principle of span of control, John Moody adds new sections in production and sales whenever the volume of business justifies the new additions. He now also finds time to concentrate more on such tasks as developing plans for the future, coordinating the work of the three departments, and supervising his managers.

After ten years, John Moody's business is employing over 700 people. During this period, Moody has promoted Martin to be in charge of five production department heads. This move has created an additional level of management in the production department. The department heads, in turn, are each responsible for four production supervisors. Each production supervisor is responsible for ten production workers. Similarly, Moody has made Cree sales manager in charge of three regional sales managers, each of whom is supervising eight salespersons.

Stage 4: The Line-and-Staff Organization. Unfortunately, increasing sales require John Moody's business to add more people in order to meet production quotas. So the profit on each unit produced declines. Finally, Beth Fields, the head of finance, reports to Moody that each $1.00 in sales is costing $1.10. In other words, a boat trailer that the business sells for $300 is costing $330 to manufacture. Although the business is now financially sound, Moody is aware that, with the way things are going, it will not take long for the business to go bankrupt. He therefore decides to call in a reputable management consultant.

The management consultant interviews managers from different levels in the company. After several days of investigation, the consultant makes the following report to John Moody:

> **My investigation reveals that you have made a mistake that many companies make: You are operating purely as a line organization, whereas at your stage of growth, you need to adopt a *line-and-staff organization*. This means that you need to hire several staff experts to perform some of the activities your line managers presently do. As it now stands, your organizational structure tends to overload your managers. They are, in effect, wearing too many hats. More specifically, I have found evidence of the following three kinds of inefficiency:**

line-and-staff organization A line organization to which staff departments have been added.

1. Your supervisors are doing their own hiring, firing, and disciplining. Consequently, you have no uniform way of screening, selecting, promoting, and disciplining employees. Moreover, a number of the supervisors are hiring friends and relatives for their departments, and other employees believe that favoritism is rampant throughout the company.

2. The several department heads independently purchase materials and supplies for their departments. This duplication of effort has caused excessive space and dollars to be tied up in raw materials inventory. In addition, this practice has opened the door for waste and pilferage of supplies and materials.

3. Your department heads and supervisors are involved in method and layout studies, maintenance and repair work, scheduling and dispatching, and, to cap it off, quality control—all on top of their primary jobs of supervising the work and motivating their employees. The old proverb that "a jack of all trades is master of none" is certainly borne out by the situation I find in your plant.

My primary recommendation, therefore, is that you hire a human resources specialist to screen and select new employees, a production control manager to do all the purchasing and inventory control, and an industrial engineering manager to do method and layout studies and the like. By adding these three staff specialists, you will give your department heads and supervisors a chance to concentrate on their primary job of overseeing production and motivating their employees. Equally important, you should receive immediate benefits and cost savings by eliminating inefficiencies and installing improved ways of operating.

The consultant went on to report that, in the future, additional staff people would be needed if the company's rate of growth continued. He also stated that the company might want to consider diversifying by adding additional product lines that would require similar skills.

The only things that evolve by themselves in an organization are disorder, friction, and malperformance.

Peter Drucker

In Chapter 1, we defined the term *organizing* and noted that it is one of the five functions of any manager or supervisor. In this chapter, we present concepts, principles, and a frame of reference for understanding this function.

Many first-level managers understand organization only from a narrow vantage point—their immediate department or perhaps one or two levels above them. We believe that it is equally important to be able to see and understand the organization from a much broader standpoint. The more completely supervisors understand the big picture, the better equipped they are to work effectively as key members of the management team. Consequently, organizing is presented from a broad, overall perspective in this chapter.

In Chapter 6, we will focus on organizing concepts that are directly applicable to the supervisory management level.

Failure to understand the organizing function from a broader viewpoint can lead to the following problems:

1. Excessive violation of the unity of command principle.
2. Failure to develop additional departments or work groups when needed.
3. Unclear and improper assignment of duties and responsibilities to new employees.
4. Ineffective use of organizational units and inadequate development of human resources because of improper decentralization of authority.
5. Excessive and unhealthy conflicts between departments and between line supervisors and staff personnel.

THE FOUR STAGES IN GROWTH OF AN ORGANIZATION

Learning Objective 1

Understand the stages of organization growth.

To see the organizing function of management in operation, let us study the growth and development of a hypothetical manufacturing business. Usually a business organization grows in four stages. Stage 1 is the one-person organization; Stage 2 is the organization with assistants added; Stage 3 is the line organization; and Stage 4 is the line-and-staff organization. Not all organizations go through all these stages. Many skip the first stage and go directly to Stage 2. For clarity's sake, however, we'll discuss each stage.

Stage 1: The One-Person Organization

Exhibit 5–1 shows that John Moody's business is in the first stage of organizational growth—that is, a one-person operation. This means that he alone performs the three basic activities common to all manufacturing operations: financing, producing, and selling.

Stage 2: The Organization with Assistants Added

Exhibit 5–2 shows that John Moody has had to hire three assistants to help carry out the three primary activities of his business. This stage is a critical one; over 50 percent of new businesses fail in their first year of operation from lack of capital, ineffective management, or both.

Demand for the trailers grows as Paul Cree focuses his efforts on sales. The volume of orders increases, and John Moody must hire more workers—first in production and then later in sales and finance also. Beginning his third year in business, Exhibit 5–3 shows Moody's company and its 19 employees.

SELF-CHECK

Before reading further, look at the organization chart in Exhibit 5–3. Can you explain why John Moody is losing control of his business?

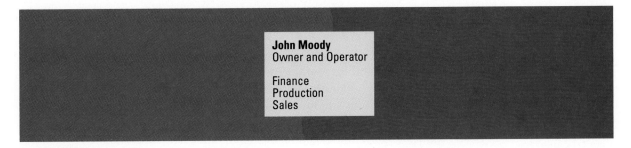

Exhibit 5–1
John Moody's One-Person Organization

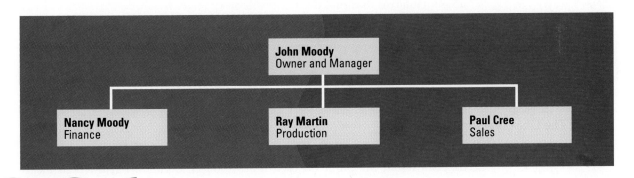

Exhibit 5–2
John Moody Hires Assistants

Exhibit 5–3
John Moody's Organization After Two Years

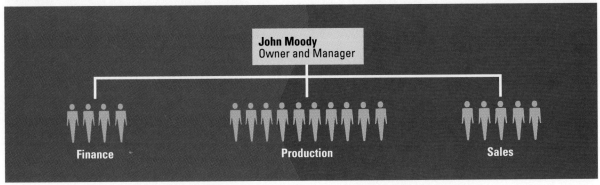

Stage 3: The Line Organization

Exhibit 5–4 shows that John Moody has selected a manager for each of the three major departments, and his span of control has been reduced from 19 to three employees. Beth Fields is responsible for three employees, Ray Martin for nine employees, and Paul Martin for four employees. In effect, John Moody's business is now structured as a **line organization.** This means that each person in the organization has clearly defined responsibilities and reports to an immediate supervisor.

line organization Has clearly defined responsibilities and reports to an immediate supervisor.

There are two advantages to having a line organization at an early stage of a business organization's growth:

1. Quick, decisive action on problems is possible because authority is centralized—it is in the hands of John Moody and his three managers.
2. Lines of responsibility and authority are clearly defined. Everyone knows what his or her job and obligations are. Thus, evasion of responsibility is minimized and accountability is maximized.

The business remains successful, and after ten years, there are over 700 employees. Exhibit 5–5 shows how a new level of management has been added. The new level includes department heads in production and regional sales managers in the sales organization structure.

Stage 4: The Line-and-Staff Organization

Increased sales force John Moody to add more people in order to meet production needs. As a result, the profit on each unit produced declines. Finally, Beth Fields reports that a boat trailer that sells for $300 is costing $330 to produce. No business can remain financially sound if it spends more to produce its product than it makes when the product is sold. John Moody hires a reputable management consultant.

Exhibit 5–4
The Span of Control in John Moody's Line Organization

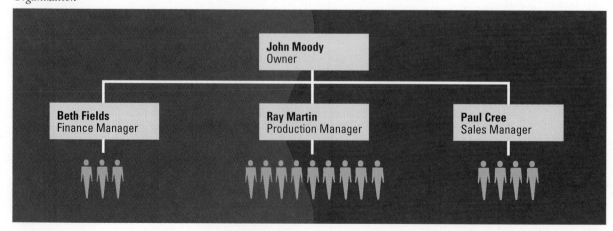

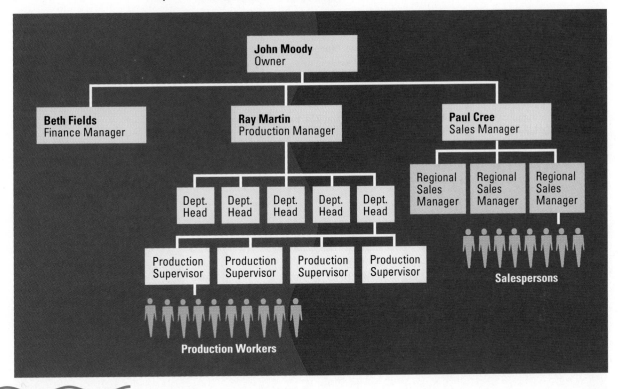

Exhibit 5–5
*John Moody's Line
Organization After
Ten Years*

Before reading the consultant's recommendations, decide what you think is the primary problem or problems causing manufacturing costs to increase in John Moody's business.

The consultant studies the situation and interviews managers from different levels in the organization. The recommendations that the consultant made are listed on page 125 at the end of the opening case. John Moody accepted the consultant's recommendations, and the resulting organization structure is shown in Exhibit 5–6.

What adjustments will the supervisors need to make to accommodate the consultant's recommended changes? Do you think these changes will help or hinder the supervisor in the job of motivating and managing his or her crew?

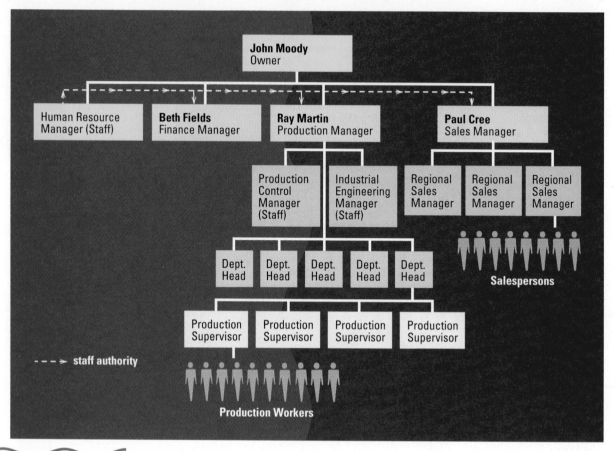

Exhibit 5–6
John Moody's Line-and-Staff Organization

The new line-and-staff organization went on to achieve not only record sales, but also record profits and growth. Ultimately, any growing business needs to pass into this fourth stage. Unfortunately, many do not, and some suffer the consequences of decline and bankruptcy.

Other Organizational Forms

There are several key ways in which organizations decide on the organizational pattern that will be used to group the various activities to be performed. The process of determining how activities are to be grouped is called departmentalization. In the Moody case the form used was by function, by sales, by production, by personnel, etc. Some examples of other forms are as follows:

- By product or service, such as a bank's loan department, a hospital's coronary care unit, and a business college, an engineering college, and an education college.
- By territory, such as southwest division, northeast division, and international operations.

Retail stores can run the gamut of departmentation; for example, one store may sell clothes for all ages, all shapes and sizes, while another may stock solely petite sophisticated career wear.

- By customer, such as industrial sales, retail sales, and government sales.
- By matrix or project, such as space projects, construction projects, and pollution control projects.

Later in the chapter we will examine in more detail the project or matrix organization along with newer forms of organizational structures.

TWO IMPORTANT ORGANIZING PRINCIPLES

Two important principles involved in the organizing function were illustrated in the case of John Moody's organizations. These are unity of command and span of control (or span of management). Let us now discuss these principles in detail.

Unity of Command

unity of command principle States that everyone should report to and be accountable to only one boss.

The **unity of command principle** states that everyone in an organization should report to and be accountable to only one boss for performance of a given activity. This supervisor should be responsible for evaluating performance, passing down orders and information, and developing employees to become better employees in the organization. It is to this person that employees should turn for help in carrying out their duties and should communicate any deviations, either positive or negative, in implementing their duties. In sum, the supervisor is the one responsible for motivating his or her employees to achieve effective results and for taking action when employees deviate from planned performance.

Adherence to the unity of command principle is important for five reasons:

1. It prevents duplication and conflict when orders and instructions are passed down.
2. It decreases confusion and "passing the buck" because everyone—including managers—is accountable to only one person for a given assignment.
3. It provides a basis whereby a supervisor and his or her employees can develop a knowledge of each other's strengths and weaknesses.
4. It provides an opportunity for a supervisor and employees to develop supportive relationships and to realize their individual and group potential in achieving organizational objectives.
5. It promotes higher morale than is generally found in organizations that do not follow the unity of command principle.

Unfortunately some managers only give lip service to this principle, although their organization chart seems to reflect it.

Recently, one of the authors of this book was working with a branch plant of a large company to tailor a management development program. Among other things, this author was examining the leadership styles practiced by key managers and their effect on employees. To determine those leadership styles, the author interviewed managers at all levels. The results showed that the plant manager, though unusually capable and generally effective, made one mistake with his employee managers: he violated the unity of command principle by periodically conducting inspections throughout the plant and making on-the-spot suggestions to operative employees. Oftentimes, he made these suggestions when the employees' supervisor was not present. As a result, operative employees were following instructions that their immediate supervisors were unaware of. Moreover, employees would stop working on their assigned duties in order to carry out the instructions of the plant manager. This practice caused a problem for supervisors, as illustrated by Exhibit 5–7.

As a result of this one error, a serious morale problem had developed. Many of the plant manager's otherwise effective managerial practices were being undermined.

Exhibit 5–7
Violating the Unity of Command Principle

When this situation was called to his attention, he was quite surprised. It seems that he had slipped into this habit without being fully aware of its long-range consequences. When this manager thereupon began passing his suggestions and instructions through lower-level managers, morale improved.

Although employees should have only one supervisor, they may, of course, have relationships with many people. For example, in a line-and-staff organization, line supervisors and department heads will have many contacts with staff personnel. These contacts are necessary so that both line and staff personnel can accomplish their duties. Later in this chapter, we will explain how these relationships can be developed without violating the unity of command principle. The important thing to remember is this: If there should be a conflict between a staff request and a line manager's command, the employee should have a single manager to turn to for clarification or a final decision.

Span of Control

Learning Objective 2

Explain the principles of unity of command and span of control.

span of control principle States that there is a limit to the number of people a person can supervise effectively.

Before World War II, experts maintained that the span of control should be three to eight people, depending on the level of management. In those days, one of the first things an organizational consultant examined when a company was having problems was the span of control at various levels. Today the three-to-eight-people limit is no longer accepted as universally applicable. This is why we state the **span of control principle** simply as follows: There is a limit to the number of people a person can manage effectively. Just as you can span only a limited number of feet and inches with your arms, your mental reach can span only a limited number of the problems, situations, and relationships that make up the activities of management.

NARROWER SPAN OF CONTROL AT THE TOP. One thing we can say without qualification: The higher the managers are in an organization, the fewer people they should have reporting directly to them. There are at least three reasons for relating span of control to management level:

1. Top-level managers must solve a variety of different, nonrecurring problems. Much mental concentration is required to solve such problems.
2. Middle managers must spend much of their time in long-range planning, working with outside interest groups, and coordinating the various activities of the organization. They cannot afford to be tied down by the excessive burden of supervision created when a large number of people report directly to them.
3. First-level managers, by contrast, tend to be concerned with more clearly defined areas of operation. Although they are responsible for a certain amount of coordination with other departments, most of their contacts are directly with their immediate employees. Hence, they are able to supervise more people than are higher-level managers.

DIFFERENT APPROACHES TO A SUPERVISOR'S SPAN OF CONTROL. Exhibit 5–8 depicts three different approaches to a supervisor's span of control, leading to quite different jobs for supervisors A, B, and C. Can we say that one of these approaches is best? No, because the correct size of a supervisor's span of control depends on a number of circumstances, as shown in Exhibit 5–9.

Exhibit 5–8
Narrow, Wide, and Very Wide Spans of Control

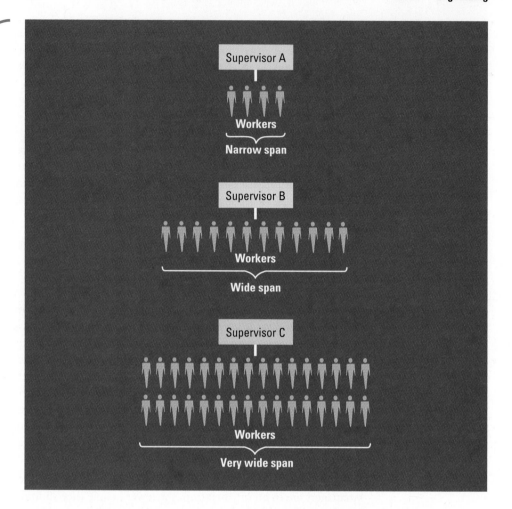

Companies that follow a policy of a narrow span of control are often hampered in achieving effective results. If an organization of, say, a thousand people rigidly adheres to a span of between three and seven, this tall, narrow organizational structure (with many, many management levels) will have some disadvantages. Numerous supervisory managers will be required, resulting in high payroll costs. Communication will have to pass up and down through many levels, increasing the possibility of distortion. Oversupervision may restrict decision making by employees and limit their opportunities to achieve their full potential. On the other hand, an advantage of tight control is that the work can be closely directed, so the company can hire relatively less skilled people.

TENDENCY TOWARD WIDER SPANS OF CONTROL. Over the years, many companies have tended to broaden their span of control at all levels. There are at least four reasons for this trend:

1. Higher educational attainment, management and supervisory development programs, vocational and technical training, and increased knowledge generally on the part of the labor force have improved the abilities and capacities of both managers and employees. The greater the supervisor's capacity, the more people he or she can supervise.

Exhibit 5–9
Factors Contributing to a Narrow or Wide Span of Control

Factor	Narrow Span Indicated	Wide Span Indicated
How physically close are the people performing the work?	Dispersed, perhaps even in different geographical locations.	Very close, perhaps all in one physical work area in a building.
How complex is the work?	Very complex, such as development of a manned space station that will orbit the earth.	Rather routine and simple, such as an assembly-line operation.
How much supervision is required?	A great deal. So many problems arise that the supervisor needs to exercise close control.	Little. Workers are well trained and able to make normal job decisions easily.
How much non-supervisory work is required of the supervisor?	Much. The supervisor spends much time planning, coordinating, and performing nonsupervisory tasks.	Little. Not much planning and coordination is required of the supervisor. The supervisor spends most of his or her time supervising employees.
How much organizational assistance is furnished to the supervisor?	Little. The supervisor may do his or her own recruiting, training, and controlling.	Much. The supervisor may be aided by a training department, quality control department, etc.

2. Research indicates that in many situations *general* supervision is more effective than *close* supervision. A supervisor practicing general supervision delegates authority and supervises by results; whereas a supervisor practicing close supervision provides detailed instructions and often does the same type of work as the workers they are supervising.

3. New developments in management have permitted businesses to broaden their span of control and supervise by results, without losing control. For example, by using a computer an organization can process information more quickly and develop more efficient information-reporting systems.

4. Finally—and sometimes this is the primary reason—wider spans of control save the company money.

RELATIONSHIPS BETWEEN LINE AND STAFF

Learning Objective 3

Describe the difference between line and staff.

line personnel Carry out the primary activities of a business.

staff personnel Have the expertise to assist line people and aid top management.

Line personnel carry out the primary activities of a business, such as producing or selling products and/or services. **Staff personnel,** on the other hand, use their expertise to assist the line people and aid top management in various areas of business activities. Line departments, therefore, are like a main stream. Staff departments are like the tributaries serving and assisting the main stream, although they should not be thought of as being secondary to the line departments. Both line and staff people are important.

Of the various jobs you've held, which were "line" and which were "staff"?

Once a business has reached the fourth stage of growth and is no longer a small organization, it becomes more complex and difficult to coordinate. A line-and-staff structure that places competent specialists in certain positions, such as human resources management, legal and governmental departments, research and development, and public relations, will help eliminate confusion, duplication, and inefficiency. But it will not solve all problems for all time. A growing organization must be continually alert to pitfalls and potential trouble spots.

Conflicts Between Line and Staff

One common problem in most large organizations is excessive conflict between line and staff personnel and between different departments. Differences in viewpoint between people and departments are natural, inevitable, and healthy, but excessive conflict can disrupt an entire organization. As shown in Exhibit 5–10, many line and staff contacts are normal.

There are many reasons excessive conflict can develop between line and staff personnel within an organization. Exhibit 5–11 summarizes some reasons for conflict between line and staff personnel.

Exhibit 5–10
Line and Staff Contacts

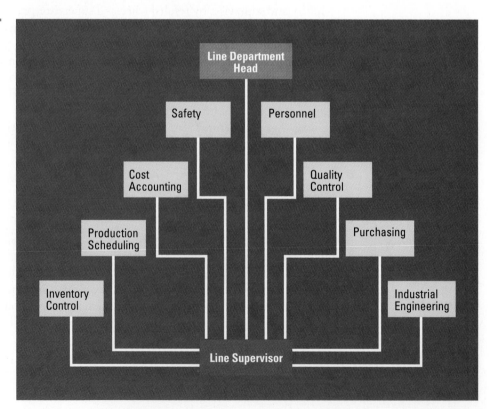

- Staff personnel give direct orders to line personnel.
- Good human relations are not practiced in dealings between line and staff personnel.
- Overlapping authority and responsibility confuse both line and staff personnel.
- Line people believe that staff people are not knowledgeable about conditions at the operating level.
- Staff people, because of their expertise, attempt to influence line decisions against line managers' wishes.
- Top management misuses staff personnel or fails to use them properly.
- Each department views the organization from a narrow viewpoint instead of looking at the organization as a whole.

Exhibit 5–11
Some Reasons for Conflict Between Line and Staff Personnel

SELF-CHECK   Before reading further, decide what you think might be done to decrease or eliminate the reasons for conflict between line and staff personnel.

How to Avoid Excessive Line-Staff Conflict: Delineating Authority

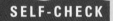
Learning Objective 4
Understand how to avoid excessive conflict between line and staff.

Learning Objective 5
Explain the three types of authority found in organizations.

Although conflict between line and staff people is not likely to be completely eliminated, a major way to avoid it is to ensure that people clearly understand the authority/responsibility relationships between individuals and departments. There are three types of authority: advisory, line, and functional.

ADVISORY AUTHORITY. The primary responsibility of most staff departments is to serve and advise the line departments. This type of authority is called **advisory authority** or the *authority of ideas*. However, some staff people may be so zealous in their efforts to sell their ideas to line personnel that they, in effect, hand out orders. If the line supervisor permits this to occur frequently, the unity of command begins to break down.

advisory authority Authority of most staff departments to serve and advise line departments.

LINE AUTHORITY. The second type of authority, **line authority,** is the power to directly command or exact performance from others. Having this power to command does not mean that you will elicit effective performance simply by giving out orders. It does mean, however, that you are directly responsible for the results of a certain department or group of workers. Line authority is not restricted to line personnel. The head of a staff department has line authority over the employees in his or her department.

line authority Power to directly command or exact performance from others.

When we think of AT&T, the first picture that may come to mind are the commercials touting service. But in addition to the customer service function are the behind-the-scenes functions of research, accounting, quality control, safety, and human resources.

FUNCTIONAL AUTHORITY. The third type of authority, **functional authority,** is usually a restricted kind of line authority. It gives a staff person a type of limited line authority over a given *function,* such as safety or quality, regardless of where that function is found in the organization.

functional authority
A staff person's limited line authority over a given function.

For example, a staff safety specialist may have functional authority to insist that line managers follow standard safety procedures in their departments. The staff safety specialist may have top management's blessing to dictate to lower-level line managers exactly what they must do and must not do concerning any matter that falls within the realm of safety. A quality control inspector may tell a line worker that certain parts need to be reworked. A human resources specialist may say to a line supervisor that the latter cannot fire a certain employee. A cost accountant may notify line departments that certain cost information must be furnished weekly, and so on.

SELF-CHECK   Can you think of some other common examples of functional authority?

Are you thinking that functional authority seems to violate the unity of command principle? It does! For this reason, it is important that all individuals clearly understand what functional authority is. Top line managers have the major responsibility for defining the nature of functional authority. Moreover, it is important for line personnel to exercise their right to appeal to higher management levels when they have disagreements with staff personnel. Functional authority is necessary, but it can be dangerous if it is granted indescriminately. Normally, it is given only to a staff area where there is a great deal of expertise and the staff expert's advice would be followed anyway.

Another way to avoid excessive conflict between line and staff people is to have effective communication between people and between departments. Key managers overseeing both line and staff people can improve the communication process by periodically bringing line and staff people together to discuss problems that cut across departmental lines. This example may inspire lower-level managers to do the same thing with their key employees. Thus, the danger of seeing only part of the picture will be minimized.

DECENTRALIZATION VERSUS CENTRALIZATION

Learning Objective 6

Distinguish between centralization and decentralization.

The concept of decentralization is closely related to the concept of delegation, which is examined in the next chapter. Briefly, delegation is the process by which managers allocate duties and authority downward to the people who report to them and assign responsibility for how authority is used.

> **An example of delegation occurred when John Moody called in assistants to help him do a better job than he could do alone. He assigned his assistants duties in finance, production, and sales.**

decentralization The extent to which authority is delegated from one unit of the organization to another.

Both delegation and decentralization are concerned with the giving of authority to someone at a lower level. **Decentralization** is the broader concept, as it refers to the extent to which authority is delegated from one level or one unit of the organization to another. In a *decentralized* organization, middle and lower levels of management make broader, more important decisions about their units. In a *centralized* organization, upper management makes most of the important decisions that concern all levels or units within the organization.

Factors Affecting Decentralization

No organization is completely centralized or decentralized. Decentralization is a relative concept and depends on a number of factors, including the following:

1. *Top management philosophy.* Some top managers have a need for tight control. They put together a strong central staff and want to make the most important decisions themselves. Others believe in strong delegation and push decisions to the lowest levels of their organization.
2. *History of the organization's growth.* Organizations that have grown by merging with other companies or acquiring them tend to be decentralized. Those that have grown on their own tend to be centralized.
3. *Geographic location(s).* Organizations that are spread out, with units in different cities or regions, tend to be decentralized so that lower-level managers can make decisions that fit their territory or circumstances.
4. *Quality of managers.* If an organization has many well-qualified, well-trained managers, it will likely be decentralized. If it has few, top management will centralize and make the most important decisions.

5. *Availability of controls.* If top management has an effective control system—good, timely information about performance at lower levels—the organization will tend toward decentralization. Without a good flow of control information for monitoring end results, it will tend to be centralized.[1]

Select one of your past employers. Would you say that the organization was centralized or decentralized? Why?

Effect of Decentralization on Organizational Structure

The degree to which an organization is decentralized will have a direct effect on the number of levels within the organization. As shown in Exhibit 5–12, Ford Motor Company, which is relatively centralized, has 12 layers of managers and supervisors between the operative employees and the chairperson. Toyota, which is relatively decentralized, has only seven levels of management. The trend in the United States is toward reducing the number of levels of management and decentralizing. Both the Japanese success in the automobile industry and the recession of the early 1990s, during which many United States companies trimmed organizational "fat," have had an impact on this trend. After Marvin Runyon retired as vice-president of Ford Motor Company, he accepted the position of chief executive officer with the Nissan Motor Manufacturing Corporation, U.S.A. When Runyon was asked how the Nissan plant

Exhibit 5–12
*Layers of Management
Reflecting a Centralized
Versus a Decentralized
Structure*

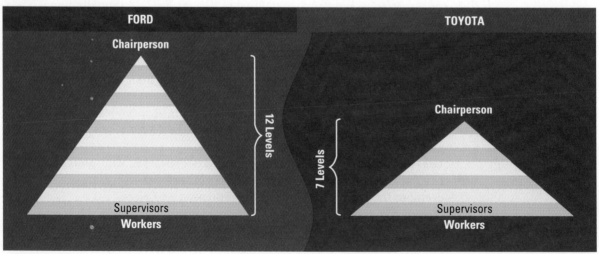

in Tennessee would be operated, he replied that the plan would take the best of both American and Japanese management concepts and methods. He went on to state:

> We are reducing the management levels that are customarily found in United States auto manufacturing companies. A lot of companies are very tiered. We're going to have five levels of management—president, vice-president, plant manager, operations manager, and supervisor. And then we have technicians. The reason we are doing that is to foster good communications, which I think is the key to running any business.
>
> We're going to have a very participative management style. What I mean is, everybody participates in what is done in this company. It will be more of a bottom-up management than top-down. Usually the top fellow decides everything that's going to happen, tells everybody, then expects everybody to march to that drummer. Japanese don't work that way. They work from a bottom-up technique. And that's what we plan to do.
>
> Now the reason for that is very simple. You go into a company and ask even a third-level person—say, the level of plant manager—"What are the problems in your operation?" He can give you about 4 percent of the real problems. Then you go to the operations-manager level, and they can give you, say, 40 percent. You go to the supervisor level, and maybe they can give you 70 percent. If you go to the technicians and ask them, they'll give you 100 percent of the problems. So, who better to participate in running the company than the people who actually know what's going on?[2]

PROJECT OR MATRIX ORGANIZATION

Learning Objective 7

Understand project or matrix organization.

project or **matrix organization** A hybrid type of organization having both functional departments and project teams.

Most organizations today are still structured as either a line or a line-and-staff organization along functional or product lines. Line organizations and line-and-staff organizations have served their purposes well for many years. They place considerable emphasis on basic organizational principles such as unity of command. However, many other organizational structures have developed. One of these is a hybrid type of organization called the **project** or **matrix organization,** in which both functional departments and project teams exist.[3] The functional departments, such as production, purchasing, and engineering, are permanent parts of the organization. The project teams are created as the need arises, and they are disbanded when the projects are completed. Let's look at an example.

> Stan Douglas is plant manager for the XYZ Company. For some time, Stan has been concerned with increasing costs, which are reducing the profit margin for the products his plant produces. The functional departments in his plant are shown in Exhibit 5–13. Under this arrangement, Stan Douglas has line authority over his functional managers, and they, in turn, have line authority over the people who report to them. The unity of command principle is adhered to throughout the company. However, Stan decides to form three project teams, composed of employees from various departments, to develop cost-reduction recommendations.

Exhibit 5–13
*The Traditional
Organization*

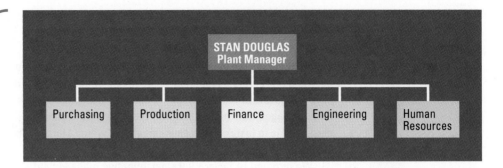

With this new assignment come the organizational changes reflected in Exhibit 5–14. The broken lines in Exhibit 5–14 show that the project supervisors have functional authority over project team members drawn from the different functional departments. Stan Douglas retains line authority over the functional departments.

The recommendations from members of the three project teams are excellent. As a result, costs are reduced. After one year, the project teams are disbanded.

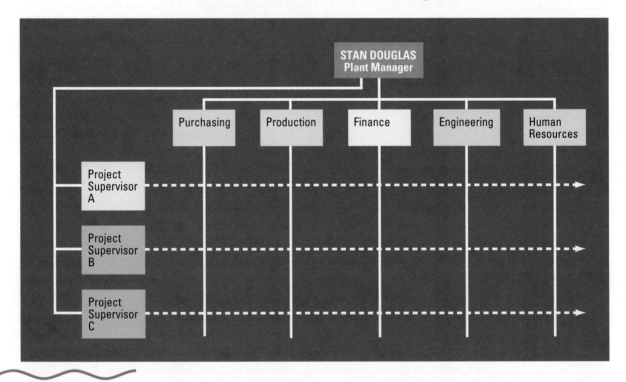

Exhibit 5–14
*The Project or Matrix
Organization*

SELF-CHECK

Under the project or matrix organization form, is the unity of command principle followed? Explain.

If your answer to the above question was "no," then you are correct. People from functional departments are working for two bosses: the line manager in the functional department and the project supervisor. Why would Stan Douglas use the matrix form, when it violates an important management principle? The answer, of course, is to increase his plant's *flexibility* in dealing with an important problem—cost reduction. The matrix form allows the plant to use expertise from several functional areas to focus on a problem. You should think of principles as guidelines and not as rigid rules.

Theoretically, one key advantage of the project or matrix approach is that it permits open communication and coordination of activities among the relevant functional specialists. Unfortunately, in reality, many companies have moved away from a matrix structure because of excessive conflicts between specialists and groups.

The Concept of Partnering

In the construction industry, on complex projects lasting a year or longer, two or more organizations are forced to use a project/matrix type of organization. Many times this leads to organizations forming joint ventures. A concept called *partnering* has been used in the public sector by the U.S. Army Corps of Engineers, the Navy and Air Force, and numerous contractors to greatly improve efficiency, effectiveness, and communications on these projects.

What Is Partnering?

Some observers have compared a construction contract to a marriage. In a marriage, two people with distinct backgrounds and different values contract to live together. Sometimes the partnership results in a "win-win" situation, in which both parties enhance each other and grow and develop together. On other occasions, differences grow into conflict, resulting in either a "win-lose" or a "lose-lose" situation. The outcome of the latter is divorce.

In large-scale construction contracts, two or more parties agree to work together for the life of the contract. The parties represent different cultures, where decisions are based on the goals and values of their respective organizations. The separate management processes followed often lead to miscommunication, distrust, and the development of adversarial relationships. Such relationships are reflected in construction delays, difficulty in resolving disputes, cost overruns, and litigation.

partnering Working together to develop trust, improve communications, and build teams.

Partnering is a process that focuses on resolving these traditional problems by developing trust, improving communication, and building teams. It identifies positive and resisting forces and then sets in motion the development of action plans to turn resisting forces into positive forces. It uses improved mutual understanding and strategic planning to develop a common set of goals and objectives, along with a partnering agreement that all parties sign.

The net result can be the creation of one culture with a common set of values, beliefs, behavior patterns, action plans, and goals that form the core of the partnering relationship.[4]

Exhibit 5–15, a partnering agreement signed by the Air Force, Corps of Engineers, and four contractors, shows how partnering was used in the construction and equipping of a tactical operation control center at Cape Canaveral.

Exhibit 5–15
TOCC Partnering Agreement

28 February 1989

We, the partners of the TOCC project, agree to work together as a cohesive team to produce a quality job on time, under budget, safely, ensuring a fair profit for the contractors. We will streamline the paperwork process, resolve conflicts at the lowest level and provide a safe work environment.

We agree to communicate and cooperate in all matters affecting the project by developing specific action plans to break down communication barriers, improve work change orders and ensure the construction, instrumentation and follow-on operation and maintenance of the TOCC meets the needs of the Eastern Space and Missle Center.

CORPS OF ENGINEERS

AIR FORCE

CSR

PAN AM

HARRIS

W & J

Source: *Organization Development Journal* 8 (Fall 1990), p.49.

DOWNSIZING

Learning Objective 8

Discuss the benefits and costs of downsizing.

In their book *In Search of Excellence,* Thomas Peters and Robert Waterman noted that one of the attributes of excellent companies is a simple organizational structure with a lean top-level staff.[5] In a 1988 article, management theorist Peter Drucker predicted that by 2008 a typical large business would have half the levels of management and one-third the managers of its counterpart today.[6]

What Is Downsizing?

downsizing Eliminating unnecessary levels of management.

Drucker's forecast is already coming true throughout the United States and Canada. **Downsizing** is the process of eliminating unnecessary levels of management and thus reducing the number of staff personnel and supervisors. A survey of 1,200 human resource managers indicated that 35 percent of them had engaged in downsizing within the past 12 months, and the average reduction was just over 10 percent.[7]

Benefits of Downsizing

One of the major benefits of downsizing is the tremendous cost reductions that occur almost immediately. Perhaps even more important are the improvements that take place in the way the organization is managed. Turnaround time in decision making is speeded up, and usually communication improves in all directions. Moreover, the organization becomes more responsive to customers and provides faster product delivery. Downsizing also removes the tendency for each level to justify its existence by close supervision and by frequently asking for reports and data from lower levels. Without excessive interference and stifling of creativity at lower levels, line managers have more opportunity to develop and use their authority to make decisions affecting the bottom line. In the final analysis, all of these things translate into higher profits.

An illustration:

A. T. Kearney analyzed management layers among both highly successful companies and others whose performance was not above average in their industry. The 15 not-so-successful companies typically had at least four more organizational layers than the 26 successful ones. Interviews confirmed that more layers in the organization inhibit productivity because the decision-making process is slower and the chances are greater that opportunities will be lost.[8]

Costs of Downsizing

Downsizing has some costs that can wreck the prospect of higher profits if the process is not accomplished ethically and efficiently. Some companies downsize so rapidly and prune staff and middle management so much that they lose control. In addition, some companies are very insensitive in the way they go about downsizing, telling a number of loyal, effective managers that they are no longer needed. A heavy-handed approach can lead to morale problems with remaining employees for years to come. Some other potential disadvantages are increased workloads, diminished chances of promotion, and threatened job security for those remaining.

Perhaps the greatest costs are the least known—the social costs. Research shows that when employees lose their jobs because of downsizing, domestic problems increase. Fifteen percent lose their homes, despite an increase in the number of hours their spouses work. Moreover, the suicide rate for laid-off workers is 30 times the national average.[9] Because of these costs, downsizing can never be painless, but thoughtful planning can minimize the pain.

Impact on Remaining Supervisors and Managers

Remaining managers and supervisors must adapt to fuzzier lines of authority and must develop skills in team building. In tall, narrow structures, middle managers and supervisors are accustomed to carrying out orders, and suddenly they must operate differently. As a first-line supervisor in an International Paper Company mill told one of the authors: "They used to tell us what to do; now they ask us." With the increasing emphasis on quality management, a supervisor has to function more as a coach, facilitator, expediter, and team developer.

EMPOWERMENT AND NEWER ORGANIZATION FORMS

In a presentation before human resource management professionals, management theorist and consultant R. E. Miles discussed the management philosophies and evolution of organization forms. Exhibit 5–16 highlights the organization forms, and Exhibit 5–17 relates form to managerial philosophy, job design, and team utilization.

Exhibit 5–17 captures the idea that most empowerment involving self-direction and control comes with the network form of organization. However, there is some overlap between the organization forms and empowerment. For example, there is considerable empowerment in some divisionalized, decentralized, structures that make use of a form of self-managing work teams. Also, in matrix structures that use partnering there is not only empowerment but also a type of network form of organization. Next, let us provide examples of specific structures that emphasize empowerment.

The Inverted Pyramid

inverted pyramid
A structure widest at the top and narrowing as it funnels down.

The creation of the **inverted pyramid** has been attributed to Nordstrom, a very successful specialty retailer. Nordstrom's structure is very flat with few levels and employs a bottoms-up management philosophy. The sales and sales support personnel, who are in direct contact with the customer, make the key decisions. The chart portrays "helping hands" symbolizing that all other levels are there to help and support the sales personnel to better serve and satisfy the customer. Exhibit 5–18 shows Nordstrom's inverted pyramid and the helping-hand concept.

The success of Nordstrom's management philosophy and empowered personnel is reflected in end results. Over the past decade its sales have increased from $769 million (39 stores, 10,000 employees) to $3.4 billion (72 stores, 30,000 employees).[10]

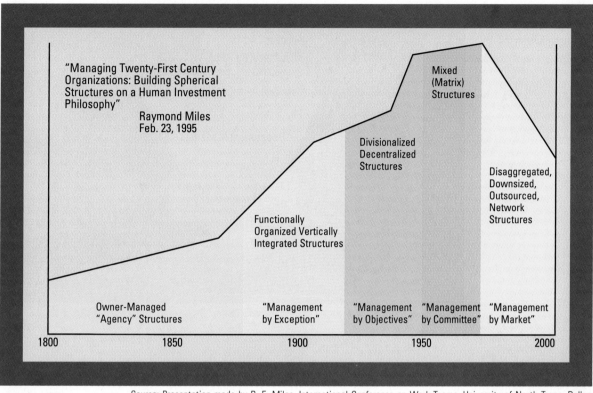

Source: Presentation made by R. E. Miles, International Conference on Work Teams, University of North Texas, Dallas, Texas, February 23, 1995.

Exhibit 5–16
Evolution of Organizational Forms

Exhibit 5–17
Managerial Philosophies: Prescriptions for Job Design and Team Utilization

Organizational Forms	Managerial Philosophies	Job Design	Team Utilization
Functional, vertically integrated	Human relations	Enlargement	Suggestions
Divisional and matrix forms	Human resources	Enrichment	Quality circles and control, limited self-direction
Network forms	Human investment	Empowerment	Full self-direction, intra-network self-control

Source: Presentation made by R. E. Miles, International Conference on Work Teams, University of North Texas, Dallas, Texas, February 23, 1995.

Exhibit 5–18
Nordstrom's Inverted Pyramid

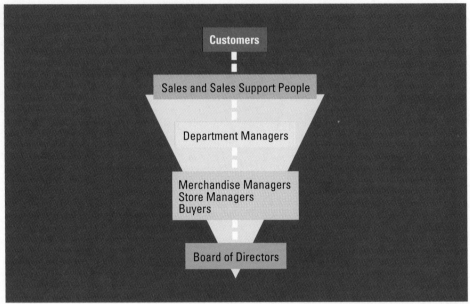

Source: Nancy K. Austin, "Reorganizing the Organizational Charts," *Working Woman,* September 1993, p. 24.

The Wagon Wheel

wagon wheel An organization form with a hub, a series of spokes radiating from the hub, and the outer rim.

Management consultant and author Nancy Austin points out that the **wagon wheel** is even more unorthodox than the inverted pyramid. In her words, "there are usually three main parts to these innovative formats: the hub of the wheel; a series of spokes, which radiate from the hub; and, finally, the outer rim. Customers are at the center. Whether you call the hub 'customers,' 'customer satisfaction,' or 'customer delight'— as AT&T Universal Card Services does—at last, customers show up inside the chart! Next come the spokes—business functions (finance, marketing, engineering) or teams (new-product development, customer satisfaction, suppliers). Keeping it all together on the outer rim—where the rubber meets the road—are the chief executive and the board, who are placed there to make sure everybody has at his or her fingertips everything needed to serve customers. Here, too, managers are coaches and supporters, not naysayers and devil's advocates. The stubborn 'Us vs. Them' antagonism spawned by the old hierarchical mentality begins to even out a bit."[11]

Network Forms

network form Uses the collective assets of several firms located at various points along the value chain.

Because international competition and rapid technological change forced massive restructuring across industries and companies, the **network form** has evolved, as documented by R. E. Miles and C. C. Snow. These two point out the following:

> Network organizations are different from previous organizations in several respects. First, over the past several decades, firms using older structures preferred to hold in-house (or under exclusive contract) all the assets required to produce a given product or service. In contrast, many networks use the collective assets of several firms located at various points along the value chain. Second, networks

rely more on market mechanisms than administrative processes to manage resource flows. However, these mechanisms are not the simple "arm's length" relationships usually associated with independently owned economic entities. Rather, the various components of the network recognize their interdependence and are willing to share information, cooperate with each other, and customize their product or service—all to maintain their position within the network. Third, while networks of subcontractors have been commonplace in the construction industry, many recently designed networks expect a more proactive role among participants—voluntary behavior that improves the final product or service rather than simply fulfills a contractual obligation.[12]

Exhibit 5–19 shows the common network types.

Exhibit 5–19
Common Network Types

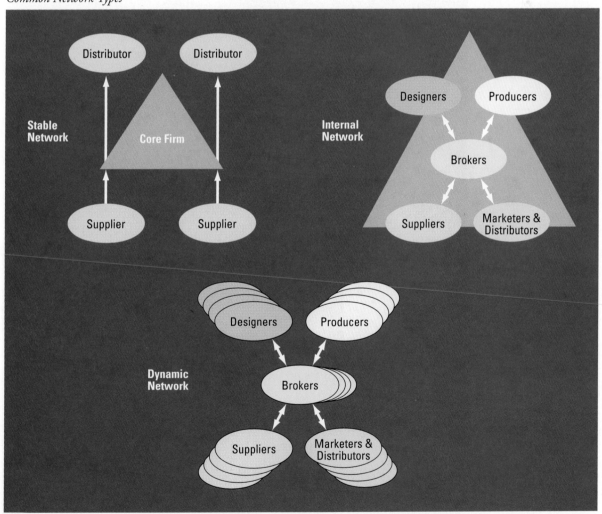

Source: R. E. Miles and C. C. Snow, "Causes of Failure in Network Organizations." Copyright 1992 by the Regents of the University of California. Reprinted from the *California Management Review,* Vol. 34, No. 4. By permission of the Regents.

Air Canada Centre

Earlier we mentioned the concept of partnering in connection with the matrix form of organization. Recently, one of the authors had the opportunity to facilitate a partnering workshop for the Air Canada Centre to be built in downtown Toronto.

Although still in the early stages, this project is going to be a tremendous success because of a very innovative and creative owner/design team working cooperatively with the city of Toronto. Experts are aware that achievement-oriented teams and

Exhibit 5–20
Air Canada Centre

individuals see clearly the vision and begin with the end in mind. They are also proactive in developing plans and strategies to ensure the end result occurs. The photo and caption in Exhibit 5–20 represent the end results. Exhibit 5–21 is the Mission Statement of the owner/design team.

Especially exciting to the facilitator is the action plan developed at the partnering workshop to ensure clear lines of communication and authority relationships. Part of that action plan is the chart shown in Exhibit 5–22, combining the wagon wheel with the network form of organization. Note the empowerment of the blue spheres where

Exhibit 5–20
Air Canada Centre
Concluded

The newest state-of-the-art stadium • Home of the hungriest team in the NBA, the Toronto Raptors • The perfect size for the greatest entertainment variety in the city • Connected to Union Station in the centre of downtown Toronto at the heart of Toronto's famous PATH walkway system • 22,500 seats featuring unparalleled views of every event • A sensory sound system so sophisticated it will make your head spin • The finest in corporate lounges and luxury suites at the centre of the action.

AIR CANADA CENTRE
Mission Statement

The theatre of sport in the heart of downtown

Create a timeless, financially viable theatre of sport that redefines the entertainment experience. Air Canada Centre will exceed the expectation of all participants, while providing professional satisfaction and financial success to each team member. We will create, demand, and maintain the highest level of mutual respect, honesty and trust through open, professional communication.

"Success of a Vision"
Requires Collaboration—Collaboration
Requires Shared Responsibility—Shared
Responsibility Requires Understanding

*   *   *

This Is Our "Vision of Success"

Exhibit 5–21
Air Canada Centre
Mission Statement

they are charged with coordination, solving problems, and implementing solutions. The small number of employees in the ownership circle is led by Jay Cross and is concerned primarily with schedule/risk/program/budgets. These concerns are essential, since this is the only stadium of this magnitude built exclusively with private funds.

Chapter Review

This chapter focused on concepts that give supervisory managers a better understanding of their organization. A continuing case illustrated several phases of organization growth, from a one-person organization to a line-and-staff organization. It is important for a growing company to evolve from a line organization to a line-and-staff organization. This evolution allows the company to take advantage of specialization in such areas as human resources, quality control, purchasing, maintenance, scheduling, and safety. It also allows line managers and supervisors to concentrate on supervising and motivating their employees.

Learning Objective 1

Understand the stages of organization growth.
Two important management principles for organizations are unity of command and span of control. Following the unity of command principle is important because it prevents duplication and conflict when orders and instructions are passed down. It also decreases confusion and "passing the buck" and provides a basis for managers and their employees to develop a better understanding of what they expect of each other. Finally, it promotes higher morale than is found in organizations that excessively violate the unity of command principle.

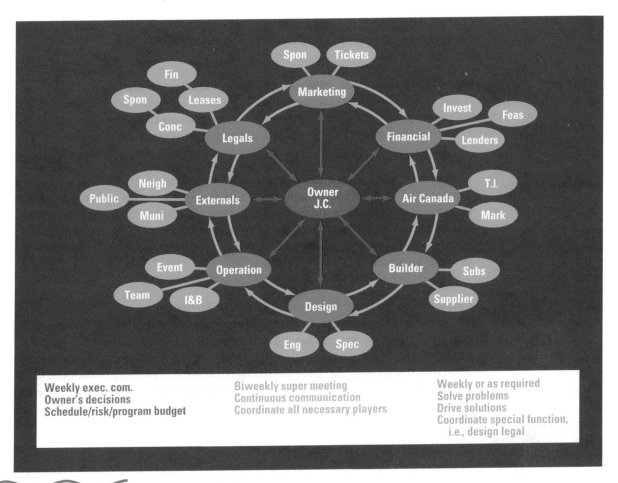

Exhibit 5–22
*Chart Showing
Communication
Relationships, Air
Canada Centre*

Explain the principles of unity of command and span of control.

The span of control principle emphasizes that there is a limit to the number of people a person can effectively manage. As one moves down the organization chart from top management to supervisory management levels, the span of control should increase. The reasons for tying span of control to management level are that (1) top management requires the freedom to solve a variety of different, nonrecurring problems; (2) higher-level managers must spend much of their time doing long-range planning, working with outside interest groups, and coordinating the various activities of the business; and (3) supervisory managers tend to be concerned with more clearly defined areas of operation.

Describe the difference between line and staff.

Though both line and staff personnel are important, their duties differ. Line personnel carry out the primary activities of a business, such as producing or selling products

specialize by separating sales from service and placing all sales personnel under Temple. Under this new arrangement, even though sales personnel operated from the local manager's office, they reported organizationally to a district sales manager, usually located in another city (see Hardy Organization Chart). The sales manager positions, since they were new, had to be staffed with office help and supplied with office space. The proposed new organization is shown as follows:

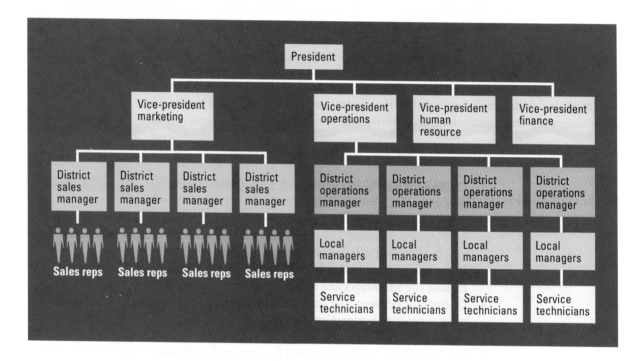

Prior to accepting the proposal, Jim Hardy decided to call in a management consulting firm to evaluate the proposal and suggest to him whether to accept or reject it.

Divide the class into teams of five to seven students who will play the role of a consulting firm, and analyze the proposal.

Answer the following questions:
1. What do you see as the pros and cons of the new structure?
2. Based on your analysis, what is your recommendation to Jim Hardy?

Skill Builder 5–2
Reducing Costs in an Accounting Firm

Divide the class into groups of five to seven students, each group representing the managing partners of an accounting firm. Have them discuss the following situation and report back to the class what their plan is, and how they would communicate it to employees.

There are 30 employees in your organization, and for the past year, sales and profits have been down. In fact, for the past six months, the firm has been operating at a loss.

Two months ago, a larger accounting firm acquired your firm in a friendly take-over. Its philosophy is to treat your smaller organization as a semiautonomous division of the accounting company, providing only general guidance and managing by results.

The accounting company CEO has asked your group, the managing partners, to develop a plan to reduce costs. It is important to note that 90% of your budget goes to salaries. Along with your plan, the accounting company CEO wants to know how you will communicate the plan to employees.

Source: Adapted from Megginson, Mosley, and Pietri, *Management: Concepts and Applications,* 4e (New York: Harper-Collins) p. 334.

CASE 5–1

Conflicting Views

Conflicts between departments occur frequently. In production facilities, these conflicts often arise between production and maintenance departments, as illustrated by the following comments:

Production Supervisor: What a job! Top management is breathing down my neck to get the work out. My people do a real good job, considering our equipment problems and how crowded we are. But what a problem I have with that crew from maintenance! You'd think they owned the whole company, the way they carry on. They act as if they're doing you a big favor to do a repair job—letting you know how important they are and how they have to schedule their jobs. And they hate for you to tell them what's wrong with the equipment, as if they have to be the ones to do a "complete diagnosis." They always seem to drag their feet for me, and yet other production departments get things done right away. I've told the superintendent about their favoritism and cockiness, but it doesn't help.

Maintenance Supervisor: What a job! I've got production people running around here all day telling me what they've got to have done. I've got six mechanics, and sometimes we'll have 20 calls a day, not to mention our scheduled maintenance. So I try to assign priorities—that's the only way to survive. And then one of those @#$%&*! production supervisors takes his or her problem to the superintendent! What really burns me up is the abuse my people get from them. You try to do what's right, and some say you play favorites. I'd like to straighten that whole bunch of production yo-yos out!

Answer the following questions:
1. What concepts presented in the chapter are involved in this conflict?
2. What do you recommend be done to resolve the problem between the two supervisors?
3. Describe how a third party might work with the two supervisors to attempt to resolve the problem.

Skill-Development Scenario
Delegation

Tony Roberts is a newly appointed supervisor of the accounting department at Lexicon Dynamics. He has years of experience as a staff accountant but none with the job of supervisor. Roberts will provide an excellent example of the need to grow into the role of supervisor.

Answer the following questions:
1. Why doesn't Roberts delegate responsibilities to his staff? How does his inability to delegate affect the department?
2. After viewing the second part of this video, discuss how Roberts uses delegation effectively and also motivates the workers in the accounting department.

Chapter 6
Delegating Authority

Joe Allegro, An Effective Developer of People

Joe Allegro is currently Deputy Director of Construction for the Massachusetts Highway Department and is responsible for supervising construction at the largest publicly funded project in the United States, the Central Artery Tunnel (CAT) in Boston. Known as the "big dig," this series of tunnels will dramatically improve transportation in the city and has the potential to transform an interesting city into one of the world's most beautiful.

Growing up in Boston was a developmental experience in which sports played a key role. From sports Allegro learned the importance of relying on and supporting one another through teamwork, the value of preparation, and the good feeling that comes with success. Allegro states that from his teachers and coaches he learned that when a leader has high expectations and sets high standards, people generally will meet the challenge. In his own career he has found this to be the case nine out of ten times. Not only did his football coach, Paul Costello, have high expectations, he treated his players with respect and was very fair. Allegro states "he was a great motivator, and I learned from him that loyalty needs to go both ways. Some kids playing football at other schools felt that they were being used. But our coach worked very hard to get our players into colleges; he did not have to make this effort."

Allegro went to Cornell primarily because it had a good engineering school; there he played three years of college football. It was in college where Allegro really developed socially and became receptive to new ideas and concepts. He became interested in leadership and discovered he had some leadership ability.

Allegro graduated with a degree in civil engineering in 1982 and entered what many would consider a career down-period, but Allegro turned it into a leadership growth experience. During this time there was an economic downturn in engineering and he could not find a job in his field, so he took a job as a cook in a restaurant. Allegro gained a valuable lesson regarding authority and responsibility. Based on his job description, his real authority was limited, and he was rather low on the totem pole. In reality, Allegro did whatever needed to be done whether it went beyond his job description or not. Soon his *perceived* authority was much greater than his *real* authority. People turned to him for guidance and assistance, and he was running things whenever the boss was absent. The lesson learned was that if you assume authority and responsibility, people will give it to you as long as it is used to improve things.

In 1984 Allegro went to work for the Massachusetts Highway Department (MHD) as an engineer. The MHD had hired a large number of engineers after WWII to meet the expansion of the interstate highway program and had not hired many since that time. The average age of their engineers when Allegro went to work was fifty-seven, and he was one of 306 new engineering hirees. After going through an extensive job rotation program, Allegro advanced rapidly and joined the massive Central Artery project in February 1989. After spending time as an area engineer on the design side, he was made area manager for construction in April 1992.

LEARNING OBJECTIVES
After reading and studying this chapter, you should be able to:

1
Recognize the importance of delegation.

2
Explain what is involved in the delegation process, including authority, responsibility, and accountability.

3
Discuss the roles of various parties in achieving effective delegation.

4
Understand why some supervisors are reluctant to delegate.

5
Indicate ways to achieve effective delegation.

Allegro had learned from sports and previous mentors that the essence of good performance and relationships is working *with* people rather than over or under people. While working on CAT, Allegro learned just how important good relationships are in getting a job done.

For example, one of the major tunnels of the Central Artery will connect downtown Boston with the Boston airport. Massport is the separate government agency that operates the airport and waterways surrounding the city. Completing the CAT project will take tremendous coordination and cooperation between Massport and Mass Highway. Allegro indicates that the only reason the project has not had excessive delays is because of the relationships that developed between people, enabling them to pick up the phone to call someone for support or assistance in solving problems.

The people who work with Allegro have commented on how cool, calm, and collected he is in difficult situations. Margaret O'Meara is assistant area manager and reports directly to Allegro. She gives Allegro excellent marks as a boss, leader, and delegator. About the way he operates, she observes:

> **Allegro has the ability and confidence to motivate and empower people. He has helped me to grow and develop, and although I have had good managers in the past, he ranks number one. He challenges me and delegates to me major responsibilities and assignments. I, in turn, try to keep him informed on key issues, and I don't hesitate to seek his guidance on exceptional issues.**

As we go through the chapter, we will return to Allegro and O'Meara to examine how they handle the delegation process.

Source: Discussions and correspondence with Joe Allegro and Margaret O'Meara and others associated with the Central Artery Tunnel Project.

The greatest challenge in life is to be who you are and to become what you are capable of becoming.

Robert Louis Stevenson

The second greatest challenge is to assist and empower other people to become what they are capable of becoming.

The authors of this book

WHY DELEGATE?

Learning Objective 1

Recognize the importance of delegation.

The previous chapter covered the fundamentals of organizing—one of the management functions discussed in Chapter 1. Delegation is at the heart of organizing. Yet it is one of the concepts least understood and most underutilized by managers, especially middle managers. Research indicates that when people are elevated to middle-level management positions, they will either remain there for the rest of their careers or be demoted unless they learn to delegate authority effectively. The best time to learn to do this is at the first managerial level—the supervisor's level.

Delegating Develops People

experiential learning
One learns by doing and uses mistakes as an opportunity to figure out how to avoid them in the future.

People cannot grow and develop if they are oversupervised or not trusted to handle their normal duties and responsibilities. It is a well-known principle that we learn not only from books, but also from doing. In learning through doing, we will make mistakes. The wise supervisor realizes this truth and uses mistakes as an opportunity to discuss with employees what happened and how it can be prevented in the future. The employees, in turn, learn from the experience. This procedure is called **experiential learning.** Exhibit 6–1 shows the steps the supervisor and employee follow in learning from successes and mistakes.

Delegating Allows a Supervisor to Do Other Things

Exhibit 6–1
Learning from Successes and Mistakes

A supervisor's job, as we have seen, involves more than just direct supervision. Effective delegation allows the supervisor to spend more time planning work and coordinating with other departments. It also allows more time for troubleshooting—dealing with problems before they get out of hand and taking advantage of opportunities in a timely manner.

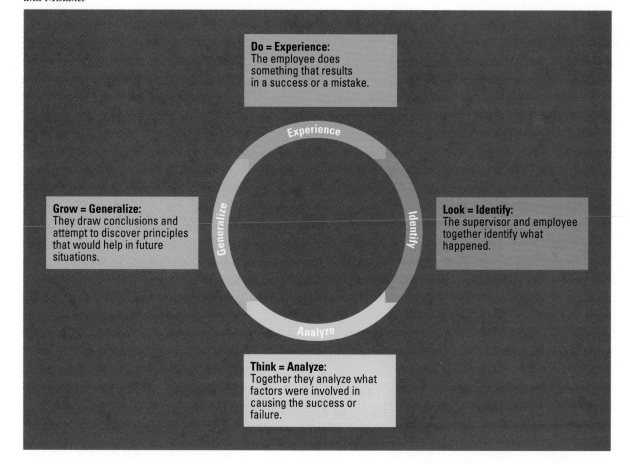

Do = Experience:
The employee does something that results in a success or a mistake.

Experience

Grow = Generalize:
They draw conclusions and attempt to discover principles that would help in future situations.

Generalize

Identify

Look = Identify:
The supervisor and employee together identify what happened.

Analyze

Think = Analyze:
Together they analyze what factors were involved in causing the success or failure.

Delegating Allows More Work to Be Accomplished

Instead of taking power away from supervisors, effective delegation expands the basis of their power. More people become knowledgeable about what the priorities are and assume responsibility for getting the job done. A climate of trust is established. In this environment, when the supervisor leaves the work area, employees continue to work effectively. They do so because of commitment and a sense of ownership in the work of the department.

Delegating Improves Control

In the effective delegation process, the emphasis is on results, not activities. Thus, the supervisor focuses on how well standards and objectives are met, not on the specific details of how they are met. In many cases, delegation also serves as a basis for evaluating people; they are compensated according to the results achieved. The key to improving control is to have an effective feedback system so that the supervisor can compare results with standards.

SELF-CHECK   Can you identify other reasons effective delegation is so important? What are they?

PROCESS OF DELEGATION

Learning Objective

Explain what is involved in the delegation process, including authority, responsibility, and accountability.

delegation of authority
Managers grant authority to the people who report to them.

Delegation of authority refers to the process by which managers bestow authority on the people who report to them. The three key aspects of the process of delegation are granting authority, assigning responsibility, and requiring accountability. As shown in Exhibit 6–2, they are like the three legs of a stool, all equally necessary. Although authority, responsibility, and accountability are all bound together, we will examine each aspect to sharpen our analysis and their interrelationship.

Granting Authority

In the previous chapter we defined line authority as the right and power to request others to carry out certain duties and responsibilities. When you delegate authority, you are granting an individual or team the power, freedom, or right to act within certain guidelines.

Exhibit 6–2
*Three Aspects of the
Delegation Process*

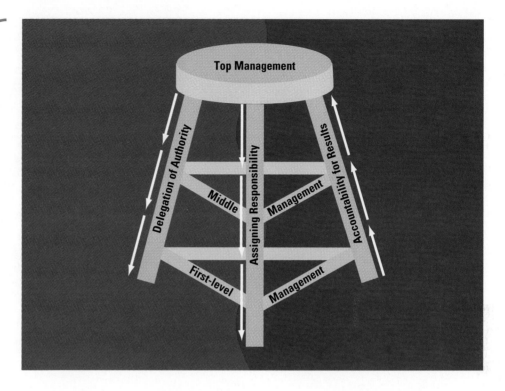

James Walker, supervisor of Department A, is concerned because four new workers have just been assigned to his department. Although normally he takes care of
indoctrinating and training new workers, his schedule is so loaded for the next
month that he cannot properly carry out the training assignments. He calls in his
two most senior workers and, after expressing his confidence in their abilities,
gives them the authority to indoctrinate and train the four new workers.

In this example, Walker has just granted authority. The example illustrates that
delegation to lower levels can occur above and beyond the normal assignment of duties
and responsibilities. It also illustrates why it is important for supervisors to know both
the weak and the strong points of their employees. James Walker knew his crew and
chose the two people who could most effectively carry out the training function.

SELF-CHECK   Can you think of other activities beyond the normal ones for which authority
might be granted to workers at lower levels? What are they?

Assigning Responsibility

The second aspect of delegation is assigning duties and responsibilities. Most jobs,
whether that of a nurse in a hospital, a teller in a bank, or an assembly worker in a

Bank tellers are assigned responsibility for servicing customers, which includes maintaining accountability for verifying identification of customers when necessary and always keeping accurate cash balances.

manufacturing plant, have certain duties and responsibilities that usually go with them. For example, a bank teller not only is responsible for providing service to bank customers, but also is expected to be friendly, to identify prospective customers who do not have proper identification for cashing out-of-town checks, and to maintain the correct cash balances.

In addition, the unique nature of the banking industry or special priorities of the employing organization may result in the assignment of duties and responsibilities beyond the traditional requirements. An aggressive bank might add the extra responsibility of selling services. For example, a teller might be asked to present to each customer a form describing the bank's new money market account. If the customer shows interest, the teller can then engage in direct selling.

In medium-sized and large organizations, the key tasks associated with many jobs are listed in job descriptions, which are usually written by a human resources specialist after interviews with the jobholder and the jobholder's immediate supervisor(s). These **job descriptions,** which spell out the primary job duties and responsibilities, as well as other job-related activities, can assist in the process of delegation. Exhibit 6–3 provides an example of a job description for a production supervisor in a paper mill. It identifies 13 key duties and responsibilities, including crew leadership (1), crew work assignments (5), and safety and health management (11). For the purpose of illustration, we have spelled out the tasks for the coaching and counseling responsibility (8).

job descriptions Written statements of the primary duties of specific jobs.

Exhibit 6–3
Job Description for a
Production Supervisor

Title: Production Supervisor, Finished Products

Purpose of job: To plan, organize, control, and exercise leadership in the efficient and effective utilization of assigned crew personnel, equipment, and material resources for timely achievement of the crew's production performance objectives and standards.

1. Crew leadership responsibility
2. Crew performance standards
3. Crew performance improvement
4. Daily shift-change management
5. Crew work assignments
6. Crew performance supervision
7. Crew education, training, and development
8. Individual coaching and counseling
9. Production relationships management
10. Maintenance relationships management
11. Safety and health management
12. Labor contract administration
13. Work environment improvement

a. Observes and carries on conversation with individual crew members at their work stations daily to determine if there are any problems that require attention.
b. Provides on-the-job coaching in job skills at operator stations to reinforce classroom training and develop specific job skills.
c. Provides counseling to crew members on job relationship attitudes to improve their performance.
d. Refers crew members to company employee assistance resources for personnel problems that require special help.

Requiring Accountability

accountability
When a person accepts duties and responsibilities from higher management.

The third aspect of delegation is holding accountable those people to whom you have granted authority and assigned responsibility. **Accountability** refers to the obligation that is created when a person accepts duties and responsibilities from higher management; the delegatee is accountable to the next higher level to carry them out effectively. Accountability flows *upward* in an organization. It is in this aspect of the delegation process that the controlling function plays an important role.

SELF-CHECK

Suppose that a department manager delegated a special assignment to a supervisor. The supervisor made a mistake in carrying out the assignment, and the mistake cost the firm $5,000. Who would you say should be held accountable for the mistake? Why?

If you answered that both the department manager and the supervisor should be held accountable, you are correct. The supervisor is, of course, accountable to the department manager, but the department manager is also accountable to her or his own supervisor.

An important fact to remember is that *accountability cannot be delegated!* Accountability is essential to maintain effective control over results. Therefore, a person who delegates an assignment should not be able to escape accountability for poor results.

It is important to keep in mind, however, that this aspect of the delegation process is one of the primary reasons some supervisors are reluctant to delegate. Sometimes higher management mistakenly reinforces this reluctance of supervisors to delegate.

SELF-CHECK

Could the $5,000 mistake mentioned earlier have been handled in such a way that it served as a learning experience and did not reinforce the manager's reluctance to delegate? How?

EFFECTIVE DELEGATION

In one of the classic books on the delegation process, Donald and Eleanor Laird point out that there is a big difference between making meaningful assignments to those below you and asking them to do the dirty jobs and meaningless activities you don't want to do yourself.[1] They emphasize that true delegation involves granting to the delegatee the authority needed to get the job done. Also, the decision making involved in the assignment is either shared or delegated entirely, and the delegatee is given freedom to handle details on his or her own initiative.

In order to ensure accountability, controls are set up to check the effectiveness of the delegation. These controls can take many forms, such as personal observation by the delegator, periodic reports by the delegatee, or statistical reports concerning output, costs, grievances, and so forth. When mistakes occur, the supervisor can use these as a basis for coaching and developing employees.

Knowing When to Delegate

It's not always easy to know when to delegate authority—and what authority to delegate—to those working for you. Although there are no absolute guidelines to go by, there are at least a lot of red flags that signal a need to delegate. Consider the following:

1. Do you do work that an employee could do just as well?
2. Do you think that you are the only one who actually knows how the job should be done?
3. Do you leave the job each day loaded down with details to take care of at home?
4. Do you frequently stay after hours catching up on work even though your peers don't?
5. Do you seem never to get through with your work?
6. Are you a perfectionist?
7. Do you tell your employees how to solve problems?[2]

If you answered "yes" to many of the questions above, you probably need to learn to delegate more effectively.

How the Delegation Process Operates

Exhibit 6–4 illustrates how an effective delegation process operates. Notice that authority, such as for performing assigned duties, carrying out special assignments, achieving objectives, and meeting standards, is granted down the line from higher management to supervisory managers, then to workers. In turn, responsibility for using that authority is created, and accountability controls are established to ensure that the authority is properly used.

The practical steps in delegating authority effectively are listed in Exhibit 6–5. Notice that the process begins with creating an organizational climate in which delegation can occur effectively and ends only when other managers, as well as the employee, know about the delegation.

The Principle of Parity of Authority and Responsibility

parity principle When duties are assigned, adequate authority is delegated to those who must carry out the assignments.

When responsibilities and duties are assigned, adequate authority should be granted to meet the responsibilities and carry out the assignments. This is known as the **parity principle.** Some management experts go so far as to say that authority should be equal to responsibility. Quite candidly, first-line managers rarely have all the authority they would like to have to meet their responsibilities. This is also true of many other positions, including staff positions.

Win Cagle, a supervisor with L. Hunter, a mail order department store, was responsible for 25 employees who worked in the customer service department. He had just walked out of a meeting where the same old line had been handed down—how supervisors were being given more authority and should be accountable for results. "I've heard it all before—many times," he said. He continued: "Human Resources will send me warm bodies. The training department will turn them loose

Exhibit 6–4
Process of Effective Delegation

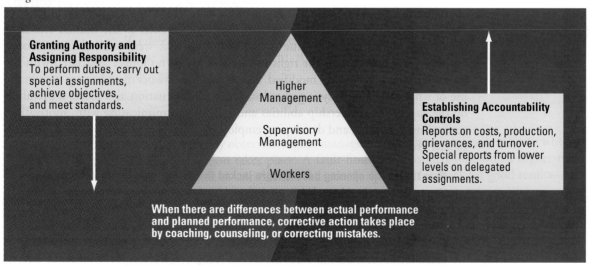

Granting Authority and Assigning Responsibility
To perform duties, carry out special assignments, achieve objectives, and meet standards.

Higher Management

Supervisory Management

Workers

Establishing Accountability Controls
Reports on costs, production, grievances, and turnover. Special reports from lower levels on delegated assignments.

When there are differences between actual performance and planned performance, corrective action takes place by coaching, counseling, or correcting mistakes.

becomes incompetent as a teacher. The competent teacher becomes incompetent as a department head or principal. The competent technician becomes incompetent as a supervisor. Naturally, incompetent employees are not promoted further. From this analysis, Peter and Hull formulated the **Peter Principle,** which states that "in a hierarchy, every employee rises to his [or her] level of incompetence."

The authors of this text agree with Savory about the importance of reframing. In fact, this book is based on our observations in working with thousands of supervisors and managers, both experienced and inexperienced, in development programs. Almost without exception, those receiving management training for the first time rated the programs exceptional in helping them to do a better job of managing. They usually added, "I wish I had received this type of training earlier."

Organizations throughout the country are realizing that they have neglected the training of managers and are beginning to spend more energy and money on correcting the situation. For example, a large hospital designed a series of management development programs around the contents of this book, thereby making the Peter Principle inoperative.

In 1995 Labor Secretary Robert Reich reported on studies conducted by researchers highlighting the considerable profits in employee empowerment. For example, Motorola estimates that it earns $30 for every $1 invested in employee training.[7]

Peter Principle States that "in a hierarchy, every employee rises to his [or her] level of incompetence."

Chapter Review

Learning Objective 1

Recognize the importance of delegation.
The delegation process is a partnering process between a supervisor and employees, bosses, and colleagues. Experiential learning is an important part of delegation, allowing employees to grow and develop by "learning through doing." If the employee's efforts result in a mistake, together the employee and supervisor can identify what happened, analyze factors involved, and discover principles to help in future situations.

Effective delegation is essential to performing the supervisory management job successfully. In addition to developing people, delegation (1) allows the supervisor to do other things, (2) accomplishes more work, and (3) improves control.

Learning Objective 2

Explain what is involved in the delegation process, including authority, responsibility, and accountability.
The process of delegation has three aspects: granting authority, assigning responsibility, and holding people accountable for results. Because accountability is essential to maintaining effective control over results, a person who delegates an assignment should not be able to escape accountability for poor results. Controls to ensure effective delegation can include personal observation by the delegator, periodic reports by the delegatee, and statistical reports concerning output, costs, and grievances.

Learning Objective 3

Discuss the roles of various parties in achieving effective delegation.
Effective delegation also requires knowing when to delegate, understanding how the delegation process operates, attempting to follow the parity principle, and taking the time required to train employees. Although higher management should be supportive

and the supervisor should delegate clearly and show trust, it is the responsibility of employees to function on their own and turn to the supervisor for help only when there is a major problem. Employees who frequently ask for advice may not be fully developing themselves or effectively carrying out responsibilities, though they may be stroking their supervisors' ego.

Employees to whom authority is delegated should (1) take the initiative, (2) relate to the supervisor, (3) make sure the delegation is realistic, (4) give feedback regarding results, (5) carry out assignments effectively, and (6) work towards handling increasingly involved assignments.

Learning Objective 4

Understand why some supervisors are reluctant to delegate.

Despite the benefits of effective delegation, some supervisors fail to do so for a variety of reasons. A supervisor, for example, may closely monitor or even perform an employee's work because of his/her accountability to a manager. However, this attitude can cause resentment among employees and leave the supervisor little time to plan and coordinate with other departments.

Learning Objective 5

Indicate ways to achieve effective delegation.

One of the solutions to ineffective delegation is to emphasize management training and development. This will reduce the probability that your organization will be subject to the Peter Principle, which states that employees rise to their level of incompetence.

Important Terms

accountability *pg. 167*
delegation of authority
164

experiential learning *163*
job descriptions *166*
parity principle *169*

Peter Principle *176*
reframing *175*

Questions for Review and Discussion

1. Discuss four reasons delegation is important.
2. Describe the process of delegation.
3. Explain the interrelationships among authority, responsibility, and accountability.
4. What is the principle of parity of authority and responsibility? How does it operate in practice?
5. Why do some supervisors fail to delegate effectively? If this situation were a common problem in an organization, what could be done to increase supervisors' skills in delegating effectively?
6. What are the roles played in effective delegation?
7. In what way or ways may higher management affect the delegation process?
8. In what way or ways may employees affect the delegation process?

Skill Builder 6–1
Test Your Delegation Habits

Assume you are a supervisor. For each of the following statements, rate your agreement with a number between 1 and 5: 5 (strongly agree), 4 (agree), 3 (undecided), 2 (disagree), and 1 (strongly disagree).

_____ 1. I'd delegate more, but the jobs I delegate never seem to get done the way I want them to be done.

_____ 2. I don't feel I have the time to delegate properly.

_____ 3. I carefully check on employees' work without letting them know I'm doing it, so I can correct their mistakes if necessary before they cause too many problems.

_____ 4. I delegate the whole job, giving the employee the opportunity to complete it without any involvement on my part. Then I'll view the end result.

_____ 5. When I have given clear instructions and the job isn't done right, I get upset.

_____ 6. I believe that the staff lacks the commitment that I have, so any job I delegate won't get done as well as I would do it.

_____ 7. I'd delegate more, but I believe I can do the task better than the person I might delegate it to.

_____ 8. I'd delegate more, but if the individual to whom I delegate the task does an incompetent job, I'll be severely criticized.

_____ 9. If I were to delegate the task, my job wouldn't be nearly as much fun.

_____ 10. When I delegate a job, I often find that the outcome is such that I end up doing the job over again myself.

_____ 11. I have not found that delegation really saves much time.

_____ 12. I delegate a task clearly and concisely, explaining exactly how it should be accomplished.

_____ 13. I can't delegate as much as I'd like to, because my employees lack the necessary experience.

_____ 14. I feel that when I delegate I lose control.

_____ 15. I would delegate more, but I'm pretty much of a perfectionist.

_____ 16. I work longer hours than I should.

_____ 17. I can give employees the routine tasks, but I feel I must personally handle the nonroutine jobs.

_____ 18. My own boss expects me to keep very close to all details of the work.

_____ TOTAL SCORE

Rate yourself:

Score

18–35   You are probably a superior delegator.

36–53   You have some room to grow.

54–71   Your delegation habits and attitudes could be substantially improved.

72–90   You are seriously failing to properly use your staff.

Source: Adapted from Theodore J. Krein, "How to Improve Delegation Habits," *Management Review* 71 (May 1982), pp. 58–61. Reprinted by permission of publisher, from *Management Review,* May 1982, © 1982, American Management Association. All rights reserved.

CASE 6–1

The Promotion Decision

Bert Ryborn is one of several candidates being considered for the position of division manager of one of the larger divisions of his insurance company. Ryborn's personnel file indicates that he joined the company as a trainee 16 years ago. His first assignment involved working in several departments on a rotation basis.

After the job rotation period, Ryborn was made a department supervisor. The work performed by his department was always in perfect order. One of the reasons for this high degree of accuracy was that Ryborn exercised close personal supervision over all aspects of the work. On more than one occasion, Ryborn became involved in the actual work to ensure that it was done correctly.

Later, Ryborn was promoted to area manager and given supervision of several departments. During his tenure in this position, there were signs that all was not well with Ryborn's supervision of his employees. In fact, one of his supervisors resigned during this period, stating that he had obtained a better position with another firm. However, during an exit interview with the human resources manager, he indicated that his real reason was Ryborn's management style. He added:

> **Bert demands personal approval of everything taking place within my department, even down to a pay change for the newest employee. He personally prepares most of the reports that provide data to the division manager. He also plans much of the work of the supervisors reporting to him.**

Ralph Johnson, the vice-president, is a staunch supporter of promoting Ryborn to division manager.

Answer the following questions:
1. Why do you think Ryborn has succeeded in his positions so far? Do you think that is the reason Johnson supports him for the promotion?
2. Do you think Ryborn will be a successful division manager?
3. Assume you are the human resources manager and Johnson has asked you for your advice on promoting Ryborn. Role play your meeting with Vice-President Johnson.

CASE 6–2

GROUP ACTIVITY

Marion Dawson's Problem

Marion Dawson was quite pleased when she graduated from Community College with an associate degree in business. While pursuing her degree, she had been employed as a worker with an international company specializing in fast foods similar to McDonald's, Wendy's, and Burger King. She was a very efficient worker and was soon elevated to handling the outside window sales where only the best employees were placed. She was also promised an opportunity to work for the organization upon completion of her associate degree program. After graduation, Dawson entered the company's management training program. From there she was placed in a busy store location as assistant manager. As an achievement-oriented person, Dawson saw this as the first step toward her long-range goal of becoming a regional manager or having her own franchise some day.

In her position as assistant manager, things went well. Dawson was familiar with all operations, and she practiced close supervision, stayed on top of things, and really stressed high production and fast service. Six months later she was promoted to manager at another busy store that was the most profitable within the region. In fact, the previous manager had just been promoted to regional manager and was now Dawson's boss.

At this stage of her career, Dawson was well ahead of schedule in her long-range program of becoming a regional manager. She had anticipated spending a minimum of two years as an assistant manager before having an opportunity to advance to manager. Her next career objective of becoming a regional manager seemed well within reach, since the industry and company were growing at a rapid rate.

Dawson surmised that what had worked for her as an assistant manager would also work for her as a manager. She was not really concerned that the assistant manager and four supervisors who would be reporting to her were older and more experienced. After all, results were what counted. At her first meeting, she stressed her high expectations and set as an objective "to increase profits by 10 percent within three months." The yearly objective was to be a 20 percent increase. She indicated that she believed strongly in the management principle of follow-up. Not only would she be closely following up on their work, but she would expect them to do the same with store employees.

Two months later, overall profits in her store were down by 7 percent, and Dawson was beginning to worry. It seemed that the more she stressed profits and service and tried to follow delegated assignments closely, the more resistance she encountered. Although the resistance was not open, it was definitely present. In fact, she sensed hostility even from the part-time workers, a group with which she had always been close.

At the end of three months, profits had decreased by 10 percent.

Instructions:

Meet in groups of six or seven people. Make a diagnosis of what the problem is, and identify the critical issues involved. Select one member of your team to present what the team thinks Dawson's boss should do. After all teams have presented, the class should vote on which approach offers the best solution.

Chapter 7
Communication

Case 7

Good News, Bad News?

This case presents a dialogue between Ann Bishop, a medical records clerk with City Hospital, and Jean Curtis, the administrative section head. As you read this, think about the communication in this situation. Do you think it's effective? Why or why not? Would Bishop or Curtis answer this question differently?

Bishop: You wanted to see me?

Curtis: Yes, I did. I'll be right with you. Have a seat. (Curtis swivels her chair, facing away from Bishop, and continues talking on the phone for about four minutes. Her tone of voice and body movements show that she is upset about something. After hanging up, she swivels around, faces Bishop, and takes off her watch, placing it face up on the desk in front of her.) Ann, this will only take a few minutes.

Bishop: Okay.

Curtis: (Opens a personnel file folder, presumably Bishop's, looks at it and begins speaking.) As you know, I like to get right to the point, Ann. We've had two people leave us in the past three weeks, one involuntarily. The point is that you're ready to move on. You've been in archives for six months; we badly need some help in coding charts. Beginning next week I'd like to work you there.

Bishop: (Looks uncomfortable, shifts in her chair.) Into coding? But I've never done coding . . . .

Curtis: Don't worry about that. Of course you don't know coding yet. You'll have to learn. It's not really that complicated. You just have to be accurate. You'll do just fine.

Bishop: But I like working in archives. It's . . .

Curtis: When you were hired you were told you'd start off in archives, but people have to work where there's the greatest need. And you'll be making about $160 a month more in coding than where you are now. I know you'll like coding . . . in a few weeks you'll feel just as comfortable in coding as you do now in archives. I've alerted Stephanie Koval that you'll be working with her next week to learn the ropes . . . (Phone rings and Curtis tells the caller she'll be right up.) I've got to get some reports to the assistant administrator. I know you'll be really pleased in coding, Ann. It will be a wonderful opportunity for you. (Puts watch on and rises. Begins gathering papers as Bishop rises, turns, and walks away.)

The opening quotations certainly apply to Case 7, don't they? Bishop will likely walk away from the meeting feeling pretty uncomfortable about the job change—perhaps not so much because of the change itself but because of the manner in which Curtis presented it. Each day, supervisors like Curtis and their organizations pay a high price for ineffective communication. These negative results include poor morale, reduced motivation, wasted money and time, lack of cooperation between people and departments, and even physical injury.

Communication plays a critical role in human relations, as well as in task-related areas of supervision. In a typical workday, supervisors assign jobs, discuss coordination efforts with people from other departments, have discussions

LEARNING OBJECTIVES
After reading and studying this chapter, you should be able to:

1 Describe the five components of the communication process model.

2 Explain the different ways in which nonverbal communications influence supervisory communication.

3 Identify the three basic flows of formal communication in an organization.

4 Explain the managerial communication style matrix.

5 Identify and explain how organizational, interpersonal, and language barriers affect supervisory communication.

6 Identify five specific actions supervisors can take to improve their communications.

7 Show how a supervisor can use feedback to improve communication.

8 Define and illustrate active listening skills.

with their own bosses, attend meetings, listen to and counsel employees—the list could go on and on. As you learned in Chapter 2, the emerging supervisor role of teacher, leader, and coach is strongly communication-linked. Studies of managers and supervisors have shown that they spend 60–80 percent of their time in some form of communication.[1]

Communication is something so simple and difficult that we can never put in simple words.

T. S. Matthews

I know you believe you understand what you think I said, but I am not sure you realize that what you heard is not what I meant.

Author Unknown

Too many people think they are wonderful with people because they have the ability to speak well. What they fail to realize is that being wonderful with people means being able to listen well.

Peter Drucker

WHAT IS COMMUNICATION?

Many supervisors think that communication is just a matter of "telling it like it is." They fail to recognize the difficulties involved in such a simple approach. When communication breakdowns occur, they are more interested in placing blame than in finding out what went wrong. To really understand a supervisor's role in communication, you must first learn about the basic communication process.

Communication Process Model

Learning Objective 1

Describe the five components of the communication process model.

communication process model Shows the five components of communication and their relationships.

Rather than define communication in words, we will use an illustration of the **communication process model** (see Exhibit 7–1). The components of the model are (1) the sender, (2) the message, (3) the channel, (4) the receiver, and (5) feedback. The barriers that interfere with the process are presented separately later in the chapter.

Exhibit 7–1
*Communication
Process Model*

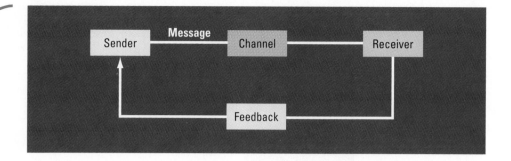

THE SENDER. The **sender** is the person who originates a message. Sometimes an inner need triggers the urge to communicate. When you say, "Pass the salt, please," you are reacting to a physical need. When you say, "I love you," you may be reflecting a need for affection. When, as a supervisor, you say, "You'll have to do this report over," you may be reflecting a need for esteem (you want to be proud of work done in your department) or a need for security (you fear that your own boss will reprimand you).

sender Originates and sends a message.

THE MESSAGE. The **message** consists of words and/or nonverbal expressions that are capable of transmitting meaning. In the preceding examples, the messages are verbal. But as in the Curtis-Bishop interaction, nonverbal messages, such as placing a watch on the desk and smiling or frowning, are equally—if not more—important.

message Words and/or nonverbal expressions that transmit meaning.

THE CHANNEL. The **channel** is the means used to pass the message. Channels include face-to-face communication, the telephone, written forms (such as memos, reports, newsletters, or E-mail), and group meetings.

channel The means used to pass a message.

> One supervisor related how his crew was working on an important machine breakdown when the plant manager chewed him out, by name, for taking too long to complete the job. "I didn't mind getting chewed out as much as I minded the way he did it," said the supervisor. "It was over the intercom, and the whole plant heard it."

THE RECEIVER. The **receiver** is the ultimate destination of the sender's message. The receiver is the one who assigns meaning to the message. On a daily basis, a supervisor frequently acts in the dual role of sender and receiver, as Exhibit 7–2 shows.

receiver The ultimate destination of the sender's message.

FEEDBACK. Frequently we send a message in response to someone else's message. The response is called **feedback.** For example, your employee may ask, "Why do I have to do the report over?" When you answer this question, you are sending feedback in response to the employee's message.

feedback The response that a communicator receives.

The communication process model makes communication appear very simple. In reality, though, the communication process is quite complicated and involves many variables.

Exhibit 7–2
The Supervisor as a
Sender and a Receiver

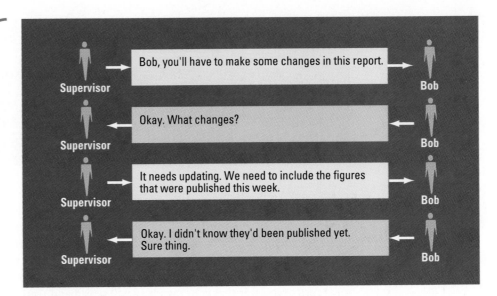

Supervisor → Bob, you'll have to make some changes in this report. → Bob

Supervisor ← Okay. What changes? ← Bob

Supervisor → It needs updating. We need to include the figures that were published this week. → Bob

Supervisor ← Okay. I didn't know they'd been published yet. Sure thing. ← Bob

Test yourself! Are the following statements true or false?

1. Meaning lies in words.
2. Words are the most important means of communication.

In the next section, you'll find the correct answers.

Do words have meaning? The answer is no; words themselves do not have meaning! A supervisor must constantly be aware that meanings lie in people, not in the words they use.

> Plant manager Peter Hampton was mad, mad, mad! Earlier in the day, at about 10 a.m., he had been notified that his boss, William Vogel, the manufacturing vice-president, planned to arrive by company plane from the company's Philadelphia headquarters to discuss a company matter with him.
>
> Hampton's operation produced elasticized stretch fabrics for a variety of garments. Seepage of the polyester residue from the process resulted in a buildup of the white, sticky, foamy substance on the plant floor around key machinery. It was not only an eyesore but also a safety concern. Knowing that the vice-president was a stickler for good housekeeping, Hampton contacted Bill Jeansonne, production manager, and told him to clean up the production areas as soon as he could, as Vogel would likely make a pass through the facility. Jeansonne indicated that he would do so.

> When Hampton and Vogel toured the plant shortly after lunch, Hampton was shocked to find the production areas untouched, the normal accumulation of several shifts' worth of residue evident. The vice-president let Hampton know in no uncertain terms that the area was disgraceful as well as a safety hazard. Hampton had no alternative but to apologize for the sloppiness and was quite embarrassed by the incident.
>
> When the vice-president left the plant, Hampton immediately called Jeansonne, who came straight to Hampton's office. "Bill," said Hampton, "I told you we needed to clean up the place—Vogel came down on me like a ton of bricks. Why wasn't it clean?"
>
> "You know, Peter," Jeansonne responded, "I said I'd get to it as soon as I could. I was getting ready to, but we had to make up some lost production time this morning. I planned on getting to it right after lunch. That was what I had in mind when I said, 'as soon as I can.'"

Who's to blame for the communication breakdown, Hampton or Jeansonne? Blaming Jeansonne allows Hampton to protect his own ego, but it represents a poor approach to his own communication responsibilities. The meaning lay not in the words "as soon as you can" but in the people saying and hearing them—Hampton and Jeansonne. Unless you realize that the meaning of your words depends on your receiver's interpretation and not on your own understanding of them, you will see all communication breakdowns as the other person's fault. Perhaps another example will drive home the point.

> "I certainly don't mean anything negative by it," said Max Jones, office supervisor for Hunter Supply Co. "But if you say so, I'm sure that's the way they must take it. I'll be careful not to do it again."
>
> What Jones was talking about was something Linda Carson had just told him. It seems that the women employees were quite turned off by Jones's referring to them as "the gals." To them this expression had a very condescending and unprofessional meaning. It especially angered the younger women in the department!

Importance of Nonverbal Messages

Learning Objective 2

Explain the different ways in which nonverbal communications influence supervisory communication.

Nonverbal messages play a big role in communication. One expert, Albert Mehrabian, found that only about 7 percent of emotional meaning is communicated verbally; the other 93 percent is communicated nonverbally.[2] In other words, your impression of someone's emotions, such as anger, happiness, or fear, is formed more strongly from that person's tone of voice, facial expression, or other nonverbal means than from the words the person uses.

Supervisors have to be careful that their verbal and nonverbal signals are consistent and do not give the wrong impression. Moreover, supervisors can obtain much information from the nonverbal signals of others.

Basically, nonverbal signals, which can send positive or negative information, fall into five categories:

SELF-CHECK

In Chapter 1 you learned of the dramatic changes taking place to make the work force much more diverse. This included increasing percentages of women and of African American, Hispanic, Asian, and Native American workers. In what ways do these changes impact the *downward communication flow* from manager/supervisor to work team members? The *upward communication flow* from team members to manager/supervisor?

MANAGERIAL COMMUNICATION MATRIX. Now that you have a good understanding of the vertical communication flows, you can better understand each supervisor's communication relationship with his or her team members. As shown in Exhibit 7–6, the managerial communication matrix, a supervisor's basic communications with team members consist of disclosing information (downward communication) and receiving information from them (upward communication). A supervisor can be considered high as an information discloser and high as an information receiver (box 4); high in one but not the other (boxes 2 and 3) or low in both (box 1).

Supervisors who are high disclosers are very visible. When you work for a high discloser, you hear frequently about performance expectations, standards, your boss's

Learning Objective 4

Explain the managerial communication style matrix.

Exhibit 7–6
The Managerial Communication Matrix

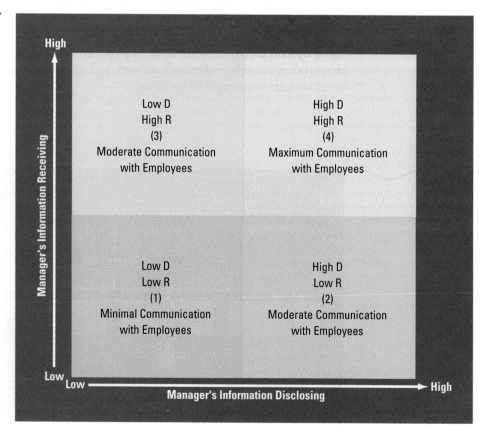

Toyota averages over 40 suggestions yearly from each of its employees, and management implements over 90% of these.

Camrys and Avalons on the production line in Georgetown, Kentucky.

BUILT WITH INCREDIBLY
sophisticated technology and
SURPRISINGLY OLD-FASHIONED IDEAS.

AT TOYOTA'S five American manufacturing plants, we employ robotics, computers and advanced technology. We also employ people who share the belief that quality is a team effort. In fact, last year alone more than 60,000 team-member suggestions were introduced into our U.S. production lines. It's this combination of technology and teamwork that is bringing world-renowned Toyota quality to everything we build here in America.

INVESTING IN THE THINGS WE ALL CARE ABOUT. **TOYOTA**

For more information about Toyota in America write Toyota Motor Corporate Services, 9 West 57th Street, Suite 4900-N8, New York, NY 10019

Source: *Forbes,* June 19, 1995, p. 168.

likes and dislikes, where you stand, and about the goings-on in the organization. Low disclosers tend to be less visible, communicating less frequently and openly about such matters.

High information-receiving supervisors are accessible and maintain an environment that encourages feedback from employees. They are apt to spend much of their time listening to employees' discussions about performance progress, problems being experienced, ideas and feelings about organizational and personal issues. In contrast, low information-receiving supervisors are less accessible and tend to create a less encouraging upward-communication environment than do high information receivers.

In this chapter's opening case, how would you rate Curtis's communication style? Let us first qualify our answer. A supervisor's communication style is based on an ongoing, continual relationship with employees, rather than a single 3–4 minute interaction. But let's do some generalizing about Curtis. Let's take the easier choice first. Curtis seems definitely to be a *low information receiver.* She doesn't appear in the least interested in what Bishop has to say about the prospective new assignment in coding. Curtis did *disclose* some facts, as we mentioned earlier in this section. However, we heard nothing about Curtis's evaluation of Bishop's past work, which must be good, since she's being promoted. There was no discussion about why Bishop was chosen over other candidates for the position or how the new position is advantageous (other than higher pay). So if we had to generalize about Curtis's style, we'd bet that her normal, daily style is that of a *low discloser, low receiver.*

What would you like your own supervisor's style to be? In our workshops and seminars, about 90 percent of managers and supervisors state a strong preference in working for a high discloser, high receiver (box 4). When given a choice of their own boss's style being either a high discloser, low receiver (box 2) or a high receiver, low discloser (box 3), most opt for a supervisor whose style falls in box 2. This choice reflects the importance managers place on knowing clearly their boss's performance expectations and his or her feelings about their performance.

Lateral-Diagonal Flows

lateral-diagonal communication Flows between individuals in the same department or different departments.

Lateral-diagonal communication takes place between individuals in the same department or different departments. This form of communication has become more important than ever in the past 25 years for several reasons. First, organizations have become greatly specialized. As indicated in the line-and-staff form of organization discussed in Chapter 5, members of staff departments such as purchasing, human resources, cost accounting, maintenance, and others interact regularly with line personnel. This may be to provide services, coordinate, advise, and sometimes actually give directives (recall the definition of functional authority in Chapter 5).

A second reason is the increased use of teams. Cross-functional, problem-solving teams comprising personnel from different departments have become an increasingly necessary approach to address problems that cut across organizational lines. As you learned in Chapter 2, one form of employee empowerment is the use of self-managed or autonomous work teams *within* departments. These teams often meet as a group on a daily basis and are highly dependent upon communications among their members as they budget, schedule, assign jobs, and control quality of their *own* work.

Informal Communication

informal communication Separate from a formal, established communication system.

The upward, downward, and lateral-diagonal communication flows that we have just presented are examples of formal communication. **Informal communication** is that which exists separately from the formal, established communication system. Some examples of informal communication are given below. Each example represents a communication channel that you will not find listed in the company's organization chart. Yet informal communications such as these are a way of life!

> **Lisa, Diane, Fred, and Roberto carpool, since they all work for the same company and live about 35 miles away. Their driving time is usually spent talking about their departments, people who work at the company, and other job-related matters. As they all work in different departments, they are very much "in the know" about a number of company matters long before the formal company communication channels carry them.**
>
> **Before seeing her boss about an important request, Mildred O'Neil dropped by to get Kathie Troy's opinion. Troy is a close friend of O'Neil's boss and would probably have some excellent advice for O'Neil as to how best to present her request.**

grapevine "The rumor mill."

THE GRAPEVINE. The best-known informal communication method is the grapevine, also called *the rumor mill.* It is called a **grapevine** because, like the plant it is named after, it is tangled and twisted and seemingly grows without direction. Yet some surveys have found the grapevine to be employees' major source of information about their company, and it has been found to be surprisingly accurate. In fact, the research of Keith Davis, an authority on human relations, has shown that in normal work situations over 75 percent of grapevine information is correct.[4]

PURPOSES SERVED BY INFORMAL COMMUNICATION. Informal communication accomplishes a number of purposes. Among these are (1) providing a source of information not ordinarily available, (2) reducing the effects of monotony, and (3) satisfying personal needs such as the need for relationships or status. Some people, in fact, take great pride in their unofficial knowledge of company matters.

LIVING WITH INFORMAL COMMUNICATION. Effective supervisors realize that informal communication serves important purposes. A supervisor must be aware that, unless employees are informed through formal channels, the informal channels will take up the slack. Keeping employees well informed is the best way to manage the grapevine, although it can never be eliminated. It will tend to be especially active when employees are concerned about job security or status.

BARRIERS TO EFFECTIVE SUPERVISORY COMMUNICATION

Learning Objective 5

Identify and explain how organizational, interpersonal, and language barriers affect supervisory communication.

Now that you understand the communication process, let's explore some typical communication barriers that a supervisor faces on the job. These barriers may be organizational, interpersonal, or language-related.

Organizational Barriers

Three types of organizational barriers to communication are (1) levels of hierarchy, (2) authority and status, and (3) specialization and its related jargon.

LEVELS OF HIERARCHY. Have you ever asked another person to give a message to a third person and found that the third person received a totally different message from the one you sent? The same thing occurs in organizations. When a message goes up or down the organization, it passes through a number of "substations" at each level. Each level can add to, take from, qualify, or completely change the original message!

At higher levels of management, messages are usually broad and general. At lower levels, these broad messages must be put into more specific terms. That's frequently the fly in the ointment, especially when lower and top levels have a gap of understanding between them.

AUTHORITY AND STATUS. The very fact that one person is a boss over others creates a barrier to free and open communication.

Do you recall your feelings, as a student in elementary or high school, when you were told to report to the principal's office? Even if you had done nothing wrong, you were probably still very anxious and defensive about the visit.

Perhaps you have witnessed situations such as this:

> **The conference room patter before the superintendent walked in was loose and jovial. Some verbal horseplay occurred among the members, and there was kidding and joking. Some made very negative remarks about the major item on the agenda, which was a discussion of proposed changes in the company's system of performance evaluation. One person joked about another's being the one to tell the boss about the flaws in the new system, even though the boss strongly favored it. But when the boss walked in, the mood shifted dramatically. He did most of the talking; those in attendance listened attentively. Even when he asked for their opinions, he received only favorable comments about the proposal.**

Since, as a supervisor, you must fill out employees' performance evaluations and determine rewards and penalties, employees will tend to give you the information that you are most likely to welcome. Information about frustrations, disagreements with your policies, job problems, below-standard work, and the like will tend to be withheld or changed to look more favorable.

SPECIALIZATION AND ITS RELATED JARGON. The *principle of specialization* states that employees are more efficient when each performs just one task or only certain aspects of a task. For example, accountants do accounting work, salespersons sell, industrial engineers prepare efficiency studies, and safety specialists see to it that working conditions are safe.

Today's increased specialization, however, also creates problems. Specialists have their own technical language or jargon, interests, and narrow view of the organization. Many special terms used by maintenance technicians, electronic data processing specialists, and other groups are completely foreign to people in other departments. This can severely hamper communication.

What are some technical words that you're familiar with that your classmates probably wouldn't understand?

Interpersonal and Language Barriers

Even if the three organizational barriers just discussed do not exist, a supervisor's communication can still be distorted by interpersonal as well as language-related problems. Exhibit 7–7 lists a number of these barriers, some of which we will discuss.

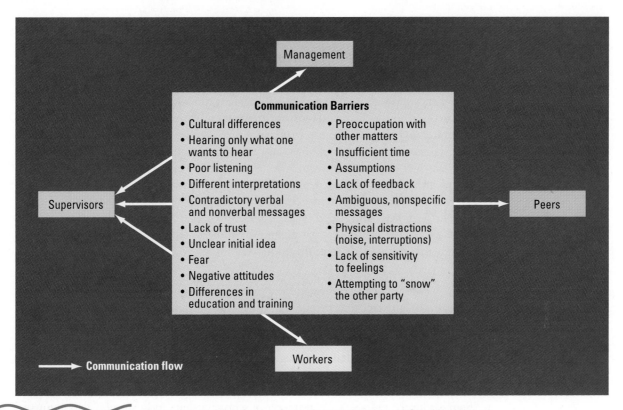

Communication Barriers

- Cultural differences
- Hearing only what one wants to hear
- Poor listening
- Different interpretations
- Contradictory verbal and nonverbal messages
- Lack of trust
- Unclear initial idea
- Fear
- Negative attitudes
- Differences in education and training

- Preoccupation with other matters
- Insufficient time
- Assumptions
- Lack of feedback
- Ambiguous, nonspecific messages
- Physical distractions (noise, interruptions)
- Lack of sensitivity to feelings
- Attempting to "snow" the other party

Management

Supervisors

Peers

Workers

➜ Communication flow

Source: Bovee and Thill, *Business Communication Today,* 4th ed., McGraw-Hill, 1995, p. 59.

Exhibit 7–7
Interpersonal Barriers to Effective Supervisory Communication

DIFFERING PERCEPTIONS. The term **perception** may be defined as the process by which one selects, organizes, and gives meaning to his or her world. All of us have a special way of filtering things around us based on our culture, needs, moods, biases, expectations, experiences, and so on.

perception How one selects, organizes, and gives meaning to his or her world.

A major barrier to communication results from the increasingly diverse work force, which reflects broad differences in age, race, sex, education, nationality, and other work force factors. These differences result in quite different perceptions and interpretations of what is seen and heard, and they often result in different styles of communicating. This poses a much stronger communication challenge to supervisors than if all team members had similar backgrounds and shared similar characteristics with their supervisor.

One factor limiting our perception is that we can't grasp the whole situation at a given time. Some matters receive greater attention than others, while some matters receive none at all. Those matters we do focus on usually serve some immediate purpose. A person's needs, moods, cultural and social influences, and attitudes all come together to determine which things are important and what they mean.

In a factory accident, for example, the following persons might "see" the accident differently: the supervisor, who may have lost a valuable worker; the safety engineer, whose safety record may have been blemished; the fellow worker, who is the

injured worker's best friend; the company physician, who attends to the injured worker; and the human resources manager, who is concerned with workers' compensation and finding a replacement for the injured worker. If these persons were to communicate about the accident, each would have a different version.

When we go about interpreting things around us, we have a tendency to put similar things in the same category, to make them easier to handle. This tendency is called **stereotyping.** There are strong negative stereotypes for various nationalities, races, religions, sexes, occupations, and other groups in our society. For example, a male manager may label all women as "emotionally weak," all union officials as "agitators," and all staff employees as "meddlers." Obviously, such stereotyping will have a strong influence on this manager's communications to and from these individuals.

On the other hand, stereotypes may be favorable. As a supervisor, you must be aware that your attitudes, biases, and prejudices—both positive and negative—strongly influence your communications with others.

stereotyping The tendency to put similar things in the same categories to make them easier to deal with.

LANGUAGE-RELATED FACTORS. We have already indicated how important language is in the process of communication. The fact that people interpret words differently may be traced to a lack of precision in the use of language. True, you can say that a drill press weighs 270 pounds, or that Sam Eggers is 5′11″ tall, or that Judy Snead has completed 10 years of service with the hospital. Language is precise in that regard, and we can verify it.

Consider, however, a salesperson selling copiers who tells an office manager that the copier is "the finest on the market." Or one supervisor who tells another that "Sam is a loyal employee." Or a supervisor who says that "Judy Snead is a good nurse." What is "loyal" or "good"? What you consider to be "loyal" (for example, turning down several job offers from competing firms) may be "complacent" or "unambitious" to someone else. A "good" nurse to you may be one who is a sympathetic listener and spends a lot of time talking with patients and being cheerful and friendly; to someone else, a "good" nurse may be one who is knowledgeable and competent and goes about her or his work without trying to make conversation.

Sometimes a supervisor uses imprecise language when more precise language is necessary. Suppose a supervisor tells an employee, "You must improve on your absenteeism, as it has been excessive. Otherwise, you'll be disciplined." What does the supervisor mean by "improve on your absenteeism" and "excessive"? What "discipline" does the supervisor have in mind?

Another language barrier is the fact that words have multiple meanings and not all people have the same level of language skill, as exemplified in Exhibit 7–8. Many terms familiar to a veteran employee, for example, may be over the heads of a new crop of employees going through an orientation program. In some cases, people even try to "snow" others by using terms they know the others will not understand!

SELF-CHECK   After examining Exhibit 7–7, which barriers do you believe were involved in the Curtis-Bishop communication in Case 7?

FIX the machine to its foundation. (anchor)
FIX that nitpicking cost accountant. (give just due)
FIX the cash register. (repair)
FIXING to go to the storeroom. (getting ready to)
FIX our position regarding overtime policy. (establish)
FIX you up with that young engineer. (arrange a date)
A banquet with all the **FIXIN'S.** (special effects, side dishes)
FIX things up with the salespeople. (make amends, patch up a quarrel)
If we don't make quota, we're in a **FIX.** (a pickle, a bad position)
FIX the data outcome. (so that it's favorable, rig)
FIX your hair before seeing the boss. (arrange, make orderly)
FIX the departmental meal on Friday. (cook, prepare)
FIX the company's mascot dog. (neuter)

Exhibit 7–8
Multiple Interpre-
tations of Words

IMPROVING SUPERVISORY COMMUNICATIONS

Learning Objective 6

Identify five specific actions supervisors can take to improve their communications.

As we've indicated, communication is too critical to your success as a supervisor to be left to chance. Improving your skills in communication will help you accomplish your "task" and "people" goals. Some specific things you can do are (1) set the proper climate with your employees, (2) plan your communication, (3) use repetition to reinforce key ideas, (4) encourage the use of feedback, and (5) become a better listener.

Setting the Proper Climate

A supervisor doesn't communicate in a vacuum. Communications take place within the entire supervisor-employee or supervisor-group relationship. A supervisor and his or her workers each bring a store of experiences, expectations, and attitudes into the communication event. These mental pictures strongly influence the meaning each person assigns to the messages sent and received. Thus, the setting is very important for good communication.

What type of setting best contributes to effective communication? We believe that two important factors are (1) mutual trust between the supervisor and employees and (2) a minimum of status barriers.

MUTUAL TRUST BETWEEN SUPERVISOR AND EMPLOYEES. Trust helps communication in two ways. First, if an employee trusts you, he or she is more willing to communicate frankly about job problems. Second, if employees trust you, they are less likely to distort your motives and make negative assumptions about your communications. If you fight for your employees' interests by bargaining with higher management, if you discipline fairly

To set the proper climate for communications, Alga Plastics' president goes on sales calls with sales reps to hear their concerns and ideas.

and consistently, and if you respect your employees' abilities, you are more likely to be trusted by them. You'll be looked upon as a source of help in reaching their goals.

A MINIMUM OF STATUS BARRIERS. Generally, the best communication occurs in a setting where people are relaxed and comfortable rather than "uptight." The way a supervisor arranges his or her office furniture has much to do with establishing a relaxed setting, as shown in Exhibit 7–9.

> One supervisor says he likes to discuss certain sensitive matters away from his own turf so as to make an employee feel more comfortable and less nervous. By design, supervisors may communicate in the employee's work area or in a neutral situation such as over a cup of coffee or lunch.
> At Honda of America, Honda President Shochiro Iramafiri wears no tie and eats in the company cafeteria. On the front of his white overalls, which are just like

Exhibit 7–9
Desk-Chair Arrangements that Affect Formality

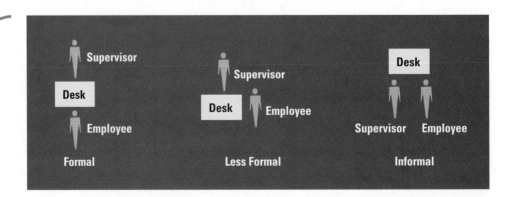

those everyone else in the plant wears, is his nickname, "IRI." He has no private office but works at a desk in the same work area as the 100 others in his white-collar work group. This represents a distinct effort to diminish the status differences between himself and all other employees.[5]

Planning Communication

How many times have you completely blown a communication situation by not being prepared for it? After it's over, you think, "Now why didn't I say this?" or "I never should have said such and such."

ANTICIPATING SITUATIONS. If you are a supervisor, many of your contacts will occur without much warning and may not allow much planning. Yet there are a number of situations you can anticipate. For example, you can give thought to the following situations before they occur:

1. Giving employees their performance evaluations.
2. Disciplining employees and making work corrections.
3. Delegating authority for a job and communicating job assignments and instructions.
4. Persuading employees to accept changes in the job or work environment.
5. Trying to sell an idea to your boss or to other staff members.

If you understand how complex good communications are, you'll be more aware of the existing barriers and try to minimize their effects. To be understood by your team members, you must put yourself in their shoes and try to see things from their viewpoint. An old Indian prayer expresses the thought this way: "Lord, grant that I may not criticize my neighbor until I've walked a mile in his moccasins."

EXAMPLES OF PLANNED COMMUNICATIONS. Once you have established an objective for a communication, make a plan to achieve it. Let's look at two examples.

> **Suppose an excellent employee has asked in advance to speak to you about a transfer to another department. Assuming that you don't know all the facts, one objective of your meeting is to gain insight into the request for transfer, including the reasons for it and the timing. This will help you make a decision or make readjustments in your department. Your plan could be to take a listening role and use active listening techniques, which will be explained shortly. This strategy will prevent you from dominating the interaction, monopolizing the communication, and hindering the achievement of your objective.**
>
> **Suppose you are going to ask a promising employee to participate in a voluntary training program. Your objective in this case is to gain the employee's acceptance of the program and to develop enthusiasm for it. Your plan, then, is to focus on how the employee will benefit from participating in the program. How will training aid the employee's development, future in the company, and so on? You would try to uncover any objections by using listening skills. And you would attempt to anticipate possible objections and determine how they can be overcome.**

These two examples show the advantage of planning your communication. If you fail to plan when you can do so, you may depend too much on your spontaneous, off-the-cuff ability to communicate. Moreover, when you attempt to do your planning while the other person is talking, you can't listen effectively. The planning stage, therefore, spills over into the act of communication itself. The nature of your communication role, the message(s), and the strategy in message content and sequence can, to some extent, be predetermined. Thus, the three major concepts presented in the rest of this chapter relate clearly to planning.

Using Repetition to Reinforce Key Ideas

Repeating a message plays an important part in communicating effectively. This is especially true when you have to communicate technical information or a direct order. Repetition, or redundancy, reduces the chance that incorrect assumptions will be made by the receiver. For example, you can state a complicated message in several ways, using examples, illustrations, or comparisons. You can also say the same thing several times, but in different words. Here, for instance, is how a supervisor might communicate an instruction to an employee.

> **Danny, we just got a telephone order for a 42-by-36-inch fireplace screen in our KL–17 series. I know you haven't done one up like it since last year, when that customer gave us so much trouble about the screen not fitting his fireplace opening. That's the same style this guy wants, with black and gold trim as shown in this catalog clipping. And you heard me right: He wants it 42 inches high by 36 inches wide—higher than it is wide. *(Hands Danny the written specifications for the screen.)* That's a new one for me, and I'm sure it's a new one for you too. Can you get it out in the next two weeks?**

Note how the supervisor used a past example and a catalog to clarify the style of the fireplace screen and how the supervisor repeated the required measurements, even though he also provided written specs!

Encouraging the Use of Feedback

Learning Objective 7

Show how a supervisor can use feedback to improve communication.

As mentioned earlier, feedback is the response that a communicator receives from the receiver of the message. Two ways in which a supervisor can encourage employees to provide feedback are (1) creating a relaxed environment and (2) taking the initiative.

CREATING A RELAXED ENVIRONMENT. Earlier in this section, we discussed the importance of establishing a favorable setting for communication. A relaxed setting is also required when the supervisor wants to obtain feedback from his or her employees. As a supervisor, you certainly should not look down on employees for asking questions or for openly stating their opinions, suggestions, or feelings on a subject. A defensive attitude on your part discourages feedback from employees. How you communicate also determines, to a large extent, the amount of feedback you will receive. For example, written instructions or memos don't allow for the immediate feedback that can be gained from face-to-face communication.

In ancient times, there was an Oriental king who hated to hear bad news. Whenever a courier reported bad news or an unfortunate event to the king, the king became furious and had him beheaded. After three couriers bit the dust, the king began hearing only good news! The moral here for supervisors is that they must be receptive to all information, both good and bad, from their employees, or they too will be surrounded by a smokescreen.

TAKING THE INITIATIVE. Although the type of communication used and the setting for the communication are important in determining what feedback is obtained, the supervisor still must take the initiative in getting responses from the work group. For example, after giving a job assignment, you might ask, "Do you have any questions?" or "Did I leave anything out?" An even better approach would be to say, "To make sure I've gotten my message across, how about repeating it to me?" Frequently this approach produces a number of clarifications that someone might otherwise be unwilling to request for fear of looking stupid. You must be careful, however, not to use a patronizing tone of voice or to put too much of the burden of understanding on the employee. Remember—effective communication is a two-way street. Finally, you can set the stage for further feedback with comments such as "If anything comes up later or if you have some questions, just let me know."

The participative leadership style (discussed in Chapter 9) relies heavily on good two-way communication, which is a form of feedback. When a supervisor allows team members to make decisions or to express opinions, their responses are a form of feedback. This style helps the supervisor better understand the team members' thinking.

Feedback can also help you learn how to better send messages in the future. When you discover that your initial message wasn't clear or that your use of persuasion was not effective, you can refine future messages. A summary of tips about feedback appears in Exhibit 7–10.

Becoming a Better Listener

It has been said that Mother Nature blessed human beings with two ears and only one mouth as a not-so-subtle hint that, unfortunately, we often ignore. "How to Be a Good Listener" has become a popular subject and is being taught today in many elementary and high schools throughout the country. Test your listening skills by completing the test in Exhibit 7–11. Studies of managers show that on average they spend a larger percentage of their work day (about 45%) in listening than in the other communication forms—speaking, writing, or reading.[6]

SELF-CHECK

Our own research reveals that of the four communication skills (writing, speaking, reading, and listening) that managers and supervisors most frequently use, listening is the skill in which they have had the least training. Why do you think this is so?

consider the receiver's frame of reference. This requires looking at things from the receiver's view, which can be difficult. Fourth, a supervisor should use repetition to reinforce key ideas. Finally, a supervisor should encourage and induce feedback and become a better listener.

Learning Objective 7

Show how a supervisor can use feedback to improve communication.

Two ways in which a supervisor can encourage employees to provide feedback are by (1) creating a relaxed communication environment and (2) taking the initiative to encourage feedback from others. A favorable feedback environment makes team members feel comfortable and relaxed and encourages open expression of their true feelings. Supervisors can take the feedback initiative by asking questions and creating situations which encourage or require their employees to communicate.

Learning Objective 8

Define and illustrate active listening skills.

Active listening, known also as *feeling listening, reflective listening* or *nondirective listening,* is a method of encouraging feedback from others. Reflective statements and probes are two forms of active listening. Reflective statements restate back to the speaker a summary of what the listener has heard the speaker express. Probes are more specific reflective statements that direct attention to a *particular* aspect of the sender's message.

Important Terms

active listening *pg. 204*
body signals *188*
channel *185*
communication process model *184*
downward communication *189*
feedback *185*
grapevine *194*

informal communication *194*
lateral-diagonal communication *194*
message *185*
object signals *188*
perception *197*
probe *206*
receiver *185*

reflective statement *204*
sender *185*
space signals *188*
stereotyping *198*
time signals *188*
upward communication *191*
voice signals *188*

Questions for Review and Discussion

1. What are the five components of the basic communication process model? Define each.
2. Explain the different ways in which nonverbal signals influence supervisory communication.
3. Identify the three major flows of communication in an organization.
4. Explain the managerial communication style matrix.
5. Identify and explain the three organizational barriers to supervisory communication.
6. How does planning aid communication effectiveness? Can you give a personal example?
7. Explain how a supervisor can use feedback to improve communication.
8. Define and give an example of active listening.

Skill Builder 7–1
Practicing Active Listening

The interaction below is a replay of Case 7, which opened this chapter. Note that some of the supervisor's dialogue is missing; you will be asked to complete it. It is okay for you to read the entire case before beginning the assignment.

Bishop: (enters Jean Curtis's office) You wanted to see me?

Curtis: Yes, I did, Ann. Come in and have a seat. (Pauses) As you know, I've been very pleased with your performance in archives since you joined us six months ago. You seem to have an excellent handle on everything we do there. We have an opening in the coding department and it would be an excellent opportunity. I want to see how you feel about moving into coding. You are first choice, and that's what I want to discuss with you.

Bishop: Into coding? Gee, I don't know; I really don't know much about coding. I don't know what to say . . . .

Curtis: (Active listening response #1) _____

_____

_____

Bishop: I mean, yeah, this is a surprise. I hear a little about what they do in coding. Everyone's heard stories about some of the charts having the wrong codes on them and people getting into trouble because of that. It seems like a lot more pressure and responsibility . . . .

Curtis: (Active listening response #2) _____

_____

_____

Bishop: Yes, that's an important factor to me in any job. Not that I don't mind some responsibility. It's just that it seems there's a lot more in coding than in archives.

Curtis: Well, Ann, you're right about that; it is more responsibility because having updated, accurately coded charts is very important to both patients and insurers. That's why we're careful about who we ask to work in coding.

Bishop: But I like working in archives. I like the other clerks and we work together well. We work our lunch breaks out to cover for each other; we all pitch in and help when one of us gets overloaded. That's one thing I really like about working here—the cooperation.

Curtis: (Active listening response #3) _____

_____

_____

Bishop: Yeah, I really like that. At the last place I worked, nobody seemed to get along. I made more money than I make here, but getting along is more important to me than money. I know some people have left coding recently. Why is that?

Curtis: One left to work as a marketing assistant downstairs. Another married and moved out of the state. I've just finished writing her a letter of reference for a similar coding position in a hospital in her new location. The third didn't work out because of several reasons, including excessive absenteeism and marginal performance when she was here. The first two had been with us for over five years each and seemed very happy in the department. (Pause) So money's not the most important thing to you in a job?

Bishop: Oh, it's important, but there are other things—the people, the work, liking what I do. I guess money just isn't the only important thing.

Curtis: I think you're wise in looking at a job in ways other than just money. As a coder you would receive a $160 monthly increase, but it also would enable you to build a record of responsibility—this helped in landing the job in marketing for the person I just mentioned. It would also provide a stepping stone for you if you wanted to work in our legal records department.

Bishop: I don't know. It's just that I know the archives, I know what's expected of me there, and I know pretty much all there is to know about it. And I really was trained well before getting started . . . .

Curtis: (Active listening response #4) _____

_____

_____

Bishop: Yeah, I'm concerned about that. I just started really feeling comfortable in archives.

Curtis: We would want you to be comfortable before putting you on your own in coding. You'd work with Stephanie Koval, one of the senior coders for two or three days to get the hang of things. And we wouldn't turn you loose until you felt comfortable about your performance. In fact, since you seem to have some reservations that are understandable, we could let you try the job for two weeks and see how things go. Would that help any? I think you're ideally suited, but I don't want you to feel that I'm pressuring you.

Bishop: So you're saying you understand some of my concerns . . . .

Curtis: Yes, Ann, I think I do. And they're certainly normal. So why don't you give this some thought? I told Koval I'd be talking with you, so feel free to ask her any questions, or if you need to see me about anything further on this, please do. You've impressed us with your work in archives and that's what has led to today's meeting. Will you be able to let me know something by this Friday?

Bishop: I really like working here, Ms. Curtis, and I'm pleased by the confidence you have in me. The chance to switch jobs is a surprise to me . . . I just wasn't expecting it. You've given me some things to think about, so a few days will be fine. I'll let you know something by Friday.

Instructions:
1. Complete Curtis's four active listening responses as requested.
2. Identify any additional uses of active listening responses in the case.
3. Compare your active listening responses with those of other students and discuss.

CASE 7–1

Developing a Communication Plan

Brenda Watson is a cafeteria manager for a large cafeteria chain with over 250 cafeterias. The cafeteria has two assistant managers. One has responsibility for the kitchen and food preparation; the other has responsibility for other functions, including the service line personnel, cashiers, and the buspersons. Approximately 45 people work at the unit.

The following four situations occurred during the past week.

a. Tuesday was Watson's day off, but she'd forgotten a novel she'd left in her office. When she dropped by to pick it up at noon, she noted that several areas of the cafeteria line were not up to standard—there was spilled food on the floor in the customer line; the food line itself was not attractively displayed, and four leftover food trays cluttered the area. Watson didn't say anything at the time, because she was in a hurry. But she was shocked, to say the least. She planned to discuss this with the assistant manager the following day.

b. Reed Barton, one of Watson's most senior, trusted head cooks, asked her to intervene with John Casey, assistant manager of the kitchen. Kitchen employees have been turned off by Casey's hard-nosed, autocratic style, which of late seems to have turned up a notch. Casey, according to Barton, runs the kitchen like it's boot camp. And he gets angry when things aren't to his liking. Today he berated a senior employee loudly in front of several other employees; the employee, carving knife in hand, yelled back. Cooler heads prevented the incident from escalating. Barton senses bad vibes between Casey and several employees, and most of it relates to Casey's aggressive style. Several employees asked Barton to tell Watson what's been going on. Watson is aware that Casey, who's been with her for four months, is very bright. However, she has noted his strong, aggressive style—a marked difference from his predecessor, one of the best kitchen managers Watson had. Since Barton had left for the evening, Watson pondered a plan for best discussing this with him.

c. At 1:30 p.m. Watson learned from her regional manager via a telephone call that the company was bought by Shoney's. The sale, totally unexpected, will be announced to the financial community within the hour and will likely make the morning paper. The regional manager knew little of the details, saying that Watson now knew as much as he did and should communicate this information to her employees.

d. Watson must communicate to her employees that a new overtime system will be installed companywide, effective in four weeks. In the past (ever since she could remember), managers would contact workers—by seniority—either in person or by phone to make sure that the most senior workers would have first opportunity for overtime. This was always slow and ineffective, since some senior workers declined overtime consistently. The new system should give each manager more flexibility in overtime assignments by getting monthly, advance overtime commitments from workers. While most employees will buy into the new system, Watson knew that several of the more senior people were likely to be upset.

Instructions:
1. In each situation, identify the major communication barriers that face Watson.
2. For each of the four situations, develop, in writing, a communication plan or strategy to help Watson in dealing with each. Include such factors as the objective, the appropriate setting, time, how she would organize her message, and other strategic factors you believe are relevant.

VIDEO

Skill-Development Scenario
Communication

Ken Foley is production development supervisor for Carson Products. In the first part of the video, he has a rather old-fashioned attitude toward supervision and communication with his staff members.

Answer the following questions:

1. What examples did you see of Foley's ineffective communications skills? What do you think the effect of his attitude is on the group members? What suggestions would you have for Foley?

2. After viewing the second part of this video, discuss how good communications skills allow Foley to run his department efficiently. How did effective communication solve or prevent problems?

Chapter 8
Motivation

The Demotivating Environment

A new president of a large, public utility firm in a southern state was concerned because his firm was not performing anywhere near its potential effectiveness. The new president believed one of the problems was that the management system was under a traditional command-and-control approach and needed to shift to a more participative, team approach. Accordingly, he contacted a management consulting firm that had an excellent reputation in facilitating an organization's culture to change toward a participative team approach.

The consulting firm's plan was to conduct a research diagnosis phase by surveying a large sample of employees and customers through questionnaires and interviews. Once the diagnosis phase was completed, the plan called for a series of training programs during which managers, supervisors, and key employees were trained in participative management concepts such as team building, leadership, coaching, and empowerment.

After the training programs were completed, the plan called for the formation of ad hoc teams to develop solutions to priority issues and problems identified in the research and diagnosis phase.

Shortly after the consulting firm started to work, it informed the president that the pay and reward system now in effect was in opposition to the planned participative team approach. They discovered that seven years prior the former president had brought in another consulting firm to study their compensation program. This firm recommended a pay system whereby each employee was evaluated by his supervisor and placed in a normal distribution of all employees of the firm. Each year, money available for raises was distributed based on one's placement in the normal distribution ranking. The recommended pay system was implemented, and the percentage in each category is shown graphically in Exhibit 8–1.

At the meeting with the new president the just-hired consulting firm indicated the pay and reward system was causing serious morale problems. During the interviews, many employees, including a number ranked in the top fifty percent, perceived the system as unfair and creating an environment of dysfunctional competition rather than a climate of cooperation and teamwork. Moreover, the way the system worked, the top management of the firm evaluated and placed their employees in the normal distribution first. Invariably they placed their employees in the top two categories of the distribution, and lower levels were left with fewer higher-ranking placements.

The new president readily agreed with the consultants that the pay system and the efforts to change the company culture were incompatible. It was decided that after the completion of the research/diagnosis and training phase, an ad hoc task force would work with the consultants and provide recommendations to the president regarding a more compatible pay and reward system.

MOTIVATION: UNDERSTANDING HUMAN BEHAVIOR

motivation The willingness to work to achieve the organization's objectives.

The opening case demonstrates the importance of both organizations and supervisors understanding the "why" of human behavior. Perhaps you've heard people say that no one can motivate someone else. They mean that **motivation** comes from within. It is the result of a person's individual perceptions, needs, and goals. We define motivation as the willingness of individuals and groups, as influenced by various needs and perceptions, to strive toward a goal. In organizations with enlightened management there is an attempt to integrate needs and goals of individuals with needs and goals of the organization. In the opening case we saw an incompatibility between the two, which resulted in a demotivating environment.

Some people believe that management can never become a science because managers have to deal with human behavior, which is often unpredictable and irrational, and with human beings, who often act out of emotion rather than reason. Few social scientists would deny that people often act emotionally, but many would dispute that

Exhibit 8–1
The Forced Distribution Reward System

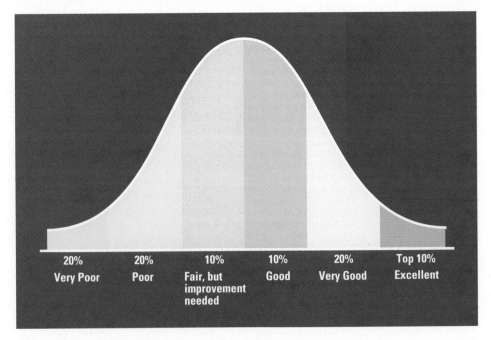

20%	20%	10%	10%	20%	Top 10%
Very Poor	Poor	Fair, but improvement needed	Good	Very Good	Excellent

most people behave irrationally and unpredictably. They would argue that, if more people understood the *why* of human behavior, other people's behavior would seem more rational and predictable.

Since the 1960s, much research has been done on the behavior of people at work. Some significant theories have been developed that are important to anyone in a position of leadership who wants to avoid unnecessary friction arising from human relationships in the organization. We will discuss some of these theories of motivation and see how they relate to supervision.

Some students do not enjoy studying theory because they believe it is abstract and unrelated to the real world. Actually, whatever the discipline, a sound theory provides a basis for understanding, explaining, and predicting what will happen in the real world. Kurt Lewin, famous for his work in the study of groups, once said that nothing is more *practical* than good theory.[1] For a person of action, such as a supervisor who has to work with and through people, an understanding of motivation theory is essential.

MASLOW'S HIERARCHY OF NEEDS THEORY

Learning Objective 1

Understand and explain Maslow's hierarchy of needs theory.

One theory that is particularly significant and practical was developed by psychologist Abraham H. Maslow.[2] This theory is known as the hierarchy of needs. Of all motivation theories, it is probably the one best known by managers.

Principles Underlying the Theory

hierarchy of needs
Arrangement of people's needs in a hierarchy, or ranking of importance.

The two principles underlying Maslow's **hierarchy of needs** theory are that (1) people's needs may be arranged in a hierarchy, or ranking of importance, and (2) once a need has been satisfied, it no longer serves as a primary motivator of behavior. To understand the significance of these principles to Maslow's theory, let us examine the hierarchy of needs shown in Exhibit 8–2.

Exhibit 8–2
Maslow's Hierarchy of Needs

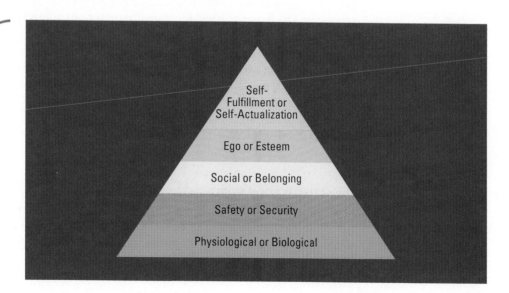

Self-
Fulfillment or
Self-Actualization

Ego or Esteem

Social or Belonging

Safety or Security

Physiological or Biological

PHYSIOLOGICAL OR BIOLOGICAL NEEDS. At the lowest level, but of primary importance when they are not met, are our **physiological** or **biological needs.** "Man does not live by bread alone," says the Bible, but anything else is less important when there is no bread. Unless the circumstances are unusual, the need we have for love, status, or recognition is inoperative when our stomach has been empty for a while. But when we eat regularly and adequately, we cease to regard hunger as an important motivator. The same is true of other physiological needs, such as those for air, water, rest, exercise, shelter, and protection from the elements.

physiological needs
The need for food, water, air, and other physical necessities.

SAFETY OR SECURITY NEEDS. When the physiological needs have been reasonably well satisfied, **safety** or **security needs** become important. We want to be protected from danger, threat, or deprivation. When we feel threatened or dependent, our greatest need is for protection or security.

safety needs The need for protection from danger, threat, or deprivation.

Most employees are in a dependent relationship at work, so they may regard their safety needs as being very important. Arbitrary or autocratic management actions such as favoritism, discrimination, or the unpredictable application of policies can be a powerful threat to the safety of any employee at any level.

SOCIAL OR BELONGING NEEDS. **Social** or **belonging needs** include the need for belonging, for association, for acceptance by colleagues,and for friendship and love. Although most supervisors know that these needs exist, many assume—wrongly—that they represent a threat to the organization. Fearing group hostility to its own objectives, management may go to considerable lengths to control and direct human efforts in ways that are detrimental to cohesive work groups. When the employees' social needs, as well as their safety needs, are not met, they may behave in ways that tend to defeat organizational objectives. They become resistant, antagonistic, and uncooperative. But this behavior is a *consequence* of their frustration, not the cause.

social needs The need for belonging, acceptance by colleagues, friendship, and love.

EGO OR ESTEEM NEEDS. Above the social needs are the **ego** or **esteem needs.** These needs are of two kinds: (1) those that relate to one's self-esteem, such as the need for self-confidence, independence, achievement, competence, and knowledge, and (2) those that relate to one's reputation, such as the need for status, recognition, appreciation, and respect from one's colleagues.

ego needs The need for self-confidence, independence, appreciation, and status.

Unlike the lower-level needs, ego needs are rarely fully satisfied, because people always seek more satisfaction of such needs once they have become important. A few years ago, the typical organization offered few opportunities for lower-level employees to satisfy their ego needs. As you will see toward the end of the chapter, well-managed and innovative companies are doing a better job in this regard today. Still, the conventional method of organizing work, particularly in mass-production industries, gives little consideration to these aspects of motivation.

SELF-FULFILLMENT OR SELF-ACTUALIZATION NEEDS. At the top of Maslow's hierarchy are the **self-fulfillment** or **self-actualization needs.** These needs lead one to seek to realize one's own potential, to develop oneself, and to be creative. It seems clear that the quality of work life in most organizations provides only limited opportunities to fulfill these needs. When higher-level needs are not satisfied, employees compensate by trying to further satisfy lower-level needs. So the needs for self-fulfillment may remain dormant.

self-fulfillment needs
Needs concerned with realizing one's potential, self-development, and creativity.

The president of Wixon/ Fontarome, a flavorings manufacturer in Milwaukee, financed a recent trip to Walt Disney World for his 150 employees. He viewed this as a way to motivate them and to reward them for years of consistent growth in sales and profits.

Qualifying the Theory

Maslow's theory is a relative rather than absolute explanation of human behavior. You should be aware of the following four important qualifiers to his theory:

1. Needs on one level of the hierarchy do not have to completely satisfied before needs on the next level become important.
2. The theory does not pretend to explain the behavior of the neurotic or the mentally disturbed.
3. Some people's priorities are different. For example, an artist may practically starve while trying to achieve self-actualization through the creation of a great work of art. Also, some people are much less security-oriented or achievement-oriented than others.
4. Unlike the lower levels, the two highest levels of needs can hardly ever be fully satisfied. There are always new challenges and opportunities for growth, recognition, and achievement. A person may remain in the same job position for years and still find a great deal of challenge and motivation in his or her work.

Bob Buschka, a computer programmer for a large bank in a midwestern state, has held his position for 20 years and would like to remain in that position. He enjoys programming and is looked upon as one of the top programmers in banking in the area. The bank sends him to various schools to keep him growing and developing on the job.

"Bob's a remarkable person," says his boss. "He's passed up promotions into management to keep his present job, he's so into it. We know what a gem he is, and we do everything we can to give him lots of room to operate—special key projects, training and developing new programmers, and keeping up with the new applications to our industry."

Maslow and Quality

Even with the qualifications, Maslow is a most useful motivational framework. Management consultants and authors Patrick Townsend and Joan Gebhardt make a strong case that Maslow's framework is a key for a successful quality program. Townsend and Gebhardt have conducted numerous quality workshops in the United States, Europe, and Asia, and Townsend serves as an examiner for the Malcolm Baldrige National Quality Award. They indicate that the top two levels of the hierarchy involving autonomy and esteem "have long been the background of a well-established quality process. What has been missing, perhaps, in so many failed or faltering efforts has been the realization that virtually no one can concentrate efforts in this area unless more basic needs are already met."

That explains one of the paradoxes of the quality movement: the ideal time to begin a quality process is when the company seems not to need it. The chances of individuals within the organization reaching level four of Maslow's hierarchy are greatly improved when the company as a whole is healthy financially and emotionally. In those stellar cases where authority is pushed down the corporate ladder to where it is equal to responsibility, as in self-managed workteams, an increasing number of employees can achieve this level.

Maslow's fifth level, self-actualization, is thought to be achieved by only a small percentage of individuals even under the best of conditions. Unless the surrounding environment ensures that the individual is thought of as a thinking, contributing adult and not just as another interchangeable part of the organization, reaching this level is virtually impossible.

When individuals take an active role in ensuring the success of the quality effort, the company, now quality-focused, will be able to create the environment that makes it possible for individuals to work their way through to a level of self-actualization at work. Along the way, the nation will benefit and the company will make a lot of money, but the gain to each person is the most dramatic and most precious. The paradox is "You can't get there unless you participate. So perhaps the best answer to WIIFM is this: WHAT'S IN IT FOR ME . . . IS A BETTER ME."[3]

How Supervisors Can Help Satisfy Employees' Needs

Learning Objective 2

Understand and explain Herzberg's theory of motivation.

Supervisors play a key role in helping employees satisfy their needs. Maslow's theory should be used by the supervisor as a general guide to motivating employees, not as a formula for routine motivation. Exhibit 8–3 shows how some of the needs at the various levels can be met with the supervisors' help.

SELF-CHECK

Referring to Exhibit 8–3, determine which needs a supervisor could help employees reach and which would be beyond her or his control.

Exhibit 8–3
How a Job Satisfies
Employee Needs

Need	Ways of Satisfying the Need on the Job
Self-actualization	Learning new skills, growing and developing, feeling a sense of accomplishment, exercising responsibility.
Esteem	Praise, recognition, promotion, getting one's name in the company paper as "employee of the month," being given more responsibility, being asked for help or advice.
Social	Work groups, group meetings, company-sponsored events.
Safety	Safe working conditions, pensions and benefits, job security, fair treatment, fair grievance system.
Physiological	Pay, rest breaks, clean air.

How can a supervisor help employees achieve satisfaction of their needs? The answer to this question amounts to a definition of what employees expect from their supervisor—namely, (1) knowledge, (2) an atmosphere of approval, and (3) consistent discipline.[4]

KNOWLEDGE PROVIDED BY THE SUPERVISOR. Most employees expect their employer to provide them with information on organizational policies, rules and regulations, and their duties and responsibilities. As a rule, companies and supervisors do a fair job of providing this type of information. However, employees today have the right to expect more, and this is where many supervisors fall down on the job. For example, new employees need to know what the probationary period is before they are accepted as full-fledged members of the organization. They also need to know the following:

1. What assistance they can count on to help them become proficient in their work.
2. On what basis they will receive promotions and pay increases.
3. How management determines who will be laid off first in slack times.
4. How much advance notice they will be given of changes that may affect them.
5. How they are performing (probably the most important information a supervisor can provide). Employees not only need this knowledge, but also expect it as part of their employment agreement.

ATMOSPHERE OF APPROVAL. An atmosphere of approval is an atmosphere free of fault-finding. This atmosphere is less dependent on a supervisor's standards of performance or strictness of discipline than on his or her attitude toward employees when correcting their errors. Does the supervisor use this opportunity to help employees do a better job in the future or to make them feel like "dummies" who made stupid mistakes?

By helping employees overcome mistakes in a positive manner, a supervisor is not necessarily being slack or easy. If new employees simply cannot master the work during their probationary period, the supervisor should let them know whether they will be transferred or dismissed.

CONSISTENT DISCIPLINE. Most employees expect and want consistent discipline. One of the worst mistakes you can make as a supervisor is to try to be a nice guy and look the other way when employees violate rules and policies, because sooner or later you will have to crack down. Then your employees will feel that you are playing favorites, because earlier you let other employees get by with rule breaking.

Discipline should be consistent not only in its application to wrong actions, but also in support of right actions. In other words, employees should have positive support when they do things beyond the normal expectations of their jobs. If you look for ways to compliment employees sincerely—to consistently give praise and acknowledgment to different people for similar types of achievement—you will be amazed at the *esprit de corps* this practice will create in your department.

Managing from the Heart

The Atlanta Consulting Group is a firm that enjoys an excellent reputation in helping firms create an environment that is personally satisfying as well as productive and profitable. The two founders along with two vice-presidents have written a book titled *Managing from the Heart.* The book is a story of the transformation of an autocratic manager, who is feared by employees, into a caring, compassionate leader who appreciates and empowers the people around him or her. The principles presented in the text embody the requests that employees should make of a supervisor or leader. These principles are:

1. Please don't make me out to be wrong, even if you disagree.
2. Hear and understand me.
3. Tell me the truth with compassion.
4. Remember to look for my good intentions.
5. Acknowledge the greatness within me.[5]

SELF-CHECK

What needs in the Maslow hierarchy do the five principles in *Managing from the Heart* address?

HERZBERG'S FINDINGS

After an environment has been provided that can satisfy employees' lower-level needs, supervisors may try to motivate them by providing opportunities to fulfill higher-level needs. It is by tapping these needs that real achievements in efficiency, productivity, and creativity can be gained in working with and through people.

Herzberg's Original Study on Job Satisfaction

Learning Objective 3

Explain the supervisor's role in helping employees achieve satisfaction of their needs.

Several research studies have demonstrated the importance of higher-level needs as motivators. The originator of these experiments is Frederick Herzberg, an American psychologist whose findings have had considerable impact on American management.

In the initial study, Herzberg and his associates conducted in-depth interviews with 200 engineers and accountants from 11 different firms in the Pittsburgh, Pennsylvania, area.[6] Those interviewed were asked to recall an event or series of related events from the past year that had made them feel *unusually good* about their work. They were also asked to speculate on how much the event(s) affected their performance and morale. Conversely, they were asked to recall an event or series of related events that had made them feel *unusually bad* and to speculate on how the event(s) affected their performance and morale.

SELF-CHECK

Try to answer Herzberg's survey questions yourself. Think about a job you've held in the past or presently hold. If you haven't had a job, think of your school work.

1. What specific incident or event (singular or recurring) in that situation gave you the most satisfaction?
2. What caused the most dissatisfaction?

From this study, Herzberg and his associates found that the top-ranking factors causing job satisfaction and the top-ranking factors causing job dissatisfaction were those shown in Exhibit 8–4. Most important, the study revealed that, in almost all cases, the factors causing job satisfaction had a *stimulating* effect on performance and morale. On the other hand, the factors causing job dissatisfaction had a *negative* effect.

Exhibit 8–4

Results of Herzberg's Original Study on Job Satisfaction

Factors That Caused Job Satisfaction	Factors That Caused Job Dissatisfaction
Achievement	Company policy and administration
Recognition	Supervision
The work itself	Relationship with supervisor
Responsibility	Working conditions
Advancement	Salary

MOTIVATORS AND HYGIENE FACTORS. Another important finding of Herzberg's study was that the factors causing job satisfaction were *intrinsic* to the job, whereas those causing job dissatisfaction were *extrinsic* to the job. That is, when people felt good about their job, it was usually because something had happened that showed that they were doing their work particularly well or that they were becoming more expert in their professions. In other words, good feelings were keyed to the specific tasks that they performed, rather than to extrinsic factors such as money, security, or working conditions. Conversely, when they felt bad, it was usually because something had happened to make them feel that they were being treated unfairly.

motivators Have an uplifting effect on attitude or performance.

hygiene factors Can prevent serious dissatisfaction or a drop in productivity.

Herzberg and his associates therefore made a distinction between what they called motivators and hygiene factors. **Motivators** are those factors that have an uplifting effect on attitudes or performance. **Hygiene factors** are those factors that can prevent serious dissatisfaction or a drop in productivity, thereby preventing loss of morale or efficiency, but cannot motivate by themselves. In other words, hygiene factors do not increase a worker's desire to do the job well.

SIGNIFICANCE OF HERZBERG'S ORIGINAL STUDY. Herzberg's study tended to support Maslow's concept of a hierarchy of needs. The motivators relate to the two highest levels of Maslow's hierarchy (self-fulfillment and esteem); the hygiene factors relate to the lower-level needs, primarily the need for security.

What all this means is that employees today *expect* to be treated fairly by their supervisors. They *expect* decent working conditions and pay comparable to that of people doing similar work in the firms. They *expect* company policies to be consistently and equitably applied to all employees. When these expectations are not realized, employees are demotivated. This condition is usually reflected in inefficiency and a high turnover rate. But fulfilling these expectations does not motivate employees. As Maslow's theory maintains, it is only when the lower-level needs have been satisfied that the higher-level needs can be used effectively in motivating employees. Exhibit 8–5 indicates ways in which a supervisor can use higher-level needs to create a motivating environment.

Exhibit 8–5
Ways to Use Motivators on the Job

- Delegate more authority to workers.
- When you have an important project to complete or are facing difficult problems, call your workers in and get their ideas.
- Cross-train your employees so that they become more broadly experienced.
- Compliment and recognize employees for good work.
- Assign workers to special projects.
- Ask the more experienced workers to assist in training new employees.
- Send employees to training courses for skill upgrading.

Additional Studies on Job Satisfaction

After the original Herzberg study of engineers and accountants, critics were quick to suggest that, although the findings might apply to professionals who sought creativity in their work, they would not apply to other groups of employees. But similar studies, conducted by different investigators in different countries, have shown surprisingly similar results. Exhibit 8–6 summarizes the results of 12 studies involving people from all walks of life—accountants, agricultural administrators, assemblers, engineers, food handlers, hospital maintenance personnel, housekeepers, manufacturing supervisors, military officers, nurses, retired managers, scientists, teachers, and technicians.

Exhibit 8–6

Factors Affecting Job Attitudes, As Reported in 12 Studies

Note: The percentage of satisfaction was based on a study of 1,753 events on the job; the percentage of dissatisfaction was based on a study of 1,844 events on the job.

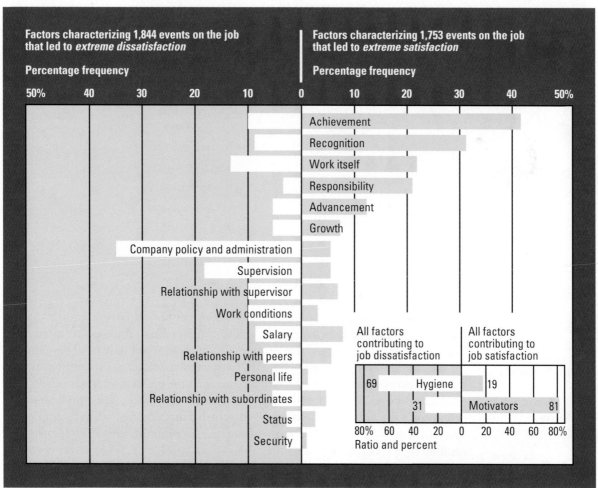

Although supervision is characterized as a hygiene factor, you should not conclude that supervision is not important in motivating employees. In the summary of the 12 studies cited in Exhibit 8–6, ineffective supervision was ranked as the second most important factor in causing job *dissatisfaction.* Moreover, one of the authors of this textbook conducted a study in New Zealand and discovered that ineffective supervision ranked as the number one factor in causing job dissatisfaction. The following quotation from a New Zealander illustrates how poor supervision can reduce motivation:

> **I was once given a job to do that involved a bit of responsibility. The job, I was told, was to take several days, and I was to be completely responsible for the job. I was told to report back at a later date and tell the boss how I was getting on. I didn't particularly worry when, a couple of hours later, the boss came down and asked me how I was doing; in fact, I was quite glad that he was taking an interest.**
>
> **However, when he repeated the process at intervals of every two or three hours, I got decidedly annoyed. In fact, I was fed up, and I was looking for ways of palming the job off on someone else. I felt that the boss thought I was incapable of doing the job properly, and I wondered why he gave it to me in the first place. The more I thought about this, the more unhappy I got. Consequently, I began to take longer on the job than I should have done, and couldn't have cared less if it was right or wrong. After all, the boss was constantly checking it; so he could pick up my mistakes.**

As you can see, supervision is one of the major influences on whether such motivators as achievement, recognition, creative and challenging work, and responsibility are operating in the work environment. In short, supervision helps determine whether the satisfaction of higher-level needs can be realized by employees in their work.

SELF-CHECK   Is money a motivator for you? Explain.

Gainsharing Reward Systems

Learning Objective 4

State the relationship among money, motivation, and the expectancy theory.

gainsharing
Employees' financial rewards are linked to the performance of an entire unit.

At a recent management development program conducted by the authors of this textbook, several first-level supervisors challenged Herzberg's finding that money was not a motivator. They argued that money was a motivator not only for them, but also for the employees in their departments. They cited as evidence a recently instituted plant bonus system tied to production quotas. After the bonus system was introduced, production increased, resulting in more money for employees. The employees were describing a pay and reward system called **gainsharing,** a system whereby employees' financial rewards are linked to the performance of an entire unit. The idea behind gainsharing is to encourage participation in solving problems and lowering costs and to enlist cooperative behaviors, where interdependency is a key in attaining desired outcomes.[7] In the opening case, the utility company decided that the most compatible

E. Rachel Hubka, president of Rachel's Bus Co., nurtures part-timers to be entrepreneurs by helping them foster a professional attitude. In addition to offering her drivers incentives to earn more, she provides them with business cards and teaches them how to deal effectively with customers.

pay and reward system, with the shift to a more participative management system, was a gainsharing plan linking pay to performance.

Although gainsharing has been in existence for many years, its use is increasing rapidly with the trend toward empowerment and more teamwork. The success of motivational gainsharing programs such as the Scanlon and Lincoln Electric plans are well known. Why are more companies turning to this approach? Again, money is tied directly to the Herzberg motivating factors of recognition, achievement, and responsibility. Management consultant and author Michael Markowich describes the motivational value of gainsharing with the following story:

> **Last year I was conducting a management program at the Marriott Marquis Hotel in New York City at the same time that the television soap opera awards were being held there. I asked one of the security guards on the scene how things were going. "Great!" he replied. "And I'm working a lot of hours."**
>
> **"I guess you're making a lot of overtime," I said.**
>
> **Needless to say, I was puzzled when he told me that he wasn't, but he explained his reasons for being so optimistic. "Look, we have profit sharing at our place; I like it when the company makes money."**
>
> **Then I understood. This security guard was not just an employee—he had an equity stake in the business. You could tell the difference in his attitude.**

Sharing the gains of the business will give employees a personal financial reason to continue thinking about what is best for the company, since it will be what is best for the employee.

How can any company lose?[8]

Qualifying Herzberg's Theory

We believe that Herzberg's theory is valuable as a general guide to understanding motivation at work. However, here are some qualifications you should bear in mind:

1. Money *can* sometimes be a motivating factor.
2. For some people, especially professionals, the absence of a motivating factor on the job can constitute dissatisfaction.
3. Research studies that use Herzberg's method support his findings; however, studies that use a different method arrive at different conclusions. This fact has led some researchers to conclude that Herzberg's theory is "method bound." On the other hand, Charles and Donna Hanson conclude from their study that Herzberg's theory has considerable validity, especially in comparison with other theories of motivation.[9]

OTHER THEORIES OF MOTIVATION

Learning Objective 5

Define and explain other theories of motivation, such as equity, positive reinforcement, and goal-setting theories.

Four popular theories of motivation that apply especially well to supervisory management are (1) expectancy theory, (2) equity theory, (3) positive reinforcement theory, and (4) goal-setting theory.

The Expectancy Theory of Motivation

expectancy theory Expectation that a good effort, resulting in effective performance, will be followed by a reward.

The **expectancy theory** of motivation (see Exhibit 8–7) states that workers expect a good effort, resulting in effective performance, to be followed by a reward. This theory was developed by Victor H. Vroom. Using the previous example of employees' improved productivity after a plant bonus system was instituted, this theory can be expressed as follows:

$$\text{Motivation} = \begin{matrix} \text{Expectancy that} \\ \text{increased effort} \\ \text{will lead to} \\ \text{increased rewards} \end{matrix} \times \begin{matrix} \text{Increased effort} \\ \text{leading to higher} \\ \text{production} \end{matrix} = \begin{matrix} \text{Year-end} \\ \text{bonus for} \\ \text{employees} \end{matrix}$$

Exhibit 8–7 is a graphic illustration of the expectancy theory. It shows that rewards based on current performance cause subsequent performance to be more effective.

SELF-CHECK

What happens to worker expectations and effort when an employer follows over a period of years a policy of across-the-board pay increases for all employees?

The Equity Theory of Motivation

equity theory Positive motivation can be achieved by reducing workers' feelings that they are treated inequitably.

Another concept that has received research support is called the **equity theory** of motivation. This theory states that one can motivate employees by reducing their feelings of inequity, if such feelings exist. The concept is especially relevant to the wage and salary system. Suppose you had started working at the same type of position at the same time as several other people with similar backgrounds, so logically they should be receiving the same wage as you. If you found out that they were making more, then you would become dissatisfied and possibly demotivated. In a case like this, salary is a hygiene factor, as revealed by Herzberg's findings.

Exhibit 8–7
Expectancy Theory

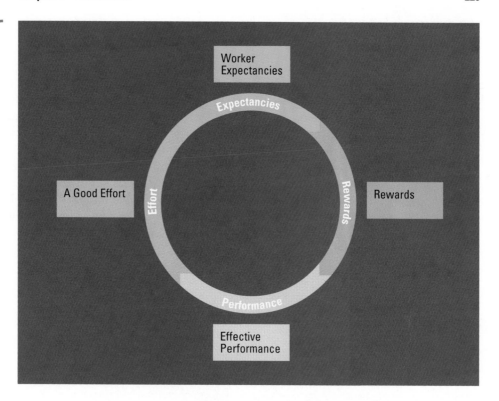

SELF-CHECK

Have you ever received a lower grade than you thought you deserved, only to find that others you considered to be poorer students had received better grades? How did you feel?

Here is an example of the equity theory in action.

> **Sue Smith had started work as an accountant at a local hospital after graduation from college. During her two years on the job, she had received excellent annual appraisals and salary increases. She had been pleased with her progress with the job until she discovered that two new college graduates without experience had been hired in the accounting department at slightly more than she was making. She immediately started looking for employment elsewhere.**

SELF-CHECK

As far as you can tell, is Sue Smith's situation a widespread problem in today's working world? Why or why not?

The Positive Reinforcement Theory of Motivation

positive reinforcement theory Favorable activities will be reinforced by a reward and discouraged by punishment.

law of effect Activities that meet with pleasant consequences tend to be repeated.

As shown in Exhibit 8–8, one of the best ways to influence and modify employee behavior in a favorable direction is explained by the **positive reinforcement theory** of motivation. We have talked about this concept indirectly throughout this chapter. It is based on the **law of effect,** which holds that those activities that meet with pleasant consequences tend to be repeated, whereas those activities that meet with unpleasant consequences tend not to be repeated.

Since the supervisor in most companies has control of the reward and discipline system for employees, he or she controls the law of effect. The immediate supervisor, more than any other person, is responsible for whether employees develop into an excellent, fair, or poor work team. This situation will in turn determine to a large degree the employees' satisfaction with their jobs.

Exhibit 8–8
In Praise of Praise

Many supervisors feel that the only way they can truly get through to their employees is via the paycheck. However, we all have at our disposal an entirely free and easy way to get our employees' attention: praise.

The basic principle of motivation is that people do what they do because they are looking for something called "positive reinforcement"—that is, praise or recognition that demonstrates that their efforts are appreciated by those in charge. If a person's actions have resulted in positive consequences, then he or she is more likely to repeat those particular actions. Thus, his or her behavior has been positively reinforced. Reinforcing consequences motivates action. If there is any other type of consequence, or none at all, the behavior is "demotivated."

A word of caution: In order for praise to be a truly effective motivator, it must be sincere, and it must be well deserved. As much as we all like a supervisor who is lavish with praise, when it comes too easily from the manager, it loses a lot of its impact. Giving praise out generously, but cautiously, requires the extra effort of observing and being aware of what your employees are doing on a daily basis. However, the side benefits are an increased understanding of how your employees work and better communication as you get to understand them and their needs better.

Look for reasons to praise. You need not worry about looking for reasons to discipline—these seldom stay hidden for long. But it is often the quiet, unassuming employees who are most deserving of praise and least likely to receive it because they don't bring their accomplishments to their supervisors' attention. If you can notice when such an employee does something a little extraordinary or very skillfully, your praise may be powerful enough to motivate that employee to continue this type of high job performance on a regular basis.

Some people find it very hard to give unsolicited praise to others. However, it gets easier with practice. Start out by complimenting an employee on a large accomplishment and work up to the smaller, less noticeable feats also worthy of recognition. Before too long, praising will become a part of your supervisory style.

Source: Philip C. Grant, "Some 'New' Motivational Techniques." Reprinted from *SUPERVISORY SENSE*, December/1987. © 1987, American Management Association, Inc. All rights reserved.

Goal-Setting Theory

goal-setting theory
Achievement-oriented people set difficult but attainable goals and appreciate positive reinforcement for achieving them.

A theory of motivation that undergirds the other motivational theories is the **goal-setting theory.** We have known for some time that one of the characteristics of achievement-oriented people is that they set difficult but attainable goals. The theory does not seem to work as well if people set either extremely easy or impossible goals. One of the reasons it works is that achieving difficult, but attainable, goals provides feedback and positive reinforcement. It seems to motivate people, regardless of whether the goals are set by the supervisors, set participatively, or set individually.

In conducting partnering workshops, one of the first things to do is to have the participants develop a common set of goals. These goals are incorporated in a partnering agreement that everyone signs; the agreement provides the participants a basis for evaluating how well they are doing throughout the project. (See the section on partnering in Chapter 5.) Individually or collectively, when people place either long- or short-term goals on paper, they seem to internalize them, and it guides them in their efforts. It is a well-known fact that the starting point for people who achieve a successful retirement from a financial standpoint start with written short- and long-term goals. Whether we are talking about retirement or improving your golf game, the use of goal setting is a powerful motivator.

But the willingness (motivation) does not come automatically; you have to have some ability and you have to work toward achieving your goals. A wonderful book by Charles Kemp develops the theme that in the world of golf and the game of life you have to have ability, plus desire, plus effort, plus knowledge, plus patience, and persistence in the face of discouragement in order to achieve your goals.[10]

MOTIVATIONAL PRACTICES AT AMERICA'S BEST-MANAGED COMPANIES

Learning Objective 6

Explain motivational practices in the best-managed companies.

Many companies and supervisors are quite adept at penalizing employees for mistakes or poor performance. A best-selling book, drawing lessons from America's best-run companies, states that "the dominant culture in most big companies demands punishment for a mistake, no matter how small."[11] The book goes on to say that the dominant culture in the *best-managed companies* is just the opposite. These companies develop "winners" by constantly reinforcing the idea that employees *are* winners. The performance targets are set so that they provide a challenge but are attainable. Recall in the Herzberg studies that recognition was one of the primary motivators. The effective supervisor continually provides recognition for good performance by employees.

In a presentation to the American Psychological Association meeting, Barry Stow noted that for years, organization psychologists have been advocating certain company actions to increase motivation of individuals. Many of America's best-managed companies have implemented these actions, which include:

1. Tying extrinsic rewards (such as pay) to performance.
2. Setting realistic and challenging goals.
3. Evaluating employee performance accurately and providing feedback on performance.

4. Promoting on the basis of skill and performance rather than personal characteristics, power, or connections.
5. Building the skill level of the workforce through training and development.
6. Enlarging and enriching jobs through increases in responsibility, variety, and significance.[12]

These actions demonstrate the practicality of the theories presented in this chapter.

On an all-encompassing basis, James O'Toole has published a book on employee practices at the best-managed companies. He shows that these companies place a lot of emphasis not only on the rights and responsibilities of employees, but also on the value of employee contribution through participative management. Specifically, these companies provide stakeholder status for unions, employee stock ownership, a fair measure of job security, lifelong training, benefits tailored to individual needs, participation in decision making, freedom of expression, and incentive pay.[13]

MOTIVATION IN THE 1990s AND BEYOND

The next twenty years may well determine who will be the world's leader in economic productivity and innovation. Will it be the United States, China, Germany, Japan, or some other country?

A big challenge facing the United States is how to manage and motivate an increasingly diverse workforce, having a higher percentage of different races and nationalities and a lower percentage of white males.

Different Nationalities

Some maintain that countries with a homogenous (having similar backgrounds and origins) population base have an advantage in creating a motivating work culture compared to a country with a heterogenous (having diverse backgrounds and origins) population base, such as the United States. Historically, this position has not been the case. Many of our immigrants have come, and are coming, because they were fleeing from oppression or lack of opportunities in their native countries. Most of these newcomers seem to have an adventuresome spirit and a high need for achievement similar to the immigrant pioneers who originally developed the United States. People with a high need for achievement flourish in organizations that use the practices found in America's best-managed companies.

Baby Busters

baby busters The generation born between 1965 and 1975; thought of as idealistic.

Perhaps a more challenging question is how do you create a motivational climate for the **baby busters,** those young employees just entering the workforce or who fall between the ages of 20–30? Chrysler President Robert Lutz maintains that the secret to international competitive success may lie in how well the baby busters are prepared by the nation's school systems.

"Just as U.S. automakers lost their way after years of supremacy, so too has the American educational system." He went on to urge that American school systems renew themselves by implementing a standardized core curriculum that would help

American kids "compete with kids from Tokyo and Stuttgard. The U.S. auto industry has a vested interest in the future of U.S. schools, because by the end of this decade, approximately half of the Big Three's domestic workforce will be eligible for retirement. At Chrysler alone that could translate into as many as 30,000 new hires in the next four to five years."[14]

SELF-CHECK   Do you agree with Lutz's position? If not, why not? If you agree, what courses would you require in the core curriculum?

If you agreed with Lutz, you are in agreement with the experts.

In spite of a higher percentage of students enrolling in colleges (59% in 1988 as compared to 49% in 1978), studies have shown that "vast numbers of them function dismally in math and science or are functionally illiterate." In addition, they are said to have a longer adolescence, with 75% of men from ages 18 to 24 living with their parents.[15] Consequently, companies are going to have to take the lead in the training and development of baby busters in certain skills until the education system improves. Exhibit 8–9 provides guidelines on how to assess the skills of baby busters.

Some very positive aspects of the baby busters is that they are generally idealistic and are concerned about quality-of-life issues. They also tend to value challenge and growth more than money or titles. Although it is difficult to generalize about any age

Exhibit 8–9
How to Assess the Skills of the Baby Busters

Here are 10 diagnostic questions to ask yourself about the skills of your twentysomething employees and your company's commitment to closing the skills gap:

1. Do you know the educational level of each employee whom you must lead?
2. Does your company have a budget set aside specifically for providing training to entry-level employees and retraining for experienced employees and managers?
3. Have you ever conducted a training needs analysis to determine the skills employees need for maximum productivity?
4. Does your company have a full-time training department that's led and staffed by qualified training and development specialists?
5. What percent of your annual budget is devoted to training?
6. When was the last time that you, as a manger or supervisor, completed a formal training session?
7. Does your company provide support for personnel who wish to further their education in after-hours classes?
8. Does your company offer short training events, such as a "Brown Bag Lunch," in which employees can have lunch and experience a short learning event?
9. Is the training and retraining of employees a priority for top management?
10. What one specific action could you initiate as a manager to begin to provide needed skills training for your employees?

Source: *Twentysomething: Managing & Motivating Today's New Work Force*

group, the authors of the book *Twentysomething: Managing and Motivating Today's New Work Force* have done a good job in analyzing today's work force. Exhibit 8–10 generalizes how the different age groups view one another, and Exhibit 8–11 presents turn-ons and turn-offs while working with baby busters.

Motivating All Employees

A supervisor has many rewards to draw from in creating an environment to motivate both individuals and groups. Many of these rewards are relatively inexpensive, and Exhibit 8–12 provides a number of examples.

Traditionalists (Born 1925–1945) See
Baby boomers as disrespectful, overly blunt, too "warm and fuzzy."
Younger workers as *very* young, impatient, unethical.

Baby Boomers (Born 1946–1964) See
Traditionalists as caught in the by-the-book syndrome, overly cautious, conservative, inflexible.
Younger workers as selfish, manipulative, aloof.

Baby Busters (Born 1965–1975) See
Traditionalists as old, outdated, rigid.
Baby boomers as workaholic, unrealistic, disgustingly "new age."

Source: *Twentysomething: Managing & Motivating Today's New Work Force*

Exhibit 8–10
How Employees Young and Old View Each Other

Exhibit 8–11
Baby Buster's Turn-ons/Turn-offs

Turn-ons	Turn-offs
• Recognition	• Hearing about the past (yours)
• Praise	• Inflexibility about time
• Time with you (manager)	• Workaholism
• Learning how what they're doing right now is making them more marketable	• Being watched and scrutinized
• Opportunity to learn new things	• Feeling disrespected
• Fun at work (structured play, harmless practical jokes, cartoons, light competition, surprises)	• Feeling pressure to "convert" to traditionalist behavior
• Small, unexpected rewards for jobs well done	• Disparaging comments about their generation's tastes and styles

Source: *Twentysomething: Managing & Motivating Today's New Work Force*

The Manager's List of Good Rewards
- Raises and bonuses
- Social functions
- Outings
- A night on the town
- A nice meal or lunch, courtesy of the manager
- Lunch as a group that the manager buys
- Dinner
- A pizza party
- Picnics for teams
- Golf or other sporting event in which both parties participate
- Direct praise
- Peer recognition
- Letters of recognition to file or place where customers can see them
- Passing on customer compliments and commendations in voice mail or in writing
- Written praise from the branch
- One-on-one verbal praise
- Day off or time off
- Cash
- Tickets to sporting events, concerts, and so on, that the employees can attend by themselves
- Certificates and plaques
- Shirts, phones, pins, hats, cups, and so on, all with the name of the company on them
- A parking space
- Additional responsibilities
- Opportunities to excel
- Additional training
- A personal call or visit from the CEO or a senior executive
- Better tools
- Allowing people to bid on projects they would most prefer

Source: Peter Meyer, "Can You Give Good, Inexpensive Rewards? Some Real-Life Answers," *Business Horizons,* November–December, 1994, p. 85.

Exhibit 8–12
The Manager's List of Good Rewards

Experts are saying that no matter what group of employees prosper in the nineties and beyond, companies must concentrate on the three R's: recruiting, retraining, and retaining high-quality people.[16] Motivation is involved in all of the R's, especially motivating people through tapping higher-level needs. A trend today in many companies is a shift toward self-managing work teams. People cannot be expected to turn into self-managers overnight; they need to be given the proper tools through development and training programs.

The following statement captures the motivation challenge in the 1990s:

The adaptive organization . . . provides openings for the creativity and initiative too often found [only] in small, entrepreneurial companies. It does this by aligning what the corporation wants—innovation and improvement—with what turns people on—namely, a chance to use their heads and expand their skills.[17]

Chapter Review

Learning Objective 1

Understand and explain Maslow's hierarchy of needs theory.
The principles underlying Maslow's theory of a hierarchy of needs are that needs are arranged in a hierarchy of importance and that, once a need has been satisfied, it is no longer a primary motivator. The lower-level needs include physiological, security, and social needs, and the higher-level needs are esteem and self-fulfillment.

Learning Objective 2

Understand and explain Herzberg's theory of motivation.
Herzberg's research discovered that motivators are those factors that have an uplifting effect on attitudes or performance, whereas hygiene factors are those factors that prevent serious dissatisfaction but do not motivate by themselves. The motivators are achievement, recognition, the work itself, responsibility, and advancement. The hygiene factors are company policy and administration, supervision, relationship with the supervisor, working conditions, and pay. The motivators relate to the two highest levels of the Maslow hierarchy, self-fulfillment and esteem. Hygiene factors relate to lower-level needs, especially the security needs. Although pay is listed as a hygiene factor, it becomes a motivator when it is directly related to achievement and/or recognition.

Learning Objective 3

Explain the supervisor's role in helping employees achieve satisfaction of their needs.
The supervisor plays a major role in whether or not an employee's needs are met. Our opening quote by Sydney Harris highlights this fact. If there is a continual fault-finding environment, there is a climate of demotivation that threatens employees' security and self-esteem needs; a climate of positive recognition for good performance provides a motivating climate. If there is a climate in which employees are empowered to achieve agreed-upon goals and are rewarded accordingly, the higher-level employees' needs and expectancies are met.

Learning Objective 4

State the relationship among money, motivation, and expectancy theory.
An example of money becoming a motivator is gainsharing, where money is directly related to achievement, increased responsibility, and effective teamwork.

The expectancy theory of motivation states that workers expect a good effort, resulting in effective performance, to be followed by a reward. If this expectation is not met, employees can be demotivated. Equity theory, which is closely related, acknowledges that employees will consider how their output and performance are rewarded as compared to other employees'. If, for example, a woman discovers that men are making more for comparable work and performance, the discovery can be demotivating—and even lead to a lawsuit.

Learning Objective 5

Define and explain other theories of motivation, such as equity, positive reinforcement, and goal-setting theories.
The positive reinforcement theory of motivation is based on the law of effect. If a supervisor provides praise and perhaps positive salary recommendations for good performance, this will tend to encourage continued good performance.

Goal-setting theory undergirds the other motivational theories and urges the setting of difficult but attainable goals. The ideal cause-and-effect relationship in motivating employees is found in Exhibit 8–13.

Exhibit 8–13
Ideal Cause-and-Effect Relationship in Motivating Employees

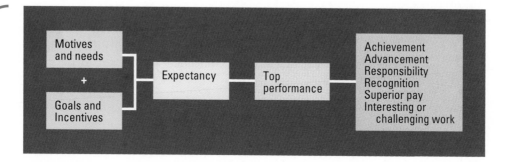

Learning Objective 6

Explain motivational practices in the best-managed companies.

We also discussed creating a climate of positive motivation in the 1990s and beyond, paying particular attention to motivating the baby busters.

The dominant culture in America's best-managed companies creates "winners" by focusing on and reinforcing effective performance. In the 1990s, the motivating culture is focusing on higher-level needs by training, providing increased responsibilities, transferring employees for purposes of growth and enrichment, and closely relating pay to performance. When this type of culture is prevalent, baby busters, along with other groups, respond very positively, resulting in win-win outcomes for both the company and the employees.

Important Terms

baby busters *pg. 232*
ego *or* esteem needs *218*
equity theory *228*
expectancy theory *228*
gainsharing *226*
goal-setting theory *231*
hierarchy of needs *217*

hygiene factors *224*
law of effect *230*
motivation *216*
motivators *224*
physiological *or*
  biological needs *218*

positive reinforcement
  theory *230*
safety *or* security
  needs *218*
self-fulfillment *or* self-
  actualization needs *218*
social *or* belonging needs
  218

Questions for Review and Discussion

1. Briefly outline Maslow's theory of the hierarchy of needs. What are the two basic principles underlying this theory? Can you relate the theory to a real situation?
2. What kinds of knowledge should a leader furnish to his or her employees? How does such information satisfy their needs?
3. What findings resulted from Frederick Herzberg's research concerning employee motivation? Can these findings be correlated with Maslow's hierarchy of needs? If so, how?

4. Is security the most important job need of blue-collar workers?
5. What is being done to improve motivation in U.S. companies?
6. Refer back to the opening case and identify the benefits of the gainsharing reward system that was recommended as opposed to the previous forced distribution reward system.

Skill Builder 8–1
Excessive Coffee Breaks

An office manager for the Hawthorne Company has a staff with high morale and generally good productivity. However, several employees have been extending their coffee breaks by five to ten minutes. The manager feels that the more conscientious employees resent this, yet wonders whether these extended coffee breaks should be stopped at the risk of alienating the employees guilty of this practice. How should the manager handle this situation?

Skill Builder 8–2
Unneeded Overtime

Irwin Bates is 53 years old and works as an installer for Midland Telephone Company. His three children are married, and his modest 1,000-square-foot home is almost paid for. His wife, Edna, enjoys working part-time in a small fabric shop. Irwin is an avid outdoorsman. He and his group of five or six buddies spend many weekend mornings at a nearby recreation area hunting or fishing. In fact, this coming Saturday is the opening day of deer season.

Do you think Irwin's supervisor will have much luck getting Irwin to work overtime this Saturday morning at time-and-a-half pay? Such overtime work is strictly voluntary and not required of Irwin. Assume that you are his supervisor. What motivational appeals would you use in trying to persuade him to work on Saturday?

Skill Builder 8–3
Distinguishing Motivators from Hygiene Factors

The items listed on the following page represent ways in which organizations attempt to meet employees' needs and increase organizational effectiveness. Using Herzberg's theory, identify which factors are motivators and which are hygiene factors.

Factor	Motivator	Hygiene Factor
Raises based on performance	_____	_____
Company-sponsored supervisors' club	_____	_____
Suggestion system with monetary rewards for cost-saving ideas	_____	_____
Pensions	_____	_____
Promotions	_____	_____
Company newsletter	_____	_____

Skill Builder 8–4
Changing the Demotivating Environment

Divide the class into teams of six or seven. Their assignment is to reread the opening case and assume they are the ad hoc task force that will recommend a more motivating pay and reward system. Each team will present their recommendations to the class, and through class discussion, the best ideas will be combined for a recommended pay and reward system.

School Teacher Bonuses: Motivators or Demotivators?

Assume that you have been called in as consultant by the president of the Harris County school board. He has asked you (or your group) to evaluate a bonus plan that the school board is considering initiating this year. He has also stated that if the proposed plan has too many problems, he would like you (or your group) to recommend an alternative bonus and/or pay plan.

The president indicates that the board was impressed with the recommendations of the National Commission on Excellence in Education. They were specifically impressed with the conclusion that "performance-based" teacher salaries were among the ways to push back the "rising tide of mediocrity" threatening U.S. education.

The board is considering paying $1,000 bonuses to 25 of its 233 teachers. Principals and department heads would select the 25 meritorious teachers who would serve as role models for the other teachers. The plan calls for the 25 teachers selected to have their names and pictures published in the local paper.

Some additional information:

- Teachers' salaries average $26,000/year.
- Starting pay begins at $20,000/year.
- Pay raises in the past have been primarily across-the-board increases.
- This year the proposed across-the-board increase is 5 percent.

Instructions:
1. Develop a profile of strong points and weak points of the proposed bonus system.
2. Write a report to the president of the school board stating whether or not you endorse the plan and why. If you do not endorse the plan, what do you recommend in its place?

Source: Adapted from L. C. Megginson, D. C. Mosley, P. H. Pietri, Jr., *Management: Concepts and Applications* (New York: HarperCollins, 4th ed.), 1992, p. 446.

Skill-Development Scenario
Motivation

Ken Foley is production development supervisor for Carson Products. Members of the department have been working significant amounts of overtime to complete some important projects. In the first part of the video, Foley's behavior makes the hours seem even longer than they really are.

Answer the following questions:
1. Using specific examples, describe how Foley's attitudes and methods are affecting the productivity and motivation of his staff members. What suggestions would you have for Foley?
2. After viewing the second part of this video, discuss how Foley motivated his employees to work extra hours and remain focused on doing a good job.

Chapter 9
Leadership

Case 9

Kenny: An Effective Supervisor

The most effective supervisor encountered by one of the authors of this textbook was named Kenny, and he was maintenance supervisor in a chemical plant of an international corporation.* The author was called in as a consultant[1] because the plant was suffering from the results of the ineffective, autocratic leadership of a former plant manager. Such leadership at the top had adversely affected all levels, resulting in low morale and losses from plant operations.

In gathering data about the plant through interviews, questionnaires, and observations, the consultant discovered that one maintenance crew, unlike the rest of the departments in the plant, had very high morale and productivity. Kenny was its supervisor.

In the interview with Kenny, the consultant discovered that Kenny was a young man in his early thirties who had a two-year associate degree from a community college. The consultant was impressed with his positive attitude, especially in view of the overall low plant morale and productivity. Kenny said that the plant was one of the finest places he'd ever worked in and that the maintenance people had more know-how than any other group he had been associated with. Kenny's perception of his crew was that they did twice as much work as other crews, that everyone worked together, and that participative management did work with them.

One thing the consultant was curious about was why pressure and criticism from the old, autocratic manager seemed not to have had any effect on Kenny's crew. The crew gave the consultant the answer. They explained that Kenny had the ability to act as a buffer between upper management and the crew. He would get higher management's primary objectives and points across without upsetting his people. As one crew member described it:

> **The maintenance supervisors will come back from a "donkey barbecue" session with higher management where they are raising hell about shoddy work, taking too long at coffee breaks, etc. Other supervisors are shook up for a week and give their staff hell. But Kenny is cool, calm, and collected. He will call us together and report that nine items were discussed at the meeting, including shoddy work, but that doesn't apply to our crew. Then he will cover the two or three items that are relevant to our getting the job done.**

Unfortunately, Kenny did have a real concern at the time of the consultant's interview. He was being transferred from the highest-producing crew to the lowest-producing one. In fact, the latter was known as the "Hell's Angels" crew. The crew members were a renegade group who were constantly fighting with production people as well as with one another. The previous supervisor had been terminated because he could not cope with them. In the course of this chapter, we will return to Kenny and what happened with the renegade crew.

*The company would not permit use of its name.

LEARNING OBJECTIVES
After reading and studying this chapter, you should be able to:

1 Describe factors that affect the leadership style used.

2 Discuss and explain two frequently used leadership models.

3 Determine which leadership style is most appropriate in different situations.

4 Contrast transformational leadership with transactional leadership.

5 Discuss how to inspire self-confidence, develop people, and increase productivity.

Chapter 10
Team Building and Managing Change

Tsoi/Kobus & Associates: The Move Toward Empowerment and Participative Teamwork

This case is about change and journey toward empowerment and the shift toward a participative management system. It is much easier to start such a journey when things are not going well and danger signals are appearing in the form of declining profits, sales, etc. An organization with declining profits is willing to initiate changes in the operation. But for the architectural firm in this case, the journey began when things were going well and end results were quite robust. As this case reveals, such a journey takes effort and time and requires courage and perseverance on the part of key leaders and supervisors.

Tsoi/Kobus & Associates (TK&A) was founded in 1983 by Edward Tsoi and Richard Kobus. Since that time, the firm has expanded from a group of six people to a staff of 86 full-time employees. This growth reflects the success of the firm during a period of slow growth and even downsizing by a number of architectural firms. The catalyst for this success has been the dynamic leadership, vision, and business acumen of the two principals, Tsoi and Kobus.

Edward Tsoi is a graduate of Massachusetts Institute of Technology, and Richard Kobus graduated from Harvard University. The management of the firm consists of the two principals and nine associates. Some of the focus and philosophy of this group is stated in the firm's customer brochure:

We are committed to two very simple objectives as a design firm: excellence in design and the highest level of comprehensive professional services to our clients.

TK&A's principals contacted one of the authors of this text about facilitating a retreat involving the firm's management team (principals and associates). On past retreats the management team had experienced difficulty completing the agenda.

The author accepted the assignment with enthusiasm—to work with a professional group noted for individual creativity and expression in design would be interesting. Would the group respond favorably or negatively to a participative/team approach? Were the two successful entrepreneurs (principals) ready to share power and leadership with the associates?

In preparation for the retreat, the consultant (author) held conversations with the two principals and was sent a list of associates' issues/questions to be addressed at the retreat. The list covered four pages and focused on three major areas—process, office organization and staffing, and TK&A's position in the marketplace. For example, in the process area, a sample issue was the perception among the staff that the office operated like two separate offices. This caused the associates to raise the following questions: Does this perception contribute to a sense of division rather than unity? Do the natural differences in Ed's and Rick's working styles create any real problems within the office? What roles do the principals, associates,

LEARNING OBJECTIVES
After reading and studying this chapter, you should be able to:

1
Define what a team is.

2
Identify what participative management is and is not.

3
Compare and contrast command-and-control (heroic) leaders with team leaders.

4
Discuss the characteristics of effective team building.

5
Identify stages of team development.

6
Identify what's involved in shifting from an autocratic system to a participative system.

7
Identify the reasons employees resist change and understand ways to overcome resistance to change.

8
Discuss ways in which a team leader can effectively manage the boss.

Skill-Development Scenario
Team Leadership and Empowerment

Tony Roberts is a newly appointed supervisor of the accounting department at Lexicon Dynamics. He has years of experience as a staff accountant but none with the job of supervisor.

Answer the following questions:
1. Roberts' inexperience and attitude may be damaging the motivation of his team members. What specific examples of alienation did you see in the first part of the video?
2. After viewing the second part of this video, discuss how Roberts improves motivation by using different leadership styles with different employees. What evidence did you see of empowerment, and what was its effect on the team?

Hans Higgins was caught flat-footed by his crew's lack of progress on the machine-overhaul job. Like Hans, many supervisors are taken by surprise when their plans blow up. It was crucial to complete the overhaul by 5 p.m. If Hans had used the principles of controlling, which will be discussed in this chapter, the job would likely have been completed as scheduled and he would not be confronting his present crisis.

In this chapter we will give you a broad overview of what is involved in the control function. Chapter 12 will examine some specific areas of control that are crucial for supervisors.

WHAT IS CONTROL?

Learning Objective 1

Define control and explain how it relates to planning.

Have you ever been driving a car on a trip and had one of the dashboard warning lights come on? Perhaps it was the oil pressure or temperature light. Basically, the light indicates that something is amiss. Without such a warning system, you would be caught by surprise when the car broke down, perhaps leaving you stranded far from home.

Managers and supervisors are often in a similar quandary! They go along not knowing whether things are as they should be or not. Unfortunately, many of them find that things are *not* as they should be only when it is too late to do anything about it. They do not have the advantage of periodic feedback or warning lights to tell them if they are on track. You might think of control as consisting of performance markers that tell you whether your unit's performance is moving in the right direction.

In Chapter 1, we defined *controlling* as the management function that involves comparing actual performance with planned performance and taking corrective action, if needed, to ensure that objectives are achieved. Basically, control has three phases: (1) foreseeing the things that could go wrong and taking preventive measures, (2) monitoring or measuring performance in some way, to compare what *is* happening with what *should* be happening, and (3) correcting performance problems that occur, which is the therapeutic aspect of control.

Control's Close Links to Planning

In Chapter 1, we also indicated that planning and controlling might be thought of as Siamese twins because they are so closely related. Planning "sets the ship's course," and controlling "keeps it on course." When a ship begins to veer off course, the navigator notices this and recommends a new heading designed to return the ship to its proper course. That's how supervisory control works. You set goals and seek information on whether they are being reached as planned. If not, you make the adjustments necessary to achieve your goals.

Thus, controlling may be thought of as the process that supervisors use to help accomplish their plans. Hans' plan was for his department to have the machine on line at a certain time. Poor control resulted in failure to achieve this goal.

make meaningful comparisons to operations standards. As wi[...]
information can be worse than too little.

5. *Controls should be accepted by people they affect.* Controls and [...]
specific situations should be communicated clearly to those r[...]
menting them and to those who will be controlled by them.

While all of these characteristics are important, a given con[...]
have all of them in order to do the job for which it is designed.

STEPS IN THE CONTROLLING PROCESS

Learning Objective 3

Discuss the four steps in the controlling process.

The steps in the controlling process are illustrated in Exhibit 1[...]
(4) may require going back to any of the previous three steps [...]
modifying the original standard, changing the frequency and m[...]
performance, or achieving more insight into the possible cause of [...]
examine the details of each of these steps.

Step 1: Establishing Performance Standards

standard A unit of measurement that can serve as a reference point for evaluating results.

The first step of the controlling process is really a planning step. [...]
on something you want to accomplish. As a supervisor, you exerci[...]
paring performance to some standard or goal. A **standard** is a u[...]
that can serve as a reference point for evaluating results. Properly [...]
accepted by employees, standards become the bases for the s[...]
activities.

Learning Objective 4

Identify the different types of standards.

TYPES OF STANDARDS. Standards can be either *tangible* or *intangible*. **Tangible standards** are [...]

tangible standards
Clear, concrete, specific, and generally measurable.

numerical standards
Expressed in numbers.

monetary standards
Expressed in dollars and cents.

physical standards
Refer to quality, durability, size, weight.

time standards Expressed in terms of time.

quite clear, concrete, specific, and generally measurable. For instan[...]
"I want the machine on line by 3 p.m.," the goal is very specific an[...]
the machine is on line at 3 p.m. or it is not.

Tangible standards can be further categorized as numerical, mo[...]
time-related. **Numerical standards** are expressed in numbers, such a[...]
produced, number of absences, percentage of successful sales ca[...]
personnel who successfully complete training. **Monetary standard[...]
dollars and cents. Examples of monetary standards are predetermin[...]
payroll costs, scrap costs, and maintenance costs. **Physical standar[...]
durability, size, weight, and other factors related to physical co[...]
standards refer to the speed with which the job should be done. [...]
standards include printing deadlines, scheduled project completio[...]
of production.

Importance of Controls

Perhaps you have heard the old adage: "Things never go as planned." That is a primary reason supervisors need to perform the controlling function effectively. Control is important in view of the many variables that can put things off track. Murphy's Laws (some of which are listed in Exhibit 11–1) seem to operate everywhere. Because anything involving humans is imperfect, supervisors must use control to monitor progress and to make intelligent adjustments as required.

Examples of Controls

We live in a world of controls. Circuit breakers in our homes and offices are examples of controls. When an electrical overload occurs, the system adjusts by shutting itself down. Security alarm systems send out signals when a protected area is violated. As mentioned earlier, the dashboard in your car contains numerous controls to warn you when something is not the way it is supposed to be—low oil pressure, overheated engine, alternator malfunction, keys left in car, seat belt not on, and so on. Exhibit 11–2 illustrates a number of other common examples of control.

SELF-CHECK

Here are four examples of poor control found in Case 11. Can you find others?

1. Hans should have checked several days before starting the job to make sure that the pump and other needed parts were on hand.
2. Since the job was an important one, Hans should have checked his crew's progress sooner.
3. If ordered parts were not delivered on time, follow-up should have been swifter.
4. Hans should have been notified that a key employee had left the job site, leaving his crew understaffed.

Exhibit 11–1
Murphy's Laws

- Left to themselves, things always go from bad to worse.
- There's never time to do it right, but always time to do it over.
- If anything can go wrong, it will.
- Of the things that can go wrong, the one that will is that which is capable of the most possible damage.
- If you think nothing can go wrong, you have obviously overlooked something.
- Of those things that "cannot" go wrong, the most unlikely one is that which will.
- Inside every large problem are many small problems struggling to get out.
- Any object will fall so that it lands in the one spot where it is capable of doing the most damage.

- At the end of the workday, a production supervisor spends 30 minutes examining a printo[...] employee's output, quality, and scrap. The supervisor notes those employees whose perfo[...] par and makes plans to discuss their performance with them the next day.
- A nursing supervisor studies a survey completed by all patients who were housed in her w[...] months. The survey lists items such as nurses' friendliness, professionalism, appearance, [...] other factors related to job performance.
- A maintenance supervisor tours the building, examining the progress of each worker or w[...]
- After a college football game, the head defensive coach views the game films several time[...] performance grades to each defensive player. Grades below 60 reflect areas to which the [...] special attention during upcoming practices.

Exhibit 11–2
Some Common Examples of Supervisory Control

CHARACTERISTICS OF EFFECTIVE CONTROL SYSTEMS

Learning Objective 2
Discuss the characteristics of effective controls.

To be effective, a control system must have certain characteris[...] following are the most important.[1]

1. *Controls need to focus on appropriate activities.* Effective c[...] critical factors that affect both the individual's and the org[...] achieve objectives. These critical objectives should include[...] production and personnel activities, as well as related costs. [...]
2. *Controls should be timely.* Information needed for compari[...] poses needs to be in a supervisor's hands in order for him [...] corrective action. Therefore, delays in generating, gather[...] information can prolong the occurrence—and extent—of d[...]
3. *Controls must be cost-effective.* The benefits controls provide[...] costs of installation and operation. Too much control can b[...] The key is that controls should be appropriate to the nee[...] greater than the costs involved. An example of this need[...] Senator William Cohen of Maine in the following statemen[...]

> The U.S. Department of Defense could save millions of [...] it revamped regulations covering employee travel voucher[...] the Pentagon has created to protect itself against travel wa[...] equivalent of assigning an armored division to guard an ATM[...] precautions cost more than the potential loss.[2]

4. *Controls should be accurate and concise.* Controls must provi[...] operations and people in sufficient quality and quantity to[...]

Exhibit 11–3
The Process of Control

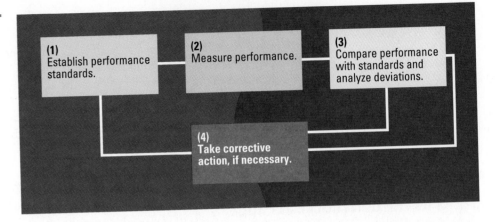

SELF-CHECK   In Case 11, what standards were involved in the machine-overhaul job?

Note that there may be some overlap among the types of tangible standards. For instance, when you say, "I want the machine on line by 3 p.m.," you have obviously communicated a time standard, but the standard is expressed numerically. Monetary standards are also expressed numerically, as are some physical standards.

In contrast to tangible standards, **intangible standards** are not expressed in terms of numbers, money, physical qualities, or time, because they relate to human characteristics that are difficult to measure. Examples of intangible standards are a desirable attitude, high morale, ethics, and cooperation (see Exhibit 11–4). Intangible standards pose special challenges to the supervisor, as the following example illustrates.

intangible standards
Are not expressed in terms of numbers, money, physical qualities, or time.

> **Supervisor Maude Leyden of the State Employment Office overheard one of her newer employment counselors, David Hoffman, berating a job applicant. The tone of his voice was domineering, as though he were scolding a child, although the applicant was perhaps 30 years his senior. She heard David conclude the interview with the words, "Now don't come back here and bother us again until you've had someone fill this form out properly. That's not what I'm paid to do!"**
>
> **After the applicant left, Maude listened to David's explanation of what had just happened. He said he'd been under a lot of pressure that day and had grown very impatient, and he acknowledged his rudeness toward the applicant. Maude told him that he had not handled himself in a professional manner and discussed what he should have done differently. Later in the day, David was to call the applicant, apologize, and offer to be of further help.**
>
> **He did call and apologize.**

It is much more difficult to clearly explain an intangible standard, such as "interviewers must observe standards of professional conduct with clients," than to tell someone that the standard is "to service six malfunctioning computer systems each day." Just what *is* professional conduct? Is it patience, friendliness, courtesy, keeping a

AT&T Universal Card's customer service representatives are monitored against time standards—how quickly they answer the telephones and how long they stay on the line with customers.

Exhibit 11–4
Controlling Intangible Standards

Certain types of jobs, such as maintenance, personnel, and sales, don't lend themselves to frequent measurement of progress. Measurement takes time, unless an automated system is in place. Moreover, some jobs are more crucial to monitor effectively. For example, the work of an emergency room nurse requires more careful monitoring than does the work of a sales representative or a clerical worker.

SELF-CHECK   Notice in Case 11 that supervisor Hans Higgins had not given much thought to establishing any strategic control points on the machine-overhaul job. What key control points would you recommend? If these had been established, do you think the job would have gone awry?

HOW TO MEASURE. There are several basic ways for a supervisor to measure performance. These are:

1. Personal observation.
2. Written or oral reports by or about employees.
3. Automatic methods.
4. Inspections, tests, or samples.

Exhibit 11–7 is an example of the second method, which could be used frequently, at very little cost. Notice how specifically the information requested is stated.

SELF-CHECK   In Case 11, supervisor Hans Higgins used personal observations as the control technique. Might he have used any other methods? Which ones? Why?

In some jobs, supervisors and their employees work in the same area. The supervisor can easily move among the workers, observing their performance. In other departments, however, the supervisor may have workers spread out in various locations, which makes direct observation impractical. Consider a sanitation supervisor whose eight work crews collect garbage on various routes throughout the city. Such a supervisor must depend on written or oral reports or occasional inspections as the primary means of measurement. Here is what one sanitation supervisor said:

> **How do I know if my crews are doing the job properly? Mainly by the complaints I get from customers. Complaints range from garbage that isn't picked up on schedule to overturned trash cans, surrounded with litter. That's how I know what's going on directly in the field. Sometimes I will drive around and make an occasional inspection. We also annually survey residents to see if our people are considered timely, friendly, and efficient.**

Sales supervisors may seldom see their employees if the sales work takes them outside the office. As a result, salespersons are required to complete reports about

Exhibit 11–7
Example of a Written Report About an Employee

Management Encourages Your Comments

Date 5/19/9-

Waiter or waitress *Phyllis*

Please circle meal   Breakfast   (Lunch)   Dinner

	Yes	No
1. Were you greeted by host or hostess promptly and courteously?	✓	—
2. Was your server prompt, courteous, and helpful?	✓	—
3. Was the quality of food to your expectations?	—	✓
4. Was the table setting and condition of overall restaurant appearance pleasing and in good taste?	✓	—
5. Will you return to our restaurant?	—	✓
6. Will you recommend our restaurant to your friends and associates?	—	✓

Comments

Food was overcooked, Potatoes were leftovers, Meat was tough, This was my second visit and I brought a friend with me. We were both very disappointed.

Name and address
(if you desire)

Please drop this in our quality improvement box located near the exit.

Thank you and have a good day.

Source: Leon C. Megginson, Donald C. Mosley, and Paul N. Pietri, Jr., *Management: Concepts and Applications,* 3rd ed. (New York: Harper & Row, 1989), p. 417.

number of calls made, sales results, travel expenses, customer comments, and numerous other matters. These reports are received by supervisors or the home office staff. Many salespersons, in fact, complain that they are required to do too much paperwork!

Supervisors who are not in frequent contact with their employees must come up with some meaningful, valid way to measure results. They need to find some means of making sure the measurements are reliable. Because of pressures to conform to standards, employees may attempt to falsify reports to make themselves appear better.

Preventive controls are key to limiting workers' compensation claims. As part of its accident-prevention program, Mid-Atlantic Packaging enables employees to load pallets of cardboard boxes without bending or lifting.

exceptional. The key idea is to set priorities for activities, depending on their importance, and to focus your efforts on top-priority items. Management by exception works essentially the same way. Your attention should be focused on exceptional, rather than routine, problems.

SELF-CHECK

Suppose you are a sales supervisor and your departmental sales goal is 800 units weekly (or 3,200 units monthly). Each of your eight sales representatives, then, has a goal of 100 units weekly (or 400 units monthly). At the end of the first week, your sales results are as follows:

Salesperson	Weekly Goal	Units Sold
A	100	105
B	100	95
C	100	90
D	100	102
E	100	102
F	100	88
G	100	98
H	100	115
Total =	800	795

What corrective action will you take?

Managers who practice management by exception might do absolutely nothing about the previous situation. "But wait!" you say. "Look at Salesperson C, who performed 10 percent below standard, and Salesperson F, who was 12 percent below standard. Shouldn't a supervisor do something about these two employees?"

Of course, a supervisor should be aware of these deviations. However, recall that only the first week has gone by. It is probably fairly normal to find such variances in a single week; the more pertinent information is how performance compares to the monthly benchmark of 3,200 units. With three weeks to go, the supervisor who gets too upset after Week 1 may be overreacting. Naturally, the supervisor should keep an eye on sales data in the upcoming weeks to seek whether Salespersons C and F improve their performances. In this situation, the assumption of management by exception is that Salespersons B, C, F, and G realize that they are below standard and will be working to improve.

SELF-CHECK

Suppose that at the end of the second week, sales results are as shown:

Salesperson	Weekly Goal	Week 1	Week 2
A	100	105	107
B	100	95	101
C	100	90	97
D	100	102	101
E	100	102	101
F	100	88	84
G	100	98	99
H	100	115	126
Total =	800	795	816

What will you do now?

Sales have perked up, and, with the exception of Salesperson F, everyone is in reasonable shape. As supervisor, you'd be justified in entering the control process with Salesperson F, as the red flag is still up on this one. You may want to discuss this person's results, try to identify actions that produce below-standard results, and develop a plan of corrective action.

Note that Salesperson H has been setting the standards on fire, averaging more than 20 percent *above* standard the first two weeks. This performance is also an exceptional departure from standard. What is behind these results? Is Salesperson H using some techniques that will work for others? Is this person's territory so choice that it becomes easy to make the standard? Should you modify the standard for Salesperson H? Management by exception can be applied to both favorable and unfavorable deviations from standard.

UNIONS. Perhaps, like many others, you believe unions to be the primary culprit in the productivity decline in the United States. We read and hear about many cases in which unions resist improved technology and new work methods, protect jobs that are considered nonproductive, and generally oppose labor-saving techniques and efficiencies. Few experts, however, place primary blame for the productivity decline on unions. If anything, unions have been losing rather than gaining influence in recent years. Many industries with little, if any, union strength—such as agriculture, wholesale trade, and retail trade—have suffered productivity declines similar to those of the more traditionally unionized industries. Although they shoulder some of the blame, unions certainly do not seem to be the major problem.

So then, who is to blame? In all probability, each of these groups has played a part in the productivity decline. Many experts, however, point the finger most strongly at management, which they say has been far too conservative and unwilling to change its ways to enhance productivity.

Unleashing the creative forces of rank-and-file employees is one of the recently discovered keys to productivity improvement. These techniques will be discussed later in the chapter.

The Supervisor's Role in Improving Productivity

Learning Objective 3

Describe some steps that supervisors can take to increase productivity.

Regardless of who is to blame, supervisory management plays an important role in improving productivity. But how do you do it? Suppose that your department has 20 employees who produced a total of 10,000 units last year. Under your plant manager's new mandate, you must increase production to 11,500 units. How would you go about this? You could do some of the things listed in Exhibit 12–3, many of which have already been discussed elsewhere in this text.

Exhibit 12–3
How Supervisors Can Improve Employee Productivity

- Train employees. Can their abilities be upgraded?
- Clearly communicate the need for high standards so that workers understand what is expected of them.
- Use motivation techniques to inspire workers to increase output. Pride, ego, and security are several important motivators available.
- Eliminate idleness, extended breaks, and early quitting time.
- Build in quality the first time work is done. Productivity is lost when items are scrapped or need to be reworked to be salvaged.
- Work on improving attendance and turnover in your work group.
- Reduce accidents. Accidents normally result in time lost to investigations, meetings, and reports—even if the employee does not suffer a lost-work-time injury.
- Seek to improve production measures. Will process or work-flow improvements help?
- Try to eliminate or reduce equipment or machinery breakdowns. Preventive maintenance is important.
- Exercise good control techniques. Follow up on performance and take corrective action promptly.
- Involve your employees in the process of improvement. Select their ideas and suggestions for improvement. Form special productivity improvement teams.

The Supervisor's Role in Cost Control

As we pointed out earlier, the productivity of a department is based on its total outputs and total inputs. Upper management is cost-conscious because costs represent major inputs. Supervisors direct the operating work of an organization; thus, they have a key role in controlling a firm's cost in labor hours and efficiency, maintenance of machinery and equipment, supplies, energy, and other matters.

Budgets are one aid that can help supervisors to control costs. Different budgets are normally prepared for sales, production, scrap, equipment, grievances, lost-work-time accidents, and the like. Moreover, they may be set for different time periods such as a week, a month, a quarter, or a year. Since a budget reflects expected performance, it becomes a basis for evaluating a department's actual performance (see Exhibit 12–4).

Exhibit 12–4
Performance Report

Name of department	Fabrication	Performance period	November 1996
Budgeted output	15,700 lbs.	**Budgeted scrap**	152 lbs.
Actual output	15,227 lbs.	**Actual scrap**	120 lbs.
Variance	−473 lbs.		+32 lbs.

Item	Actual	Budgeted	Variance
Direct labor	$32,000	$32,000	$ 0
Overtime	1,500	1,000	−500
Supplies	500	385	−115
Maintenance and repairs	4,250	3,000	−1,250
Utilities	1,300	1,200	−100
Scrapped material	1,200	1,520	+320
Total	$40,750	$39,105	−$1,645

SELF-CHECK

Assume that you are supervisor of the fabrication department in Exhibit 12–4. If you were really trying to tighten up costs, which activities in your department would you focus on? Why?

Note in Exhibit 12–4 that the supervisor's department has performed well in some cost areas and not so well in others. Output is off by 473 pounds, overtime is 50 percent higher than budgeted, and maintenance and repairs are also over budget. On the plus side, the department has been efficient in using raw materials.

Understanding Variance in Controlling Quality

Learning Objective 5

Describe the role of variance in controlling quality.

Every product and service is the output or result of a process. You might consider a process to be a set of related activities designed to accomplish a goal. The nature of processes is to exhibit variation; for example, items produced in a machining or manufacturing process are not all exactly alike. Some measurable dimensions, such as length, diameter, or weight will vary. These variations may be quite small and imperceivable by the naked eye, but sophisticated gauges or test equipment will reveal these differences. Similarly, service processes are also subject to variation. Fast food customers wait different periods of time before being served. Some luggage checked in on a commercial airline will not arrive with its owner. At a steakhouse, there is considerable variation among steaks prepared as "rare."

Two types of variation exist: common cause and special cause. Let's use a classic example to illustrate process variation: writing. Note the variations of handwritten letters below, though each one was carefully written by the same author.

You needn't use a magnifying glass to note that differences exist. The differences in each "P" are normal and to be expected. This we call *common cause variation*. Now look at the "a's." Note that the middle one is clearly different from the others. Perhaps the writer was bumped, or the paper quality in that one spot was different, or a different pen was used. (Actually, it was made by the same writer but using the other hand.) The variation is not routine or expected; clearly there was excessive variation, or *special cause variation*. Common cause variation is a general, routine variation that is built into the system. Special cause variation occurs intermittently and is associated with a specific event.

Effective control of quality can have two focuses: (1) reducing common cause variation and (2) reducing special cause variation. As Deming and other quality experts note, special causes can sometimes be addressed by individual workers, but common causes can ordinarily only be corrected through management action to improve the process. This might include such things as upgrading raw materials, using more sophisticated equipment, additional training, and so on. Importantly, much of the effort by organizations to seek continuous quality improvement is aimed at reducing common cause variation by improving processes.

Reducing special cause variation entails identifying the problem, isolating it, examining the cause and remedying it. This might mean, for instance, replacing an erratic piece of equipment, reassigning an employee who cannot keep pace with job demands, or reassigning personnel to handle peak customer demand periods. As a supervisor, it is important to understand variation and the extent to which different levels of quality performance can be attributed to normal or special cause variables. Statistical sampling is one useful tool for doing so, but is beyond our scope here. However, we will examine some other important tools.

Some Tools of Quality

Identify some important tools in managing quality.

A number of tools are available to assist in effective control of quality. Often, these are used by individuals who are part of special problem-solving or quality-improvement teams. Among the tools discussed here are flowcharts, histograms, run charts, Pareto charts, control charts, and fishbone diagrams. Keep in mind that these tools apply not just to quality of manufacturing processes (although this is perhaps the most common application), but to service processes as well.

FLOWCHART. A **flowchart** is a visual representation of the sequence of steps needed to complete a process. Its purpose is to help individuals understand the process with which they are involved. Flowcharts are frequently used by problem-solving teams to address quality issues involving processes with a number of sequential steps to complete (see Exhibit 12–5). Often such processes cut across departmental lines. The visual representation of the process enables team members to examine the relevant steps and note where improvements can be made, as reflected in the following example:

flowchart Visual representation of the sequence of steps needed to complete a process.

Exhibit 12–5
Flowchart of a Fast-Food, Drive-Thru Process

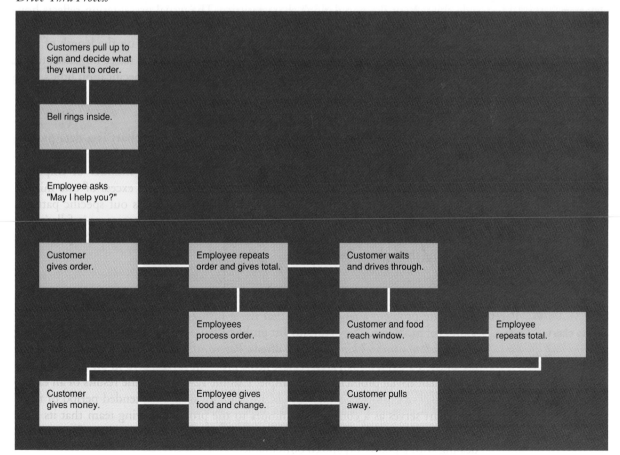

Exhibit 12–14
*Occupational Injury
and Illness Rates:
Selected Industries,
1991*

Industry	Total Cases	Lost Workdays
Mining	7.4	129.6
Food processing	19.5	207.2
Lumber and wood products	16.8	172.0
General building contractors	12.0	132.0
Fabricated metal products	17.4	146.6
Transportation	9.3	140.0
Textile mill products	10.0	88.3
Chemicals and related products	6.4	62.4
Printing and publishing	6.7	74.5
Retail trade	7.7	69.1
Tobacco products	6.4	52.0
Communications	2.8	26.4
Finance, insurance, and real estate	2.4	24.1

Source: U.S. Department of Labor, *Monthly Labor Review,* December 1994, pp. 118–119.

The Supervisor's Role in Promoting Safety

Learning Objective 9

Describe the
supervisor's role in
promoting safety.

Good safety practices among employees help the supervisor in many ways. For one thing, on-the-job injuries can take up much of a supervisor's time as he or she may have to fill out accident reports, attend meetings to investigate the injury, and make recommendations (see Exhibit 12–15). Furthermore, safety is linked to productivity. The work group's productivity suffers when an injured employee is being treated or is recovering from an accident. Temporary or full-time replacements must be recruited, selected, and trained, and an inexperienced worker is unlikely to be as productive as the more experienced employee being replaced.

The supervisor, as top management's link with operating employees, plays a crucial role in employee safety. He or she is accountable for safety, just as for output or quality. Good safety control by the supervisor begins with a positive attitude.

"Safety is very important around here and especially in my work unit," said Vera Edwards, a machine tender for Supreme Manufacturing. "When you drive into the parking lot, a large sign shows our company's safety record for the week and the year. Our supervisor is always talking safety, we have safety meetings monthly, and there are posters and signs throughout the work area. Our supervisor also makes us toe the line in following safety rules. He can really be tough on you when

Exhibit 12–15
*Personal Injury
Investigation*

Injured:	Fred Hanna
Position:	Lab Assistant
Presiding:	L. C. Smithson, Technical Supt.
Date of meeting:	4/15/96
Time of meeting:	2:34 P.M.
Place of meeting:	Plant Conference Room
Present:	L. C. Smithson (Technical Supt.), Fred Hanna (injured), Jim Berry (Housekeeping), Tom Ahens (Safety Director), Kim Jernigan (Supervisor)
Nature of injury:	Fractured distal end of radius, right arm
Lost time:	42 days (estimated)
Accident time and date:	4/13/96 at 7:15 A.M.
Cause of injury:	Floor was wet—appeared to be water. Investigation revealed that bags of Seperan (a synthetic polymer) had been rearranged during the 11 p.m.–7 a.m. shift. One bag was torn, and its contents had trickled onto the floor, causing it to be exceptionally slippery when washed at the end of the shift. Janitor noticed but did not flag it or attempt to remove hazard, as he noted at the end of his shift.

Corrective steps/recommendations:

1. Apply grit to slippery areas; mark with appropriate warning signs.
2. Remind incoming shift personnel of hazardous conditions.
3. Communicate to incoming shift personnel any job priorities.
4. Store Seperan in a more remote area of the plant.

he catches you bending a rule such as not using your goggles or failing to put on your machine guard."

Exhibit 12–16 shows a number of steps that supervisors can take to improve safety performance in their departments. Even though supervisors play a critical role in controlling safety, they cannot do it alone. Top management must be committed to factors such as proper plant layout and design, safe machinery and equipment, and good physical working conditions.

- Push for upgraded safety equipment and safer work methods.
- Establish and communicate safety goals for the department.
- Clearly communicate safety requirements to all employees.
- Listen to employee job complaints about safety-related matters, including noise, fatigue, and working conditions.
- Make sure new employees thoroughly understand equipment and safety rules.
- Prohibit use of unsafe or damaged equipment.
- Encourage safety suggestions from your workers.
- Post safety bulletins, slogans, and posters to reinforce the need for safety.
- Refuse to let rush jobs cause relaxed safety standards.
- Set a proper example. Don't bend safety rules yourself.
- Conduct periodic safety meetings, with demonstrations by employee safety specialists or insurance representatives.
- Refuse to tolerate horseplay.
- Compete with other departments in safety contests.
- Report to employees any accidents that occur elsewhere in the company.
- Review past accident records for trends and insights.
- Encourage reporting of unsafe conditions.
- Make regular safety inspections of all major equipment.
- Enforce the rules when they are broken—take appropriate disciplinary action to demonstrate your safety commitment.
- Look for signs of fatigue in employees, such as massaging shoulders, rubbing eyes, and stretching or shifting position to relieve pain or fatigue. In such a case, relief for the employee may be warranted.
- Thoroughly investigate all accidents and attempt to remedy the causes.
- Develop a system for rewarding or acknowledging excellent safety conduct.

Exhibit 12–16
*What Supervisors Can
Do to Improve Safety*

Chapter Review

Explain the concept of productivity.

Productivity is a measure of outputs compared to inputs. Companywide, it refers to the total value of the units or services a company produced as compared to the total cost of producing them. Productivity can be increased by increasing output with the same input, decreasing input and maintaining the same output, or increasing output while decreasing input.

Identify causes of the declining productivity growth rate in the United States.

The federal government's measure of productivity is based on the ratio of total output to total labor hours input by the nation's industrial and business firms. The United States has the highest productivity per labor hour in the world. However, the rate of increase in U.S. productivity has been declining yearly until recently. Among the causes of this decline were the unwillingness of industry to invest in upgraded equipment; federal and state government regulations requiring increased capital spending on environmental and health and safety issues rather than productivity; and workforce characteristics such as a changed work ethic.

Learning Objective 3

Describe some steps that supervisors can take to increase productivity.

Actions that supervisors can take to increase productivity include upgrading workers' skills through training, improving worker motivation, using machinery and equipment better, improving quality, and preventing accidents.

Cost control is an important measure of a supervisor's productivity. One helpful device is a budget, which shows expected outcome for a given period expressed in numbers. Robotics, just-in-time inventory systems (JIT), and computer-assisted manufacturing (CAM) are three recent productivity enhancement measures.

Learning Objective 4

Differentiate between quality assurance and quality control.

A second major area discussed in this chapter was quality. Quality assurance (total quality management or TQM) is the entire system of policies, procedures, and guidelines an organization institutes so as to attain and maintain quality. Quality control, on the other hand, consists of after-the-fact measurements to see if quality standards are actually being met.

Learning Objective 5

Describe the role of variance in controlling quality.

It is important for supervisors to understand the concept of variance as it relates to measurement of quality. Common cause variance is built into processes and is "normal."

Learning Objective 6

Identify some important tools in managing quality.

Special cause variance is nonroutine and occurs intermittently. Among the tools of quality are flowcharts, histograms, run charts, Pareto charts, cause-and-effect diagrams, and control charts.

Learning Objective 7

Describe how employee involvement programs function.

Two important ways supervisors can improve quality are (1) to communicate their high quality expectations and standards and (2) to involve workers in helping improve the quality process. Employee involvement teams are an effective way to enlist employees in improving quality.

Learning Objective 8

Explain what the Occupational Safety and Health Administration (OSHA) does.

Employee safety has become important to organizations in recent years, especially since the passage of the Occupational Safety and Health Act in 1970. The Occupational Safety and Health Administration, charged with enforcing compliance with the law, sets standards and regulations, requires organizations to maintain safety logs and records, conducts inspections, and has the authority to issue citations and penalties for violations found. Generally, the smallest and the largest organizations are the safest places to work. The nature of some industries makes them much more likely than others to have high injury incidence rates.

Learning Objective 9

Describe the supervisor's role in promoting safety.

The supervisor can be active in controlling safety in a number of ways. Among these are clearly communicating safety standards, emphasizing the importance of safety through meetings, identifying and fixing unsafe equipment or conditions, and taking corrective action when safety rules are violated.

representatives and routed to other individuals as appropriate. A number of customers had complained about long waits when calling for service. A market research study found that customers became irritated if the call was not answered within five rings. Scott Welz, the company president, authorized the customer service department manager, Tim Nagy, to study the problem and find a method to shorten the call-waiting time. Tim met with his service representatives, Robin Coder, Raul Venegas, LaMarr Jones, Mark Staley, and Nancy Shipe, who answered the calls, to attempt to determine the reasons for long waiting times. The following conversation ensued:

Nagy: This is a serious problem. How a customer phone inquiry is answered is the first impression the customer receives from us. As you know, this company was founded on efficient and friendly service to all our customers. It's obvious why customers have to wait: You're on the phone with another customer. Can you think of any reasons that might keep you on the phone for an unnecessarily long time?

Coder: I've noticed quite often that the person to whom I need to route the call is not present. It takes time to transfer the call and to see if it is answered. If the person is not there, I end up apologizing and transferring the call to another extension.

Nagy: You're right, Robin. Sales personnel often are out of the office on sales calls, away on trips to preview new products, or away from their desks for a variety of reasons. What else might cause this problem?

Venegas: I get irritated at customers who spend a great deal of time complaining about a problem that I cannot do anything about except refer to someone else. Of course, I listen and sympathize with them, but this eats up a lot of time.

Jones: Some customers call so often, they think we're long lost friends and strike up a personal conversation.

Nagy: That's not always a bad thing, you realize.

Jones: Sure, but it delays my answering other calls.

Shipe: It's not always the customer's fault. During lunch, we're not all available to answer the phone.

Venegas: Right after we open at 9 a.m., we get a rush of calls. I think that many of the delays are caused by these peak periods.

Coder: I've noticed the same thing between 4 and 5 p.m.

Nagy: I've had a few comments from department managers who received calls that didn't fall in their areas of responsibility and had to be transferred again.

Staley: But that doesn't cause delays at our end.

Shipe: That's right, Mark, but I just realized that sometimes I simply don't understand what the customer's problem really is. I spend a lot of time trying to get him or her to explain it better. Often, I have to route it to someone because other calls are waiting.

Venegas: Perhaps we need to have more knowledge of our products.

Nagy: Well, I think we've covered most of the major reasons why many customers have to wait. It seems to me that we have four major reasons: the phones are short-staffed, the receiving party is not present, the customer dominates the conversation, and you may not understand the customer's problem. Next, we need to collect some information about these possible causes. Raul, can you and Mark set up a data collection sheet that we can use to track some of these things?

The next day, Venegas and Staley produced a sheet that enabled the staff to record the data.

Over the next two weeks the staff collected data on the frequency of reasons why some callers had to wait. The results are summarized as follows:

	Reason	Total Number
A	Operators short-staffed	172
B	Receiving party not present	73
C	Customer dominates conversation	19
D	Lack of operator understanding	61
E	Other reasons	10

Instructions: Form a group of three to five students and based on the conversation between Nagy and his staff,

1. Draw a cause-and-effect diagram.
2. Perform a Pareto analysis of the data collected.
3. Develop some possible actions that the company might take to improve the situation.

Source: Adapted from "The Quest for Higher Quality: The Deming Prize and Quality Control," by RICOH of America, Inc., and presented in James W. Dean and James R. Evans *Total Quality* (Minneapolis/St. Paul: West Publishing Company, 1994), pp. 96–98.

Chapter 13
Coaching for Higher Performance

Case 13

Coaching in Action

Manager: Jeff, thanks for coming. I know you're getting ready for our one-week Supervisory Skills course at the Training Center next week. I see that you've read over the pretraining outline and materials. I always like to meet with participants before and after each course to discuss how I can help you put the skills into operation. Having looked over the outline and read the pre-course materials, what would you most like to get from the course that would help you?

Jeff: Well, one thing I'd like to do better is to delegate tasks. Sometimes I'm too eager to do things myself. I guess it's just hard to let go.

Manager: Being pretty new to supervision, that's not unusual. It's especially a challenge to someone who is a strong technician, as you are.

Jeff: I must admit I could sometimes spend my whole day still interfacing with the departments working out their management information system problems. I'm afraid if you were to ask my technicians, they'd probably say I spend *too* much time still doing that, rather than delegating the challenging jobs to them. I guess it's my insecurity in supervision . . . .

Manager: So, you'd like the delegation session to help overcome some of this insecurity about your technicians . . . .

Jeff: Well, no, I wouldn't say it's so much insecurity about them, as it is about me. I guess I'm insecure about some of them; I mean they're younger and not as experienced. However, my key people are really talented professionals. Some of them know a lot more than I do about phases of our system. I've been doing this for only six months, and sometimes I feel as if I'm getting behind in my own technical expertise, which is to install and debug our systems. It's hard reconciling that. That's why I may assign a job, then follow up on it too closely. They probably see it as a lack of trust, when in fact, it's just my personal need to learn as much as I can to keep my own skills up.

Manager: Oh, I see what you're saying now. You feel as if you're losing some of your technical edge and miss doing the troubleshooting yourself . . . .

Jeff: Yeah, that's pretty much it . . . .

Manager: It seems as if that comes with your first management job. Technical expertise is a big plus, but it can also get in the way of your own employees' development.

Jeff: Yeah, so that's why in looking over the pre-course materials, being able to delegate better was one of the skill areas that jumped at me.

Manager: I think that's an excellent insight, Jeff. Our new culture is shifting to managers and supervisors becoming facilitators and developers and away from being the technical hub of expertise in their own departments. Our job now is to allow our people to run with the ball and help them do it. From what I know of the course, there's a strong emphasis on empowerment and delegation that will help you. Did any other areas particularly interest you? (The discussion continued for another 10–15 minutes.)

INTRODUCTION TO COACHING

Did you ever play an organized sport, such as football, basketball, soccer, or volleyball? Or take individual lessons in piano, karate, or math? In each case you had a coach whose goal was to improve your performance. The essence of supervisory coaching—just as in those situations—is helping individuals become more effective performers. In the case that began this chapter, Jeff's manager is performing coaching—helping Jeff grow and learn new skills as a supervisor. The manager will also perform coaching during the follow-up meeting with Jeff after he returns from the course. That is the objective of this chapter: to help you learn more about coaching and the skills required to perform it effectively.

coaching Supervisors helping individuals to reach their highest levels of performance.

You might think of **coaching** as the interpersonal process that supervisors and managers use to help individuals continually reach their highest levels of performance. It is a personal activity, a one-to-one relationship that starts when a new employee joins the team and continues throughout his or her tenure in the work unit. It may seem that new employees would be the primary focus of supervisory coaching. However, this is no longer true, given today's goals of *continuous* performance improvement. It is the job of supervisors to continually coach individuals to help them achieve increasingly higher levels of performance throughout their careers. As one well-known coaching expert puts it:

> **Coaching is the process by which managers stay in touch with subordinates. All the walking around in the world will not help managers to get the best from their employees unless they are walking around as coaches. Coaching is "eyeball to eyeball" management. Every conversation between managers and employees is potentially a coaching conversation. It is a chance to clarify goals, priorities, and standards of performance. It is a chance to reaffirm and reinforce the group's core values. It is a chance to hear ideas and involve employees in the processes of planning and problem solving.[1]**

Coaching Is Performance-Linked

The focus of coaching conversations is employee performance. The underlying assumption is that through effective coaching, the supervisor can help an employee become an increasingly effective performer, as shown in Exhibit 13–1. If a topic has a

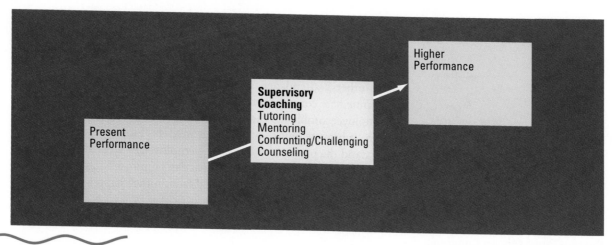

Exhibit 13–1
*Performance-
Linked Coaching*

present or future impact on an employee's performance, then it should be considered suitable for a coaching situation. Some situations are more obviously performance-linked, such as helping an employee learn a new skill or addressing a problem of substandard work. Others are less directly performance-related, such as helping an employee to prepare for advancement or to better understand and overcome insecurities. Notice the wide-reaching range of coaching situations shown in Exhibit 13–2 and how each is in some way performance-linked. Quite a broad list, isn't it?

In the 1940s, a number of large organizations experimented by employing professionals to serve as organizationwide counselors. Their job was not to give advice, but essentially to become the organization's primary vehicle to listen to employees' job-related, personal, and emotional problems. Granted, it helped employees to vent their feelings about job frustrations and conflicts as well as personal problems, but the success of these programs was limited. Today, while a number of large organizations

Exhibit 13–2
*Examples of
Coaching Situations*

- Assigning a new challenging task; reviewing results.
- Determining with an employee his/her training needs.
- Showing an employee how to perform a task.
- Discussing a plan for employee career advancement.
- Listening to an employee's fears of job cutbacks.
- Providing an employee insight into company politics.
- Helping an employee adapt psychologically to job changes.
- Discussing poor employee performance.
- Helping an employee manage stress.
- Discussing how a long-term, excellent employee can reach an even higher performance level.
- Conducting a disciplinary interview.
- Discussing a problem of poor work or failure to follow organization rules/policy.
- Conducting a performance appraisal.
- Allowing an employee to "blow off" some emotional "steam."

employ full-time counselors, it is the individual supervisor who is considered the "first line" of counseling. They are seen by employees as best able to help someone adjust to working conditions, work load and assignments, and employee-supervisor relationships. A team member's problems often affect his or her work performance (as well as the performance of others), attendance, and relationships on the job. Therefore, the supervisor has an immediate concern in these matters and assumes the legitimate role to address such employee problems. Supervisors cannot resolve personal problems such as poor health, substance abuse, or financial matters. However, the supervisor must at least understand the problem and urge the employee to seek adequate help if such a problem has the potential to negatively impact an employee's job performance. The supervisor's role in these situations is discussed later in the chapter.

Current Emphasis on Coaching

Coaching has only recently received recognition as a key supervisory activity. It first appeared in the mid-1970s, gained momentum in the 1980s, and is widely used in organizations today. In Chapter 2 you learned how the supervisor's role has changed from the autocratic, no-nonsense, technically proficient supervisor to a developer of people and a facilitator whose job is to help team members maximize their potential.

Because organizations and work units have become more culturally diverse, managers and supervisors must understand their people as individuals, taking into consideration their needs, competencies, goals, attitudes, insecurities, and concerns. Understanding individuals allows a supervisor to target his or her coaching efforts. In turn, coaching becomes an important vehicle for the supervisor to further his own understanding of his employees. Organizations also recognize that coaching efforts should be tailored to the individual being coached. Coaching directed toward the younger, more insecure employee, who must learn many job essentials, differs dramatically from coaching directed toward the senior employee, who values advancement to the next level.

Why Supervisors Reject Coaching

Coaching appears to be a natural activity; however, in actual practice there is a tendency for supervisors to neglect their coaching role. First, many lack confidence. They may feel uncomfortable counseling employees and embarrassed to discuss problems of substandard performance. There is always the risk that confronting a performance problem with an employee will create more problems than it resolves. The supervisor may have to deal with an employee's excuses, anger, or hurt feelings; the quality of a good relationship may be jeopardized. Ignoring a performance problem in the hope that it will resolve itself is often seen as a more desirable alternative.

Second, many supervisors see coaching as a passive process. They are more inclined through experience, and perhaps the expectation of their own managers, to have ready answers for everyone's problems and to deal with performance matters expeditiously. As one supervisor related in one of our coaching seminars:

All this listening makes coaching seem like a weak, "touchy-feely" approach that's too soft on people. When somebody's not doing his job, you get on his case and he'd better shape up. There's no way I can see myself sitting around saying "Oh, really."

My own boss would think I've lost it. I've always been direct with people—you tell them exactly what they're to do, see that they do it, and get on them when they don't.

We are all products of our past. Our parents told us what to do when we were young, as did our teachers. For those of us with military service experience, platoon leaders took over the telling. Then, when we went to work, our bosses told us what to do. When we become supervisors, it is only natural that we tend to become "tellers," which is an active, expeditious way to handle things.

However, as pointed out throughout this text, today's supervisory environment has changed considerably. The supportive relationship required for effective coaching does indeed involve more open, two-way communication and greater emphasis on the supervisor's listening skills. However, as you will see throughout this chapter, coaching behavior always distinctly addresses continually improving performance.

Third, coaching takes considerable time. Faced by many pressures, supervisors are not prepared to abandon their heroic firefighting pace. Many are so immersed into managing "details" that they cannot effectively employ coaching on the personal, one-to-one level that is required.

THE COACHING FUNCTIONS

Learning Objective 2

Identify the four major coaching functions.

There are different ways to understand effective coaching. One is to examine *why* someone conducts a coaching session, that is, the *function* that coaching intends to serve. Another is to examine what *skills* a coach uses during a coaching session. We will examine the functions first, then the skills. Coaching serves four fundamental functions: (1) tutoring, (2) mentoring, (3) counseling, and (4) confronting/challenging.[2]

Tutoring

tutoring Helps a team member gain knowledge, skill, and competency.

Tutoring involves a large range of coaching situations that help a team member gain knowledge, skill, and competency. Tutoring encourages team members to learn, grow, and develop. The goal is to avoid complacency with present skill levels and to develop a commitment to continuous learning. It also encourages members to put into practice those skills that are learned.

SELF-CHECK

Note in Case 13 that tutoring was the primary function being performed. The manager supported Jeff's attendance at the training course and drew out the major needs that Jeff hoped the course would address. The coach also established a follow-up meeting to review the course and discuss Jeff's plans for implementing the skills learned.

A supervisor's tutoring, one of the four fundamental coaching functions, can encourage an employee to learn and develop skills and to put them in practice.

Mentoring

mentoring Helps develop careers in others.

Mentoring is the coaching activity that helps develop careers in others. Mentoring may teach political savvy, understanding of the organization's culture, and the ways to advance one's career. It may also mean:

1. Helping an employee see the potentially negative impact of behavior he or she is considering.
2. Understanding how to approach and gain influence with powerful organization members.
3. Learning who key players are in given circumstances.
4. Understanding how relevant past or current events should impact the team member's actions and behavior.

Successful supervisory coaches help their team members to make key organizational contacts and to develop their own networks. They aid in giving good career guidance, and they keep a watchful eye out for effective development of their team members' careers.

Confronting/Challenging

confronting/challenging Establishes clear performance standards, compares actual performance against them, and addresses performance that doesn't meet those standards.

The **confronting/challenging** coaching function is most directly performance-related. Supervisory coaches establish clear performance standards, compare actual team member performance against those standards, and address performance that does not meet those standards. Through confronting/challenging, successful coaches help less-than-successful performers become successful and challenge successful ones to reach even higher levels.

Often supervisors, though they may be good, sensitive listeners and effective tutors and mentors, experience difficulty in confronting and challenging team members in the area of performance. They may find it uncomfortable to establish clear, concrete performance standards and to talk about performance directly. They may not be willing to address performance problems when a team member's behavior falls below standard. Confronting/challenging sessions, when finally held, may be superficial, apologetic, and may skirt the poor performance problem. We will discuss confronting/challenging in greater detail later in the chapter.

Counseling

counseling Supervisors helping an individual recognize, talk about, and solve either real or perceived problems that affect performance.

Counseling is the coaching function whereby the supervisor helps an individual recognize, talk about, gain insight into, and solve either real or perceived problems that affect performance. The manager's role is essentially to help the individual determine his or her own course of action. Many supervisors feel inept and poorly trained to deal with employees' personal problems. Perhaps the most common mistake is the tendency to give advice rather than to help the employee think through, understand, and develop alternatives to solving problems.

In conducting counseling, it is especially important to show sensitivity and to help a team member understand how personal problems impact, or potentially impact, job performance. It is also important to help a team member gain confidence in his/her ability to handle problems. In serious cases—such as drug abuse, financial problems, or health issues—this would mean recommending that the individual seek help through the company's employee assistance program or an outside professional.

You can gain more insight into the four coaching functions by examining the different outcomes associated with each function, as shown in Exhibit 13–3.

SELF-CHECK   Re-examine Exhibit 13–1 and discuss which functions—tutoring, mentoring, confronting/challenging, and counseling—are reflected by some of the coaching situations described.

All four functions have much in common and are often combined in a single coaching session. For example, when a new employee is struggling to perform, a single coaching session may involve confronting/challenging, counseling, and tutoring. Many of the skills and processes involved in all four functions are similar—the need for sensitivity, listening, and movement toward some form of closure.

Exhibit 13–3
*Outcomes of the Four
Coaching Functions*

Tutoring	Mentoring
1. Increased technical know-how	1. Developing political understanding/savvy
2. Increased understanding of processes and systems	2. Sensitivity to the organization's culture
3. Increased pace of learning	3. Expanded personal networks
4. Movement to expert status	4. Increased sensitivity to key players' likes/dislikes
5. Commitment to continual learning	5. Greater proaction in managing own career
Counseling	**Confronting/Challenging**
1. Accurate descriptions of problems and their causes	1. Clarification of performance expectations
2. Technical and organizational insight	2. Identification of performance shortcomings
3. Ventilation of strong feelings	3. Acceptance of more-difficult tasks
4. Commitment to self-sufficiency	4. Strategies to improve future performance
5. Deeper personal insight about own feelings and behavior	5. Commitment to continual performance improvement
6. Changes in point of view	

Source: Adapted form Dennis C. Kinlaw, *Coaching for Commitment*, (San Diego, CA: Pfeiffer & Company, 1993), pp. 22–23.

THE SKILLS OF COACHING

Learning Objective **3**

Describe some of
the important skills
used in coaching.

When a supervisor initiates a formal coaching session, he or she should have an objective to achieve and establish a basic framework for the session, adapted to the coaching function and the circumstances. However, the coaching process largely involves a number of spontaneous interactions that occur in a relaxed, personal setting. Many coaching interactions are initiated by the team member rather than the supervisor, and these may include requests for help, advice, or informal discussion of a work-related matter. In some cases, such as those of a personal nature, work may not be directly involved.

The supervisor must create a supportive atmosphere that encourages contact. He or she must maintain a climate that makes people feel welcome, respects their views and feelings, and shows patience when communicating with them. A supportive climate exists when a supervisor understands what team members want to accomplish and when members are encouraged to try new approaches without fear of reprisal. Effective listening is a critical coaching skill. It is difficult for many individuals to approach their supervisor for advice or to acknowledge job-related or personal problems that affect their job. Supervisors must establish an open, receptive communication climate.

Coaching: The Core Skills

The core coaching skills are discussed in the following sections. No single coaching session will necessarily involve all, or even most, of these. As you read through these skills, note the importance of an atmosphere of respect and understanding and a clear need for an outcome of the coaching effort.

ACKNOWLEDGING. Acknowledging is showing through a range of nonevaluative verbal responses that you have listened to what the employee has stated. These comments may range from brief "uh huhs," "ohs," "hmmmms," or "I sees," to longer phrases like "I can understand that" or "So that's how it happened." The acknowledging skill is designed to bounce the communication ball back to the employee and allow him or her to further develop the information.

acknowledging Showing by nonevaluative verbal responses that you have listened to what the employee has stated.

ATTENDING. Attending is showing through nonverbal behavior that you are listening in an open, nonjudgmental manner. In attending, your body language, such as alert posture, head nods, eye contact, and facial expressions, conveys full interest and attention. Nonattending behavior would include blank stares, nodding off, being distracted, glancing at your watch, or exhibiting other body language that displays uneasiness or disagreement with the topic being discussed. Effective attending behavior clearly communicates, "I am interested and I am listening."

attending Showing through nonverbal behavior that you are listening in an open, nonjudgmental manner.

AFFIRMING. Affirming is communicating to an employee his or her value, strengths, and contributions or other positive factors. An example might be "You have made excellent progress learning the new system." Or "It always amazes me how quickly you catch on." Or "I've always valued your willingness to share your feelings with me about things. It's good knowing you'll level with me about the proposed changes."

affirming Communicating to an employee his or her value, strengths, and contributions.

CONFIRMING. Confirming is making sure that an employee understands what has been said or agreed upon. The coach can do this by summarizing and repeating the key points or by requesting the person being coached to do so. The coach might ask, "How about going over these steps in your own words and telling me how you would proceed?" Confirming may also occur with an eye to the future: "How about modifying your estimates as we've discussed, using the highest-quality materials available, and let's take a look at this at 3 p.m. tomorrow."

confirming Making sure an employee understands what has been said or agreed upon.

PINPOINTING. Pinpointing is providing specific, tangible information. For instance, "You did a poor job on the write-up," is a vague general statement that covers wide territory. It is not as helpful as "The write-up used figures that were three years old, contained over 20 spelling and typographical errors, and lacked a specific recommendation."

pinpointing Providing specific, tangible information about performance to an employee.

A supervisor's probing, a core coaching skill, can lead to additional information being exchanged and clearer understanding of the topics and tasks at hand.

PROBING. Probing is asking questions to obtain additional information or exploring a topic at greater length, such as the following: "So you feel your group is ready to take on more responsibility. In what ways have they signaled this?" Or "So you would do it differently next time, given what you now know. Just what would you do differently?"

probing Asking questions to obtain additional information.

REFLECTING. Reflecting is stating in your own words your interpretation of what the employee has said or feels, such as "So you feel that you should have received more help from your team-mates on this?" or "It seems like you're really upset with them for not helping out."

reflecting Stating your interpretation of what the employee has said.

RESOURCING. Coaches should act as resources for their team members. **Resourcing** can be done by providing information, assistance, and advice: "I really wouldn't recommend by-passing Mason on this. It cost someone his job about five years ago when he did it." or "Talk to the human resources people. They should be able to answer your question." or "Let me show you how to do that."

resourcing Providing information, assistance, and advice to employees.

REVIEWING. At the end of a coaching session, reinforcing key points to ensure common understanding is the skill of **reviewing**. This can be done by the coach or coachee. "Let's pull this together. It seems we've identified three things you'll do with the survey data. First, you'll send your supervisors their individual results and the overall company results. Then you'll conduct one-on-one meetings with them to discuss their results. Following this, they'll develop a written plan, accepted by you as to what they'll do to improve." or "Let's make sure we're together on this. How about summarizing what you'll do with the survey results?"

reviewing Reinforcing key points at the end of a coaching session to ensure common understanding.

Case 14

The Quiet Meeting

Debra Ronson, sales supervisor of the Comzat Cable Company, was just opening a meeting she had called for members of her department. Ronson did most of the talking for the first five minutes, recounting her group's performance over the past week. Then she asked, "Are there any questions?" No one responded.

Ronson then changed subjects. "As you know, in two weeks we'll be going to a new format for scheduling our sales calls. This was outlined in the memo from the vice-president, copies of which I sent to each of you. This is going to alter your calling schedules and significantly change the way we've been doing things. I have some ideas on how we can best work into this new system. But before getting into that, I'd like to see if anyone here has any ideas . . . (*pause*). Anyone care to contribute anything?" No one in the group responded.

Ronson continued, "Well, here's what I think we should do . . . ." Ronson then spent eight minutes outlining her plan. After the meeting was over, Ronson discussed it with one of her fellow supervisors. "I don't know what it is," she said, "but I can never get my people to say much at meetings. I try to give them a chance, but I always end up doing most of the talking. It seems they're either shy or uninterested, but I really don't know if that's the reason or not. I just wish they'd contribute their ideas."

LEARNING OBJECTIVES
After reading and studying this chapter, you should be able to:

1
Identify the characteristics and processes of group dynamics.

2
Explain the four basic purposes of meetings.

3
Explain the process of consensus decision making in meetings.

4
Differentiate between the leader-controlled approach and the group-centered approach used in meetings.

5
Identify the advantages and disadvantages of meetings.

6
Describe the actions that a supervisor can take before, during, and after a meeting to make it effective.

7
Discuss the important principles to remember in making presentations at meetings.

Chapter 15
Facilitation Skills, Managing Conflict and Stress

Case 15

Chuck Dansby, Facilitator "Extraordinaire"

Facilitators are being called on increasingly to help groups and organizations become more effective. One of the best facilitators around is Chuck Dansby, total quality management supervisor with the Navy's Public Works Center in the San Francisco Bay area. Some public works representatives have suggested that a number of awards received by the Center from 1992–1994 could not have been achieved without expert facilitation. The most prestigious of these awards was the Meritorious Unit Commendation Award issued by the Secretary of Defense.

After graduating from Chattanooga State Technical Institute, Chuck spent twelve years in the Navy, ending his tour as a First Class E6 Petty Officer. In 1988 he joined the Public Works Center, and in 1991 he was named the first Quality Improvement Coordinator. During this time, the center was going through a period of expansion, and Chuck soon found himself operating a quality improvement department with a staff of seven people. Chuck and his team made helping units and groups to permanently improve processes their primary task. Even though Chuck and his group were in a staff capacity with no command authority, the following comments reveal why various managers called on him for assistance and what they said about him as a facilitator.

- Lt. Commander Bryan Johnson asked for Chuck's assistance when he needed to get the environmental group and construction group to work more effectively together. He states, "Chuck was very helpful in teaming with me to get key people to talk through issues and concerns and in getting the groups to cooperate in achieving objectives." He especially appreciated Chuck's ability to ask questions, getting people to brainstorm and rethink alternatives. Program Manager Steve Worthington echoes these observations and states, "Chuck is an excellent listener and is very good at getting people to 'see the big picture.'"
- Security Officer Mike Shanlas states, "He gets people to rethink their ways of operating and does it by asking questions. In this manner, people stay focused on the process, and they come out with improved ways of operating. People become indebted to him because he helps them to succeed; he does not set people up for failure.
- Contract Manager John Teetsov gives insight as to the ideal quality of a facilitator when he states that Chuck can come into an unfamiliar area and "not knowing the business, can extract the right ideas and answers. Very importantly, he does things in a manner so that the group feels that they are being helped rather than manipulated."

Chuck has attended a number of schools while with the Navy, but the one that had the greatest impact on him as a future effective facilitator was W. Edward Deming's four-day workshop on continual quality improvement. Deming and the

LEARNING OBJECTIVES
After reading and studying this chapter, you should be able to:

1 Define group facilitation.

2 Explain the role of group facilitator.

3 Differentiate between process consultation and other models of consultation.

4 Identify conflict causes.

5 Discuss conflict management styles and identify when each one would be appropriate.

6 Describe principled negotiation.

7 Explain why modern life makes us particularly vulnerable to stress.

8 Describe both the costs and benefits of stress.

9 Explain the major causes of stress.

course taught Chuck the value of asking the right questions. Today, the Navy's Public Works Center is going through a process of downsizing. In carrying out this process in a fair and humanistic manner, Chuck is being called on for his expert facilitation skills in meeting the Public Works Center's greatest challenge.

Source: Conversations and correspondence with Chuck Dansby and others with the Navy's Public Works Center, San Francisco Bay area.

Rule No. 1 is, don't sweat the small stuff. Rule No. 2 is, it's all small stuff. And if you can't fight and you can't flee, flow.

Robert Eliot, University of Nebraska Cardiologist

I would I could stand on a busy corner, hat in hand, and beg people to throw me all their wasted hours.

Bernard Berenson

WHAT IS GROUP FACILITATION?

Learning Objective 1

Define group facilitation.

group facilitation The process of intervening to help a group improve in goal setting, action planning, problem solving, conflict management, and decision making in order to increase the group's effectiveness.

Group facilitation is a process of intervening to help a group improve in goal setting, action planning, problem solving, conflict management, and decision making in order to increase the group's effectiveness. Although an outside facilitator can be helpful, as we saw in the opening case, the ideal is for managers and supervisors to gain facilitation skills and utilize shared leadership in carrying out the process.

As organizations cope with the world of increasingly rapid change, the need for facilitation to improve their effectiveness increases. Examples run the gamut from empowering employees, developing shared visions, and creating self-managing work teams to changing to a more participative organizational culture. It is hard to imagine successful change efforts in the areas of total quality management, reengineering, partnering, mergers, or downsizing without some form of facilitation.

Role of the Facilitator

Learning Objective 2

Explain the role of group facilitator.

In our discussion of group dynamics and conducting meetings in Chapter 14, you were introduced to facilitation challenges and suggestions for handling inappropriate behavior at meetings. A good foundation for being an effective facilitator requires experience and knowledge, not only of dynamics of the group but also of decision making, problem solving, communications, motivation, and leadership. In addition, the core skills shown in Exhibit 15–1 are essential.

- Communication skills—listening and asking the right questions.
- Leadership skills—participative management and developmental leadership.
- Problem-solving skills.
- Group dynamics skills.
- Conceptual and analytical skills.
- Conflict management skills—principled negotiation.
- Process consultation skills—intervention and diagnostic insights.

Exhibit 15–1
*Core Skills for the
Effective Facilitator*

It is important to keep in mind that the effective facilitator is primarily a helper and wants the group to achieve long-term development and continuous process improvement. Exhibit 15–2 highlights this emphasis by showing the distinction between basic facilitation and developmental facilitation.

Process Consultation

Learning Objective 3

Differentiate between process consultation and other models of consultation.

Among the many roles facilitators must play is that of process consultant. In fact, process consultation skills are identified as being among the core skills of an effective facilitator. This role involves sitting in on team or task force meetings, observing the group's process, and intervening, if needed, to help the group function more effectively. Skill Builder 15–2 is designed to help you better understand when and how to intervene. Increasingly, facilitators are being used in major change efforts of total quality management, reengineering, and partnering. In essence, a facilitator becomes a consultant. The following sections describe three consultation models, and we draw extensively from author/consultant Edgar Schein in comparing them.

THE PURCHASE-OF-EXPERTISE MODEL. The most widely used form of consultation is the purchase of expert information. The organization, or someone within the organization, decides there is a need to call on an expert to help solve a problem or add a service. For example, someone to initiate an organizational attitude survey or introduce a performance evaluation system may be called. An individual who specializes in conducting marketing surveys or initiating total quality improvement programs may also be needed. Schein points out that this model has problems in that there is frequently a low rate of implementation of the consultant's recommendations. Further, this model is based on many assumptions that have to be met for it to succeed, and therein lies its weakness. The assumptions are:

1. The manager has correctly diagnosed the organization's needs.
2. The manager has correctly communicated those needs to the consultant.
3. The manager has accurately assessed the capabilities of the consultant to provide the information or the service.
4. The manager has considered the consequences of having the consultant gather such information and is willing to implement changes that may be recommended by the consultant.[1]

Exhibit 15–2
*Basic and
Developmental
Facilitation*

Characteristic	Basic Facilitation	Developmental Facilitation
Group objective	Solve a substantive problem or problems.	Achieve group goals along with solving substantive problems while learning to improve processes.
Facilitator role	Help group temporarily improve its processes.	Help group permanently improve its processes.
	Take primary responsibility for managing the group's processes.	Help group assume primary responsibility for achieving goals and managing processes.
Outcome for group	Emphasize dependence on facilitator for solving future problems.	Reduce dependence on facilitator for solving future problems.

Source: Roger M. Schwartz, *The Skilled Facilitator: Practical Wisdom for Developing Effective Groups*, Table 1.1, page 7, adapted as submitted. Copyright © 1994 Jossey-Bass Inc., Publishers.

Another weakness is the fact that the model is based on a "tell and sell" method by the expert and there is no "ownership" or commitment by the client.

THE DOCTOR-PATIENT MODEL. A relationship between a consultant and an organization can be likened to that of a doctor and a patient. When an organization suffers symptoms such as declining sales or profits, low morale, or high turnover, a consultant may be brought in to check these problems. After the "checkup," the consultant prescribes what needs to be done to "get well" again. As Schein points out, this model places a great deal of power in the hands of the consultant in that he or she makes a diagnosis and also prescribes a treatment. The success of the model then depends on the following:

1. The initial client has accurately identified which person, group, or department is "sick."
2. The "patient" has revealed accurate information.
3. The "patient" accepts the prescription, that is, does what the "doctor" recommends.[2]

THE PROCESS CONSULTATION MODEL. In contrast to the other models, **process consultation** involves others in making a joint diagnosis and eventually provides others with the skills and tools to make their own diagnoses. Also, even though the consultant may be an expert in the area of consultation, he or she refrains from solving the problem for the client. The emphasis is on facilitating the process so the client learns problem-solving skills. Although the facilitator may make suggestions or raise questions that broaden the diagnosis or develop more alternatives, the client makes the ultimate decision and develops the action plan or remedy. A summary of the underlying assumptions of the process consultation model follows:

process consultation
A consultation model that involves others in making a joint diagnosis of the problem and eventually providing others with the skills and tools to make their own diagnoses.

1. Clients/managers often do not know what is wrong and need special help in diagnosing what their problems actually are.

2. Clients/managers often do not know what kinds of help consultants can give to them; they need to be informed of what kinds of help to seek.

3. Most clients/managers have a constructive intent to improve things, but they need help in identifying what to improve and how to improve it.

4. Most organizations can be more effective if they learn to diagnose and manage their own strengths and weaknesses.

5. A consultant probably cannot, without exhaustive and time-consuming study or actual participation in the client organization, learn enough about the culture of the organization to suggest reliable new courses of action. Therefore, unless remedies are worked out jointly with members of the organization, who do know what will and will not work in their culture, such remedies are likely either to be wrong or to be resisted because they come from an outsider.

6. Unless the client/manager learns to see the problem for himself and thinks through the remedy, he or she will not be willing or able to implement the solution. More importantly, he or she will not learn how to fix such problems should they recur. The process consultant can provide alternatives, but decision making about such alternatives must remain in the hands of the client.

7. The essential function of process consultation, or PC, is to teach the skills of how to diagnose and fix organizational problems. In this way, the client is able to continue on his or her own to improve the organization.[3]

How do facilitators determine whether or not they are being effective? One group that facilitates partnering workshops always asks the participants to evaluate both the effectiveness of the workshop and the facilitator(s). The following comments demonstrate that the facilitator provided good process consultation skills.

> **"The facilitators did an excellent job in serving as catalysts for dialogue."**
>
> **"The facilitator took the time to help each person or group with problem solving and with staying focused."**
>
> **"The techniques of the workshop leader improved communications and helped us to solve our problems in a collaborative manner."**
>
> **"The facilitator provided good, constructive, visionary thinking and identified personal and group blind spots."**
>
> **"The facilitator was collaborative, but firm enough to keep things focused and keep things moving."**
>
> **"The facilitator's people skills were exceptional. He was genuinely interested in the individual and group needs, which made the workshop most effective."**
>
> **"The facilitator achieved the goal of allowing *us* to solve our problems."**
>
> **"The facilitator kept us focused without inhibiting the interaction of the participants."[4]**

In two of the skill builders at the end of the chapter, you will have an opportunity to develop your process consultation and facilitation skills.

CONFLICT MANAGEMENT

conflict management
Becoming aware of the causes and appropriate levels of conflict for various situations and reacting accordingly.

As we have seen, facilitators must possess a variety of skills and be knowledgeable about many subjects. One of the most critical areas is **conflict management.** Conflict is a part of everyday life. It exists in professional and personal relationships. Usually, there are negative connotations associated with the term conflict. When emotion is not tempered by reason, a situation can easily get out of hand. However, not all conflict is bad. A certain amount of conflict is healthy, because it can lead to more effective decision making. When conflict is present, the status quo is examined. Individuals grapple with various solutions through their analysis of the situation. In many cases, this evaluation leads to better decisions. As the graph in Exhibit 15–3 indicates, performance actually increases as the level of conflict intensifies.

This concept is true until the appropriate level of conflict is reached, and then performance diminishes.[5] It is the facilitator's responsibility to become aware of the causes and appropriate levels of conflict for various situations in order to utilize the most effective conflict management style.

Causes of Conflict

Learning Objective 4
Identify the causes of conflict.

A facilitator must have a basic understanding of the causes of conflict before he or she can determine what is functional or dysfunctional. The following sections look at some of the causes.

DIFFERENT OBJECTIVES. An individual's actions tend to support his or her personal goals or objectives. If an employee's personal objectives differ from those of the organization, then conflict may exist. An example of this type of situation is when the organization's incentive or

Exhibit 15–3
Balanced View of Conflict

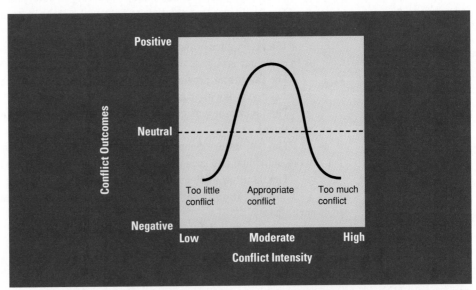

Source: Adapted from L. D. Brown, *Managing Conflict at Organizational Interfaces.* Reading, Mass.: Addison-Wesley, 1983, p. 8. Adapted and used with permission.

reward system encourages internal competition through individual incentives, while the company attempts to switch to a participative, team-based management approach.

Insecure feelings may also play a role in creating and fostering conflict. For example, a plant supervisor may aspire to be plant manager. If the person has been passed over twice for promotion, then the probability of achieving that personal goal may be low. It would be quite normal for the individual to question his or her abilities. That person might also wonder where he or she "fits" in the organization's long-term plans. A facilitator that works with this supervisor on a task force, cross-functional team, etc., needs to be aware of this conflict and know how to deal with it. Conflict caused by feelings of insecurity can have a positive effect on the supervisor's performance. If provided with feedback about the reasons for being passed over for promotion, the individual can work to improve in those areas. There is a good chance that the individual's insecurities will motivate him or her to work harder to improve.

COMMUNICATION. Communication breakdowns may be the number one reason for most conflict situations. Consider the following case of a facilitator/consultant who consulted with a prominent organization located outside the continental United States. The company was involved in a large-scale construction project with several major players. The project management team included the owner, the general contractor, and subcontractors. They had developed an issue resolution model at the outset of the project, which provided a course of action in dealing with unexpected problems. The model indicated the process of escalation, including which individuals were to be involved and the amount of time that each management level had to resolve the dispute. Legal action was the final step, but it was a last resort.

During the project, a claim was filed by the general contractor because of a disagreement with the owner on a particular issue. The claim was so substantial that it endangered the success of the overall project. The problem was in the final stages of the issue-resolution process. If the issue was not solved at the present level, then the next step was litigation. Even though Spanish was the main language for most of the participants, all of the negotiations up to this point had been conducted in English. The project manager made a final effort to resolve the dispute, in suggesting that the project management team conduct the final negotiations in Spanish.

After months of disagreement, the team was able to develop a solution within 48 hours. This is an extreme case, but it demonstrates the relationship between communication and conflict. The project manager was intuitive enough to realize that the language differences were causing communication barriers. Combine the fact that words and phrases have different meanings and connotations in different languages with the fact that each party had emotional ownership in the outcome of the issue, and it is easy to see how communication breakdowns occur.

SIMILARITIES. The book *Getting Together* by Roger Fisher and Scott Brow accurately describes the relationship between similarities and conflict.

> **When people in a relationship are further apart—in terms of distance, culture, background, and role—the contrast between their perceptions will be greater, and each will find it more difficult to appreciate how the other sees things.... [Individuals have] to recognize that partisans will perceive their differences differently. In this respect, the United States/Russia relationship is particularly difficult. Officials of the two countries cannot possibly have the same perceptions, due to living in**

different cultures, observing some facts at close range and others at a distant, and approaching those facts with different ideologies, values, and interests.[6]

Diversity, in the form of differing perceptions, can be a strength or a weakness depending on how an individual or group chooses to handle the issue. Is the glass half full or half empty? The challenge for the facilitator is to utilize these differences so that they enhance the performance of the individual or group. In order for the facilitator to be effective at this task, an understanding of conflict management styles is necessary. Therefore, the next section of this chapter is devoted to understanding the different ways of dealing with conflict.

Conflict Management Styles

Learning Objective 5

Discuss conflict management styles and identify when each one would be appropriate.

Individuals must cope with all forms of interpersonal and intergroup conflict. It is important to properly diagnose the conflict situation so that it can be dealt with in a most-effective manner. Exhibit 15–4 is a diagram of five conflict handling styles which are based on the concern an individual has for oneself and for others. The five styles are:[7]

- **Avoiding**—Avoiding is an unassertive, uncooperative style in which the individual's concern for self and others is low. It is a useful style when dealing with trivial issues or when the negative consequences of confrontation outweigh the need for resolution.
- **Accommodating**—Accomodating is an unassertive, cooperative style in which the individual's concern for self is low while the concern for others is high. The accommodating approach downplays the parties' differences. It is an appropriate style to use when the issue is more important to the other party or the other party is right.

Exhibit 15–4
Interpersonal Conflict Management Styles

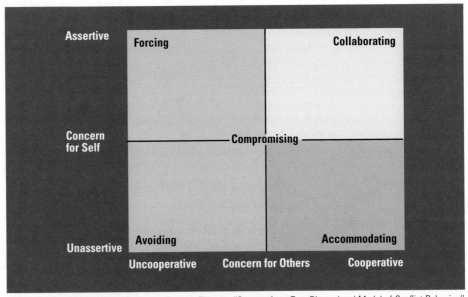

Source: Adapted from Thomas Ruble and Kenneth Thomas, "Support for a Two-Dimensional Model of Conflict Behavior," *Organizational Behavior and Human Performance*, vol. 16 (1976), p. 145. Used with permission of Academic Press, Inc.

Firefighters must rely on the most effective management style when dealing with life-threatening situations, which in this case would be the forcing style.

- **Forcing**—Forcing is an assertive, uncooperative style in which the individual's concern for self is high while the concern for others is low. This approach uses power to resolve conflict. A forcing style is useful in an emergency situation, where quick decisions are necessary.
- **Compromising**—Compromising is a somewhat assertive, cooperative style in which the individual has a moderate amount of concern for both self and others. The objective is to find a middle ground. The compromising style is appropriate when the parties have reached an impasse due to mutually exclusive goals.
- **Collaborating**—Collaborating is an assertive, cooperative approach in which the individual has a high concern for self and others. Collaboration is a problem-solving style. It is effective when dealing with conflict "head on," trying to surface all of the pertinent issues, and attempting to interpret differing points of view.

Conflict management theory during most of the 1960s and 1970s supported collaboration as the appropriate approach to resolve conflict. Since collaboration in many cases leads to win/win outcomes, it is easy to discern why collaboration advocates supported this approach as "the model" for handling conflict. During the 1970s and 1980s, the contingency movement gained momentum. Proponents of this theory maintained that collaboration in all situations is unrealistic. For example, a management student, who is a member of a local emergency response team, made the following observation when conflict management styles were covered in class.

Her unit was activated shortly after a tragic train wreck occurred. The emergency response team prepares for these types of situations regularly. However, unanticipated problems arise that must be dealt with effectively as quickly as possible in order to save lives. Although the team members may utilize the collaborative approach during the planning stages, they do not have time to rely on this method while in the field. She indicated that the approach most often used by the team in the field was the forcing style, because it was the most effective.

The avoiding, accommodating, forcing, and compromising conflict management styles are usually best used when dealing with tactical, day-to-day, short-term problems. Whereas, collaboration (and compromising, to a limited extent) is a conflict management style more appropriate for ad hoc task forces and long-term strategic problems.

Using Principled Negotiation to Resolve Conflict

Learning Objective 6

Describe principled negotiation.

A real breakthrough in conflict management and resolution is found in the concepts proposed by Roger Fisher and William Ury of the Harvard negotiation project. They emphasize that, whether negotiation involves a peace settlement among nations or a business contract, people often engage in *positional bargaining.* This common form of negotiation involves proposing and then giving up a sequence of positions. The idea is to give up things that are not very important. Hence, proposals are "padded" initially. For this form of negotiation to succeed, it must meet three criteria of fair negotiation, which are: "It should produce a wise agreement if agreement is possible; it should be efficient; and it should improve, or at least not damage, the relationship between the parties."[8]

When people bargain over positions, they tend to back themselves into corners defending their positions, which results in a number of either *win-lose* or *lose-lose* outcomes. Moreover, arguing over positions often endangers an ongoing relationship by straining and sometimes shattering relationships. In a marriage this results in divorce, and in business the result can be the breakup of an otherwise successful operation. Many negotiations involve more than two parties, and in these cases positional bargaining compounds the problem of negotiating an agreement.

principled negotiation

Negotiation on the merits.

In their work with the Harvard negotiation project, Fisher and Ury developed an alternative to positional bargaining that they call **principled negotiation,** or negotiation on the merits. The four basic components of principled negotiation are:

1. Separating the people from the problem.
2. Focusing on interests, not positions.
3. Generating a variety of possibilities before deciding what to do.
4. Insisting that the result be based on some objective standard.

Consultant facilitators for a number of joint ventures and partnerships involving multiple parties have noted that educating the joint venture parties in the concepts of principled negotiation has resulted in a high percentage of win-win resolutions in dispute settlements. Exhibit 15–5 illustrates the difference between positional bargaining and principled negotiation. Notice that in positional bargaining, one can either play "hardball" or "softball."

WHAT IS STRESS?

A number of concepts presented earlier in this chapter and in previous chapters lend insight into how to manage stress. Organizations and supervisors can suffer serious consequences if stress is not understood and managed. We now examine the topic in more depth.

Exhibit 15–5

Contrast of Positional Bargaining and Principled Negotiations

Problem Positional Bargaining: Which Game Should You Play?		Solution Change the Game— Negotiate on the Merits
Soft	**Hard**	**Principled**
Participants are friends.	Participants are adversaries.	Participants are problem-solvers.
The goal is agreement.	The goal is victory.	The goal is a wise outcome reached efficiently and amicably.
Make concessions to cultivate the relationship.	Demand concessions as a condition of the relationship.	**Separate the people from the problem.**
Be soft on the people and the problem.	Be hard on the problem and the people.	Be soft on the people, hard on the problem.
Trust others.	Distrust others.	Proceed independent of trust.
Change your position easily.	Dig in to your position.	**Focus on interests, not positions.**
Make offers.	Make threats.	Explore interests.
Disclose your bottom line.	Mislead as to your bottom line.	Avoid having a bottom line.
Accept one-sided losses to reach agreement.	Demand one-sided gains as the price of agreement.	**Invent options for mutual gain.**
Search for the single answer: the one *they* will accept.	Search for the single answer: the one *you* will accept.	Develop multiple options to choose from; decide later.
Insist on agreement.	Insist on your position.	**Insist on using objective criteria.**
Try to avoid a contest of will.	Try to win a contest of will.	Try to reach a result based on standards independent of will.
Yield to pressure.	Apply pressure.	Reason and be open to reason; yield to principle, not pressure.

Definition of Stress

Learning Objective 7

Explain why modern life makes us particularly vulnerable to stress.

stress Any external stimulus that causes wear and tear on one's psychological or physical well-being.

For many years the medical community failed to take stress seriously. One of the reasons for this failure was the lack of an adequate definition of stress and of research into its effects. **Stress** may be defined as any external stimulus that causes wear and tear on one's psychological or physical well-being.[9]

Stress researchers point out that modern men and women sometimes react to the strains of work and everyday life the same way our primitive ancestors did. In the days of the caveman, when there was danger, a chemical reaction in the body geared our ancestors for either fight or flight. The problem for some modern men and women is that their bodies still react the same way to external stimuli, causing them to maintain a constant fight-or-flight readiness. The anxiety is similar to that of soldiers in combat, and it causes wear and tear on our bodies.

Jane Coleman was driving to work during the morning rush hour. An irresponsible driver nearly caused an accident by cutting into her lane. By the time Jane arrived at work, she was already tense; the problem was compounded when she discovered that one of her key employees was out with the flu. Two emergencies during the day caused her to end the day anxious and exhausted.

Many of us face situations similar to Jane's. Note that stress can be caused by an external stimulus such as driving on the freeway or by conditions on the job. An excellent definition of job stress is "a condition arising from the interaction of people and their jobs and characterized by changes within people that force them to deviate from their normal functioning."[10] Under normal conditions, our bodies and minds are in a state of equilibrium (see Exhibit 15–6). As a result of occurrences on or off the job, however, our equilibrium may be disrupted. In attempting to recover from this imbalance, we function differently and sometimes generate a fight-or-flight chemical reaction. Obviously, Jane, as a supervisor, cannot leave her job or pick a fight with someone, but the chemical reaction in her body occurs anyway.

The Costs of Stress

Learning Objective 8

Describe both the costs and the benefits of stress.

It has been estimated that two-thirds of all visits to doctors can be traced to stress-related symptoms. Stress, for example, is a major contributor to heart disease, cancer, lung problems, accidents, cirrhosis of the liver, and suicide.

Even the common cold and skin rashes are sometimes related to a person's experiencing prolonged and severe stress. Industry leaders are aware that such symptoms play a major role in absenteeism, accidents, and lost productivity.

Certainly a person under severe and/or prolonged stress cannot function as effectively as a person leading a more balanced life. We are not implying that stress is all negative, however, because a certain amount of stress adds zest to life.

Exhibit 15–6
*Equilibrium and
Disequilibrium*

Exhibit 15–6
*Equilibrium and
Disequilibrium*

The Positive Aspects of Stress

Some amount of stress is necessary to accomplish anything meaningful. The teams that play in the Super Bowl are certainly in a stressful situation. Anyone who has played a sport or spoken in front of a large group has been in a stressful situation. Without question, moderate amounts of stress improve performance. For example, difficult but attainable objectives motivate better than easy objectives.

People who seek types of work and leisure that engage their skills find life zestful and interesting. The secret is to involve oneself in challenging work and active leisure accompanied by sufficient rest and retreat. Life is full of stressors that can stimulate, energize, and aid in such positive outcomes as individual health and high productivity. We call the constructive dimensions of positive stress *entress,* which can be a powerful motivator. Examples of entress include going to an athletic event or participating in sports events.

MAJOR CAUSES OF STRESS

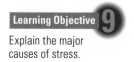

Learning Objective **9**

Explain the major causes of stress.

A number of factors contribute to individual stress. Among these are (1) life events, (2) personal psychological makeup, and (3) organizational and work-related factors. Especially in the case of organizational and work-related factors, the result is likely to be burnout.

Life Events

Stress occurs whenever we face situations that require changes in behavior and a higher level of activity. It would be impossible to list all the situations that place stress on human beings, since the mere fact of living does so. However, researchers have identified major life events, both positive and negative, that require drastic changes in a person's behavior. If many of these events occur within a year's time, a person becomes particularly susceptible to unpleasant physical or psychological consequences of excessive stress.

life event Anything that causes a person to deviate from normal functioning.

Exhibit 15–7 lists a number of stress-provoking life events. A major **life event** is anything that causes a person to deviate from normal functioning. The events are ranked in order of impact on a person's life. The death of a spouse has the most impact; minor violations of the law, such as receiving a traffic ticket, cause the least stress.

Researchers have discovered a statistical correlation between scores on the SRRS and illness among managers and the general population. Individuals scoring 150 points or below have less than a 33 percent chance that a serious illness will occur in the next two years. With scores of 150–300, the probability increases to about 50 percent, and those who score over 300 have an 80 percent chance of serious illness.[11] Steps and action plans can be initiated to offset the probability of a high score, and thus a serious illness. We discuss this later in the chapter.

> **Patrick Hogan was a 34-year-old supervisor who seemed to have it all. He had a good job, was happily married, had two children, and was on top of the world. At work, he was highly productive and outgoing and was considered a leading candidate for advancement.**
>
> **In the course of a year, several events occurred in Patrick's life that completely disrupted his patterns of living. A long-time friend enticed him to invest in a steak house that the friend would operate. The restaurant lost money, and the friend left town, leaving Patrick responsible for the bank note. To save his investments, he started moonlighting at the restaurant, not getting home many nights until 1 a.m.**
>
> **While Patrick was struggling with the restaurant, his mother died after a lingering illness. Two weeks after the funeral, his wife had an accident and was confined to bed with a slipped disc. For the first time in his life, Patrick had to prepare meals, wash clothes, and care for the children while at the same time carrying on with his regular job and struggling with the restaurant.**
>
> **At work, Patrick's behavior changed drastically. He was impatient with his employees and lost his temper quickly. He became depressed and found it difficult to reach decisions about matters that he had previously handled decisively.**

SELF-CHECK

Based on the above description of what happened in Patrick Hogan's life within the past year, calculate his score on the SRRS. Assume you are his supervisor and Patrick comes to you to talk about his situation. What advice would you give him?

Exhibit 15–7

Life Events from the Social Readjustment Rating Scale (SRRS)

Event	Scale of Impact
Death of spouse	100
Divorce	73
Marital separation	65
Jail term	63
Death of close family member	63
Personal injury or illness	53
Marriage	50
Fired at work	47
Marital reconciliation	45
Retirement	45
Change in health of family member	44
Pregnancy	40
Sex difficulties	39
Gain of new family member	39
Business readjustment	39
Change in financial state	38
Death of close friend	37
Change to different line of work	36
Change in number of arguments with spouse	35
Foreclosure of mortgage or loan	30
Change in responsibilities at work	29
Son or daughter leaving home	29
Trouble with in-laws	29
Outstanding personal achievement	28
Wife begins or stops work	26
Begin or end school	26
Change in living conditions	25
Revision of personal habits	24
Trouble with boss	23
Change in work hours or conditions	20
Change in residence	20
Change in schools	20
Change in recreation	19
Change in church activities	19
Change in social activities	18
Change in sleeping habits	16
Change in number of family get-togethers	15
Change in eating habits	15
Vacation	13
Christmas	12
Minor violations of the law	11

Source: "The Stress of Adjusting to Change," from *The Relaxation Response,* by Herbert Benson, M.D., with Miriam Z. Klipper. Copyright 1975 by William Morrow Company, Inc. By permission of the publisher.

Personal Psychological Makeup

Learning Objective 10

Compare and contrast
Type A behavior and
Type B behavior.

Americans have long been noted for their emphasis on work. The United States has a justifiable reputation as a country where individuals, through hard work, can achieve considerable economic success. Some people, however, have become so caught up in the work ethic that work becomes the end itself rather than the means to an end. New Zealanders say that "Americans live to work and New Zealanders work to live." Our point is that some Americans have become workaholics, and this excessiveness has behavioral consequences that take a toll over a period of time.

Researchers have identified two basic types of behavior characterizing people in our society: Type A and Type B.

TYPE A BEHAVIOR. Cardiologists Meyer Friedman and Roy Rosenman first defined the term **Type A behavior.** Individuals who exhibit Type A behavior tend to try to accomplish too many things in a short time. Lacking patience, they struggle against time and other people to accomplish their ends. As a consequence, they become irritated by trivial things. Type A people also tend to be workaholics. Because of their psychological makeup they may be subject to stress over prolonged periods. For this reason, Type A people have a much higher risk of heart disease than Type B people.[12]

Type A behavior A behavior pattern characterized by (a) trying to accomplish too much in a short time and (b) lacking patience and struggling against time and other people to accomplish one's ends.

TYPE B BEHAVIOR. People exhibiting **Type B behavior** tend to be calmer, to take more time to exercise, and to be more realistic than Type A in estimating the amount of time needed to complete an assignment. Type Bs also worry less and, in general, desire more satisfaction from their work.[13]

Type B behavior A behavior pattern characterized by (a) tending to be calmer than someone with *Type A behavior,* (b) devoting more time to exercise, and (c) being more realistic in estimating the time it takes to complete an assignment.

Studies of Type A and B behaviors indicate that 60 percent of managers and supervisors fall into the category of Type A people. Many supervisors respond to all events as if they were emergencies or life-threatening situations. Managers and supervisors who exhibit extreme Type A behavior patterns tend to practice close supervision and find it difficult to delegate. They are concerned that errors might reflect on past achievements, and so they become excessively task-oriented.[14]

SELF-CHECK

Do you think of yourself as a Type A or a Type B personality? Exhibit 15–8 provides a quiz that will give you a rough idea of your behavioral pattern.

Organizational and Work-Related Factors

Throughout this book we have discussed many organizational and work-related factors that may cause excessive stress. As shown in Exhibit 15–9, these range from having poorly defined job descriptions to having autocratic or permissive leadership. If these factors exist in an organization over a period of time, they will cause extensive damage in the form of dissatisfaction, high turnover, low productivity, incomplete goal accomplishment, and job burnout.

Exhibit 15–8
Behavior Type Quiz

To find out which behavior type you are, circle the number on the scale below for each trait that best characterizes your behavior.

Casual about appointments	1	2	3	4	5	6	7	8	Never late
Not competitive	1	2	3	4	5	6	7	8	Very competitive
Never feel rushed even under pressure	1	2	3	4	5	6	7	8	Always rushed
Take things one at a time	1	2	3	4	5	6	7	8	Try to do many things at once, think about what I'm going to do next.
Slow doing things	1	2	3	4	5	6	7	8	Fast (eating, walking, etc.)
Express feelings	1	2	3	4	5	6	7	8	"Sit on" feelings
Many interests	1	2	3	4	5	6	7	8	Few interests outside work

Total score: _____ Total score multiplied by 3: _____

The interpretation is as follows:

Number of Points	Type of Personality
Less than 90	B
90 to 99	B+
100 to 105	A—
106 to 119	A
120 or more	A+

Source: A. P. Brief, R. S. Schuler, and M. V. Sell, *Managing Job Stress* (Boston: Little, Brown & Co., 1981), p. 87.

Exhibit 15–9
Organizational and Work-Related Factors that Cause Excessive Stress

- A highly centralized organization with decision making concentrated at the top.
- Many levels and narrow spans of control.
- Excessive and continuous pressure from higher levels.
- Conflicting demands on lower levels.
- Lack of clarity with respect to organizational and work objectives.
- Widespread autocratic leadership and close supervision.
- Little or no participation in decision making by supervisor and workers.
- Inconsistent application of company policies.
- Favoritism in decisions regarding layoffs, salary increases, promotions, and the like.
- Poor working conditions.
- Poor communication.
- Lack of structure and job descriptions.
- Widespread permissive leadership.

As the following example shows, stress can even create an opportunity for union activity.

A union organizer approached several employees from the home office of XYZ Life & Casualty Insurance Company. He was quickly told that they were not interested in joining a union, since they had excellent pay, good working conditions, and a high regard for their supervisors.

Six months later, a supervisor retired in the claims department. The new supervisor, after being on the job a month, called two long-time employees into the office and gave them dismissal notices without a reason for doing so. That night, five employees drove 90 miles to a meeting in another city with the union organizer. Upon their return, they obtained enough employee signatures to force an election to determine whether the union would represent employees in the XYZ home office.

Burnout

burnout A malady caused by excessive stress in the setting where people invest most of their time and energy.

One of the most common results of excessive stress is burnout. **Burnout** is a stress-related malady that generally originates in the setting where people invest most of their time and energy. This setting is usually the work environment but could just as well be the home or the golf course.

The seriousness of the burnout problem has been highlighted by researchers Robert Golembiewski and Robert Munzenrider. Utilizing an adapted version of the *Maslach Burnout Inventory* (MBI), they discovered that 40 percent of more than 12,000 respondents in 33 organizations suffered from advanced phases of burnout.[15] Exhibit 15–10 explains the subscales used in the MBI and charts the eight phases of burnout.

A person scoring in Phase I would be highly energized and motivated by the positive aspects of stress. In Maslow's terms, such a person would be operating at the esteem and self-fulfillment level of the need hierarchy. To a lesser extent, the same would be true of a person in Phases II, III, IV, and V. Difficulties occur when a person reaches Phases VI, VII, and VIII, the advanced stages of burnout.

Candidates for job burnout have three distinguishing characteristics. First, they experience stress caused predominantly by job-related stressors. Second, they tend to be idealistic and/or self-motivated achievers. Third, they tend to seek unattainable goals.[16]

Although over the long term the ideal way to deal with burnout is to address the factors that are causing it, in the short term burnout can be managed through use of any of a variety of strategies for coping with stress.

WAYS TO COPE WITH PERSONAL STRESS

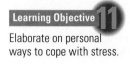

Learning Objective 11

Elaborate on personal ways to cope with stress.

Four methods that have helped many supervisors to cope with stress are (1) engaging in physical exercise, (2) practicing the relaxation response, (3) gaining a sense of control, and (4) developing and maintaining good interpersonal relationships.

Exhibit 15–10
MBI Subscales and Phases of Burnout

The adapted Maslach Burnout Inventory, or MBI, consists of 25 items, rated on a scale of 1 (very much *unlike* me) to 7 (very much *like* me). There are three subscales.

Depersonalization: Individuals with high scores on this subscale tend to view people as objects and to distance themselves from others. Example: "I worry that this job is hardening me emotionally."

Personal Accomplishment (reversed): Respondents with high scores on this subscale see themselves as not performing well on a task that they perceive as not being particularly worthwhile. Example: "I have accomplished few worthwhile things on this job."

Emotional Exhaustion: Individuals with high scores on this subscale see themselves as operating beyond comfortable coping limits and as approaching "the end of the rope" in psychological and emotional senses. Example: "I feel fatigued when I get up in the morning and have to face another day on the job."

Emotional exhaustion is considered most characteristic of advanced phases of burnout, and depersonalization is considered least virulent. Ratings of high or low on the three subscales determine the progressive phases of burnout, generating an eight-phase model of burnout:

	Progressive Phases of Burnout							
	I	II	III	IV	V	VI	VII	VIII
Depersonalization	Low	High	Low	High	Low	High	Low	High
Personal accomplishment	Low	Low	High	High	Low	Low	High	High
Emotional exhaustion	Low	Low	Low	Low	High	High	High	High

Source: Adapted from Robert T. Golembiewski and Robert F. Munzenrider, *Phases of Burnout* (Praeger Publishers, an imprint of Greenwood Publishing Group, Inc., Westport, CT, 1988), pp. 19–28. Reprinted with permission. All rights reserved.

Physical Exercise

People who exercise a minimum of two or three times a week are much less prone to the adverse symptoms of stress than those who do not. The exercise should be vigorous to the point of inducing perspiration. A person's muscles and circulatory system are not designed for a life of inactivity. People who revitalize their bodies are much less likely to worry and become upset over events and problems. The exercise can take many forms—tennis, handball, jogging, walking, swimming, gardening, or workouts at a health and exercise spa.

Earlier in the chapter, we highlighted the problems that Patrick Hogan was facing and saw how the stress of dealing with these problems had drastically changed his behavior. Patrick's manager noticed the change and counseled him regarding the situation. After Patrick had discussed his circumstances, the manager asked him if he engaged in regular exercise. Patrick answered that he simply did not have the time as a result of having to moonlight at the restaurant.

Patrick's manager persuaded him to work out three times a week in the company exercise room (see Exhibit 15–11). Within two week's time, Patrick's

Workers on the Tenneco gas rig in Louisiana used to load up on artery-clogging food, such as deep-fried crawfish and sausage-laden gumbo. Their employer, fearing a medical time bomb, began encouraging employees to get healthy.

Exhibit 15–11
Coping with Stress

on-the-job behavior was back to normal, and he had begun developing a plan to cope with some of the problems outside of work.

The Relaxation Response

Several years ago, in *The Relaxation Response,* Dr. Herbert Benson and Miriam Klipper described a simple meditative technique that helps relieve tensions, enables one to deal more effectively with stress, lowers blood pressure, and, in general, improves physical and emotional health. This technique is particularly useful to supervisors because it is neither time-consuming nor costly. All that is involved is finding a quiet place and practicing the technique for 10 to 20 minutes once or twice a day.

relaxation response
A meditative technique that helps relieve tensions, enables one to deal more effectively with stress, lowers blood pressure, and, in general, improves physical and emotional health.

Research by Benson and others validates that the **relaxation response** is a meditative state that not only relieves hypertension but also counteracts the fight-or-flight response provoked by the stressful events of life (see Exhibit 15–12).

Benson describes his method of bringing forth the relaxation response as follows:

1. Sit quietly in a comfortable position.
2. Close your eyes.
3. Deeply relax all your muscles, beginning at your feet and progressing up to your face. Keep them relaxed.
4. Breathe through your nose. Become aware of your breathing. As you breathe out, say the word "one" silently to yourself. For example, breathe in . . . out, "one," in . . . out, "one," etc. Breathe easily and naturally.
5. Continue for 10 to 20 minutes. You may open your eyes to check the time, but do not use an alarm clock. When you finish, sit quietly for several minutes, first with your eyes closed and later with your eyes opened. Wait a few minutes before standing up.
6. Do not worry about whether you are successful in achieving a deep level of relaxation. Maintain a passive attitude and permit relaxation to occur at its own pace.

Exhibit 15–12
Relaxing as a Means of Coping with Stress

Describe principled negotiation.
Principled negotiation holds promise in keeping personalities out of conflict by focusing on the problem rather than the person.

Explain why modern life makes us particularly vulnerable to stress.
Stress is any external stimulus that causes wear and tear on a person's psychological or physical well-being. Modern men and women react to stress as our primitive ancestors did, with a chemical reaction designed to ready the body for fight or flight. This chemical reaction is not helpful in normal situations today, so we need to develop ways to cope with and manage stress.

Describe both the costs and the benefits of stress.
When we are unsuccessful in coping with stress, the costs are enormous. Stress is a major cause of many illnesses, from the common cold to heart disease. It plays a role in absenteeism, accidents, and lost productivity. Not all stress is negative, however. Small and great achievements occur as a result of moderate amounts of stress.

Explain the major causes of stress.
Major causes of stress are life events, personal psychological makeup, and organizational and work-related factors. The death of a spouse or a divorce places tremendous stress on most individuals. Similarly, working in an extremely high-pressure environment under prolonged autocratic leadership can cause stress and job burnout.

Compare and contrast Type A behavior and Type B behavior.
A person's psychological makeup influences how that person handles stress. Type A people try to accomplish too many things in a short period of time and tend to lack patience in dealing with people. Type B people tend to be calmer and more realistic in their assessment of the length of time needed to complete an assignment.

Elaborate on personal ways to cope with stress.
Fortunately, many of us can do a better job of managing stress if we develop certain strategies and behaviors. On a personal level, we can (1) exercise, (2) practice the relaxation response, and (3) gain a sense of control over our lives.

On the job, a supervisor can apply many of the concepts discussed throughout this book. Techniques particularly helpful in reducing stress in a work unit are to practice the concept of balance through participative management, when appropriate, and to delegate effectively without losing control.

Important Terms

burnout *pg. 418*
conflict management
   styles *406*
group facilitation *402*

life event *414*
principled negotiation
   410
process consultation *404*

relaxation response *421*
stress *412*
Type A behavior *416*
Type B behavior *416*

Questions for Review and Discussion

1. Discuss the purpose of group facilitation and the role of the facilitator.
2. How does process consultation differ from other models of consultation?
3. Identify the conflict management styles and describe when each one would be appropriate.
4. Discuss what is involved in principled negotiation. How does it differ from hard or soft negotiation?
5. Compare and contrast Type A behavior and Type B behavior.
6. What are the major causes of stress on the job? off the job?
7. Explain why exercise and the relaxation response are helpful in coping with stress.
8. What can a supervisor do to prevent stress in his or her work unit?

GROUP
ACTIVITY

Skill Builder 15–1
Developing Skills as a Facilitator/Consultant

In preparation for this class, go back and reread the section on process consultation. Keep in mind that the primary role of the facilitator/consultant is that of helper to an individual, group, or organization.

Instructions:

1. Each member of the class is to identify a problem or issue on which he or she needs help. It may be that you need help improving your study habits and grades. It may be that you are having a problem at work with your boss or with someone who works with you or for you. The guideline is that it must be a real problem or issue and that you "own" the problem.
2. The class is to be divided into groups of three. Each member of the trio will take turns being the client and receiving help from the other two members. The client will start the process by stating the issue or problem and will have 20 minutes to receive help.
3. The other two members will ask questions to clarify, expand on, and sharpen the diagnosis. In carrying out the questioning, the facilitators will play an active listening role and ask questions that not only help them in understanding the problem, but also help the class to better understand. Examples of such questions would be: "When did you first start having this problem? Can you expand on the history of your relationship with this co-worker?"
4. Ask the client what steps, if any, have been initiated to solve the problem.
5. Move into a joint problem-solving framework where all three of you engage in brainstorming ideas on how to deal with the problem.
6. Put together an action plan using the best ideas on specific actions the client can take to solve the problem.

Skill Builder 15–2
Facilitator Training

Assume you are in training to become an external facilitator/consultant and are faced with the following situations:

Your Task

First you are to choose the correct answer from the three alternatives and write the letter (a, b, c) that corresponds to the answer provided under the heading "Your Answer." You will have ten minutes to complete the task.

Team Task

You will be assigned to a small team of trainees to develop a team answer. Although the team will arrive at its answer through consensus, remember that consensus does not always mean unanimity. It means everyone has an opportunity to have their views considered before a choice is made. You will have 30 minutes to complete the team task.

How would you handle the following situations if you were the facilitator?

1. You are the facilitator at a workshop with 35 participants. The participants have agreed upon a common set of goals, and they have also identified five issues they need to deal with to achieve their goals. Five ad hoc subgroups of seven participants have been assigned to develop a plan to solve one of the top issues. The first step in the problem-solving process is to clearly state the problem. The members of one of the subgroups approach you as facilitator and state that they are having difficulty defining the problem and need your help.
   a. Tell them to do the best they can. (Your logic is that people learn from experience—success as well as failures.)
   b. Ask a few questions, and then write your version of the problem on the flip chart.
   c. Suggest that each person write a statement of the problem and then record all of them on the flip chart to see if one stands out or if there is a central theme.

Your Answer   *Team's Answer*   *Expert's Answer*

_____   _____   _____

2. You are facilitating a two-day workshop between the Navy and a contractor regarding the environmental clean-up progress of a Pacific island. There are several former Navy personnel that now work for the contractor. Toward the end of the first day, during a break, a public works civilian from the Navy approaches you and expresses a concern that a former Navy captain, who now works for the contractor, always begins a suggestion or recommendation with the following comment: "When I was Captain of XYZ installation and we were faced with this situation, we did so and so."
   a. Do nothing.
   b. As facilitator, talk with the former captain and level with him about the concern of a member of the Navy's group. Suggest he make recommendations without mentioning his former leadership positions in the Navy.

    c. As facilitator, mention the problem to the former captain's boss with the contractor. Leave it to him to decide whether or not he wants to say anything to the former captain.

Your Answer   *Team's Answer*   *Expert's Answer*

_____   _____   _____

3. You are facilitator for a group of 25 participants of two organizations who must work together to complete a major task such as building a dam. The two groups are having difficulties. As facilitator, you have taken them through a process where the group has identified and prioritized five issues they need to work on to ensure they will achieve their goals. After this task is completed, the group takes a short break before they start work on the priority issues. During the break, a key manager of one of the organizations comes to you and says that unless the lack of trust issue is addressed, very little progress will be made in resolving the other issues.

    a. Tell the key manager to trust the process and that by working on the five prioritized issues, team building will occur and trust will develop.

    b. Prior to reconvening, have a short meeting between four of the leaders, two from each organization, to gain their opinion on adding the trust issue to the list. Have the key manager present his case to them, and you, as facilitator, point out that developing trust is an important factor in successful teamwork and task accomplishment.

    c. When the group reconvenes, you as facilitator add the trust issue to the list to be worked on.

Your Answer   *Team's Answer*   *Expert's Answer*

_____   _____   _____

4. Assume you are facilitating a quarterly improvement meeting between representatives from the production and maintenance departments of a chemical plant. There are seven participants: four from production and three from maintenance. The meeting has become bogged down and is not making progress because of the strong views of two participants—one from production and one from maintenance. It appears to you that although both views have merit, neither one is hearing what the other is saying, and each is strictly focusing on his or her own viewpoint.

    a. Intervene and remind the participants of the time constraints and suggest they move on to something else.

    b. Intervene and request to hear the views of the other participants.

    c. Intervene by asking the production representative to summarize the maintenance representative's viewpoint to be sure the viewpoint was understood correctly by the production representative; then reverse the process.

Your Answer   *Team's Answer*   *Expert's Answer*

_____   _____   _____

5. Assume you are the facilitator/consultant for two medical firms located in a U.S. city with a population of 300,000 people. The firms are considering a merger; there are a number of win-win outcomes from such a merger (lower costs, better offices and facilities, more complete medical coverage, etc.). You are facilitating an

a young engineering graduate named Bobbi, whom Paul had trained, was promoted to the superintendent's job. It was then that Paul's personality changed. He began sleeping longer each night, often falling asleep in front of the television set. He also developed a tightness in his stomach that was creating a burning sensation.

Bobbi, the engineer who had been promoted to maintenance superintendent was worried. For the past several months she had been concerned about the performance and health of one of her maintenance supervisors, Paul Williamson. Paul had been Bobbi's boss at one time, and she had always admired his ability as a supervisor and his knowledge of the maintenance area.

Recently, while attending a regional meeting of maintenance managers from different plants of the ABC Company, Bobbi ran into the former maintenance manager at her plant, who was now at another plant. He asked how Paul was doing. Bobbi, glad to share her concern with someone, said that she was really worried about him. "His performance has slipped, for one thing. Also, he used to have perfect attendance, but lately he's been calling in sick a lot."

The maintenance manager replied, "I wonder if disappointment over not being promoted to maintenance superintendent has affected his performance. No reflection on you, of course, but before I left, the plant manager and I had agreed that Paul would be promoted to maintenance superintendent. Then the home office changed its corporate policy so that only college graduates could be promoted to superintendent. This made Paul ineligible, and you got the job instead."

Bobbi hadn't realized that Paul had been the first choice for the position she now held. Upon reflection, she decided to have a coaching and counseling session with him when she returned to the plant, as she certainly didn't want to lose him.

Answer the following questions:
1. How should Bobbi approach Paul about the situation?
2. What do you think Paul's reaction(s) will be?
3. Do you agree with the company's policy of promoting only college graduates to the maintenance superintendent position? Why or why not?

Chapter 16
Selecting, Training, and Compensating Employees

Case 16

Bill Waldorf: Selecting and Supervising a Diverse High-Tech Work Team

William L. (Bill) Waldorf, Marketing Production Manager, handles advertising for the 25 Gayfers/Maison Blanche Department Stores located throughout Alabama, Mississippi, Florida, and Louisiana. Gayfers/Maison Blanche is a subsidiary of Mercantile Stores Company, Inc., which is based in Cincinnati, Ohio. Waldorf reports to the advertising director, who, in turn, reports to the president of Gayfers.

Waldorf is responsible for recruiting, interviewing, hiring, evaluating, rewarding, and disciplining his "associates," as employees are called. He selects his people from within the company, if feasible. His staff consists of 22 full-time employees who handle the creative and conceptual portion of the advertising and marketing activities for all the stores. There are an art director, four designers, a print production manager, a traffic manager, two copywriters, a photo studio manager, three photographers, three support personnel, three electronic pagination experts, a scanner operator, a darkroom technician, and a clerical/technical worker. The staff is composed of a diverse group of men and women, including minorities, who are highly skilled, conscientious, and largely self-motivated. While most of the employees are paid on an hourly basis, a few are paid a monthly or yearly salary.

Waldorf, who believes in empowering his associates, gives them freedom to make their own decisions and encourages them to come up with suggestions for work improvement throughout the company. He also uses the double incentives of (1) providing recognition for a job well done and (2) granting merit increases when deserved. Since most of his associates are creative people, he uses a *laissez-faire leadership style*. They mutually agree on what is to be done and what each person is to do; then he leaves them alone to do it—unless the job is not done effectively and on time.

As mentioned earlier, Waldorf is responsible for the creative portions of Gayfers' advertising operations. He frequently meets with the merchandise managers, their divisional managers, and the president of the company—if needed—to plan their marketing strategy. After they tell him what items they think will sell, Waldorf helps them identify who their customers are and what makes the items attractive to them. He then suggests themes, layout, color, artwork, and other factors that will make the items appealing.

Waldorf is also responsible for planning and supervising the photography activities and for the preparation and placement of ads in the electronic and print media used to advertise the merchandise. He checks daily sales figures on his e-mail terminal, by which internal letters are sent directly, quickly, and confidentially to him. He communicates via internet with headquarters in Ohio, which permits quicker and easier decision making.

Among his other activities, Waldorf supervises all TV, radio, and newspaper production, in addition to preparing and distributing direct mailing pieces. He also has access to the company's charge account list. Software programs can analyze many different types of information about these customers, which he can then use for various direct mail promotions.

Waldorf does extensive strategic and operational planning—part of which involves researching competitive marketing in other stores in order to evaluate their marketing strategy. In addition, he does weekly, monthly, quarterly, and annual planning, including evaluating which previous promotions were successful and which were not—and why. He then discusses with the merchandise managers which promotions to repeat.

Waldorf majored in commercial art at the University of Southern Alabama. He has also taken courses in illustration and design and computer courses in three-dimensional graphics and multimedia. As he has moved up in the company, he has attended leadership courses at Mercantile Stores University (MSU). At MSU, empowerment is highly stressed, as is decision making. Quality control is another subject he has studied.

One of the leadership techniques Waldorf learned at MSU was the use of management by objectives (MBO). He and each of his associates sit down at the beginning of the year to jointly set attainable goals. Then, they evaluate their own performance each quarter. At the end of the year, each associate fills out a self-evaluation form, giving specific examples of performance. That evaluation plays an important part in salary adjustments.

Here lies a man who knew how to enlist in his service better men than himself.

Andrew Carnegie's Epitaph

To prosper in the nineties and beyond, companies must concentrate on the three Rs: recruiting, retraining, and retaining high-quality people.

Nancy J. Perry

It is not the employers who pay wages— they only handle the money. It is the product that pays wages.

Henry Ford

We have discussed the functions of planning, organizing, and leading employees. Now we will look at the process of staffing the organization. When Art Linkletter, owner of over 75 companies, was asked the secret of his success, his answer was "I bet on people!" As the great industrialist Andrew Carnegie realized, an organization consists not merely of physical and financial resources but, most importantly, of people. As Nancy Perry indicates in one of the opening quotations, the challenge of the immediate future will lie in properly selecting and developing people. Management must emphasize putting the right employees in the right jobs and then motivating them to perform.

Candidates for a given job can be obtained from inside or outside the organization, but there must be some method of selection to find capable people. Then, the organization must improve employees' performance through training and developing their abilities adequately and then compensating them. These and other aspects of human resource management are covered in this chapter.

We believe that supervisors need to "see the big picture" of the staffing process. Certainly not all supervisors are involved in the activities presented in this chapter, but, if they understand the total process of staffing, they will be in a better position to perform their part of this process.

RESPONSIBILITY FOR SELECTING, TRAINING, AND COMPENSATING EMPLOYEES

Learning Objective 1

Explain who is responsible for selecting, training, and compensating employees.

An organization can be successful only if it has the right number and types of people to do the required work. Therefore, a primary duty of all supervisors is the proper selection, placement, training and development, compensation, and utilization of competent employees. How well—or poorly—supervisors perform these functions is a major factor in their success or failure.

A Shared Responsibility

Like almost all aspects of supervision, selecting and training employees are shared tasks, though the primary responsibility should be left to supervisors. In general, the responsibilities are divided as follows:

1. *Top managers* set human resources objectives, establish policies, and do long-range planning and organizing.
2. *Middle managers* control the operating procedures needed to achieve these objectives and carry out personnel policies.
3. *Supervisors* interpret policies for employees and carry out higher management's wishes as to selecting and training employees. Also, they interpret and transmit workers' interests to higher management.

With today's emphasis on *empowerment,* teams are often used at all three of these levels. It is especially important to have potential fellow-employees involved in an advisory role, at least.

The Supervisor's Role

Operative employees usually have little contact with high-level managers. Therefore, they tend to think of their supervisor as being "management" or "the organization." Because employees interpret their supervisor's actions, attitudes, and methods as representing those of all managers, supervisors are probably the most important people in achieving an organization's human resources objectives. Supervisors usually have the final word in selecting employees. Then they supervise and control the employees' daily activities. Finally, they appraise the employees' performance, often as the basis for giving employees further rewards and promotions.

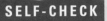

SELF-CHECK

In the Johnson Company, a large department store, sales positions are filled directly by the personnel office. When a selection decision is made, the sales department supervisor is notified, and the new employee reports to her or him for a job assignment. Typically, the new employee first meets his or her supervisor on the first day of work. What are the pros and cons of this system?

PLANNING HUMAN RESOURCE NEEDS AND FINDING EMPLOYEES TO FILL THE JOBS

Learning Objective 2

Describe how to plan human resource needs and how to find employees for specific jobs.

Most organizations cannot afford to have more workers than they need. Yet neither can they afford to do without the needed number of employees. Therefore, the beginning of the staffing function is planning personnel needs. There are two aspects to this step: (1) deciding what jobs need to be filled and what they involve and (2) determining the personal characteristics employees need to handle these jobs successfully. The first aspect involves the preparation of a *job description,* whereas the second aspect calls for a *job specification.* Both should be the responsibility of the supervisor, who best knows the job to be done and the knowledge and skills needed to do it.

Types and Number of Employees Needed

job description Spell out the primary duties and responsibilities of specific jobs.

job analysis Gathering information and determining the elements of a job by observation and study.

job specification Minimum standards a person should meet to perform the job satisfactorily.

A **job description** is a written statement covering the duties, authority, responsibilities, and working conditions of a particular job. The supervisor can obtain information about the job from experience in performing it, by observing other people performing it, or by doing a job analysis. **Job analysis** is the process of gathering information and determining the elements of a job through observation and study.

The job description also shows the relationship of the described job to others. Thus it becomes the basis not only for selecting someone for the job but also for further training workers and appraising their performance of the job. Exhibit 16–1 lists some typical components of a job description.

The personal characteristics required to perform a job are set forth in a **job specification,** which can be used to select the proper person for the job. Some of the categories of qualifications are education and training, aptitudes, temperament, interests, physical capabilities, experience, and attitudes. The job specification should state the minimum standards the person should meet in order to perform the job satisfactorily. One major reason for this is to be in compliance with the guidelines of the Equal Employment Opportunity Commission (EEOC).

Finally, the number of people to be selected to fill each of the job and skill categories must be estimated. The supervisor first determines the total number of workers needed and then subtracts the number already employed; the difference is the number to be hired. (See Exhibit 16–2, "Job Specification?")

Once the number and type(s) of employees needed for given jobs have been determined, the next step is to decide where to look for them. As Exhibit 16–3 shows, there are only two basic sources: within and outside the organization. A balanced

- *Identification of job:* Job title, department, code, salary range, supervisor, etc.
- *Job description:*
    a. Physical demands of the job and the minimum physical requirements needed to fill it.
    b. Working conditions, including psychological conditions such as relationships with others and responsibilities for other people, money, and equipment.
    c. Summary of the duties and responsibilities of the job.
    d. Days and hours of work.
    e. Machines, tools, formulas, and equipment used.
- *Job specifications:*
    a. Educational background and knowledge, skills and techniques, and training and experience required to perform the job, as well as special training and development needed.
    b. Personal characteristics such as sociableness, articulateness, or aggressiveness.

Exhibit 16–1

Components of a Typical Job Description and Job Specification

Exhibit 16–2

Job Specifications?

"I CAN REMEMBER WHEN ALL WE NEEDED WAS SOMEONE WHO COULD CARVE AND SOMEONE WHO COULD SEW."

Source: Copyright © 1980 by Sidney Harris for *The Wall Street Journal.*

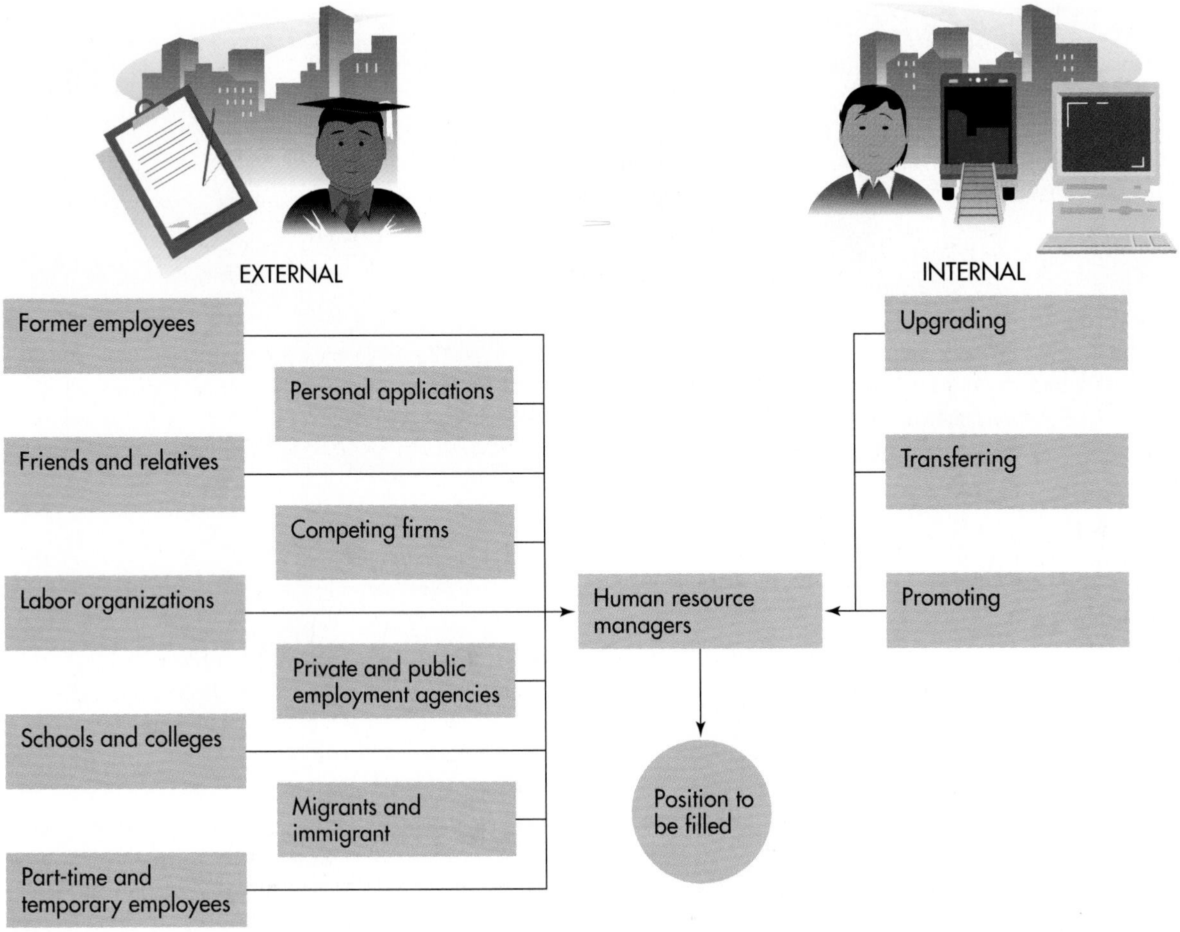

EXTERNAL

INTERNAL

| Former employees |
| Personal applications |
| Friends and relatives |
| Competing firms |
| Labor organizations |
| Private and public employment agencies |
| Schools and colleges |
| Migrants and immigrant |
| Part-time and temporary employees |

| Upgrading |
| Transferring |
| Promoting |

Human resource managers

Position to be filled

Exhibit 16–3
Where to Look for Employees

program of acquiring people from both sources is better than relying on either source exclusively. A policy of promoting from within whenever possible and recruiting from outside when necessary provides for both continuity and new ideas.

SELF-CHECK

In Case 16, where did Bill Waldorf obtain his employees? Do you think this is the best source for filling positions such as these? Explain.

If personal qualifications have been established, then the sources most likely to produce people with such qualifications must be consulted. Some of these sources are more costly in both time and money than others. Although search costs should be taken into consideration, the source chosen should be the one that provides the best results from the standpoint of employee performance.

Filling Jobs From Within

There are many specific outside sources from which employees can be recruited, as you will soon see. However, most managers try to fill jobs from within, if possible.

REASONS FOR AND AGAINST USING INTERNAL SOURCES. The reasons *for* using internal sources include (1) lower cost and (2) knowledge of the person's capabilities, strengths, and weaknesses. Promotion from within will probably provide continuity, enhance motivation, and also build the morale of other employees (except if an individual is bypassed and becomes jealous). The reasons for *not* using internal sources include (1) the lack of anyone capable of filling a job or willing to take it, (2) the conformity that may be produced by excessive reliance on internal sources, and (3) the possibility of developing complacency among current employees.

METHODS OF OBTAINING EMPLOYEES FROM WITHIN. There are three methods of securing employees internally: (1) upgrading the employee currently holding the position, (2) transferring an employee from a similar position elsewhere in the organization, and (3) promoting an employee from a lower-level job. A good training program throughout the organization is needed to provide the capable people needed for promotion.

technological un-employment When employees can no longer perform their jobs because the educational or skill demands are beyond their capacity.

Increasing skill requirements in various areas have led to **technological unemployment,** a situation in which employees can no longer perform their jobs because educational or skill demands have increased beyond their capacity. Such virtual vacancies can be dealt with by **upgrading** present employees—that is, retraining unskilled or semiskilled workers in their present positions. This method was very effective during World War II. For this method to work, employees must be willing to make the sacrifice of time and effort required to take the training.

upgrading Retraining unskilled or semi-skilled workers to meet changing demands.

> **A large church decided to computerize its accounting processes after having always used conventional ledgers, journals, and office machines to keep its books. The woman who kept the books was not qualified to do the new job, but she was not replaced. Instead, she was given a leave of absence to take an intensive course from the computer vendor to prepare herself to learn the new system. When the change was made, she successfully made the transition.**

transferring Moving employees to a different job at the same organizational level.

Positions can also be filled by **transferring** employees from the same organizational level elsewhere in the organization. The transferee may have outgrown the position he or she previously held, or the transfer may provide greater potential for advancement. Essentially, a transfer involves a change in responsibilities and duties, either with or without a change in pay. Transfers are often requested for reasons other than pay increases.

> **Van Ludwig was the purchasing clerk at Tri-State Distribution Company. In this capacity he served and became familiar with other departments of the company, especially city sales. He was a good worker—rapid, efficient, and reliable. But even though his pay increased steadily during his five years in the position, he**

Allen-Bradley Co. utililized obtaining employees from within when it promoted Larry Hanson, a cell specialist, from a tedious assembly job to high-tech circuitboard manufacturing.

became dissatisfied with the working hours, which required him to remain at the office until 6:00 or 7:00 p.m.

When a position opened up at city sales, Van applied for it. But his transfer was rejected because he hadn't cleared it with his supervisor. Furthermore, he had done nothing to prepare himself for a sales career.

A few months later Van applied for the next opening in city sales. This time the city sales supervisor pointed out to Van his lack of experience and training in sales. This supervisor suggested that Van would have to accept a considerable reduction in pay, and it would take Van two years in city sales to reach the level of pay he was currently receiving in purchasing. Finally, there was Van's worth to the company to be considered. In purchasing he was a trained, efficient clerk; in city sales he would be a new trainee.

SELF-CHECK   Would you have accepted Van as a transferee if you had been the city sales supervisor?

---

promoting Moving a person from a lower- to a higher-level job.

Promoting is moving a person from a lower- to a higher-level job. Thus, a position is filled, but another one is vacated. The person who is promoted will need more skill and/or have more responsibility but may also gain more status, prestige, and income. One important reason for using promotion to fill higher positions is that the morale and motivation of employees are enhanced by this process.

seniority An employee's length of service in a company.

There are three bases for promotion: (1) **seniority,** or length of service, (2) **merit,** which refers to the employee's ability to do the job better than others, and (3) a combination of the two. In theory, promotions based on merit are more desirable from a motivational standpoint because they encourage employees to produce more in order to demonstrate their merit. For lower-level jobs, however, particularly where unions are involved, seniority is the more common basis for promotion. There is considerable value in using a combination of length of service (seniority), which provides a good understanding of the job and the company, and merit, which guarantees that the employee has the mental and physical ability to do the job effectively.

merit An employee's ability to do the job better than others.

job posting Announcing available job openings on a bulletin board.

If the employees are represented by a union, the firm will probably be required to post available job openings on a bulletin board to give present employees a chance to bid on them. This procedure, called **job posting,** has also been found to be a good method of complying with equal employment opportunity laws if there is no evidence of discrimination in the selection process later. Many nonunion firms are using it to foster employee growth and to prevent unionization.

electronic job posting A software program to make filling jobs from within more efficient.

Many companies are now using **electronic job posting,** and computerized skills inventory systems to make filling jobs from within more efficient. For example, when Household International wanted to fill jobs from within during a growth spurt in the mid-1980s, the company used *Inside Tracks,* a job-posting software program, to help 1,300 displaced workers find another job somewhere in the company. All employees received a brochure with instructions for using the system.[1] The program was so successful that the employer made it available to all 14,500 employers at 450 offices around the country.[2]

dual promotion ladders Enables skilled technical and scientific workers to get salary increases and higher job titles without becoming managers.

Often, employees do not want to take a management job. So many companies are now using **dual promotion ladders,** whereby skilled technical and scientific workers can get salary increases and higher job titles without becoming managers. This practice is similar to the one used in professional sports, where outstanding players make far more than their coaches or management.

Filling Jobs From the Outside

Even if an employer has a policy of hiring from within, outside sources are often needed. As individual positions are filled by upgrading, transferring, or promoting employees, some vacated positions must be filled externally, as shown earlier in Exhibit 16–3. Some external sources of new employees are:

1. Former employees.
2. Personal applications received in person or through the mail.
3. Friends and relatives of employees.
4. Competing firms.
5. Labor organizations.
6. Employment agencies, either public or private.
7. Educational institutions, including high schools, business schools, vocational-technical schools, junior colleges, colleges, and manufacturers' training schools.
8. Migrants and immigrants.
9. Part-time employees.

REASONS FOR USING EXTERNAL SOURCES. A growing organization must go outside to obtain employees for at least its lowest-level jobs. But there are also reasons for going outside for higher-level personnel, and many of these reasons are associated with problems caused by computers and automation. When new skills are needed in a hurry, they must often be found in people from outside the organization who have the required education, training, and experience. Moreover, even when an internal promotion policy is followed, mistakes are inevitably made. It is almost impossible to anticipate all the skills that will be needed in the future. It is just as difficult to hire someone with those skills to join the organization at an entry-level position and progress through the organization at such a rate as to be available just when needed.

METHODS OF RECRUITING FROM THE OUTSIDE. Methods used to recruit new employees include:

1. Scouring at schools or colleges.
2. Advertising through newspapers, trade journals, radio, billboards, and window displays.
3. Using the services of private and public employment agencies.
4. Acting on employee referrals.
5. Electronic employment bulletin boards.

The choice of the proper method to use is not an easy one, but it can be very important. The following example shows some problems with each of the more frequently used methods.

> **A store manager put a "Help Wanted" sign in the window. She found this practice time-consuming because many unqualified applicants inquired about the job. Furthermore, when she rejected an applicant, she stood the risk of losing the applicant as a customer, and possibly that person's family and friends as well. The manager found that newspaper advertising also reached large groups of job seekers but still brought in many unqualified people. If the store's telephone number was given in the ad, calls tied up the line and customers couldn't reach the store.**

COMPLYING WITH EQUAL EMPLOYMENT OPPORTUNITY LAWS

Learning Objective 3

State the laws providing equal employment opportunity for protected groups of employees.

All aspects of employment are affected by federal, state, and local laws, regulations, and court decisions. Some of the federal regulations and court decisions, and their effects on recruiting and selection, will now be explained. It should be emphasized at this point, however, that EEO laws build upon—and enhance—good human resource practices by most employers.

Equal Employment Opportunity (EEO) Laws

The Civil Rights Act of 1866, the Civil Rights Act of 1964, Executive Order 11246, the Civil Rights Act of 1991, and other legislation prohibit discrimination based on race, color, religion, sex, or national origin in all employment practices. There are also laws protecting the disabled, older workers, and Vietnam veterans. Exhibit 16–4 shows who is covered by these laws and regulations. It also shows the laws' basic requirements and the agencies that enforce them.

Enforcement of EEO Laws

affirmative action programs (AAPs) Programs to put the principle of equal employment opportunity into practice.

The Equal Employment Opportunity Commission (EEOC) is the primary agency enforcing EEO laws. It receives and investigates charges of discrimination, issues orders to stop violations, and may even go to a U.S. District Court to enforce its decrees. The Commission encourages **affirmative action programs (AAPs),** which

Exhibit 16–4

Legal Influences on Equal Employment Opportunity (EEO) and Affirmative Action (AA)

Laws	Basic Requirements	Coverage	Enforcement Agencies
Section 1981 of Civil Rights Act of 1866	Prohibits racial discrimination in employment.	All private employers, labor unions, and employment agencies	Judicial system
Title VII of Civil Rights Act of 1964	Prohibits employment discrimination based on race, color, religion, sex, or national origin.	Private employers engaged in interstate commerce with 15 or more employees, labor unions, employment agencies, federal government workers, and state and local government workers	Equal Employment Opportunity Commission (EEOC)
Executive Order 11246 of 1965, as amended	Prohibits employment discrimination based on race, sex, color, religion, or national origin, and requires contractors employing 50 or more workers to develop affirmative action plans (AAPs) when contracts exceed $50,000 a year.	Federal contractors and subcontractors holding contracts of $10,000 or more	U.S. Department of Labor's Office of Federal Contract Compliance Programs (OFCCP)
Age Discrimination in Employment Act of 1967, as amended	Prohibits employment discrimination against persons over age 40.	Same as those under Title VII, except that private employers with 20 or more employees are covered	EEOC
Vocational Rehabilitation Act of 1973	Prohibits employment discrimination against otherwise qualified handicapped persons, requires reasonable accommodation, and requires development of AAPs.	Federal contractors and subcontractors holding contracts in excess of $2,500, organizations that receive federal assistance, and federal agencies	OFCCP
Vietnam Era Veterans' Assistance Act of 1974	Requires contractors to develop AAPs to recruit and employ qualified disabled veterans and veterans of the Vietnam War.	Federal contractors and subcontractors holding contracts in excess of $10,000	OFCCP

Exhibit 16–4 concluded

Laws	Basic Requirements	Coverage	Enforcement Agencies
Immigration Reform and Control Act of 1986	Prohibits recruiting, hiring, or referring aliens who are not eligible to work in the United States; prohibits employment discrimination based on national origin or citizenship.	Private employers, labor unions, and employment agencies	U.S. Department of Justice's Special Counsel for Unfair Immigration-Related Employment
Americans with Disabilities Act of 1990	Prohibits employment discrimination against qualified individuals with a disability and requires reasonable accommodation.	Same as Title VII	EEOC
Civil Rights Act of 1991	Amends Title VII and the Americans with Disabilities Act to allow for punitive and compensatory damages in cases of intentional discrimination and more extensive use of jury trials.	Same as Title VII	EEOC

Source: Leon C. Megginson, Geralyn M. Franklin, and M. Jane Byrd, *Human Resource Management* (Houston, TX: Dame Publications, Inc., 1995), pp. 58–59.

are plans to put the principle of equal employment opportunity into practice. These programs are required by the Office of Federal Contract Compliance Programs (OFCCP) in the Labor Department, which enforces Executive Order 11246; by the Vocational Rehabilitation Act; and by the Vietnam Era Veterans Readjustment Assistance Act.

In essence, an organization, through an AAP, promises to do the following:

diverse groups Groups such as women, African-Americans, Hispanics, Vietnam-era veterans, the disabled, and older workers.

1. Make good-faith efforts to recruit from **diverse groups** (which include women, African-Americans, Hispanics, Vietnam-era veterans, native Americans, the disabled, and older workers) through state employment services.
2. Limit the questions that are asked of applicants on their application forms or during interviews (see Exhibit 16–5).
3. Set goals and timetables for hiring the protected groups.
4. Avoid testing applicants unless the tests meet established guidelines.

Here is an up-to-date summary of 10 of the most dangerous questions or topics you might raise during an interview.

1. *Children.* Do not ask applicants whether they have children, or plan to have children, or have child care.
2. *Age.* Do not ask an applicant's age.
3. *Disabilities.* Do not ask whether the candidate has a physical or mental disability that would interfere with doing the job.
4. *Physical Characteristics.* Do not ask for such identifying characteristics as height or weight on an application.
5. *Name.* Do not ask a female candidate for her maiden name.
6. *Citizenship.* Do not ask applicants about their citizenship. However, the Immigration Reform and Control Act does require business operators to determine that their employees have a legal right to work in the United States.
7. *Lawsuits.* Do not ask a job candidate whether he or she has ever filed a suit or a claim against a former employer.
8. *Arrest Records.* Do not ask applicants about their arrest records.
9. *Smoking.* Do not ask whether a candidate smokes. While smokers are not protected under the Americans with Disabilities Act (ADA), asking applicants whether they smoke might lead to legal difficulties if an applicant is turned down because of fear that smoking would drive up the employer's health care costs.
10. *AIDS and HIV.* Never ask job candidates whether they have AIDS or are HIV-positive, as these questions violate the ADA and could violate state and federal civil rights laws.

Source: Adapted by permission, *Nation's Business,* July 1992. Copyright 1992, U.S. Chamber of Commerce.

Exhibit 16–5
*Topics to Avoid When
Interviewing Applicants*

SELECTING EMPLOYEES FOR SPECIFIC JOBS

Learning Objective 4

Describe the steps in the employee selection procedure, including the proper orientation of new employees.

A suggested procedure for selecting employees is shown in Exhibit 16–6. Individual employers may find it desirable to modify this procedure—or depart from it—under certain conditions. In this section, each of the steps listed in the exhibit is briefly explained.

Requisition

Selection really begins with a requisition from the supervisor to the human resource department. This requisition (see Exhibit 16–7), which is based on the previously prepared job description and specification, is the authorization the department needs to recruit applicants for the position(s) available. In many small and medium-sized firms, the supervisor makes an informal visit or phone call to the senior officer who is authorized to make the final job offer.

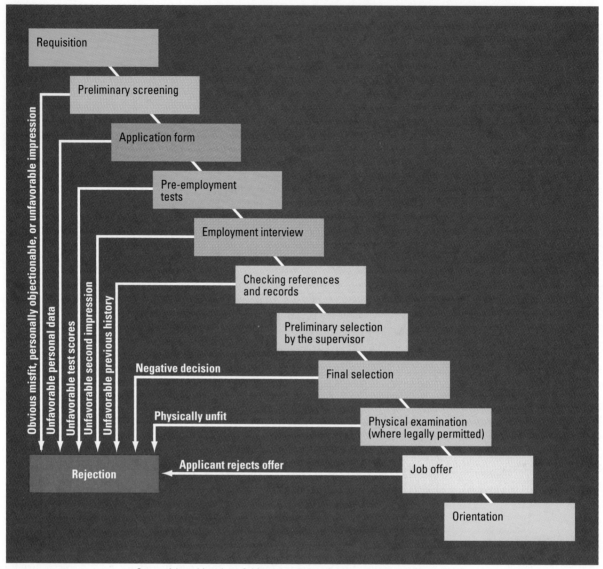

Source: Adapted from Leon C. Megginson, Donald C. Mosley, and Paul H. Pietri, Jr., *Management: Concepts and Applications,* 4th ed. (New York: HarperCollins, 1992), Figure 10.5, p. 357.

Exhibit 16–6
Flow Chart of a Suggested Selection Procedure

A reminder is needed at this point! If you, as a supervisor, are involved in selecting job applicants, all aspects of your procedure must conform to the EEOC's *Uniform Guidelines on Employee Selection Procedures.* Notice that the Guidelines cover *all selection procedures,* not just testing. Your procedures should also comply with your affirmative action program for hiring people from various groups. The human resource officer, in particular, should be certain that the selection procedure conforms to national and local laws and customs.

Preliminary Screening

Whether formal or informal, some form of preliminary screening helps weed out those persons who do not seem to meet the employer's needs—thus saving their time

HUMAN RESOURCE REQUISITION

Job Title: Warehouse worker   Job Code Number: 7-103

Number of employees needed   2   Date needed   2 March 1996

    Full-time ☐   Part-time ☐   Temporary ☑
                                                              approx. 2 weeks
Whom to report to: Norma Mills, Supervisor

Where to report: #1 warehouse, main office

Time to report: 8 AM

Requesting supervisor: Norma Mills   Date 20 Feb. 1996

(For use by Human Resource Department)

	Applicant's Name	Soc. Sec. No.	Date Available	Hire?
1.	Mike A. Johnson	344-62-9307	2 March	OK
2.	Carmen Carreon	433-54-3470	2 March	OK
3.	William S. Lloyd	460-65-0719	9 March	
4.	Laura Y. McGhee	478-60-3181	24 February	
5.				

Exhibit 16–7
*Sample Human
Resource Requisition*

and yours. This step deals with such obvious factors as educational background, training, experience, physical appearance, grooming, and speech—if these are relevant to job performance. Also, the applicant should know something about the organization and the job being sought.

An early study found that 9 percent of college applicants were eliminated at this point for "personal reasons." Some of the reasons cited for not hiring were bad breath, dirty fingernails, and uncombed hair.[3]

> **Mike, a bright young college student, applied at a local hotel for employment while home on summer break in 1994. He was rejected at the preliminary interview because his hair was below his collar—even though it was neatly pulled back. He was told that even the grounds keepers and dry cleaning plant workers had to have their hair above their collars.**
>
> **In 1995, he was rejected by a grocery chain because he had a beard. He did find a lucrative job waiting tables at an English pub—with great tips and free meals.**

Application Form

After passing the preliminary screening, the job applicant usually completes an application form. (Some applications are submitted by mail or in person before preliminary screening.) The applicant lists employers for whom he or she has worked, titles of jobs held, and length of employment with each one. Background, education, military status, and other useful data are listed. The form should be carefully designed to provide the information needed about the applicant's potential performance; it should not be a hodgepodge of irrelevant data. The completion of the form in longhand will provide you with a simple test of the applicant's neatness, thoroughness, ability to answer questions—and literacy.

> The manager of a tire store once told one of the authors that he requires all applicants to fill out an application in person on the premises. "When they ask to take it home," he said, "I can be almost sure they're illiterate and need help in reading it and filling it out."

The EEOC and many states have restrictions concerning the kinds of questions that may be included on an application form (refer back to Exhibit 16–5). Therefore, you should check any laws that your state may have on such practices.

Pre-employment Testing

Various tests can be used to assess an applicant's intelligence quotient (IQ), skills, aptitudes, vocational interests, personality, and performance. However, the tests must be EEOC-approved and be valid and reliable. Only the most popular will be discussed here.

TYPES OF TESTS. **IQ tests** are designed to measure the applicant's capacity to learn, to solve problems, and to understand relationships. They are particularly useful in selecting employees for supervisory and managerial positions. **Aptitude tests** are used to predict how a person might perform on a given job and are most applicable to operative jobs. **Vocational interest tests** are designed to determine the applicant's areas of major work interest. While interest does not guarantee competence, it can result in the employee's working and trying harder. **Personality tests** are supposed to measure the applicant's emotional adjustment and attitude. These tests are often used to evaluate interpersonal relationships and to see how the person might fit into an organization.

Probably the most effective tests the supervisor can use in selecting operative employees are **achievement, proficiency,** or **skill tests.** These tests measure fairly accurately the applicant's knowledge of and ability to do a given job. They can also spot *trade bluffers*—people who claim job knowledge, skills, and experience that they don't really have. One type of proficiency test is a **work sampling** or **work preview,** in which the prospective employee is asked to do a task that is representative of the work usually done on the job. In addition to showing whether the person can actually do the job, the test gives the applicant more realistic expectations about the job.

Perhaps the most frequently used test at present is for drug use. About 63 percent of companies now use some form of **drug testing.** Since January 1995, around 7.5 million truck drivers, pilots, and other transportation workers have faced random alcohol breath tests as well as drug screens. The U.S. Department of Transportation enforces the new law, the Omnibus Transportation Employee Testing Act of 1991.[4]

IQ tests Measure the applicant's capacity to learn, solve problems, and understand relationships.

aptitude tests Predict how a person might perform on a given job.

vocational interest tests Determine the applicant's areas of major work interest.

Personality tests Measure the applicant's emotional adjustment and attitude.

achievement tests Measure the applicant's knowledge of and ability to do a given job.

work sampling A test in which the prospective employee must perform a task that is representative of the job.

drug testing Determines whether an applicant is a drug abuser.

VALIDITY OF TESTS. If tests are used in making the selection decision, employers must be prepared to demonstrate their validity. **Validity** is demonstrated by a high positive correlation between the applicant's test scores and some identifiable measure of performance on the job. Furthermore, the tests must be designed, administered, and interpreted by a professional (usually a licensed psychologist); be culturally neutral so that they don't discriminate against any ethnic group; and be in complete conformity with EEOC guidelines.[5] Tests must also have **reliability;** that is, the results will be the same if the test is given to the same person by different testers or by the same tester at different times. Care should be exercised in interpreting test results, as some persons are adept at faking answers. Because of these and other problems, many firms are dropping testing in favor of other selection techniques.

It should be reemphasized at this point that *all selection techniques are subject to scrutiny by the EEOC.* It should also be mentioned that the most frequently used selection criteria are supervisory ratings and job performance.

validity A high positive correlation between the applicant's test scores and some objective measure of job performance.

reliability The probability that test results won't change if given to the same person by different individuals.

USE OF THE POLYGRAPH. The **polygraph (lie detector)** is a device used to evaluate a person's truthfulness by measuring physical changes in response to questioning (see Exhibit 16–8). It is now being used sparingly to deal with the surge in employee thefts. It can be used for this purpose on three occasions: (1) during the pre-employment security clearance exam, (2) when there is a specific loss, and (3) when a periodic spot check is made. Because the polygraph hasn't been proven beyond a shadow of a doubt to be reliable, its use is severely restricted by federal and state laws.

Polygraph (lie detector) Evaluates a person's truthfulness by measuring physical changes in response to questioning.

Employment Interviewing

In preparing for the employment interview, which is the only two-way part of the selection procedure, you should use the information on the application form and the test results to learn as much as you can about the applicant. A list of questions prepared before the interview can help you avoid missing information that might be significant in judging the applicant. Compare your list of questions with the job specification to ensure that you are matching the individual's personal qualifications with the job requirements. Some specific questions you might ask are:

1. What did you do on your last job?
2. How did you do it?
3. Why did you do it?
4. Of the jobs you have had, which did you like best? Which the least?
5. Why did you leave your last job?
6. What do you consider your strong and weak points?
7. Why do you want to work for us?

If you are observant and perceptive during the interview, you can obtain some impressions about the candidate's abilities, personality, appearance, speech, and attitudes toward work. You should also provide the applicant with information about the company and the job. Remember, the applicant needs facts to decide whether to accept or reject the job, just as you need information to decide whether or not to offer it.

Exhibit 16–8

Source: Baton Rouge Sunday Advocate, DIN.

structured interviews
Standardized and controlled with regard to questions asked.

unstructured interviews The pattern of questions asked, the conditions under which they are asked, and the bases for evaluating results are not standardized.

The interview may be carried out individually by the supervisor or in cooperation with someone else—the human resource officer or some other senior manager. It may be structured or unstructured. **Structured interviews** are standardized and controlled with regard to questions asked, sequence of questions, interpretation of replies, and weight given to factors considered in making the value judgment as to whether or not to hire the person. In **unstructured interviews,** the pattern of questions asked, the conditions under which they are asked, and the bases for evaluating results are determined by the interviewer.

Checking References and Records

The importance of carefully checking applicants' references cannot be overemphasized. Reference checks provide answers to questions concerning a candidate's performance on previous jobs. They are helpful in verifying information on the application form and other records, as well as statements made during the interviews. They are also useful in checking on possible omissions of information and in clarifying specific points. Yet, a Robert Half survey found that 68 percent of employers now find that former employers, fearing lawsuits, tend to say nothing—or only nice things—about past employees.[6] In fact, most former employers will only give dates of employment and position(s) held.

Reference checks made in person or by telephone are greatly preferable to written ones, as past employers are sometimes reluctant to commit to writing any uncomplimentary remarks about a former employee. Be sure to ask specific questions about the candidate's performance. The type of information you are allowed to seek is restricted by laws such as the Fair Credit Reporting Act and the Privacy Act. But you can check on dates and terms of employment, salary, whether termination was voluntary, and whether this employer would rehire the candidate.

Many organizations are now using credit checks to obtain information about prospective employees. If this source is used and is the basis for rejecting a candidate, he or she has the right to see the report.

Preliminary Selection by the Supervisor

By this point in the selection process, you—the supervisor—have narrowed the number of candidates to one or a very few. If there is only one, the applicant can be hired on a trial basis. If you have more than one qualified candidate, a review of the information collected should reveal the best choice. Although your preliminary selection may be subject to approval by the human resource department or some higher authority, usually the person will be offered the job.

Final Selection

Human resource officers are usually brought in on the final hiring decision because of their expertise. They ensure that all laws and regulations, as well as company policies, are followed. Also, they have a voice in such questions as salary and employee benefits to be offered to the applicant.

Physical Examination

Formerly, the final step in the selection procedure was a physical examination to see if the applicant could do the job. However, the Americans with Disabilities Act (ADA) has limited this part of the process. Employers may not now require an exam before a preliminary job offer is made.[7] Even then, the exam may only determine whether the worker can do the job being sought, and no medical history may be taken.[8]

Job Offer

Job offers to applicants for nonmanagerial and nonprofessional positions are usually made by the human resource office. They are often in writing and contain the terms and conditions of employment. At this point, the offer is either accepted or rejected. If it is rejected, an offer may be made to the next most qualified applicant. If there are no other qualified candidates, the selection procedure must start all over again.

After a candidate has accepted the job offer, those not hired should still be kept in mind for any possible future openings. It is common courtesy to notify them that someone else has been selected, and a diplomatic rejection will maintain their goodwill.

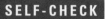

SELF-CHECK

Have you ever applied for a job and been told, "We'll let you know within a week if we want you"? Even when the week was up, were you still hoping you might get a call, if only to say definitely that you had not been hired? How did this uncertainty make you feel toward the employer?

Orientation

orientation Procedures of familiarizing a new employee with the company surroundings, policies, and job responsibilities.

The first day on a new job is confusing for anyone. Therefore, a new employee should be given a proper **orientation.** A job description should be given to him or her and explained in detail. Proper instructions, training, and observation will start the employee off on the right foot. A tour of the facilities and a look at the firm's product or service will help the new employee understand where he or she fits into the scheme of things.

The new employee needs to know the firm's objectives, policies, rules, and performance expectations. Frequent discussions should be held with him or her during the orientation program to answer questions and to ensure proper progress.

A formal interview with the new employee may be appropriate at some point during the first week. Other interviews can be held during the probationary period, which is usually from three to six months. The purpose of these interviews should be to correct any mistaken ideas the employee may have about the job and to determine whether he or she feels that you and your people are fulfilling your commitments.

After orientation is completed, a check list is usually gone over with the new employee. Then, the employee and a representative of the employer sign it, and it is placed in the employee's file as proof of knowledge of rules.

If done properly by the supervisor, orientation should accelerate the building of a positive working relationship with the new employee.

TRAINING AND DEVELOPING EMPLOYEES

Learning Objective 5

Explain why training and development are necessary and how they are done.

One of the basic responsibilities of supervisors is training and developing employees. If they have the job skills and knowledge, supervisors can be the best trainers. Not only must new workers be trained in the details of the new job, but current employees must be retrained and their skills updated to meet rapidly changing environments and job requirements.

> **John Hancock Financial Services is one of the largest employers in the city of Boston. The company has found that "it used to be that managers expected people to come in the first day on the job ready for work; today's managers must accept the fact that they have no choice but to lengthen the learning curve for new employees. They can find workers if they are willing to spend the time necessary to train them."[9]**

Why train employees? Training should result in (1) reduced employee turnover, (2) higher job satisfaction, (3) increased productivity, (4) increased earnings for the employee—and the employer, (5) less supervision as the employee becomes more self-reliant, and (6) decreased costs for materials, supplies, and equipment needed to correct errors.

> According to Bill Saul, chairman of Remmele Engineering, Inc., an automation-equipment manufacturer, it can be profitable to train new employees. The Minneapolis, Minnesota, employer said: "Every time we bring in a new, well-trained employee, he can . . . bring in $90,000 in new sales. [At that rate] it doesn't take long to recoup training costs."[10]

How to Determine Training Needs

training needs survey
Supervisors state their needs on a prepared form or in interviews.

A major problem with training is identifying *who* needs *how much* and *what type* of training. There are many ways to identify training needs. Some of the more practical ways are (1) supervisor's recommendations, (2) analysis of job requirements, (3) analysis of job performance, (4) test results, and (5) employee suggestions. A **training needs survey** may be conducted by asking supervisors to state their needs on a prepared form or by interviewing supervisors.

How to Train Employees

Once you know the employees' training needs, how do you train them? There are many ways a supervisor can train employees, including (1) on-the-job training, (2) apprenticeship training, (3) internship training, and (4) outside training.

ON-THE-JOB TRAINING. The most widely used method of training and developing employees is **on-the-job training (OJT),** in which the employees actually perform work under the supervision and guidance of the supervisor or a trained worker or instructor. Thus, while learning to do the job, the person is also a regular employee producing the good or service that the business sells. This form of training always occurs, whether or not it is consciously planned. Although the techniques depend on the one doing the training, in general OJT involves:

On-the-job training (OJT) employees actually perform the work under the guidance of a supervisor.

1. Telling the worker what is to be done.
2. Telling him or her how to do the job.
3. Showing how it is to be done.
4. Letting the worker do the job under the trainer's guidance.
5. Telling—and showing—the learner what he or she did right, what he or she did wrong, and how to correct the wrong actions.
6. Repeating the procedure until the learner has mastered the job.

As with other aspects of supervision, there are many advantages and disadvantages of OJT. The main *advantages* are that production is carried on while the employee is being trained and that OJT results in low out-of-pocket costs. Also, no transition from classroom learning to actual production is required.

On the other hand, the *disadvantages* of OJT are the poor learning environment provided by the production area and the excessive waste caused by mistakes and/or lack of skill. Supervisors handle most OJT, but they are not necessarily the best ones to do it. As their primary emphasis is on performing the operating tasks of the job, they are only secondarily concerned with training. If possible, another capable employee—or even an outside trainer—should be assigned this responsibility. Also, there should be a follow-up procedure to evaluate the results of the training and to serve as a basis for improving future development.

If the job of training is entrusted to fellow employees, they should be (1) *able* to do the training and (2) *willing* to do it. Also, arrangements should be made to ensure that they don't lose income by doing it. If a worker is paid at piecework rates or is required to fill a certain quota, time spent helping a new employee may cause the experienced worker to get less work done and hence earn less, which will certainly generate resentment and reluctance to help with future training.

Despite its disadvantages, OJT is still the best way to learn job skills. A structured OJT program not only trains and educates employees, it can also motivate them to produce more effectively.[11]

APPRENTICESHIP TRAINING. **Apprenticeship training** blends the learning of theory with practice in the techniques of the job. If job proficiency can be developed only over a long period of classroom instruction and actual learning experiences on the job, this method should be used. It usually encompasses two to seven years of both classroom learning and on-the-job training.

apprenticeship training
Blends the learning of theory with practice in the techniques of the job.

> In 1992, Serigraphics Inc., a high-tech graphics and printing company in West Bend, Wisconsin, started cooperating with West Bend High School's new state-of-the-art apprenticeship program. The program is copied from the German program of "dual education," with two days a week at a high-tech center, namely Serigraphics Inc.[12]

INTERNSHIP TRAINING. Combining on-the-job training at a cooperating business with education at a school or college, **internship training** is generally used for students who are candidates for marketing or clerical positions or who are being prepared for management positions. This method can also be used for higher-level positions. For example, the Georgia Institute of Technology's co-op program, which alternates quarters of academic work and internship with a cooperating employer, prepares students for engineering positions and also provides income to help them meet the cost of their education. Internship training gives students a chance to see if they would like to go to work for the company, and it gives management a chance to evaluate the student as a prospective full-time employee.

internship training
On-the-job training at a cooperating business is combined with classwork at a college.

OTHER TYPES OF TRAINING. Some job activities are so technical or specialized that they cannot be taught effectively on an informal basis by the supervisor. Instead, learners are sent to some outside source, such as a school, college, or equipment manufacturer, to learn the job. Drafting, computer programming, legal aid, and income tax accounting are some jobs of this nature. Some other types of development activities are extension courses, programmed (or video) instruction, closed-circuit television, job rotation, and college and university short courses and conferences.

Outside Assistance Available for Training

vocational-technical education programs Regular or special training classes conducted by vocational-technical schools.

Where can you go for help in training employees? There are many outside programs available to help with training. For example, the National Apprenticeship Act of 1937, administered by the Bureau of Apprenticeship and Training in the Labor Department, sets policies and standards for apprenticeship programs. Also, all states have some form of **vocational-technical education programs,** in which vocational-technical schools, business schools, and junior colleges conduct regular or special training classes. Through such programs, potential employees can become qualified for skilled positions such as machinist, lathe operator, computer service technician, and legal assistant.

vocational rehabilitation programs Provide counseling, medical care, and vocational training for the physically and mentally handicapped.

Other training activities for new employees are the **vocational rehabilitation programs** sponsored by the U.S. Department of Health and Human Services (HHS) in cooperation with state governments. These programs provide counseling, medical care, and vocational training for physically and mentally handicapped individuals.

private industry councils (PICs) Groups headed by company executives and local business people that help employers with training activities.

The popular Job Training Partnership Act (JTPA) underwrites the most important public programs currently being used to help employers with training activities. These programs are developed and effectively controlled by **private industry councils (PICs)** and funded by block grants to the states. The PICs are headed by company executives and local business people, who probably know more than anyone else about what is needed to train people in the skills used in their areas. The funds provided must go for training, including on-the-job training; none of the funds can be used for stipends or wage supplements. In addition to getting cash reimbursement for hiring and training through PICs, firms can also get an investment tax credit to offset the cost of hiring eligible workers.

COMPENSATING EMPLOYEES

Learning Objective **6**

Explain why employee compensation is so important and how it is determined.

An important aspect of human resource management is employee compensation. It is also an integral part of supervisory management.

Importance of Compensation

Of all supervisory problems, compensating employees is probably the most complex and difficult because it involves many emotional factors as well as economic and rational ones.

Compensation, in the form of wages and benefits, is very important to employees, as it is the primary—and often the only source of income for them and their families. It is generally accepted that employees should receive "a fair day's wages for a fair day's work." Yet there are probably as many complaints from emloyees about the *relative* amount of their income as about the *absolute* amount, for everyone wants to be treated fairly when it comes to pay. Employees' *absolute level of income* determines their standard of living, but their *relative income* indicates status, prestige, and worth.

Wages and benefits are also becoming increasingly important to U.S. businesses because of foreign competition, deregulation of the transportation, finance, and energy industries, and the tightening of the economy. No longer can wages be increased without a corresponding increase in productivity unless the cost is passed along to consumers in the form of higher prices. In fact, employers paying a noncompetitive wage rate will soon find themselves in financial trouble because employee compensation and other types of costs interact with revenue to determine an employer's profit or loss, and the primary way to increase employee earnings is to increase productivity and the company's sales and profits.

In summary, the ideal situation is for employers to pay wages high enough to attract, motivate, and retain qualified employees, while at the same time keeping wages low enough to ensure adequate profits to expand productive facilities, attract new capital, and permit consumer satisfaction with the price.

Roles Played by Compensation

Appropriate compensation plays several roles:(1) it attracts capable employees, (2) it motivates employees to perform more effectively, and (3) it helps retain capable employees.

SELF-CHECK

Before you read any further, complete Skill Builder 16–2: What Do You Want from Your Job? at the end of this chapter. Then, return to this section and continue your reading.

wage surveys Determine the "going rate" for jobs in the local labor market and the industry.

Most employers try to remain competitive, both in their industry and in their community, by paying salaries and benefits that are similar to those paid by other employers. Thus, they try to find out what the average salaries are for different types of positions in their industry and local area. They do this by using **wage surveys,** which determine the going rate for jobs in the local labor market and in the industry. If it is not feasible to conduct a wage survey, an employer may use published wage survey information from sources such as trade associations and the U.S. Department of Labor.

It can be argued that most job applicants do not know the exact wages and benefits offered by different employers for similar jobs, and therefore the compensation rate isn't important to them, but we believe that prospective employees *do* compare job offers and pay scales before making decisions about where to work.

SELF-CHECK

Which of the preceding arguments do you think is correct? Consider your own answers to Skill Builder 16–2. What did you put as the number one factor in choosing your first job? Was it "good salary"? You might want to compare notes with some of your fellow students to see how they answered the question. In our research with upper-level business students since the 1957–58 school year, we have found that "good salary" was number one in over 97 percent of the cases.

Compensation can also be used to motivate employees to improve performance. According to the *equity theory of motivation,* employees who believe that the employer's pay system, including wages and benefits, is fair and equitable to them will do a better job than those who do not. Moreover, the *expectancy theory of motivation* states that employee behavior that leads to reward tends to be repeated, whereas behavior that is not rewarded—or leads to punishment—tends not to be repeated. Thus, when an employee's income is what he or she expects, the employee will perform better.[13]

Our answer to the question "Does money motivate?" is yes it does, at least to the point that an employee's physical and safety needs have been satisfied. Above that level, money (especially day wages) tends to decline in importance.

Compensation can also act to retain employees, especially if it is in the form of favorable employee benefits. Although many factors cause employees to leave an organization, inadequate compensation is certainly an important one. Therefore, to retain good employees, employers must be sure that their compensation package is equitable not only in relation to that offered by other employers, but also in relation to that of other employees in the same organization.

Types of Wages

There are many types of wages used to compensate employees. Among the more commonly used types are (1) a single rate, (2) a rate range, (3) day work, or time wages, and (4) incentive wages.

single rate A compensation plan under which everyone who performs the same job is paid the same wage.

When a **single rate** is used, everyone who performs the same job is paid the same wage, regardless of the level of performance. The single rate is used in many industries, especially those that are unionized, such as the automobile assembly, trucking, steel, trade, and service industries. It is also used for many occupations associated with crafts, production work, and maintenance.

rate range Minimum and maximum wage rates for a given job.

A **rate range** offers a minimum and maximum wage rate for a given job, with employees paid at different rates depending on performance. The rate paid to an individual is usually determined by some form of performance appraisal, as will be discussed in the next chapter. Rate ranges are used for most technical, professional, and office workers, as well as for most government employees.

time wages Pay for the amount of time spent on the job, regardless of output.

incentive wages Wages determined by the amount of goods and services the employee produced.

The two most common bases on which to compensate employees are (1) time worked and (2) output produced. The first of these methods, **time wages** or **day work,** pays the employee for the amount of time spent on the job, regardless of the output during that period. The second method, **incentive wages** or **performance pay,** pays the employee according to the amount of goods and services produced during a given period. The latter method links compensation to individual, team, or company performance. This form of payment is becoming more popular: the number of companies using it increased from under 50% to over 70% from 1990 to 1994.[14]

In general, unions prefer single rates to rate ranges for the same type of job because rate ranges tend to cause competition among workers. Unions also tend to favor day work, or time wages, over incentive wages. Although unions will accept incentive wage plans that are based on group output rather than individual output, they insist that such plans be established according to the union's standards.

Factors Affecting Wage Rates

What most employers think they *should* pay is "competitive wages," but some specific factors affect what they actually pay. Most of these factors relate to what employers *have* to pay, but a final factor is what they are *able* to pay. These factors include (1) governmental factors, (2) collective bargaining, (3) cost-of-living adjustments (COLAs), (4) comparable wages, (5) market conditions, and (6) ability to pay.

GOVERNMENTAL FACTORS. Governmental laws, rules, and regulations largely determine what an employer *has to pay* workers. Some of these laws are the Fair Labor Standards Act, commonly called the Wage and Hour Law; the Walsh-Healey Act; the Davis-Bacon Act; the Equal Pay Act; and various EEO/AA laws, such as the Civil Rights Act, the Vocational Rehabilitation Act, the Americans with Disabilities Act, and the Vietnam Era Veterans Readjustment Assistance Act.

exempt employees Not covered by the provisions of the Fair Labor Standards Act.

nonexempt employees Covered by the provisions of the Fair Labor Standards Act.

The Fair Labor Standards Act covers all employees working in interstate commerce, federal employees, and some state employees. Some employees, referred to as **exempt employees,** including executives, administrative and professional employees, outside sales personnel, and other selected groups, are not covered by the provisions of this law. All other employees, called **nonexempt employees,** are covered and must be paid at least the basic minimum wage ($4.25/hour at this writing). If employees work over 40 hours in a given work week, they must be paid one and a half times their regular rate of pay for each hour worked over 40 hours. However, there are provisions for employing full-time students at rates lower than the minimum wage. This law also prevents child labor. Age 14 is the minimum working age for most nonfarm jobs. On nonhazardous jobs, persons of age 14 and 15 can work no more than 3 hours on a school day, 8 hours on any other day, or 40 hours per week. Those who are 16 and 17 years old can work in nonhazardous jobs for unlimited hours.

The Davis-Bacon Act and the Walsh-Healey Act have different provisions. Construction firms with government contracts or subcontracts in excess of $2,000 are covered by the Davis-Bacon Act; other employers with government contracts exceeding $10,000 are covered by the Walsh-Healey Act. These acts differ from the Fair Labor Standards Act in that the rate of pay is set by the Secretary of Labor. This rate

prevailing wage rate
Approximates the union wage scale for the area in the given type of work.

of pay is called the **prevailing wage rate** in the area and approximates the union scale for the area in the given type of work. Moreover, overtime is paid at "time and a half" for all hours worked over 8 hours in one day as well as over 40 hours in a given week.

Public policy now prohibits discrimination in pay unless it is based on performance. For example, the Equal Pay Act prohibits different rates of pay for men and women doing the same type of work. Title VII of the Civil Rights Act prevents discrimination based on race, color, religion, sex, or national origin. The Age Discrimination in Employment Act prohibits discrimination against persons 40 years of age and older. Finally, the Vocational Rehabilitation Act and Americans with Disabilities Act prohibit discrimination against handicapped persons.

COLLECTIVE BARGAINING. When unions are involved, basic wages, job differentials, individual rates of pay, and employee benefits tend to be determined through the collective bargaining process. The actual amount of compensation is determined by the relative strength of the union and the employer. However, even nonunionized employers are affected by the wage rates and the amounts of benefits paid by unionized firms.

Cost-of-living adjustments increases in wages in direct proportion to increases in the consumer price index.

consumer price index
Measures changes in the price of a group of goods and services that make up the typical consumer's budget.

COST-OF-LIVING ADJUSTMENTS. Ever since 1948, **cost-of-living adjustments (COLAs)** have been included in many union contracts. Under a COLA arrangement, wages rise in direct proportion to increases in the **consumer price index (CPI),** which measures changes in the price of a group of goods and services that make up the typical consumer's budget. Such arrangements have been popular in the automobile, communications, electrical, mining, steel, transportation, and rubber industries. Many government employees have similar arrangements. COLAs are more popular when inflation increases rapidly, as it did in the late 1970s and early 1980s.

COMPARABLE WAGE RATES. As indicated earlier, an employer must pay wage rates that are comparable to those paid in the area, the industry, and the occupation. If an employer in a given area pays less than the prevailing area rate, employees will move to higher-paying jobs. The same is true for employers in given industries, such as steel, rubber, and automobile manufacturing, which are known as high-pay industries. Finally, there tends to be a relationship between wages for people in given occupations, such as professional and technical workers, managerial personnel, and sales personnel, regardless of who their employer is.

MARKET CONDITIONS. The basic law of economics applies to wages. That is, as the supply of workers goes up relative to demand, wage rates tend to go down; and when the supply of workers goes down relative to demand, wage rates go up.

EMPLOYER'S ABILITY TO PAY. In spite of the above factors, individual wages are based ultimately on what the employer can afford to pay, or the amount of profit the private employer makes. This profit, in turn, is based on the productivity of the employees, prices charged, and the volume of goods sold or services provided. Without profit, there cannot be higher wages, regardless of what happens outside the organization.

The Comparable Worth Issue

In spite of the Equal Pay Act of 1963, which prohibited unequal pay for men and women doing the same job, women are still paid substantially less than men for *similar* jobs. There is much controversy as to the cause of this disparity. The problem, according to advocates of "pay equity," goes far beyond equal pay for the same job. The real issue is, *Are women being systematically underpaid for work that requires the same skills, knowledge, and responsibility as similar jobs performed by men?*

comparable worth
Jobs with equal points for the amount of education, effort, skill, and responsibility have equal pay.

Advocates say the solution lies in a system of **comparable worth,** or **pay equity,** in which a formula is used to assign points for the amount of education, effort, skill, and responsibility required for an individual job.[15] These points are then used, along with job evaluation, to set salary rates. Critics say such wage adjustments would destroy the market forces of supply and demand. The arguments of advocates and critics of comparable worth are shown in Exhibit 16–9.

SELF-CHECK   Do you think jobs of comparable worth should receive comparable pay? Which arguments in Exhibit 16–9 do you accept and why?

Using Job Evaluation to Set Job Rates

job evaluation Determines the relative value of jobs to an employer so the appropriate earnings for employees doing given jobs can be determined objectively.

Job evaluation is a process used to determine the relative value of jobs to an employer to more objectively establish the earnings of employees doing different jobs. It is used to develop a fair and equitable scale of wages, especially for new employees. The relative value of each job to the organization is established as a basis for determining individual wage rates and satisfying EEO requirements. Job evaluation also provides information on the qualifications needed for a given job, thus helping supervisors to make more effective employee selections, promotions, demotions, and job changes.

While it is possible to obtain a reasonable degree of equity by using job evaluation, there are several problems with the process. First, the value of various occupations to an employer cannot be precisely measured by means of the same yardstick. Also, it is difficult to measure the relative value of work done by scientific, technical, professional, and managerial personnel. Finally, the worth of one job to the organization cannot be properly evaluated without considering its relationship to other jobs.

The usual procedure for using job evaluation to arrive at job rates or ranges is to do a job analysis, grade the jobs, price each job, and administer the resulting program. As shown in Exhibit 16–10, the process of *job analysis* results in *job descriptions,* which are then translated into *job specifications* that can be used as the basis for hiring new employees. These job specifications are then grouped into job *grades,* with jobs of the same relative value in the same grade. These job grades are then assigned a *price* based on the company's overall wage rate. These wage rates or ranges become the value of the job. By appraising the performance of each employee, management determines his or her individual wage rate within the wage range.

Some women's groups believe that the principle of equal pay for work of equal value has been violated in that whole classes of jobs—such as those in the clerical area—are undervalued because they have traditionally been held by women. They want this practice changed so that pay for all jobs will be based on their value to the business or community, rather than on who holds the jobs.

The arguments *for* comparable pay for comparable work are:

1. If one employee contributes as much to the firm as another, the two should be paid the same.
2. It is needed to raise women's pay, which is now only about 65 percent of men's.
3. It will give women greater internal job mobility.
4. This is one way to further women's career ambitions.
5. It would serve to motivate women to be more productive.

The arguments *against* comparable pay are:

1. Federal law only requires equal pay for equal jobs.
2. It violates a firm's structured job evaluation system.
3. Employers must pay salaries competitive with those of other employers, which are based on what employees produce and on the economic value of the work performed.
4. Women receive less than men because two-thirds of new employees are women, and they always receive less than more senior employees.
5. It is practically impossible to determine accurately the real value of a job.

Source: Leon C. Megginson, Geralyn M. Franklin, and M. Jane Byrd, *Human Resource Management* (Houston: Dame Publications, 1995), p. 404.

Exhibit 16–9
Should Jobs of "Comparable Worth" Receive Comparable Pay?

Exhibit 16–10
Steps in the Job Evaluation Procedure

Step	Procedures and Products Used	Resulting Product
Step 1: Analysis	Job analysis → job description →	Job specifications*
Step 2: Grading	Job specifications + job evaluation, or appraisal of the worth of the job →	Job grades
Step 3: Pricing	Job grades + overall wage rate →	Job wage rates or ranges
Step 4: Administering	Job wage rates or ranges + appraisal of performance or qualities of each employee →	Individual wage rate

*These specifications can be used as the basis for performing the job evaluation procedure, or they can be used to prepare a statement of the personal qualifications needed to perform the job. This statement then becomes the basis for the recruitment and selection procedure.

Deere & Co., after successfully founding its own HMO, opened a primary-care clinic in Moline, Illinois. This clinic treats patients on site rather than passing them on to more costly specialists.

Flexible Benefits

flexcomp Providing employees with flexible benefit packages.

Many employers are now using some method of providing employees with flexible benefit packages. Called **flexcomp** or **cafeteria benefit plans,** these packages give each worker an individualized benefit package. Under these plans, all employees receive a statement of the total dollar amount of benefits they are entitled to, along with the amount earmarked for legally required benefits. Each employee then tells the employer how to allocate the balance among the programs available. Some advantages of this program are that (1) workers are more aware of the total value of their benefits, and (2) workers can choose which programs they want. As a result, workers are better satisfied and benefit packages are better tailored to individual needs.

Chapter Review

Explain who is responsible for selecting, training, and compensating employees.
This chapter has presented ways to select, train and develop, and compensate employees. In general, the human resource department is responsible for overall planning, recruiting, and handling the details of staffing. The role of supervisors is to requisition needed workers, interview applicants, orient new workers, and train new and current employees.

Describe how to plan human resource needs and how to find employees for specific jobs.
As part of planning human resource needs, the supervisor helps prepare job descriptions, which show the duties, authority, responsibilities, and working conditions of

the job, as well as a set of job specifications, which lists the personal characteristics required, such as education, aptitudes, and experience.

Employees are obtained from within an organization by upgrading present employees or by transferring or promoting people from other units, using job posting if feasible. Workers are recruited from outside by using such sources as former employees, personal applications, friends and relatives of present workers, competing firms, labor organizations, public or private employment agencies, equational institutions, migrants and immigrants, and part-time employees.

Learning Objective 3

State the laws providing equal employment opportunity for protected groups of employees.

Minorities, women, older workers, the disabled, and Vietnam veterans are protected by various laws and regulations. The Equal Employment Opportunity Commission (EEOC) is the primary agency for enforcing these laws.

Learning Objective 4

Describe the steps in the employee selection procedure, including the proper orientation of new employees.

The procedure for selecting employees for specific jobs includes (1) a requisition from the supervisor, (2) a preliminary screening-out of the obvious misfits, (3) the applicant's completion of an application form, (4) pre-employment tests, (5) various interviews by the supervisor and human resource officer, (6) checking records and references, (7) a preliminary selection made by the supervisor, (8) physical exam, if legal, and (9) a job offer. If the offer is accepted, the new employee is given a job orientation by the supervisor.

Learning Objective 5

Explain why training and development are necessary and how they are done.

One of the basic supervisory responsibilities is training and developing employees—both new and currently employed—as such development has many benefits for both employees and employer. Training methods include (1) on-the-job training, (2) apprenticeship training, (3) internship training, and (4) training given by outside institutions. Assistance in training is available from many sources, especially state and federal government agencies. Apprenticeship programs are covered by the National Apprenticeship Act of 1937. The Job Training Partnership Act underwrites local training efforts developed by private industry councils. The federal government also works with states to provide vocational rehabilitation programs for the disabled, and most states offer some form of vocational-technical education programs to train workers for skilled occupations.

Learning Objective 6

Explain why employee compensation is so important and how it is determined.

Another important management task is providing compensation for employees. Compensation is important to employees because it determines both their standard of living and their status, and it is important to employers because it represents a large proportion of costs. Appropriate compensation plays several roles: it attracts capable employees, it motivates employees to perform more effectively, and it helps retain employees.

Types of wages include a single rate for a given job and a rate range, with the actual pay based on seniority, performance, or some other criterion, including performance appraisal. Rates may be paid on a straight hourly basis—day work or time wages—or they may be based on output—incentive wages or performance pay.

Chapter 17
Appraising and Disciplining Employees

Case 17

When the Transfer Backfires (A)

Jane Smith abruptly rose and stormed out of the office of Robert Trent, the director of purchasing at a major eastern university. As she made her hasty exit, Trent began to wonder what had gone wrong with a seemingly perfect plan—one that would have rid his department of a "problem" employee. How could his well-constructed plan, using the university's formal transfer system, have failed so miserably, leaving him with an even more unmanageable situation?

It had all begun in January, when Trent decided that something must be done about Smith's performance and attitude. The process was made a little more awkward by the university's not having a formal employee performance-appraisal policy and program. Each department was left with the right to develop and conduct its own employee appraisals. This meant that each department could choose whether or not to appraise an employee, as well as choose the format and procedure to be used.

In January, Trent decided to conduct an appraisal of Smith. After writing down some weaknesses in her performance and attitude, he called her in to discuss them. He cited the various weaknesses to her, but, admittedly, most were highly subjective in nature. In only a few instances did he give specific and objective references, and he did not give Smith a copy of his findings. During the appraisal interview, he even hinted that possibly she didn't "fit in" and that she "probably would be much happier in some other place." In any event, he was satisfied that he had begun the process for eventually ridding the department of her. He reasoned that, if all else failed, this pressure would ultimately force her to quit. At the time, he hardly noticed that she was strangely quiet through the whole meeting.

As time went by, Smith's attitude and performance did not improve. In March, Trent was elated to learn that an opening existed in another department and that Smith was most interested in transferring. The university's formal transfer policy required that Trent complete the Employee Transfer Evaluation Form—which he gladly did. As a matter of fact, he rated Smith mostly "outstanding" on the performance and attitude factors. He was so pleased at having the opportunity to use the transfer system that he called the other department manager and spoke glowingly of Smith's abilities and performance. Although he had been the purchasing director for only eight months, having been recruited from another college, he even pointed with pride to Smith's five years' experience. In April, much to Trent's dismay, it was announced that Smith had lost the transfer opportunity to a better-qualified candidate.

Source: Prepared by M. T. Bledsoe, Associate Professor of Business, Meredith College, Raleigh, North Carolina.

LEARNING OBJECTIVES
After reading and studying this chapter, you should be able to:

 Explain what employee performance appraisal is and who performs it.

 Describe some methods of appraising employee performance.

 State why performance appraisal interviews are difficult for both the employee and the supervisor.

 Define discipline and explain why it is necessary.

 Discuss the differences between positive and negative discipline.

 Describe how discipline is imposed under due process.

 Explain the supervisor's disciplinary role.

shifts. Another possibility is to transfer one of them to another department. A last resort would be to discharge one or both of them.

The real problem is to decide what to do and then to do it. It will be a difficult problem determining which one will be transferred or fired, since help for this department is not readily available. The factors to be considered in the solution are fault, seniority, capability, and individual personality. These factors will have to be considered carefully, and a suitable decision will have to be made, based on the facts.

Answer the following questions:

1. If you were the division superintendent, what would you recommend doing with the two bickering employees? Why?
2. How would you implement your decision? In what order would you implement it?
3. What does this case illustrate about the need for a disciplined work environment?

Chapter 18
The Supervisor and Labor Relations

Case 18

In Union There Is Strength

A wise man had seven sons who were intelligent, personable, and otherwise attractive, but they had one common fault—they were constantly fighting and squabbling with one another, even when being attacked by others outside the family. One day, the father decided to teach them a lesson. He called them together, gave each one of them a long wooden stick, and said to each one, in turn, "Break this stick over your knee." Each one of the sons broke his stick with very little effort.

Again, the wise man handed each son a stick, but this time said to them, "Bind the seven sticks together in a bundle." They did as he asked. "Now try to break the sticks," he said to each son as he handed him the bundle. None of them could break the bundle of sticks. "Remember," he said, "In union there is strength."

Source: Aesop's Fables, "The Bundle of Sticks."

LEARNING OBJECTIVES
After reading and studying this chapter, you should be able to:

1

Explain what is meant by labor relations.

2

Trace the development of unions in the United States.

3

Explain why union membership is declining.

4

Name and explain the basic laws governing labor relations.

5

Describe union objectives and discuss the methods used to achieve those objectives.

6

Name three things that a supervisor must know in order to live with the union agreement.

All your strength is in your union,
All your danger is in discord;
Therefore be at peace henceforward,
And as brothers live together.

Henry Wadsworth Longfellow

Long ago we stated the reason for labor
organizations. We said that union was
essential to give laborers opportunity to
deal on an equality with their employer.

U.S. Supreme Court

Fight labor's demands to the last ditch, and
there will come a time when it seizes the
whole of power, makes itself sovereign,
and takes what it used to ask.

Walter Lippman

The opening quotations and Case 18 illustrate one of the most basic reasons unions are needed. Just as individual sticks can be broken, so individual employees cannot compete with the employer's resources by themselves. But when united, as the sticks were united into a bundle, individual employees can successfully contend with management.

A **labor union** is an organization of workers banded together to achieve economic goals, especially increased wages and benefits, shorter working hours, improved working conditions, and both personal and job security. The individual employee has very little bargaining strength when negotiating with the employer. But when employees band together to form a labor union, they are better able to protect their interests and to obtain economic benefits.

It is impossible to cover everything about dealing with unions in one chapter, but we will include the most important ideas to help you understand the supervisor's role in labor relations. Even if you are—or expect to be—a supervisor in a nonunion firm, you need to understand how labor relations affect supervisory activities and relationships, for they affect nonunion employers as well as unionized ones.

SELF-CHECK Did you notice in Chapter 17 that, even in nonunion firms, supervisors use due process in applying discipline? This approach by enlightened supervisors improves labor-management relations.

WHAT ARE LABOR RELATIONS?

Learning Objective 1

Explain what is meant by labor relations.

labor relations The relationship between an employer and unionized employees.

Terms such as **labor relations, union-management relations,** and **industrial relations** are often used to refer to the relationships between employers and their unionized employees. In this text, these terms will be used interchangeably.

The growth of unionism has forced managers—especially supervisors—to change many of their ways of dealing with employees, especially in matters concerning wages, hours, working conditions, and other terms and conditions of employment. Managers of unionized companies are constantly challenged by union leaders in these areas. These challenges force supervisors to consider the rights of workers when developing and applying policies. Thus, management's freedom of choice has been greatly limited. For example, managers can no longer reward an employee on the basis of favoritism or punish one without just cause.

Labor relations are more than a power struggle between management and labor over economic matters that concern only themselves. Instead, hurt feelings, bruised egos, disappointments, and the hopes and ambitions of workers, managers, and labor leaders are involved. Also, these relationships affect and are affected by the total physical, economic, social, technological, legal, political, and cultural environment in which they occur.

SELF-CHECK

Think about the last serious strike you can remember, such as the Major League Baseball strike of 1994–95 or a public transportation or teachers' strike. Did it affect you in any way, either directly or indirectly? Even if it didn't affect you, what were the economic, social, political, and cultural effects on your community? on the nation? Did any workers in affected organizations lose jobs or wages? Did any companies lose output or go out of business? Were the sales at retail stores hurt? Were tax receipts reduced? Was there any violence? Did it affect any social or cultural events?

HOW UNIONS DEVELOPED IN THE UNITED STATES

In general, employees were treated well in the early colonies because of the severe shortage of skilled labor. By the end of the nineteenth century, however, the situation had changed. The high birthrate, rapid and uncontrolled immigration, the concentration of wealth and industry in the hands of a few businessmen, political abuses by some employers, and the large numbers of workers in crowded industrial areas led to many abuses. These included long hours, hard labor, unsafe and oppressive working conditions, crowded and unsanitary living conditions, low pay with no job security, and abuses of working women and children.

Early Union Activities

Learning Objective 2

Trace the developments of unions in the United States.

craft unions Workers in a specific skill, craft, or trade.

There were labor unions in the United States as early as 1789, but they tended to be small, isolated, and ineffective **craft unions,** which are unions of workers in specific skills, crafts, or trades.

More concerted action and stronger efforts were needed to improve the workers' plight. So several of the craft unions joined together in 1869 to form the Knights of Labor—the first nationwide union. Because its leadership was considered quite radical, it was only moderately successful. A more conservative national union was formed in 1881, and it was named the American Federal of Labor (AFL) in 1886. Under the leadership of Samuel Gompers, the AFL grew and had great impact through World War I and World War II. The basic concepts of a labor union were developed under his leadership. When asked what unions wanted for their members, Gompers invariably replied, "More!"

Period of Rapid Union Growth

During the 1920s and early 1930s, business became so powerful that workers again felt they were being exploited. They were hired, rewarded, punished, and fired at the whim of first-line supervisors, many of whom acted unfeelingly. Therefore, several laws were passed in the 1930s that forced management to recognize unions and protected workers from exploitation (see the next section for details).

Until that time, the AFL and its affiliates had been organized on a craft basis. Union growth was thus limited, as there were few craft workers left to organize. But some workers had started organizing **industrial unions,** in which all the workers in an industry—such as iron, coal, and autos—belonged to the same union, whether they were craftsmen, unskilled workers, or clerical employees. These unions broke away from the AFL in 1936 to form the Congress of Industrial Organizations (CIO).

Because of laws favorable to workers, the demand for workers resulting from World War II, and the prosperity that followed that war, union membership grew rapidly until 1945, when 35.5 percent of the work force was unionized. Then, as Exhibit 18–1 shows, membership increased more slowly through the mid-1950s.

industrial unions Unions composed of all the workers in an industry.

Recent Limited Union Growth

Although total union membership was increasing through the 1970s, the percentage of all workers belonging to unions started leveling out shortly after World War II and peaked in 1955 (see Exhibits 18–1 and 18–2). For this and other reasons, the AFL and the CIO combined in 1955. Membership continued to grow in the 1960s and 1970s, when new types of unions developed. Government, white-collar, agricultural, and service employees, as well as professionals, formed **employee associations,** which functioned as labor unions, as the following example illustrates. But, as shown in Exhibit 18–2, the percentage of the total labor force that belonged to unions steadily declined. There has been a 40 percent drop in the last four decades and a 20 percent drop in just the last decade.[1]

employee associations Organizations that function as labor unions.

> It was once believed that the problems and frustrations of female clerical workers were their own concern—to be borne in silence. This attitude changed in 1973, when Karen Nussbaum, a clerk-typist at the Harvard Graduate School of Education, organized 10 clerical workers into the women's rights group known as "9 to 5." Now, 9 to 5 is a nonunion-membership advocacy group, and many of its members belong to District 925 of the Service Employees International Union (SEIU). Karen Nussbaum, who was once one of the top women in the AFL-CIO, is now director of the Women's Bureau of the U.S. Department of Labor.[2]

To summarize the current dilemma for unions, there are only about 17 million people—approximately 15.5 percent of the total labor force—who belong to unions and employee associations. Also, only about 11 percent of private employees belong to unions.

SELF-CHECK

Over four out of five workers *do not* belong to a union. Why do you think this is so?

Exhibit 18–1
Membership of National Unions as a Percentage of the Total Labor Force

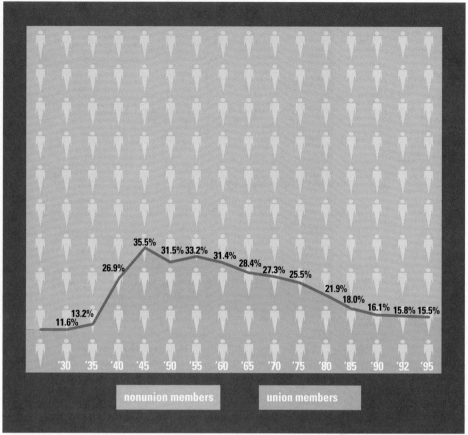

Sources: U.S. Department of Labor, Bureau of Labor Statistics; and "Union Membership," *Bulletin to Management* (a publication of the Bureau of National Affairs), March 4, 1993, pp. 68–70. Adapted from Leon C. Megginson, Geralyn M. Franklin, and M. Jane Byrd, *Human Resource Management* (Houston: Dame Publications, 1995), p. 480.

Exhibit 18–2
Unionized Labor Declining

AFL-CIO unions represent half the share of the workforce that they did in 1955, when the AFL and CIO merged:

Year	Non-Farm Wage Earners	% Union
1955	(50,675,000)	33.2%
1963	(56,702,000)	29.1%
1971	(71,222,000)	27.0%
1979	(89,823,000)	22.3%
1987	(99,303,000)	17.0%
1994	(107,989,000)	15.5%

Source: Bureau of Labor Statistics

In appointing Linda Chavez-Thompson as the first executive vice-president of the AFL-CIO, the union is trying to respond to changes that have made women and minorities organized labor's fastest-growing segments.

Some Reasons for Declining Union Membership

Learning Objective 3

Explain why union membership is declining.

There are many reasons for these declines. First, a major reason is the shift in the economy from manufacturing jobs, which are relatively easy to unionize, to service work, which is more difficult to organize. For example, there has been nearly a 40 percent drop in union membership in the auto, machine-working, and steel industries in just the last 15 years.[3]

Second, there is a new kind of service worker—more educated and technologically oriented. These mobile employees are less interested in long-term union contracts, with payments in the distant future, than in such things as portable pensions and employer contributions to retirement plans. They also enjoy "employee involvement" schemes such as quality circles and self-managing teams, which traditional unions tend to oppose. A 1994–95 Worker Representation and Participation Survey of 3,500 low- to mid-level workers found them feeling powerless and impotent. While wanting some type of representation, they preferred a blend of Europe's "works councils" and Japan's company-sponsored unions instead of U.S.-style unions.[4]

Another problem for U.S. unions is the growing global economy. U.S. firms are under pressure to cut costs in order to compete. Consequently, many employers have become more aggressive in opposing union organizing drives.[5] Also, they feel that they cannot compete with foreign competitors if they are bound by the industrywide bargaining required by U.S. unions.

For example, Caterpillar, a leading producer of earth-moving equipment, recently accepted a prolonged strike from the United Auto Workers union rather than sign an agreement that its U.S. competitors had already accepted. Its management believed that the company would lose sales to "competitors with more flexible labor deals abroad."[6]

Fourth, the growing emphasis on part-time and temporary workers has also contributed to the decline in union membership. Currently there are 20 million part-time employees out of a work force of 108 million.[7] Also, the telecommuting "explosion" makes it difficult to organize workers.

Next, the growing "small is beautiful" world of business is working to discourage union membership. U.S. small businesses are providing most of the new jobs in the United States. In fact, it has been estimated that "small companies added all net new jobs in the United States" from 1988 through 1991.[8] As an indication of the problem this trend poses for unions, there are now more small business *owners* (around 20 million) than there are union members, and small firms are very difficult for unions to organize.[9]

Finally, the decline in union membership is partially due to the passage and enforcement of laws to protect employees. Also, some laws are designed to prevent union violence and corruption. For example, nearly every president of the Teamster's Union has been convicted of a felony while serving as president of the union.

LAWS GOVERNING LABOR RELATIONS

Learning Objective 4

Name and explain the basic laws governing labor relations.

The legal basis of union-management relations is provided by the National Labor Relations Act of 1935 (also called the Wagner Act), as amended by the Labor-Management Relations Act of 1947 (the Taft-Hartley Act), the Labor Management Reporting and Disclosure Act of 1959 (the Landrum-Griffin Act), and others. This complex of laws sets public policy and controls labor relations. Exhibit 18–3 shows the coverage, basic requirements, and agencies administering these laws. We'll provide only a few more details about them in the text.

Basic Labor Laws

In this section we will examine why the basic labor laws were passed. We will also point out the important features of these laws and explain how they are administered.

WAGNER ACT. The National Labor Relations Act (Wagner Act) was passed to protect employees and unions by limiting management's rights. It gave workers the right to form and join unions of their own choosing and made collective bargaining mandatory. It also set up the National Labor Relations Board (NLRB) to enforce the law. The act defined specific **unfair labor practices** that management could not commit against the workers and the union, but it had no provision for unfair practices that unions might commit against workers and management. As a result, many union abuses arose. One major abuse was that unions could impose requirements as to how employees could get or keep a job. Many managers, as well as employees, assumed that the right to join a union carried with it the right *not* to do so. This assumption was changed during World War II, when agreements such as the union shop, the closed shop, and the agency shop became legal.

unfair labor practices
Specific acts that management may not commit against the workers and the union.

Laws	Coverage	Basic Provisions	Agencies Involved
National Labor Relations Act (NLRA) as amended (Wagner Act)	Nonmanagerial employees in nonagricultural private firms not covered by the Railway Labor Act; postal employees	Asserts the right of employees to form or join labor organizations (or to refuse to), to bargain collectively through their representatives, and to engage in other concerted activities such as strikes, picketing, and boycotts; establishes unfair labor practices that the employer cannot engage in.	National Labor Relations Board (NLRB)
Labor-Management Relations Act (LMRA) as amended (Taft-Hartley Act)	Same as above	Amended NLRA; permits states to pass laws prohibiting compulsory union membership; sets up methods to deal with strikes affecting national health and safety.	Federal Mediation and Conciliation Service
Labor-Management Reporting and Disclosure Act (Landrum-Griffin Act)	Same as above	Amended NLRA and LMRA; guarantees individual rights of union members in dealing with their union; requires financial disclosures by unions.	U.S. Department of Labor

Source: U.S. Department of Labor publications and the basic laws themselves, as amended.

Exhibit 18–3
Basic Laws Governing Labor Relations

union shop All employees must join the union within a specified period.

closed shop All prospective employees must be members of the recognized union before they can be employed.

agency shop All employees must pay union dues even if they choose not to join the union.

maintenance-of-membership clause An employee who has joined the union must maintain that membership as a condition of employment.

Under a **union shop** agreement, all employees must join the union within a specified period—usually 30 days—or be fired. Under **closed shop** agreement, all prospective employees must be members of the recognized union before they can be employed, and all current employees must join within a specified time in order to retain their jobs. In an **agency shop,** all employees must pay the union dues even if they choose not to join the union. The **maintenance-of-membership clause** says that once an employee joins the union, he or she must maintain that membership as a condition of employment.

SELF-CHECK

Do you have trouble seeing the difference between a union shop and a closed shop? In a union shop, management employs the people it chooses and then these people become members of the union. In a closed shop, management must accept the workers sent by the union.

TAFT-HARTLEY ACT. Following World War II, with evidence of abuse of power by some union leaders, Congress passed the Labor-Management Relations Act (Taft-Hartley Act). Enacted in 1947, this act greatly changed the Wagner Act, making it more evenhanded, so that unions as well as management could be charged with unfair labor practices.

The Taft-Hartley Act prohibited the closed-shop agreement, except in the construction and shipping industries. Also, Section 14(b) of this act gave states the right to pass laws prohibiting the union shop. By 1996, 21 states had used Section 14(b) to pass **right-to-work laws,** which give workers the right to join or refuse to join a union without being fired. The states with right-to-work laws are highlighted in Exhibit 18–4.

right-to-work laws The right of employees to join or refuse to join a union without being fired.

LANDRUM-GRIFFIN ACT. In 1959, Congress passed the Labor-Management Reporting and Disclosure Act (Landrum-Griffin Act) in an effort to prevent corruption and abuse of employees by some union leaders and managers. It provided an **employees' bill of rights,** which protects employees from possible abuse by unscrupulous managers and union leaders.

employees' bill of rights Protects employees from possible abuse by unscrupulous managers and union leaders.

Employees, unions, and employers all have certain specified and implied rights and privileges under the basic labor laws. Exhibit 18–5 contains the rights of employees. Exhibit 18–6 shows what unions may not do, and Exhibit 18–7 lists what employers may not do under these laws.

Administration of the Basic Labor Laws

The five-person National Labor Relations Board (NLRB) has the power to enforce the basic labor laws. The functions of the NLRB are (1) to certify unions as the exclusive bargaining agent for employees and (2) to see that unfair labor practices either are not committed or are punished. Its specific duties are:

- To hold an election to establish the bargaining agent for employees of a given firm.
- To investigate charges of unfair labor practices against the employer or the union.
- To issue complaints against either management or labor.
- To prosecute unfair labor practices and determine guilt.
- To assess fines and prison sentences.
- To ask federal courts to control activities of both management and labor by citing them for contempt.

Exhibit 18–4
States with Right-to-Work Laws

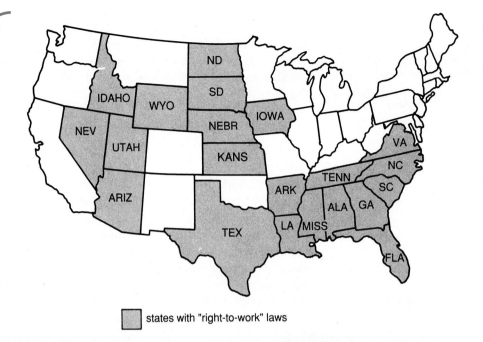

☐ states with "right-to-work" laws

- To organize.
- To bargain collectively.
- To expect no discrimination against them by management because they are union members.
- To expect no discrimination against them by management if they bring charges of unfair labor practices against the employer.
- To get a job without first being a member of a union.
- Not to have to join a union unless the union and the employer have signed a valid union shop agreement in one of the states that do not have right-to-work laws.
- Not to be charged exorbitant initiation fees and dues by a union with a valid union-shop agreement.
- To receive financial reports from the union.

Exhibit 18–5
Rights of Employees

Exhibit 18–6
Unfair Labor Practices of Unions

- To coerce employees into or restrain them from engaging in union activities.
- To force management to discriminate against employees in violation of the law.
- To refuse to bargain in good faith.
- To require managers to pay money for work not done.
- To engage in a strike or boycott to force management to commit illegal acts.
- To charge excessive initiation fees and dues where there is a union shop.

- To interfere with, restrain, or coerce employees who are exercising their rights under the law.
- To dominate or interfere with the forming or administering of unions, or to contribute support to them.
- To discriminate in hiring or in any other terms of employment in such a way as to encourage or discourage membership in a union.
- To discharge or otherwise discriminate against employees for filing charges against the employer or testifying under the law.
- To refuse to bargain with the union representative.

Exhibit 18–7
*Unfair Labor
Practices of Employers*

UNION PRINCIPLES, OBJECTIVES, AND METHODS OF ATTAINING OBJECTIVES

Learning Objective 5

Describe union objectives and discuss the methods used to achieve those objectives.

The main reason unions exist is to protect individual workers from the economic power of an employer or employer groups. Unions try to achieve certain objectives for their members and follow certain principles to achieve them.

Samuel Gompers, the AFL's first president, identified the following basic principles upon which unionism is based: (1) strength through unity, (2) equal pay for the same job, and (3) employment practices based on seniority. If any one of these principles is threatened, the union and its members will fight back, as these are cardinal, non-negotiable beliefs. (A two-tiered wage system was introduced in airline bargaining during the 1980s, but it is now being revoked.)

These principles of unionism lead to the practical objectives unions have for their members. These goals are (1) higher pay, (2) shorter hours of work on a daily, weekly, or annual basis, (3) improved working conditions, both physical and psychological, and (4) improved security, both of the person and of the job.

How do unions achieve their objectives? The usual methods they employ are (1) to organize a firm's employees, (2) to become recognized as the employees' exclusive bargaining agent, (3) to engage in collective bargaining, (4) to go on strike or threaten to strike, and (5) to process grievances. Let us look at each of these methods.

Organizing Employees

union authorization card Authorizes a particular union to be an employee's collective bargaining representative.

First, the union leader must persuade the employees of a firm to organize and join the union. The union organizer tries to get the employees to sign a **union authorization card,** which states that the employee wants the specified union to be his or her bargaining representative. An example of such a card is shown in Exhibit 18–8.

UNDERSTANDING THE SITUATION. Supervisors should first of all recognize that most union organizers are competent professionals who are committed to their work. By attending seminars and other programs, union organizers become expert in the provisions of the labor laws

Exhibit 18–8

*Example of a
Representation
Authorization Card*

COMMUNICATIONS WORKERS of AMERICA, A.F.L.-C.I.O.

Name _____
     (Please Print)   First   Middle   Last

Address _____
         Street

_____
      City   State   Zip Code

Tel. No. _____ Job Title _____

I am an Employee of _____ ,

Department _____ , Section _____ , Shift _____
and I hereby designate the Communications Workers of America, as my
collective bargaining representative.

Date _____ Signature _____

FORM O-100   **REPRESENTATION AUTHORIZATION**   150
1-77

---

and in organizing techniques. Their international headquarters conducts continual research and supplies the organizers with current and effective information and carefully conceived and tested techniques. Carefully planned, methodically executed, and well-financed campaigns have replaced the heavy-muscled past attempts by amateurs to organize workers through intimidation or force.

The employer, and the conscientious supervisor in particular, may be shocked when first hit by the realization that a union is moving in to organize employees. Arriving at the plant gates one morning, the supervisor may be greeted by workers—including some of the oldest and most trusted employees—carrying placards. The manager is often personally hurt, angered, and confused by this sudden defection. A natural reaction would be to strike back hard and fast against this threat. But precipitous action can cause management to lose the contest before the issues are drawn. Managers must know what to do—and, perhaps even more important, what not to do.

Bobby Sutton managed Quality Service, a small hauling and delivery firm in California.* His father had just bought it from an aging proprietor who had let the business slide. The elder Sutton had retained the employees—a secretary, a clerk, two warehouse workers, and three drivers. A month had passed when Marvin Wiley, an organizer for the Teamsters Union, came in and demanded that Bobby recognize the union as the bargaining agent for the firm's warehouse workers and drivers. Marvin said that most of them had joined the union and wanted it to represent them. Also, the firm owed each of them $800 in back wages in order to bring them up to the union scale. Bobby indicated that he had no evidence that the workers either belonged to or wanted to belong to a union. When Marvin threatened to take the workers out on strike, Bobby said he'd consider them absent without permission and fire them if they walked off the job. Marvin said, "You'd better not do that," and left.

*The names have been changed at the company's request.

> Bobby was quite upset and shaken by the incident. While he was trying to figure out what to do, Joe, a driver, came in to talk about the situation. Joe said he and the two warehouse workers did not want to join but that they were being pressured by Marvin and Bill, another driver. Bill was quite dissatisfied and was actively pushing the others to sign up. The third driver, Tony, was neutral and would do what the majority wanted to do.
>
> Going back to his office, Bobby felt betrayed by Bill and Tony.

WHAT ORGANIZERS DISLIKE TO FIND IN AN ORGANIZATION. Union organizers have found that certain factors effectively reduce their chances of organizing employees and gaining union recognition. They dislike finding the following in a targeted firm:

1. Employees who strongly believe that managers and supervisors are fair and are not taking advantage of them.
2. Employees who take pride in their work.
3. Good performance records kept by the management, for employees feel more secure when they know that their efforts are recognized and appreciated.
4. No claims of high-handed treatment, for employees respect firm but fair discipline.
5. No claims of favoritism.
6. Supervisors who have established good relationships with employees, for union leaders know that good supervisor-employee relations stifle organizing attempts.

As you can see, *supervisors are the key persons as far as employees are concerned, so they are an employer's first line of defense against the entry of a union.* The wise selection of supervisors is obviously very important; leadership abilities should be given more consideration than production abilities in the selection of supervisors.

THINGS TO DO BEFORE THE UNION CALLS. There are many things supervisors and other managers can do to minimize the chances of employees' joining a union—if that's their wish. The most important ones are these:

1. The company and its higher-level managers must pay close attention to supervisors, for they are the key to successful labor relations. Supervisors should receive substantially more pay than their employees. They should also get support from their boss for the orders they give and the decisions they make, because unhappy supervisors can do tremendous harm to an employer's labor relations. Treat supervisors right, keep them well informed, and make them an integral part of the management team.
2. Make sure that no item in the wage-benefit package lags far behind the norm for the area and industry.
3. Improve employee benefits as quickly and as extensively as is feasible.
4. Review jobs frequently to see if they need to be upgraded because responsibilities or working conditions have changed.
5. Make sure employee facilities are adequate, safe, well lighted, well ventilated, and reasonably clean.
6. Keep records of good—and bad—performance by employees, and have programs for boosting employee performance, loyalty, and morale.
7. Be firm but fair when imposing discipline.
8. Provide a practical release valve, such as a grievance committee, for employee frustrations and complaints.

9. Be alert for any complaints of abuse or favoritism by employees or supervisors.
10. Establish clear-cut lines for two-way communications with all employees.
11. Have clear, definite, and well-communicated work rules, making sure that their wording doesn't violate NLRB or EEO/AA rules.
12. Use discretion in hiring new employees.

Notice throughout the above list the importance of good supervisory practices. It cannot be said too strongly that first-line supervisors play an integral role in making unions unnecessary!

A classic research study found some marked differences in attitude between pro-union and pro-employer workers. In general, pro-employer workers showed a greater need for achievement, perfection, and success; a higher level of independence; and an identification with management. Pro-union workers showed a greater need for and dependence on attention, sympathy, and support from someone other than themselves. Their achievement level was low, as was their endurance.[10]

> **About a week after the incident at Quality Service took place, Marvin Wiley walked in, slapped a contract on Bobby Sutton's desk, and said, "Sign it!" After reading it, Bobby refused, explaining that he would go broke if he signed it. He said he was already paying near the union scale; he would pay the workers more when he could afford it and if they deserved it. Marvin said, "We'll see about that!" and angrily stalked out with the unsigned contract in his hand.**
>
> **Although he could not do it legally, Bobby decided that if he was to keep the union out, he'd have to get rid of Bill. As business was slow during the winter months, Bobby laid Bill off, telling him he would rehire him when things picked up. Bobby would drive the third truck if this became necessary.**
>
> **Things went well for Bobby during the next four years. Business grew and he had to add personnel. Each time he interviewed an applicant, he'd inquire as to the applicant's attitude toward various organizations, including unions. If the applicant showed a favorable attitude toward unions, Bobby would find a reason for not hiring him or her.**

WHAT TO DO—AND NOT DO—WHEN THE UNION ENTERS. A tactic frequently used to gain recognition is for the union organizer to meet with the supervisor and hand over some signed authorization cards. Then, as illustrated in the case of the Quality Service firm, the union representative says that he or she represents the workers and asks to be recognized as the workers' exclusive bargaining agent to sign or negotiate a contract.

Most labor-relations specialists suggest that supervisors not touch or examine the cards, for if they do, this action can be construed as acceptance of the union as the workers' agent. Nor should supervisors make any comments to the union representative. If the representative says, "Are you refusing to recognize the union?" the supervisor should reply, "Any comment concerning the company's position must await full consideration of the matter by higher levels of management." If the representative asks, the supervisor should give the name, address, and phone number of the company's labor relations manager. Of course, as soon as the representative leaves, the supervisor should inform his or her boss about the visit. Exhibit 18–9 contains some suggestions as to what you *may* legally do when a union tries to organize your employees. Some things you should *not* do are listed in Exhibit 18–10.

Exhibit 18–9

*Things You May Do
When a Union Tries
to Organize Your
Company*

- Keep outside organizers off premises.
- Inform employees from time to time of the benefits they presently enjoy. (Avoid veiled promises or threats.)
- Inform employees that signing a union authorization card does not mean they must vote for the union if there is an election.
- Inform employees of the disadvantages of belonging to the union, such as the possibility of strikes, serving on a picket line, dues, fines, assessments, and rule by cliques or one individual.
- Inform employees that you prefer to deal with them rather than have the union or any other outsider settle grievances.
- Tell employees what you think about unions and about union policies.
- Inform employees about any prior experience you have had with unions and whatever you know about the union officials trying to organize them.
- Inform employees that the law permits you to hire a new employee to replace any employee who goes on strike for economic reasons.
- Inform employees that no union can obtain more than you as an employer are able to give.
- Inform employees how their wages and benefits compare with those in unionized or non-unionized concerns where wages are lower and benefits are less desirable.
- Inform employees that the local union probably will be dominated by the international union, and that they, the members, will have little say in its operations.
- Inform employees of any untrue or misleading statements made by the organizer. You may give employees corrections of these statements.
- Inform employees of any known racketeering or other undesirable elements that may be active in the union.
- Give opinions on the unions and union leaders, even in derogatory terms.
- Distribute information about unions such as disclosures of congressional committees.
- Reply to union attacks on company policies or practices.
- Give the legal position on labor-management matters.
- Advise employees of their legal rights, provided you do not engage in or finance an employee suit or proceeding.
- Declare a fixed policy in opposition to compulsory union membership contracts.
- Campaign against a union seeking to represent the employees.
- Insist that no solicitation of membership or discussion of union affairs be conducted during working time.
- Administer discipline, layoff, and grievance procedures without regard to union membership or nonmembership of the employees involved.
- Treat both union and nonunion employees alike in making assignments of preferred work or desired overtime.
- Enforce plant rules impartially, regardless of the employee's membership activity in a union.
- Tell employees, if they ask, that they are free to join or not to join any organization, so far as their status with the company is concerned.
- Tell employees that their personal and job security will be determined by the economic prosperity of the company.

Source: Leon C. Megginson et al., *Successful Small Business Management*, 6th ed. (Homewood, IL: Richard D. Irwin, 1991). pp. 821–822. Reprinted with permission of Richard D. Irwin.

Exhibit 18–10

Things You May Not Do When a Union Tries to Organize Your Company

- Engage in surveillance of employees to determine who is and who is not participating in the union program; attend union meetings or engage in any undercover activities for this purpose.
- Threaten, intimidate, or punish employees who engage in union activity.
- Request information from employees about union matters, meetings, etc. Employees may, of their own volition, give such information without prompting. You may listen but not ask questions.
- Prevent employee union representatives from soliciting memberships during nonworking time.
- Grant wage increases, special concessions, or promises of any kind to keep the union out.
- Question a prospective employee about his or her affiliation with a labor organization.
- Threaten to close up or move the plant, curtail operations, or reduce employee benefits.
- Engage in any discriminatory practices, such as work assignments, overtime, layoffs, promotions, wage increases, or any other actions that could be regarded as preferential treatment for certain employees.
- Discriminate against union people when disciplining employees for a specific action, while permitting nonunion employees to go unpunished for the same action.
- Transfer workers on the basis of teaming up nonunion employees to separate them from union employees.
- Deviate in any way from company policies for the primary purpose of eliminating a union employee.
- Intimate, advise, or indicate in any way that unionization will force the company to lay off employees, take away company benefits or privileges enjoyed, or make any other changes that could be regarded as a curtailment of privileges.
- Make statements to the effect that you will not deal with a union.
- Give any financial support or other assistance to employees who support or oppose the union.
- Visit the homes of employees to urge them to oppose or reject the union in its campaign.
- Be a party to any petition or circular against the union or encourage employees to circulate such a petition.
- Make any promises of promotions, benefits, wage increases, or any other items that would induce employees to oppose the union.
- Engage in discussions or arguments that may lead to physical encounters with employees over the union question.
- Use a third party to threaten or coerce a union member, or attempt to influence any employee's vote through this medium.
- Question employees on whether or not they have been affiliated or signed with the union.
- Use the word *never* in any predictions or attitudes about unions or their promises or demands.
- Talk about tomorrow. When you give examples or reasons, you can talk about yesterday or today instead of tomorrow, to avoid making a prediction or conviction which may be interpreted as a threat or promise by the union or the NLRB.

Source: Leon C. Megginson et al., *Successful Small Business Management*, 6th ed. (Homewood, IL: Richard D. Irwin, 1991). pp. 823–824. Reprinted with permission of Richard D. Irwin.

Becoming Recognized as the Employees' Exclusive Bargaining Agent

exclusive bargaining agent Deals exclusively with management over questions of wages, hours, and other terms and conditions of employment.

Once the cards have been signed, the union tries to become recognized as the employees' exclusive bargaining agent. An **exclusive bargaining agent** is the employees' representative who has the exclusive right to deal with management over questions of wages, hours, and other terms and conditions of employment. A certified union has the sole right and legal responsibility to represent all of the employees—nonunion members as well as union members—in their dealings with management.

Management may voluntarily recognize the union or may be forced to accept it because of the union's superior bargaining strength. Ordinarily, a secret-ballot election is conducted by the NLRB when requested by the union or the company. If 30 percent or more of the eligible employees sign authorization cards or a petition requesting a representation election, the NLRB will conduct one. If a majority of the voting employees vote for the union, it is named the exclusive representative of the employees in their dealings with management.

APPEALS USED BY UNION ORGANIZERS. The technique most commonly employed by union organizers to obtain union recognition is to compare the target company's practices to items in contracts that the union has with other companies, perhaps in an entirely different industry. If the terms of employment in the target company lag far behind, the union has a ready-made argument. Of course, the organizer will focus on those parts of the wage-benefit package that will make the employer look bad.

Union organizers appeal to five main desires of employees:

1. *Job protection.* Unions stress that they continually try to ensure that employees have a job—or at least an income—for a lifetime. With most employees already enjoying generous benefits, many seem more interested in job security than in higher pay rates. But there are exceptions to this generalization.

   > **Unionized employees at an Alcoa plant in Mobile, Alabama, voted to permit the plant to close rather than take cuts in income and benefits. They received quite high unemployment compensation, as well as supplemental payments from the company, for three years.**

2. *Interference running.* Unions assure employees that they will act as their agents in grievances and disputes. They will go to bat for employees, and they claim to have the know-how to protect employees' interests.

3. *Participation in management.* Unions insist that they can and will give employees a greater voice in deciding the policies, procedures, and rules that affect them and the work they do.

4. *Economic gains.* Higher wages, reduced hours, and better benefits are still at the top of an organizer's checklist.

5. *Recognition and participation.* Knowing that pro-union workers need and are dependent on attention, sympathy, and support, union organizers promise employees that they'll have greater recognition and participation through union activities.

ADDITIONAL PRECAUTIONS FOR SUPERVISORS. Besides observing the "dos" and "don'ts" given in Exhibits 18–9 and 18–10, management should make sure there is nothing in personnel policies and work rules that the NLRB can construe as being anti-union. For example, suppose a company has the following sign displayed: "No solicitation at this company." This prohibition can actually be ruled an unfair labor practice unless it is enforced against all types of solicitation—even by charitable groups—not just union organizing. A company is obliged to permit solicitation and distribution of literature by union organizers in nonwork areas such as locker rooms and parking lots. Of course, managers can prohibit nonemployees from being on company property at any time.

Next, supervisors and anyone else in a position to reward or punish voting employees should stay away from the voting area during a representation election.

Finally, neither threat of reprisal nor any promise of reward should be given before the election, although it is permissible to tell employees what has happened at other plants where workers unionized—if it is factual.

> **During its fifth year of operation, business was booming for Quality Service. Bobby Sutton had 22 employees, including 3 office employees, 7 warehouse workers, and 12 truck drivers. His father had bought another firm in a nearby city, and Bobby was running both businesses, with a supervisor at each location. Bobby had contracted to buy five new trucks and was trying to hire new drivers for them, but the number of capable drivers available for employment was quite limited.**
>
> **After hearing nothing from the union for four years, Bobby was surprised when Marvin Wiley walked in and laid down authorization cards from five warehouse workers and two drivers. Marvin said, "Bobby, the last time I was here, you said you couldn't afford to unionize. But now you're the largest delivery firm in town. I think your people had better be working under a contract."**
>
> **Again, Bobby refused to accept the union as the representative of his employees. The seven employees subsequently petitioned for an NLRB election, but lost it by a vote of 6 for the union and 13 against it. From then on, Bobby and his supervisors became more concerned about employee relations.**

Engaging in Collective Bargaining

collective bargaining
Conferring in good faith over wages, hours, and other terms and conditions of employment.

Once the union has been recognized as the employees' bargaining agent, it starts negotiating with management to try to reach an agreement (which in effect is a contract between the company and the union). In general, **collective bargaining** is the process by which representatives of the employer and the employees meet at reasonable times and places to confer in good faith over wages, hours, and other terms and conditions of employment. Note that the representatives of the two parties are only required to meet in a "reasonable place," usually a conference room at a hotel or motel, and at a "reasonable time," usually the firm's normal daily working hours. They must negotiate "in good faith" by making valid offers and counteroffers about any question involving wages, hours, and other "terms and conditions of employment." Once an agreement has been reached, both parties must have the opportunity to sign it if they want to—which they usually do.

It's a "must" that supervisors be consulted at each step of this bargaining procedure. They should carefully examine every union proposal—and management counterproposal—to see how they would affect the supervisors' relationships with the employees. Also, supervisors should be consulted about concessions to be asked of the union negotiators.

A recent strike by a machinists' union emerged from workers' disputes with Boeing for exporting jobs to Asia.

mediator Tries to bring the parties together when collective bargaining has reached an impasse.

arbitrator Will make a binding decision when collective bargaining reaches an impasse.

If no agreement is reached, an impasse develops. At this point there are three alternatives: (1) to call in an outside **mediator,** provided by the Federal Mediation and Conciliation Service, who will try to bring the parties together; (2) to agree to bring the issue to an outside **arbitrator,** who will make a binding decision; or (3) for the union to go on strike or for management to stage a lockout.

Conducting a Strike or Lockout

strike When employees withhold their services from an employer.

picketing Walking back and forth outside the place of employment, usually carrying a sign.

The ultimate strategy used by unions to achieve their objectives is the strike. A **strike** occurs when employees withhold their services from an employer in order to achieve a goal. The employees tell the public why they are striking by means of **picketing**—walking back and forth outside the place of employment, usually carrying signs (see Exhibit 18–11).

Most union leaders *do not like to use the strike.* It is costly, it carries a certain stigma for those walking the picket line, and it is potentially dangerous to the union because of the possible loss of membership and power if the strike fails. In fact, only a very small percentage of the thousands of contract negotiations conducted annually result in strikes. Although the strike itself is the ultimate device in collective bargaining and

Exhibit 18–11

Source: Reprinted with permission of Tribune Media Service.

is the technique resorted to when all other methods of resolving differences fail, the *threat of a strike* is a continuing factor in almost all negotiations. Both the union and the employer frequently act as if one could occur.

Just as the union can call a strike if it isn't satisfied with the progress of negotiations, so can management stage a lockout. A **lockout** is the closing of company premises to the employees and refusal to let them work.

lockout A closing of a company's premises to the employees and refusing to let them work.

Reaching an Agreement

agreement Prepared when an accord has been reached to bind the company, union, and workers to specific clauses in it.

When an accord has been reached, a document is prepared which becomes the **agreement** or **contract** among the company, the union, and the workers. It usually contains clauses covering at least the following areas:

1. Union recognition
2. Wages
3. Vacation and holidays
4. Working conditions
5. Layoffs and rehiring
6. Management prerogatives
7. Hours of work
8. Seniority
9. Arbitration
10. Renewal clause

Specifics are set forth in each of these areas, and rules are established that should be obeyed by management and the union. The management prerogatives clause defines the areas in which supervisors have the right to act, free from questioning or joint action by the union.

LIVING WITH THE AGREEMENT

Learning Objective 6

Name three things that a supervisor must know in order to live with the union agreement.

Once the agreement has been signed, managers and supervisors have to live with the contract until it is time to negotiate a new one. Therefore, all management personnel—especially first-level supervisors—should be thoroughly briefed on its contents. The meaning and interpretation of each clause should be reviewed, and the wording of the contract should be clearly understood. Supervisors' questions should be answered to better prepare them to deal with labor-relations matters. Also, it should be impressed on supervisors that their counterpart—the union steward—will probably be better trained, know the contract provisions in greater detail, and be better equipped in the practice of contract administration.

Supervisors' Rights Under the Agreement

Supervisors should view the agreement as the rules of the game, for it spells out what they may and may not do. They should take a positive view of what they *may do* rather than a negative one of what they *may not do*. Although agreements differ in detail, most give supervisors the following rights:

1. To decide what work is to be done.
2. To decide how, when, and where it will be done.
3. To determine how many workers are needed to do the work safely.
4. To decide who will do each job, as long as the skill classifications and seniority provisions are observed.
5. To instruct, supervise, correct, and commend employees in the performance of their work.
6. To require that work performance and on-the-job personal behavior meet minimum standards.
7. To recommend promotions and pay increases, as long as they do not violate the union agreement.
8. To administer discipline according to the agreed-upon procedure.

If uncertain as to their authority, supervisors should check with the firm's human resources or labor relations experts. Supervisors need to have a working knowledge of the agreement's details because the employees and their advocate, the union steward, will be aware of these details.

SELF-CHECK

Would you rather be a supervisor in a unionized or a nonunionized company? Why?

The Supervisor and the Union Steward

union steward A union member elected by other members to represent their interests in relations with management.

The **union steward,** a union member who has been elected by other members to represent their interests in relations with management, is the supervisor's counterpart. He or she is the link between the workers and their union and between the union and the company, especially in case of controversy. The supervisor represents the company and its interests to workers, who play the dual roles of employees of the company and members of the union. The steward represents the union's position to the workers and to the company. The steward is at the same level in the union hierarchy as the supervisor is in the company hierarchy.

As equals, the steward and the supervisor must maintain production operations within the framework of the agreement. Frequently, the goals of the steward and the supervisor conflict, for the supervisor's job is to obtain maximum productivity, whereas the steward's aim is to protect the workers' interests—including not working too hard and not working themselves out of a job.

The Role of Seniority

seniority An employee's length of service in a company; a basis for promotion.

One of the most basic union principles is **seniority,** which means that workers who have been on the job the longest get preferred treatment and better benefits. One of the supervisor's greatest challenges is to maintain high productivity while assigning work, especially preferred jobs and overtime, to the most senior employee, who is not necessarily the most capable worker. Also, whom does the supervisor recommend for promotion—the most capable worker or the most senior employee? These issues, plus discipline, lead to most grievances against supervisors.

Handling Employee Complaints

grievance procedure A formal way of handling employees' complaints.

In unionized companies, employees' complaints take the form of grievances. The **grievance procedure** is a formal way of handling these complaints. In nonunionized companies, employees may present their complaints to their supervisors for proper disposition.

GRIEVANCE PROCEDURES. Exhibit 18–12 shows a typical grievance procedure, such as is usually found in unionized organizations. The form and substance of the grievance procedure depends on several factors:

1. The type of industry (the old-line, "smokestack" industries, such as steel, auto, and transportation, have the most formal and rigid procedures).
2. The size and structure of the organization (the larger, more highly structured organizations have the most formal and inflexible procedures).
3. The type of union (the older, craft-oriented unions tend to have a highly structured procedure).

There are usually five steps in a formal grievance procedure in a unionized organization. However, the *actual* number of steps taken will depend on the number of managerial levels in the organization and whether or not the grievance is submitted to arbitration.

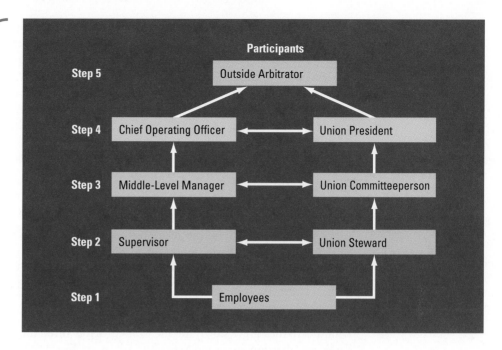

Exhibit 18–12
Typical Grievance Procedure in a Unionized Organization

1. Step 1 begins when an employee complains to the supervisor about a presumed wrong. From the employee's viewpoint, the supervisor may be violating the labor agreement or doing something that dissatisfies the employee. If the supervisor straightens out the matter satisfactorily, that's the end of the grievance.
2. Frequently, though, the issue is not resolved, so the employee goes to the union steward to present a grievance. The steward then tries to obtain satisfaction from the supervisor. This is Step 2. The vast majority of grievances are settled at this stage.
3. In Step 3, the union committeeperson or business agent tries to resolve the complaint with middle management, such as a department head.
4. In Step 4, the union president and the chief operating officer try to resolve the difference. If they succeed, that ends the grievance.
5. If the chief operating officer and the union president cannot resolve the grievance, it is submitted to outside arbitration. A mutually agreed upon arbitrator makes the decision. This is Step 5.

COMPLAINT PROCEDURES IN NONUNIONIZED ORGANIZATIONS. Many nonunion organizations have formal complaint procedures that are comparable in many ways to the formal union grievance procedures. These procedures permit complaints to go beyond the supervisor to committees composed of higher-level executives, including the personnel officer and sometimes even top executives. However, they do not provide for arbitration, since the primary purpose of these procedures is to ensure fairness in employee relations and to improve employee attitudes, rather than to interpret human resources policies and practices. Such procedures are frequently found in public organizations such as government agencies.

Supervisors can improve employee-employer relationships if they understand the types of employees who are prone to file complaints or grievances. For example, an early study found that the more sensitive people are, the more apt they are to file. Young employees who are well-educated but not well-paid tend to file grievances, as do employees who have not been with the company long but are military veterans.[11] Supervisors have two alternatives for dealing with employees of these types. In some cases they may try to avoid hiring them; alternatively, they can try to find ways to accommodate them.

Chapter Review

Learning Objective 1

Explain what is meant by labor relations.
Labor relations, which are the relationships between employers and their unionized employees, are particularly important to supervisors, for they are the managers who must deal with operative employees on a day-to-day basis. An employer usually has good labor relations if the supervisors have good relationships with employees.

Learning Objective 2

Trace the development of unions in the United States.
Union activities grew slowly in the United States until the formation of the AFL. Then membership increased steadily until after World War I, when it leveled off. Membership mushroomed during the period from 1935 to 1950, when favorable laws were passed and industrial unions became popular. Since then, union membership has grown more slowly.

Learning Objective 3

Explain why union membership is declining.
Some of the reasons for declining interest in unions among U.S. employees are: (1) the economy has shifted from manufacturing jobs, which are relatively easy to unionize, to service work, which is more difficult to organize; (2) today's more educated and technologically oriented service workers are more interested in empowerment-type activities; (3) the global economy is forcing U.S. companies to cut costs by resisting organizing drives; (4) the influx of part-time workers resists unionization; and (5) the proliferation of small businesses makes organizing more difficult.

Learning Objective 4

Name and explain the basic laws governing labor relations.
The basic law governing labor relations is the Wagner Act, which gives workers the right to freely join unions of their choosing and to engage in concerted actions to achieve their goals. The Taft-Hartley Act prohibits the closed shop and provides for states to pass right-to-work laws prohibiting the union shop. The Landrum-Griffin Act provides employees with a bill of rights that protects them from exploitation by management and unscrupulous union leaders. These laws are administered by the National Labor Relations Board (NLRB), the Federal Mediation and Conciliation Service (FMCS), and the U.S. Department of Labor. The NLRB tries to prevent both unions and management from engaging in unfair labor practices.

Learning Objective 5

Describe union objectives and discuss the methods used to achieve those objectives.
Union objectives are higher pay, shorter hours of work, improved working conditions, and improved personal and job security. In order to achieve those objectives, unions organize (or recruit) an employer's workers into a union, then try to become their exclusive bargaining agent in dealing with management, usually through an NLRB-

conducted, secret-ballot election. Unions have greater difficulty organizing employees in firms that have effective supervisors and good employee relations. Management can try to keep the union out as long as its policies and actions stay within the law.

When the union becomes the bargaining agent, it bargains collectively with representatives of management over wages, hours, and the other terms and conditions of employment. Supervisors are critical to success at this point, so they should help formulate demands to be made of the union, evaluate proposals made by the union bargaining team, and be kept informed of progress made in the negotiations.

If the two parties cannot agree and reach an impasse, there are several options: (1) they can call in an outside mediator, (2) they can agree to send the issue to an arbitrator, who will make a binding decision, or (3) the union can conduct a strike or management can stage a lockout. Most negotiations end with an agreement, which becomes the contract between management and the employees.

 **6**

Name three things that a supervisor must know in order to live with the union agreement.

It is then up to the supervisor to live with the contract. Disagreements over interpretation of the agreement are settled through the grievance procedure. If agreement is not reached within the company, the issue goes to an arbitrator for resolution.

Important Terms

agency shop *pg. 512*
agreement *or* contract *524*
arbitrator *523*
closed shop *512*
collective bargaining *522*
craft unions *507*
employee associations *508*
employees' bill of
   rights *513*
exclusive bargaining
   agent *521*

grievance procedure *526*
industrial unions *508*
labor relations *or* union-
   management relations *or*
   industrial relations *506*
labor union *506*
lockout *524*
maintenance-of-
   membership clause *512*
mediator *523*
picketing *523*

right-to-work laws *513*
seniority *526*
strike *523*
unfair labor practices *511*
union authorization
   card *515*
union shop *512*
union steward *526*

Questions for Review and Discussion

1. Define labor relations.
2. When did unions grow the fastest? Why?
3. Why has union growth slowed?
4. How do you interpret the union membership trends shown in Exhibits 18–1 and 18–2?
5. Do you believe that union power will increase or decrease in the future? Why?
6. Name the laws that form the legal basis for labor relations, and explain their general provisions.

7. What are the differences among the union shop, the closed shop, and the agency shop? Are these differences really significant? Explain.
8. What are some unfair labor practices that management sometimes commits?
9. What are some unfair labor practices that unions sometimes commit?
10. What are the primary objectives of unions?
11. What are the methods used by unions to achieve their objectives?
12. What provisions are usually included in a labor agreement?
13. Describe the typical grievance procedure.

Skill Builder 18–1
The Union Organizer

Refer back to the examples in the chapter and assume that you are Marvin Wiley and are trying to get the employees of Quality Service to organize and vote for your union. What would you do? How would you go about getting the 13 employees who voted against the union (and any new ones) to sign authorization cards and vote for the union?

Skill Builder 18–2
Would You Sign a Union Authorization Card?

Situation A: Assume that you encounter the following independent situations. You are 30 years old and have a job paying $6.50 per hour. Because of your personal situation, this is a fairly good job for you and will probably be the best job you can hold. Your spouse also does similar work at the company, so your combined income is about $26,000 per year (2,000 hours per person per year × $6.50/hour × 2 persons). Some of the workers are talking about joining a union.

Situation B: You hear that some layoffs have recently been made to improve company profits. You also know that about once a month someone is injured.

Answer the following questions:
1. Would you sign a union authorization card in Situation A? Why or why not?
2. Would you sign a union authorization card in Situation B? Why or why not?

Source: H. Giles Schmid, Winona State University.

CASE 18–1

A Rebellion in Labor's Camp

As a young man, Lane Kirkland studied foreign relations at Georgetown University. During his 15 years as America's No. 1 labor leader, he became a patron of labor figures from Poland to Indonesia. But unions back home suffered bruising defeats. In 1968, labor's share of the U.S. work force stood at 30.5 percent. In 1995, it was 15.5 percent—and Kirkland, at 73, was on the verge of becoming the first head of the AFL-CIO or its predecessors in this century to draw a challenger. When he announced his intention to seek a new term in October, leaders of 11 big AFL-CIO unions asked him not to.

AP photo by Marcy Nighswander.

His friends-turned-foes wanted someone who would rebuild labor's organizing machinery, punish political adversaries, and spend more time on picket lines than in the AFL-CIO headquarters a few blocks from the White House. They were not to be ignored: the dissenters represented four of the federation's five largest unions, including the Teamsters and the United Auto Workers, and boasted some of its savviest leaders, including John J. Sweeney of the Service Employees International Union and Richard Trumka of the United Mine Workers. Fielding a candidate who could unite labor's 13 million diverse members—carpenters, teachers, factory hands, nurses—against a seasoned incumbent would not be easy. And a change in leadership would not ensure a reversal of labor's long decline. But the dissenters' challenge would have guaranteed a historic battle. As it turned out, however, the challengers were successful in persuading Kirkland not to run.

Answer the following questions:

1. From what you have studied in this chapter, do you think Kirkland could have done anything else to prevent the AFL-CIO's decline? Explain.
2. What would you suggest that Kirkland's successor do to reverse the union's declining membership?

Source: Adapted from "A Rebellion in Labor's Camp," *U.S. News & World Report*, May 22, 1995, p. 18.

Skill-Development Scenario
Process vs. Task Orientation

Ken Foley is production development supervisor for Carson Products. A production line that Foley's department designed and implemented is not working properly, and as a result, about 20 percent of the parts made are not usable.

Answer the following questions:

1. How has the initial problem been magnified as a result of Foley and Jones' behavior? What do you think is happening to the motivation and productivity of the assembly and production workers?
2. After viewing the second part of this video, discuss the importance of focusing on the process by Foley and others. From your own experience, how will the worker empowerment influence motivation?

ENDNOTES

Chapter 1

1. Henry Mintzberg, "The Manager's Job," *Harvard Business Review* 53 (July–August 1975), pp. 49–61.
2. "The Old Foreman Is on the Way Out, and the New One Will Be More Important," *Business Week,* April 25, 1983, pp. 74–75.
3. A. Janice Klein and Pamela A. Posey, "Good Supervisors Are Good Supervisors—Anywhere," *Harvard Business Review* 64 (November–December 1986), pp. 125–128.
4. "Tomorrow's Jobs," from *Occupational Outlook Handbook,* 1992–1993 edition, U.S. Department of Labor, Bureau of Labor Statistics, p. 3, and Leon C. Megginson, Geralyn M. Franklin,

and M. Jane Byrd, *Human Resources Management* (Houston, Tex.: Dame Publications Inc., 1995), p. 46.
5. Jon Katzenbach, "The Right Kind of Teamwork," *The Wall Street Journal,* November 9, 1992, p. A–10.
6. Susan Caminiti, "A Quiet Superstar Rises in Retailing," *Fortune,* October 23, 1990, pp. 167–174.
7. John Hillkirk, "Challenging Status Quo Now in Vogue," *USA Today,* November 9, 1993, pp. 1B and 2B.
8. Ibid., p. 2B.
9. John Hillkirk, "Reengineering Movement in Infancy," *USA Today,* November 9, 1993, p. 2B.
10. Sue Shellenbarger, "In Re-Engineering, What Really Matters Are Workers' Lives,"

The Wall Street Journal, March 1, 1995, p. B1.
11. James E. Ellis, "Why Overseas? Because That's Where the Sales Are," *Business Week,* January 10, 1994, pp. 62–63; and Warren Cohen, "Exporting Know-How," *U.S. News & World Report,* September 6, 1993, p. 53.
12. John J. Keller, "AT&T to Unveil Management Shakeup Stressing Globalization and Multi-Media," *The Wall Street Journal,* July 22, 1993, p. A2.
13. Leon C. Megginson, Donald C. Mosley, and Paul H. Pietri, Jr., *Management: Concepts and Applications,* 4th ed. (New York: HarperCollins, 1992), p. 670.
14. Donald C. Mosley, Paul H. Pietri, Jr., and Leon C.

Megginson, *Management: Empayerment and Leadership* 5th ed (New York: Harper-Collins, 1996), p. 151.

Chapter 2

1. Peter Drucker, "Twilight of the First Line Supervisor," *The Wall Street Journal,* June 7, 1983, p. 1b.
2. A. B. Fisher, "Morale Crisis," *Fortune,* November 18, 1991, p. 7; J. Schmit, "ARM Quarterly Loss Totals $253 Million," *USA Today,* January 20, 1994, p. 2b.
3. David E. Bowen and Edward E. Lawler, III, "The Empowerment of Service Workers: What, Why, How and When," *Sloan Management Review* (Spring 1992), p. 34.
4. David A. Garwin, "Quality on the Line," *Harvard*

Business Review, September–October 1993, pp. 41–54.

5. James W. Dean and James R. Evans, *Total Quality* (St. Paul, Minn.: West Publishing Co., 1994) p. 7.

6. Les L. Landes, "Down with Duality Program-itis," *IABC Communication World,* February 1992, pp. 29–32.

7. Thomas J. Peters and Robert H. Waterman, Jr., *In Search of Excellence* (New York: Harper and Row, 1982). See especially Chapter 6: "Close to the Customer."

8. Charles N. Weaver, *TQM: A Step by Step Guide to Implementation* (Milwaukee, Wis.: ASQC Press, 1991), p. 4.

9. Dean and Evans, p. 248.

10. Ibid., p. 13.

11. Fred Luthans, *Organizational Behavior,* 7th ed. (New York: McGraw-Hill, Inc., 1995), p. 40.

12. See Kenneth R. Thompson, "A Conversation with Robert W. Galvin," in Joseph G. VanMatre, *Foundations of TQM* (Fort Worth, Tex.: Dryden Press, 1995) pp. 349–369.

13. Luthans, p. 35.

14. Adapted from Dean and Evans, pp. 26–28.

Chapter 4

1. For further details, see *A Matter of Judgment and Ethics at Work,* videos produced by the Ethics Resource Center.

2. Patricia Haddock and Marilyn Manning, "Ethically Speaking," *Sky,* March 1990, p. 128.

3. See Mortimer R. Feinberg and Aaron L. Wenstein, "How Do You Know When to Rely on Your Intuition?" *The Wall Street Journal,* June 21, 1982, p. 16.

Chapter 5

1. James A. F. Stoner, *Management* (Englewood Cliffs, NJ: Prentice-Hall, 1978), p. 284.

2. "Theme and Variation," *The Owen Manager* (Owen Graduate School of Management, Vanderbilt University) 4 (Spring 1983), p. 2.

3. James L. Mercer, "Organizing for the '80s—What about Matrix Management?" *Business* 31 (July–August 1981), pp. 25–33.

4. Donald Mosley, Carl Moore, Michelle Slagle, and Don Burns, "The Role of the O.D. Consultant in Partnering," *Organization Development Journal* 8 (Fall 1990), pp. 43–49.

5. Thomas J. Peters and Robert Waterman, *In Search of Excellence: Lessons from America's Best-Run Companies* (New York: Harper & Row, 1982).

6. Peter Drucker, "The Coming of the New Organization," *Harvard Business Review* 76 (January–February 1988), pp. 45–53.

7. Richard L. Bunning, "The Dynamics of Downsizing," *Personnel Journal* 69 (September 1990), p. 69.

8. Phillip R. Nienstedt, "Effective Downsizing Management Structures," *Human Resources Planning* 12 (1989), p. 156.

9. Bunning, "The Dynamics of Downsizing," p. 70.

10. Nancy K. Austin, "Reorganizing the Organization Chart," *Working Woman,* September 1993, p. 24.

11. Ibid., pp. 24–25.

12. R. E. Miles and C. C. Snow, "Causes of Failure in Network Organizations," *California Management Review* (1992), Vol. 30, No. 4, p. 55.

Chapter 6

1. Donald A. Laird and Eleanor C. Laird, *The Techniques of Delegating: How to Get Things Done Through Others* (New York: McGraw-Hill Book Co., 1957), pp. 107–108.

2. Claude S. George, *Supervision in Action: The Art of Managing Others,* 4th ed. (Englewood Cliffs, NJ: Prentice-Hall, 1985), p. 283. Reprinted by permission.

3. Dale D. McConkey, *No-Nonsense Delegation* (New York: AMACOM, 1974), pp. 90–100.

4. "Tom Peters' Formula for Supervisory Excellence," *Supervisory Management* 30 (February 1985), pp. 2–3.

5. Suzanne Savory, "Ineffective Delegation—Symptom or Problem?" *Supervisory Management* 24 (June 1979), p. 28.

6. Laurence Peter and Raymond Hull, *The Peter Principle* (New York: William Morrow & Co., 1969).

7. Peter Reuters, "Study Finds Profit in Employee Empowerment," *USA Today,* June 6, 1995, p. 4B.

Chapter 7

1. Robert Kreitner and Angelo Kinicki, *Organizational Behavior,* 3rd ed. (Chicago, Ill.: Irwin, 1995), p. 368.

2. Albert Mehrabian, "Communication Without Words," *Psychology Today 2* (September 1968), pp. 53–55.

3. According to a Toyota advertisement in *Forbes,* June 19, 1995, p. 168.

4. Keith Davis, *Human Behavior at Work,* 8th ed. (New York: McGraw-Hill Book Co., 1989), p. 371.

5. "The Difference Japanese Management Makes," *Business Week,* July 14, 1986, p. 47.

6. J. Hart Seibert, "Listening in the Organizational Context," Robert Bostrom ed., *Listening Behavior: Measurement and Application* (New York: The Guilford Press, 1990), pp. 119–127.

Chapter 8

1. Alfred J. Marrow, *Behind the Executive Mask: Greater Managerial Competence through Deeper Self-Understanding,* Report No. 79 (New York: AMACOM, 1964), p. 7.

2. Abraham H. Maslow, *Motivation and Personality* (New York: Harper & Row, 1954).

3. Patrick L. Townsend and Joan E. Gebhardt, "What's In It for Me?" *Journal for Quality and Participation,* March 1992, p. 10.

4. Adapted and updated from Douglas McGregor, "Conditions of Effective Leadership in the Industrial Organization," *Journal of Consulting Psychology,* March–April 1944, pp. 55–63.

5. Hyler Bracey, Jack Rosenblum, Aubrey Sanford, and Roy Trueblood, *Managing from the Heart* (New York: Delacorte Press, 1990), p. 13.

6. Frederick Herzberg, Bernard Mausner, and Barbara Snyderman, *The Motivation to Work,* 2d ed. (New York: John Wiley & Sons, 1959).

7. Theresa M. Welbourne, David B. Balkin, Luis R. Gomez-Mejia, "Gainsharing and Mutual Monitoring: A Combined Agency—Organizational Justice Interpretation," *The Academy of Management Journal,* Vol. 38, No. 3, June 1995, p. 881.

8. M. Michael Markowich, "Does Money Motivate?" *H.R. Focus,* (American Management Association's Human Resources Publication), No. 70, No. 8, August 1993, p. 7.

9. Charles A. Hanson and Donna K. Hanson, "Motivation: Are the Old Theories Still True?" *Supervisory Management* 23 (June 1978): 14.

10. Charles F. Kemp, *The World of Golf and the Game of Life* (St. Louis: The Bethany Press, 1978), p. 20.

11. Thomas J. Peters and Robert H. Waterman, Jr., *In Search of Excellence: Lessons from America's Best-Run Companies* (New York: Harper & Row, 1982), p. 48.

12. Barry M. Stow, "Organizational Psychology and the Pursuit of the Happy/Productive Worker," *California Management Review* 28 (Summer 1986), p. 48.

13. James O'Toole, "Employee Practices at the Best-Managed Companies," *California Management Review* 28 (Fall 1985), pp. 35–66.

14. "Reinventing Schools," *USA Today,* Section 1B, June 19, 1995.

15. Charlene M. Solomon, "Managing the Baby Busters," *Personnel Journal,* Vol. 71, No. 3, p. 52.

16. Nancy J. Perry, "The Workers of the Future," *Fortune,* Special Issue, Spring/Summer 1991, p. 68.

17. James A. Anderson, "The Bureaucracy Busters," *Fortune,* June 17, 1991, p. 37.

Chapter 9

1. Douglas McGregor, *The Human Side of Enterprise* (New York: McGraw-Hill Book Co., 1960), pp. 33–42.

2. Notes from Workshop on Process Consultation conducted by Edgar Schein, Albert Einstein Institute, Cape Code, August, 1991.

3. *Trainer's Bookshelf,* Interview with Dr. Paul Hersey (San Diego, Calif.: Leaning Resources Corporation, 1982).

4. Robert R. Blake and Jane S. Mouton, *The Managerial Grid III: The Key to Leadership Excellence* (Houston: Gulf Publishing, 1985).

5. Paul Hersey and Kenneth H. Blanchard, *Management of Organizational Behavior: Utilizing Human Resources,* 3d ed. (Englewood Cliffs, N.J.: Prentice-Hall, 1977), pp. 161–162.

6. Hersey and Blanchard acknowledge that they were strongly influenced by William J. Reddins, "3-D Management Style Theory," found in William J. Reddins, *Managerial Effectiveness* (New York: McGraw-Hill, 1970).

We use Hersey and Blanchard's model because it is better known.

7. Robert Tannenbaum and Warren Schmidt, "How to Choose a Leadership Pattern," *Harvard Business Review 51* (May–June 1973), pp. 162–180.

8. Leonard M. Apcar, "Middle Managers and Supervisors Resist Moves to More Participatory Management," *The Wall Street Journal,* September 16, 1985, p. 25.

9. John McGregor Burns, *Leadership* (New York: Harper & Row, 1978).

10. Bernard Bass, *Leadership and Performance Beyond Expectations* (New York: Free Press, 1985).

11. B. M. Bass, B. J. Avolio, and L. Goodheim, "Biography and the Assessment of Transformational Leadership at the World Class Level," *Journal of Management 13* (Spring 1987), p. 7.

12. Ibid., p. 16.

13. William D. Hitt, "The Model Leader: A Fully Functioning Person," *Leadership and Organization Development Journal,* Vol. 14, No. 7, December, 1993, p. 10.

Chapter 10

1. Glenn M. Parker, *Team Players and Teamwork* (San Francisco: Jossey-Bass Publishers, 1991).

2. William G. Dyer, *Team Building: Issues and Alternatives* (Reading, Mass.: Addison-Wesley Publishing Co., 1977), p. 4.

3. Don Hellriegel and John W. Slocum, Jr., *Management* (Cincinnati, Ohio: South-Western Publishing Co., 7th ed.), p. 52.

4. Rosabeth Moss Kanter, "Dilemmas of Managing Participation," *Organizational Dynamics* 11 (Summer 1982), pp. 4–27.

5. David L. Bradford and Allen R. Cohen, *Managing for Excellence* (New York:

John Wiley & Sons, 1984), pp. 10–11.

6. Rensis Likert, *The Human Organization: Its Management and Value* (New York: McGraw-Hill Book Co., 1967), p. 47.

7. Donald C. Mosley, "System Four Revisited: Some New Insights," *Organizational Development Journal,* Spring 1987, p. 19.

8. Don Hellreigel, John W. Slocum, Jr., and Richard Woodman, *Organization Behavior,* 5th ed. (St. Paul: West Publishing, 1989), p. 210.

9. Jan Grant, "Women as Managers: What They Can Offer to Organizations," *Organizational Dynamics* 16 (Winter 1988), pp. 56–63.

10. Carol Pearson, *The Hero Within* (New York: Harper & Row, 1986), p. 88.

11. Nancy K. Austin, "Now About This Female Management Style . . . ," *Executive Female,* Sept.–Oct. 1992, Vol. 15, No. 5, p. 48.

12. Charles C. Manz and Henry P. Sims, Jr., "Superleadership: Leading Others to Lead Themselves to Excellence," *The Manager's Bookshelf,* ed. Jan L. Pierce and John W. Newstrom (New York: Harper & Row, 1988), p. 328.

13. Robert A. Zawacki and Carol A. Norman, "Successful Self-Directed Teams and Planned Change: A Lot in Common," Reading 28, p. 311, found in W. L. French, C. H. Bell, Jr., R. A. Zawacki, *Organization Development and Transformation* (Burr Ridge, Ill.: Irwin, 4th ed., 1994).

14. *The Wall Street Journal,* November 28, 1995, p. 1.

15. Manz and Sims, "Superleadership," p. 328.

16. Zawacki and Norman, "Successful Self-Directed Work Teams and Planned Change: A Lot in Common," p. 315.

17. Randall Hanson, Rebecca

Porterfield, and Kathleen Ames, "Employee Empowerment at Risk: Effects of Recent NLRM Rulings," *The Academy of Management Executive,* Vol. IX, No. 2, May 1995, pp. 45–54.

18. John J. Gabarro and John P. Kotter, "Managing Your Boss," *Harvard Business Review* 58 (January–February 1980), pp. 92–100.

Chapter 11

1. Leon C. Megginson, Donald C. Mosley, and Paul H. Pietri, Jr., *Management: Concepts and Applications,* 4th ed. (New York: Harper Collins, 1992), pp. 579–581.

2. "Pentagon Travel Costs," *USA Today,* March 28, 1995, p. 4A.

Chapter 12

1. *The Wall Street Journal,* March 9, 1995, p. A2.

2. L. P. Sullivan, "Quality Function Deployment: The Latent Potential of Phases III and IV," in A. Richard Shores, *A TQM Approach to Achieving Manufacturing Excellence,* Milwaukee: ASQC Quality Press, 1990.

3. Lynda Radosevich, "EDI Spreads Across Different Business Lines," *Computerworld,* October 18, 1993, pp. 69–73; also, "Dillard Stores' Profit in April Quarter Was Flat, Disappointing Some Analysts," *The Wall Street Journal,* May 12, 1994, p. B4.

4. James W. Dean Jr. and James R. Evans, *Total Quality* (Minneapolis/St. Paul: West Publishing Co., 1994, p. 133.

5. Gerald Langley, Devin Nolan, and Thomas Nolan, "The Foundation of Improvement," Sixth Annual International Deming User's Group Conference, Cincinnati, Ohio, August, 1992.

6. *Accident Facts* (1993), Chicago National Safety Council.

Chapter 13

1. Dennis C. Kinlaw, *Coaching for Commitment* (San Diego, Calif.: Pfeiffer & Co., 1993), p. 19.
2. Dennis C. Kinlaw, *Coaching Skills Inventory* (San Diego, Calif.: Pfeiffer & Co., 1993), pp. 1–13.
3. Thomas Gordon, *Leader Effectiveness Training* (New York: Dryden Books, 1977), pp. 92–107.
4. Wayne F. Cascio, *Managing Human Resources,* 4th ed. (New York: McGraw-Hill, Inc., 1995), p. 550.

Chapter 14

1. Quoted in Alfred J. Marrow, *Behind the Executive Mask: Greater Managerial Competence Through Deeper Self-Understanding,* Report No. 79 (New York: AMACOM, 1964), p. 7.

Chapter 15

1. Edgar H. Schein, *Process Consultation,* Vol. 1, 2nd ed. (Reading, Mass.: Addison-Wesley Publishing Co., 1988), p. 6.
2. Ibid., p. 9.
3. Ibid., pp. 10–11.
4. Brochures, Synergistic Group, Inc., Mobile, AL, 1995.
5. Scott Brow and Roger Fisher of the Harvard Negotiation Project, *Getting Together, Building Relationships as We Negotiate,* Penguin Books, 1988, pp. 27–28.
6. M. Afzalur Rahim, Jan Edward Garrett, and Gabriel F. Buntzman, "Ethics of Managing Interpersonal Conflict in Organizations," *Journal of Business Ethics,* May 1992, VII, n5–6, p. 425.
7. Roger Fisher and William Ury, *Getting to Yes* (New York: Penquin, 1993) pp. 3, 4.
8. Claudia Wallis, "Stress: Can We Cope?" *Time,* June 6, 1983, pp. 48–54.

9. A. P. Brief, R. S. Schuler, and M. W. Sell, *Managing Job Stress* (Boston: Little, Brown, & Co., 1981) p. 2.
10. "The Road to Happiness," *Psychology Today,* July/August 1994, Vol. 27, No. 4, p. 34.
11. S. C. Kobasa, "Stressful Life Events, Personality, and Health: An Inquiry into Hardiness," *Journal of Personality and Social Psychology,* 1979, 37, pp. 1–12.
12. Wallis, "Stress: Can We Cope?" p. 52.
13. Brief, Schuler, and Sell, *Managing Job Stress,* p. 86.
14. W. W. Suoganen and Donald R. Hudson, "Coping with Stress and Addictive Work Behavior," *Business* (College of Business Administration, Georgia State University), 31 (January–February 1980), p. 11.
15. Robert T. Golembiewski and Robert F. Munzenrider, *Phases of Burnout* (New York: Praeger, 1988), p. 220.
16. Oliver I. Niehouse, "Controlling Burnout: A Leadership Code for Managers," *Business Horizons,* July–August 1984, pp. 81–82.
17. Herbert Benson and Miriam Z. Klipper, *The Relaxation Response* (New York: William Morrow & Co., 1975), pp. 114–115.
18. "The Road to Happiness," *Psychology Today,* July–August 1994, Vol. 27, No. 4, p. 37.

Chapter 16

1. Sharon M. Tarrant, "Setting Up an Electronic Job-Posting System," *Training & Development* 48 (January 1994), pp. 39–42.
2. Shari Caudron, "Online Job-Posting Facilitates Lateral Transfer at Household International," *Personnel Journal* 73 (April 1994), p. 64J.
3. "Taking Advantage," WGN TV station (Chicago), February 19, 1984.
4. "Is the DOT Guilty of Overkill?" *Railway Age* 195

(May 1994), pp. 65–67; and Lori Sharn, "Transport Workers Face Breath Tests," *USA Today,* February 4, 1994, p. 3A.
5. See "Adoption by Four Agencies of Uniform Guidelines on Employee Selection Procedures (1978)," *Federal Register* 43 (August 1978), pp. 290–315.
6. "Labor Report," *The Wall Street Journal,* February 23, 1993 p. A1.
7. Julia Lawlor, "Disabilities No Longer a Job Barrier," *USA Today,* June 22, 1993, pp. 1A and 1B.
8. Michael A. Verespej, "How Will You Know Whom to Hire? No More Questions About Medical History," *Industry Week,* September 17, 1990, p. 70.
9. J. Fraser, "The Making of a Work Force," *Business Month,* September 1989, pp. 58, 60–61.
10. "In Search of Survival," *Inc.,* November 1985, p. 90.
11. Jerry McLain, "Practice Makes Perfect," *Office Systems 9512* (April 1995), pp. 74 and 76–77.
12. Hedrick Smith, "Future Jobs Less College-Oriented," *USA Today,* June 19, 1995, p. 11A.
13. William E. Reif, "Intrinsic versus Extrinsic Rewards: Resolving the Controversy," *Human Resources Management* 14 (Summer 1975), p. 7.
14. Shawn Tully, "Are You Paid Enough?" *Fortune,* June 26, 1995, p. 72.
15. George Ming, "All the Parts of Comparable Worth," *Personnel Journal* 69 (November 1990, p. 99.
16. *Employee Benefits, 1992 Edition* (Washington, D.C.: U.S. Chamber of Commerce, 1992).

Chapter 17

1. Robert Cyr, "Seven Steps to Better Performance Appraisals," *Training & Developing*

47 (January 1993), pp. 18–19.
2. Ren Nardoni, "Corporate-wide Management Staffing," *Personnel Journal* 69 (April 1990), pp. 52–58.
3. Kenneth M. Golden, "Dealing with the Problem Manager," *Personnel* 66 (August 1989), pp. 54–59.
4. "Evaluations Get a Makeover as Employers Seek to Make Them Useful," *The Wall Street Journal,* May 2, 1995, p. A1.
5. *Appraising Managerial Performance: Current Practice and Future Directions,* Conference Board Report No. 723 (New York: Conference Board, 1977), p. 26.
6. Robert L. Mathis and John H. Jackson, *Personnel/Human Resource Management* (St. Paul, Minn.: West Publishing Co., 1991), p. 299.
7. Leon C. Megginson, Geralyn M. Franklin, and M. Jane Byrd, *Human Resource Management* (Houston: Dame Publications, 1995), pp. 365–368.
8. Mary Mavis, "Painless Performance Evaluations," *Training & Development* 48 (October 1994), pp. 40–44.
9. Douglas McGregor, "An Uneasy Look at Performance Appraisals," *Harvard Business Review* 35 (May–June 1957), p. 90.
10. L. Stockford and W. H. Bissell, "Factors Involved in Establishing a Merit Rating Scale," *Personnel* 26 (September 1949), p. 97.
11. H. H. Meyer and W. B. Walker, "A Study of Factors Relating to the Effectiveness of a Performance Appraisal Program," *Personnel Psychology* 14 (August 1961), pp. 291–298.
12. For further details, see Irwin H. McMaster, "Universal Aspects of Discipline," *Supervision* 36 (April 1974), p. 19.
13. Walter Kiechel, "How to Discipline in the Modern Age," *Fortune,* May 7, 1990, p. 179.

14. Laurie Baum, "Punishing Workers with a Day Off," *Business Week,* June 16, 1986, p. 80.

15. "Entry-Level Job Requirements Get Stiffer Every Year," *The Wall Street Journal,* May 16, 1995, p. A1.

16. M. Michael Markowich, "A Positive Approach to Discipline," *Personnel* 66 (August 1989), pp. 60–65.

17. "Degree of Discipline," *Manager's Legal Bulletin,* April 15, 1991, pp. 1–2.

18. *Employee Conduct and Discipline,* Personnel Policies Forum Survey No. 102 (Washington, D.C.: The Bureau of National Affairs, Inc., August 1973), pp. 1–2.

19. Dennis Lindsey, "Of Sound Mind? Evaluating the Workforce" *Security Management* 38 (September 1994), pp. 69–71.

20. Equal Employment Opportunity Commission, *Guidelines on Discrimination Because of Sex,* 29 C.F.R., Section 1064.11 (July 1, 1992).

21. Constance Johnson, "Court Cases Give Firms Guidance on Sexual Harassment," *The Wall Street Journal,* May 17, 1995, p. B2.

22. Margaret A. Jacobs, "Del Laboratories Agrees to Record Sum for Settling Sexual-Harassment Lawsuit," *The Wall Street Journal,* August 4, 1995, p. B2.

23. *Payne v. Western & A.R.P. Co.,* 81 Tenn. 507 (1884).

24. S. A. Youngblood and G. L. Tidwel, "Termination-at-Will: Some Changes in the Wind," *Personnel* 58 (May–June 1981), p. 24.

25. For a state-by-state guide to how easily an employer can fire a worker, contact Jill Henderson, CUE, 1331 Pennsylvania Avenue NW, Suite 1500, North Lobby, Washington, DC 20004, for a copy of the National Association's publication *Employment Law in the 50 States.*

Chapter 18

1. Michael Gartner, "Unions Can Still Speak for the Little Guy," *USA Today,* June 20, 1955, p. 11A.

2. "Washington Watch: Power Without Press," *Working Woman,* July 19, 1994, p. 12.

3. "Unions on the Ropes," *USA Today,* June 14, 1995, p. 12A.

4. Susan Dentzer, "Anti-Union, but Not Anti-Unity," *U.S. News & World Report,* July 17, 1995, p. 47.

5. "Are Unions Striking Out?" *U.S. News & World Report,* June 12, 1995, p. 26.

6. "Unions on the Ropes."

7. "Union 'Downsizing' Fuels Struggle at Top," *Mobile (Alabama) Press Register,* July 5, 1995, p. 6–B.

8. R. Wendell Moore, "The Smaller They Are, the Better They Grow," *USA Today,* March 20, 1992, p. A13; and Constant J. Pritchard, "Forget the Fortune 500," *The Wall Street Journal,* "Managing Your Career," Fall 1992, p. 12.

9. Mortimer B. Zuckerman, "The GOP's New Bedfellows," *U.S. News & World Report,* April 24, 1995, p. 72.

10. Joseph P. Cangemi et al., "Differences Between Pro-Union and Pro-Company Employees," *Personnel Journal* 55 (September 1976), pp. 451–453.

11. Phillip Ash, "The Parties to the Grievance," *Personnel Psychology* 23 (Spring 1970), pp. 13–37.

A

accountability the obligation that is created when a person accepts duties and responsibilities from higher management.

achievement, proficiency, or skill tests a test that measures fairly accurately the applicant's knowledge of and ability to do a given job; used to spot trade bluffers.

acknowledging showing through a range of nonevaluative verbal responses that you have listened to what the employee has stated.

active listening a listening technique in which the listener makes a response so as to encourage feedback.

administrative skills managerial skills that permit managers at all levels to use their other skills effectively in performing the managerial functions; include the ability to establish and follow policies and procedures and to process paperwork in an orderly manner.

advisory authority the authority of most staff departments to serve and advise the line departments.

affirmative action programs (AAPs) programs encouraged by the Equal Employment Opportunity Commission to put the principle of equal employment opportunity into practice.

affirming communicating to an employee his or her value, strengths, and contributions or other positive factors.

agency shop an agreement under which all employees must pay union dues even if they choose not to join the union; compare to *closed shop, union shop*.

agreement or contract the document prepared when an accord has been reached to bind the company, union, and workers to specific clauses, which it spells out.

alternatives possible courses of action that can satisfy a need or solve a problem.

anchors brief statements of actual worker behavior on the job.

androgynous leadership behavior leadership styles that mix so-called masculine characteristics (such as assertiveness, competition, and independence) with so-called feminine characteristics (such as cooperation, accommodation, and nurturance).

appraisal interview an interview in which the supervisor communicates the results of a performance appraisal to an employee.

appraiser bias(es) conscious or unconscious educational, racial, or interpersonal conflict.

apprenticeship training training that blends the learning of theory with practice in the techniques of the job; combines classroom instruction with hands-on experience.

aptitude tests employment tests used to predict how a person might perform on a given job; most useful for operative jobs.

arbitrator an outside agent, called in when collective bargaining reaches an impasse, who will make a binding decision.

attending showing through nonverbal behavior that you are listening in an open, nonjudgmental manner.

authority the right to tell others to act or not act in order to reach objectives.

authority compliance or **task management** a leadership style based on the leader's having a high concern for production results and using a directive approach; position 9,1 on the *Leadership Grid®*.

B

baby busters the generation of the workforce born between 1965 and 1975; they are thought of as idealistic and concerned about quality-of-life issues.

behaviorally anchored rating scales (BARS) scales designed to specify more objectively the actual job behaviors being evaluated.

benchmarking the process of comparing company practices and methods against the practices of firms who are world-class performers.

body signals nonverbal signals such as slumped posture, clenched fist, raised eyebrows, or the act of kicking a piece of equipment.

budget a forecast of expected financial performance over a period of time.

burnout a malady caused by excessive stress in the setting where people invest most of their time and energy.

C

cause-and-effect diagram a graphical display of a chain of causes and effects; also called a fishbone or Ishikawa diagram.

central tendency the tendency for the ratings to cluster around some intermediate point on the scale.

change the process of altering, modifying, or transforming one state, condition, or phase to another.

channel the means used to pass a message in the communication process.

closed shop an agreement under which all prospective employees must be members of the recognized union before they can be employed and all current employees must join within a specified time in order to retain their jobs; compare to *agency shop, union shop*.

closure successfully accomplishing the objective for a given item on the agenda.

coaching the interpersonal process that supervisors and managers use to help individuals continually reach their highest levels of performance.

coaching and selling style in the Hersey-Blanchard *Situational Leadership Model*, a high-task and high-relationship leadership style, used with individuals or groups that have potential but haven't realized it fully.

cohesiveness the degree to which group members pull in the same direction and have unity.

collective bargaining the process in which the representatives of the employer and the employees meet at reasonable times and places to confer in good faith over wages, hours, and other terms and conditions of employment.

communication process model a model that shows the five components of communication (*sender, message, channel, receiver*, and *feedback*) and their relationships.

comparable worth or pay equity the evaluation of work based on a formula whereby points are assigned for the amount of education, effort, skill, and responsibility required for an individual job; jobs with equal points have equal pay.

computer-assisted manufacturing (CAM) a manufacturing system in which special computers assist automated equipment in performing the processes necessary for production.

conceptual skills managerial skills that involve the ability to acquire, analyze, and interpret information in a logical manner.

confirming making sure that an employee understands what has been said or agreed upon.

conflict management the facilitator's responsibility to become aware of the causes and appropriate levels of conflict for various situations and react accordingly.

confronting/challenging the coaching function most directly performance-related and establishes clear performance standards, compares actual performance against the standards, and addresses performance that doesn't meet those standards.

consensus the acceptance by all members of the decision reached.

constructive criticism criticism offered in a spirit of helpfulness toward correction of a condition that can be corrected.

consumer price index (CPI) a government indicator that measures changes in the price of a group of goods and services that make up the typical consumer's budget.

contingency planning thinking in advance about possible problems or changes that might arise so that we are prepared to deal with them smoothly when they do arise.

continuum of leadership behavior a leadership model devised by Robert Tannenbaum and Warren Schmidt to show the full range of leadership behaviors in terms of the relationship between the use of authority by a supervisor and the area of freedom for employees.

control chart the "backbone" of statistical process control (SPC) and displays the "state of control" of a process.

controlling comparing actual performance with planned standards and taking corrective action, if needed, to ensure that objectives are achieved.

cost/benefit analysis estimating what each alternative will cost in terms of human, physical, and financial resources and then estimating the benefits and comparing the two.

cost-of-living adjustments (COLAs) increases in wages in direct proportion to increases in the *consumer price index (CPI)*.

counseling the coaching function whereby the supervisor helps an individual recognize, talk about, gain insight into, and solve either real or perceived problems that affect performance.

country club management a supportive, permissive leadership style characterized by high concern for people and little concern for production; position 1,9 on the *Leadership Grid*.

craft unions a union of workers in a specific skill, craft, or trade.

D

decentralization the extent to which authority is delegated from one level or one unit of the organization to another.

decision making the conscious considerations and selection of a course of action from among available alternatives in order to produce a desired result.

delegating style in the Hersey-Blanchard *Situational Leadership Model*, a low-relationship and low-task leadership style, used with exceptionally mature and capable individuals and groups.

delegation of authority the process by which managers grant authority to the people who report to them.

Deming's 85-15 rule a rule embodying the theories of Dr. W. Edwards Deming, a world-renowned statistical quality control advocate; this rule assumes that when things go wrong, 85 percent of the time the cause is attributed to elements controlled by management (such as machinery, materials, or processes), while only about 15 percent of the time are employees at fault.

disciplinary layoff or suspension time off without pay given to serious disciplinary offenders to allow them to consider the possible consequences of their actions.

discipline training that corrects, molds, or perfects knowledge, attitudes, behavior, or conduct.

distribution the *organizational activity* of marketing and distributing the organization's product or service.

diverse groups groups that employers should make good-faith efforts to recruit under affirmative action programs; include women, African-Americans, Hispanics, Vietnam-era veterans, the disabled, and older workers.

downsizing the process of eliminating unnecessary levels of management and thus reducing the number of staff personnel and supervisors.

downward communication communication flows that originate with managers and supervisors and pass down to employees.

drug testing an employment test to determine whether an applicant is a drug abuser.

dual promotion ladders an advancement plan whereby skilled technical and scientific workers can get salary increases and higher job titles without becoming managers.

due process a procedure which guarantees (a) that the individual accused of violating an established rule or law will get a hearing to determine the extent of guilt and (b) that the established penalties will be imposed only after the hearing is conducted.

E

ego *or* **esteem needs** the fourth level in Maslow's *hierarchy of needs*, including such needs as self-confidence, independence, recognition, appreciation, and status.

electronic job posting a job-posting software program to make filling jobs from within more efficient.

Employee Assistance Program (EAP) formal professional counseling and medical services programs for an organization's employees confronted by unresolved personal or work-related problems.

employee associations organizations composed of government, white-collar, agricultural, or service employees, as well as professionals, that function as labor unions.

employee benefits financial rewards and services provided to employees in addition to their regular earnings.

employee comparison method a traditional method of *performance appraisal* in which supervisors are required to rank the performance and value to the organization of each of their employees in comparison to the others.

employees' bill of rights provisions of the Labor-Management Reporting and Disclosure Act (Landrum-Griffin Act) that protect employees from possible abuse by unscrupulous managers and union leaders.

empowerment the granting of authority to employees to make key decisions within their areas of responsibility.

equity theory the theory that positive motivation can be achieved by reducing workers' feelings that they are treated inequitably relative to other workers.

ethical dilemmas situations where a person is not certain what is the correct behavior expected.

ethics the standards used to judge the "rightness" or "wrongness" of one person's behavior toward others.

exclusive bargaining agent the employee's representative who deals exclusively with management over questions of wages, hours, and other terms and conditions of employment.

exempt employees employees not covered by the provisions of the Fair Labor Standards Act; includes executives, administrative and professional employees, outside sales personnel, and other selected groups.

expectancy theory the theory that workers expect that a good effort, resulting in effective performance, will be followed by a reward.

experience rating an employer's record of unemployed workers, which is used, along with the state's unemployment rate, to determine the amount the employer must pay into the state's unemployment insurance fund.

experiential learning the procedure through which one learns by doing and uses mistakes as an opportunity to figure out how to avoid them in the future.

F

fact-finding meeting a meeting held to seek out relevant facts about a problem or situation.

feedback the response that a communicator receives from the receiver of a message.

feeling decision process a decision style that gives greater weight to the human issues involved or the "people" side of a decision.

financial resources the money, capital, and credit required by an organization for its operations.

financing the *organizational activity* of providing or using funds in order to produce and distribute the organization's product or service.

flexcomp or cafeteria benefit plans a method of providing employees with flexible benefit packages.

flowchart a visual representation of the sequence of steps needed to complete a process.

formal roles behaviors within a group that are written out in job descriptions.

full empowerment a level of empowerment in which the total organization is involved.

functional authority a staff person's limited line authority over a given *function*, such as safety or quality, regardless of where that function is found in the organization.

G

gainsharing a system whereby employees' financial rewards are linked to the performance of an entire unit.

Gantt chart a visual progress report that identifies work stages or activities on a vertical axis and scheduled completion dates horizontally.

glass ceiling jargon for invisible barriers that limit the advancement of women into higher levels of the organization.

goal-setting theory the theory of motivation that undergirds the other motivational theories that states achievement-oriented people set difficult but attainable goals and appreciate feedback and positive reinforcement for achieving these goals.

graduated scale of penalties a plan whereby punishment for a given violation becomes progressively more severe each time the violation is repeated.

grapevine a type of informal communication in organizations, also called "the rumor mill".

grievance procedure a formal way of handling employees' complaints; usually outlines the steps to be taken.

group dynamics the social process by which people interact in small groups.

group facilitation the process of intervening to help a group improve in goal setting, action planning, problem solving, conflict management, and decision making in order to increase the group's effectiveness.

group-centered approach an approach used at meetings in which group members interact freely and address and question one another, with no one dominating the discussions.

H

halo effect rater's tendency to rate an employee *high* on all factors being evaluated as a result of the rater's impression of the employee's worth to the organization.

heroic leaders (command and control) leaders who have a great need for control and influence and who want to run things.

hierarchy of needs the theory of psychologist Abraham Maslow that (a) people's needs may be arranged in a hierarchy, or ranking of importance, and (b) once a need has been satisfied, it no longer serves as a primary motivator of behavior.

hierarchy of objectives a network of objectives, beginning with broad goals at the top level of the organization and becoming more specific and narrower for individual divisions, departments, or employees.

histogram a graphical representation of the variation found in a set of data.

horn effect rater's tendency to rate an employee *low* on all factors being evaluated as a result of the rater's impression of the employee's worth to the organization.

hot-stove rule a concept that compares a good disciplinary system to a hot stove in that discipline should (a) carry advance warning, (b) be immediate, (c) be consistent, and (d) be impersonal.

human relations skills managerial skills needed to understand other people and to interact effectively with them.

human resources the people required by an organization for its operations.

hygiene factors factors in a job situation that can prevent serious dissatisfaction or a drop in productivity, thereby preventing loss of morale or efficiency, but cannot motivate by themselves; compare to *motivators*.

I

"I" message an appeal, rather than a demand, that the other person change; focuses on behavior, effect, and how it makes you feel.

impoverished management a leadership style with little concern for people or production; position 1,1 on the *Leadership Grid®*.

incentive wages or performance pay a compensation method in which an employee's wages are determined by the amount of goods and services the employee produced (output).

industrial unions unions composed of all the workers in an industry, such as coal, whether they are craftsmen, unskilled workers, or clerical employees.

informal communication communication that occurs separately from the formal, established communication system.

informal roles behaviors for group members that are not stated in writing but develop as a result of the dynamics within the group.

information exchange meeting a meeting held to make announcements of new programs and policies or to update the present ones.

information-giving meeting a meeting held to make announcements of new programs and policies or to update the present ones.

intangible standards standards that are not expressed in terms of numbers, money, physical qualities, or time

because they relate to human characteristics that are difficult to measure, such as a desirable attitude, high morale, ethics, and cooperation.

intermediaries go-betweens who act as mediators; for example, supervisors are intermediaries between their employees and higher levels of management.

internship training a method of learning in which on-the-job training at a cooperating business is combined with classwork at a school or college.

intolerable offenses disciplinary problems of such a drastic, dangerous, or illegal nature that they severely strain or endanger employment relationships.

intuition a basis for decision making derived from the unconscious influence of a person's cultural background, education, and training, as well as knowledge of the situation.

inverted pyramid an organization form with a structure widest at the top and narrowing as it funnels down.

IQ tests tests designed to measure the applicant's capacity to learn, to solve problems, and to understand relationships.

ISO 9000 registration certifying that a company meets certain quality standards in such areas as product design and development, manufacturing processes, testing, final inspection, installation, and service.

J

job analysis the process of gathering information and determining the elements of a job by observation and study.

job descriptions written statements that spell out the primary duties , authority, responsibilities, and working conditions of specific jobs, as well as other job-related activities.

job dimensions a group of duties, activities, and responsibilities that are part of the job.

job evaluation a process used to determine the relative value of jobs to an employer in order to determine more objectively the appropriate earnings for employees doing given jobs.

job involvement a level of empowerment in which jobs are defined so that employees use a broad variety of skills and control the work content of their jobs.

job posting the procedure of placing announcements of available job openings on a bulletin board to give current employees a chance to bid on them.

job specification a statement of the personal characteristics required of a person to perform a described job.

just-in-time inventory control (JIT) a system in which needed materials arrive as close as is feasible to the time they are needed in the production process.

K

KISS principle a general guide for public speaking; stands for "Keep It Short and Simple."

L

labor relations or union management relations or industrial relations the relationship between an employer and unionized employees.

labor union an organization of workers banded together to achieve economic goals, especially increased wages and benefits, shorter working hours, improved working conditions, and both personal and job security.

lateral-diagonal communication communication that takes place between individuals in the same department or in different departments.

law of effect a law which holds that activities that meet with pleasant consequences tend to be repeated, whereas activities that meet with unpleasant consequences tend not to be repeated.

leader-controlled approach an approach used at information-giving meetings or meetings of large groups in which the leader clearly runs the show and the open flow of information is impeded.

leadership a process of influencing individual and group activities toward goal setting and goal achievement.

Leadership Grid® a leadership model devised by Robert Blake and Jane Mouton that categorizes leadership styles according to two factors-concern for people and concern for production results-which are used as the axes of a graph or grid; originally published as the Managerial Grid.

leading conducting, guiding, enhancing, and supervising employees in the performance of their duties and responsibilities; coaching and empowering employees; facilitating their activities; communicating ideas and instructions; and motivating employees to perform their work efficiently.

life event anything that causes a person to deviate from normal functioning.

life-cycle theory of leadership a situational theory of leadership which holds that leadership behaviors (*task behaviors* and *relationship behaviors*) should be based on the maturity level of employees.

Likert's System 4 a system in which management views its role as ensuring the best decisions are made through a decentralized participate-group structure.

line authority the power to directly command or exact performance from others.

line organization an organizational structure in which each person has clearly defined responsibilities and reports to an immediate supervisor.

line personnel employees who carry out the primary activities of a business, such as producing or selling products and/or services.

line-and-staff organization a line organization to which staff departments have been added.

lockout a company's closing its premises to the employee and refusing to let them work.

M

maintenance-of-membership clause a statement in a union agreement which says that an employee who has joined the union must maintain that membership as a condition of employment.

major violations disciplinary problems that substantially interfere with orderly operations.

Malcolm Baldrige National Quality Award an award symbolizing America's best in quality; named for the much admired former U.S. Secretary of Commerce, Malcolm Baldrige, who died in 1987, the award is administered by the National Institute of Standards and Technology, with endowments covering costs of administration and judging of applicants.

malicious obedience a reaction in which an aggrieved employee follows instructions exactly, knowing that the order is faulty and will cause problems.

management the process of working with and through people to achieve objectives by means of effective decision making and coordination of available resources.

management by exception a control procedure or philosophy in which a supervisor focuses attention on the most critical control needs and allows employees to handle most routine deviations from the standard.

management by objectives (MBO) a system in which managers and their employees jointly establish objectives and develop a systematic approach for monitoring results.

managerial functions the acts or operations expected of a manager in a given situation, including *planning, organizing, staffing, leading,* and *controlling.*

maturity level the state of a person's drive or need for achievement as a result of experience, education, attitudes, and willingness and ability to accept responsibility; should be considered only in relation to a specific task to be performed.

mediator an outside agent, provided by the Federal Mediation and Conciliation Service, who tries to bring the parties together when collective bargaining has reached an impasse.

mentoring the coaching activity that helps develop careers in others and may teach political savvy, understanding of the organization's culture, and the ways to advance one's career.

merit an employee's ability to do the job better than others; a basis for promotion.

message words and/or nonverbal expressions that are capable of transmitting meaning.

middle management the management level responsible for a substantial part of the organization (perhaps a program, project, division, plant, or department).

middle of the road management a leadership style placing equal emphasis on people and production; position 5,5 on the *Leadership Grid*.

minor infractions violations of rules that do little harm or result in few serious consequences.

minutes a written record of the important points discussed and agree upon at a meeting.

mission a part of a plan that defines the fundamental purpose the organization attempts to serve and identifies its services, products, and customers.

monetary standards standards expressed in dollars and cents, such as predetermined profit margins, payroll costs, scrap costs, and maintenance costs.

motivation the willingness of a person or a group, with distinctive needs and personality, to work to achieve the organization's objectives, while also working to achieve individual objectives.

motivators factors in a job situation that have an uplifting effect on attitude or performance; compare to *hygiene factors*.

N

negative discipline an outside force or influence designed to change a person's behavior.

network form an organization form that uses the collective assets of several firms located at various points along the value chain.

nonexempt employees employees covered by the provisions of the Fair Labor Standards Act.

norms of behavior standards that define what is and is not acceptable behavior within the group.

numerical standards standards expressed in numbers, such as number of items produced, number of absences, percentage of successful sales calls, or number of personnel who successfully complete training.

O

object signals nonverbal messages sent by physical objects such as office furniture, protective helmets, plush carpet, plaques and awards on the wall, clothing or jewelry worn.

objectives or goals the focus toward which plans are aimed; a definition of where the organization is going or what it wants to accomplish.

Occupational Safety and Health Administration (OSHA) a federal agency that was created by the Occupational Safety and Health Act in 1970 and went into operation in April 1971.

on-the-job training (OJT) training in which employees actually perform the work under the supervision and guidance of the supervisor or a trained worker or instructor.

operational planning a management level of planning that consists of intermediate and short-term planning that facilitates achievement of the long-term strategic plans set at higher levels.

operations the *organizational activity* of producing the organization's product or service.

opportunity a chance for development, progress, or advancement.

organization a group of people working together in a structured situation to achieve a common objective.

organization change the way an organization adapts to its external and internal environment.

organizing deciding what activities are needed to reach goals and objectives, dividing human resources into work groups, and assigning each group to a manager; also, bringing together the physical, financial, and human resources needed to achieve the organization's objectives.

orientation procedures of familiarizing a new employee with the company surroundings, policies, and job responsibilities.

P

paired-comparison technique a variant of the employee comparison method of *performance appraisal* in which an employee is compared, in turn, to each of the other employees in the work group.

Pareto chart problem-analysis charts that use a *histogram* to graphically illustrate the sources of problems.

parity principle the principle that, when responsibilities and duties are assigned, adequate authority should be delegated to those who must meet the responsibilities and carry out the assignments.

participating and supporting style in the Hersey-Blanchard *Situational Leadership Model*, a high-relationship and low-task leadership style, best used with mature individuals or groups.

partnering a process used by disparate organizations working together to develop trust, improve communications, and build teams; turn resisting forces into positive forces; and develop a common set of goals and objectives along with a partnering agreement that all parties sign.

peer rating or mutual rating system a traditional method of *performance appraisal* wherein each employee anonymously appraises the performance of the other members of the work group.

perception the process by which one selects, organizes, and gives meaning to his or her world.

performance appraisal or merit rating or efficiency rating or service rating or employee evaluation the process used to determine to what extent an employee is performing a job in the way it was intended to be done.

performance objectives objectives that tell employees what they must do to make their performance acceptable.

personality tests employment tests that are supposed to measure the applicant's emotional adjustment and attitude; often used to evaluate interpersonal relationships and to see how a person might fit into an organization.

Peter Principle a management principle, enunciated by Laurence J. Peter and Raymond Hull, which states that "in a hierarchy, every employee rises to his [or her] level of incompetence."

physical resources buildings, furnishings, machinery, equipment, tools, materials, and supplies required by an organization for its operations.

physical standards standards that refer to quality, durability, size, weight, and other factors related to physical composition.

physiological *or* **biological needs** the lowest level in Maslow's *hierarchy of needs*, including the need for food, water, air, and other physical necessities.

picketing demonstrating dissatisfaction with one's employer by walking back and forth outside the place of employment, usually carrying a sign explaining the reasons for one's dissatisfaction.

pinpointing providing specific, tangible information to an employee.

planning selecting future courses of action for the organization as a whole and for each of its subunits and deciding how to achieve the desired results; involves gathering and analyzing information.

policy a guide to decision making designed to provide consistency among decision makers.

polygraph (lie detector) a device used to measure a person's changes in respiration, blood pressure, and electrothermal response under extensive questioning; these changes may indicate when a person is lying.

positive discipline an inner force that promotes emotional satisfaction instead of emotional conflict.

positive reinforcement theory a theory of motivation, based on the *law of effect*, which holds that favorable activities will be encouraged (reinforced) by a reward and discouraged by punishment or lack of reward.

prevailing wage rate a rate of pay set by the Secretary of Labor that approximates the union wage scale for the area in the given type of work.

preventive controls actions taken before or during the course of a job to prevent things from going wrong.

principle of supportive relationships a principle which holds that the team leader's actions with employees should be supportive and maintain employees' sense of personal worth and importance.

principled negotiation an alternative to positional bargaining that is composed of the following: (1) separating the people from the problem; (2) focusing on interests, not positions; (3) generating a variety of possibilities before deciding what to do; and (4) insisting that the result be based on some objective standard.

private industry councils (PICs) groups headed by company executives and local business people that help employers with training activities.

proactive quality approach an aggressive approach to managing quality that focuses on building quality into the process in advance rather than on "inspecting it into" the system.

probe an *active listening* technique that is more specific than the *reflective statement*, directing attention to a particular aspect of the speaker's message.

probing asking questions to obtain additional information or exploring a topic at greater length.

problem an existing unsatisfactory situation causing anxiety or distress.

problem-solving meeting a meeting held to identify the major elements of a problem, to discuss alternative solutions and evaluate them, and ultimately to make a decision as to the proper action to take.

problem-solving quality approach an approach to managing quality that emphasizes identification of defects through the traditional approach while rigorously seeking remedy to these problems through team problem-solving techniques such as quality teams.

procedure an outline of the steps to be performed when a particular course of action is taken.

process consultation a consultation model that involves others in making a joint diagnosis of the problem and eventually providing others with the skills and tools to make their own diagnoses.

productivity a measure of efficiency in terms of inputs as compared to outputs.

program a large-scale plan composed of a mix of objectives, policies, rules, and projects; outlines the specific steps to be taken to achieve its objectives, including the time, money, and human resources required; essentially a set of single-use plans that are carried out over a period of time.

Program Evaluation and Review Technique (PERT) a management scheduling tool which shows relationships among a network of activities and events to determine the completion time of a project.

programmed decisions decisions that are routine and repetitive.

progressive discipline discipline that uses a *graduated scale of penalties*.

project a distinct, smaller part of a *program*.

project or **matrix organization** a hybrid type of organizational structure in which both functional departments and project teams exist.

promoting moving a person from a lower- to a higher-level job; usually involves an increase in pay as well as responsibilities.

punishment a negative treatment that a person receives after an undesirable act or omission.

Q

quality the features and characteristics of a product that improve its ability to satisfy the requirements of customers.

quality assurance the entire system of policies, procedures, and guidelines that an organization institutes so as to attain and maintain quality; compare to *quality control*.

quality control defined measurements that are designed to check whether the desired quality standards are being met; compare to *quality assurance*.

R

rate range a range of minimum and maximum wage rates for a given job, with employees paid at different rates, depending on how well they perform.

rating scale a point scale used in a traditional method of *performance appraisal* to rate an employee on a number of characteristics.

receiver the ultimate destination of the sender's message in the communication process.

reengineered wiping the slate clean as far as current operations are concerned and revamping the organization.

reengineering a fundamental rethinking and redesign process to achieve improvements in a critical area of performance, such as cost, quality, service, or speed.

reflecting stating in your own words your interpretation of what the employee has said or feels.

reflective statement an active listening technique in which the listener repeats, in a summarizing way, what the speaker has just said.

reframing an aspect of management education emphasizing management training and development programs.

reinvention recasting something old or familiar into a different form.

relationship behaviors leadership behaviors such as providing people with support, giving them positive feedback, and asking for their opinions and ideas.

relaxation response a meditative technique that helps relieve tensions, enables one to deal more effectively with stress, lowers blood pressure, and, in general, improves physical and emotional health.

reliability the probability that the results of a test will be the same if it is given to the same person by different individuals.

resourcing providing information, assistance, and advice to employees.

responsibility the obligation that is created when an employee accepts a manager's delegated authority.

reviewing reinforcing key points at the end of a coaching session to ensure common understanding.

right-to-work laws state laws giving employees the right to join or refuse to join a union without being fired.

risk the possibility of defeat, disadvantage, injury, or loss.

robot a machine, controlled by a computer, that can be programmed to perform a number of repetitive manipulations of tools or materials.

roles (1) parts played by managers in the performance of their functions, classified as (a) interpersonal roles, (b) informational roles, and (c) decision-making roles; (2) behaviors expected among group members.

rule a policy that is invariably enforced.

run chart a data presentation that shows the results of a process plotted over a period of time.

S

safety or **security needs** the second level in Maslow's *hierarchy of needs*, including the need for protection from danger, threat, or deprivation.

schedule a plan showing activities to be performed and their timing.

self-fulfillment or **self-actualization needs** the highest level in Maslow's *hierarchy of needs*, including needs concerned with the realization of one's potential, self-development, and creativity.

self-managing work teams teams to which control of work and process is transferred from the traditional control manager.

sender the person who originates and sends a message in the communication process.

seniority an employee's length of service in a company; a basis for promotion.

sexual harassment unwelcome sexual advances and requests for sexual favors or other physical or verbal conduct, by a member of either sex, when such actions interfere with an employee's work performance or create a hostile, offensive, or intimidating work environment.

"Siamese twins" of management the managerial functions of planning and controlling, so called because planning is such an integral part of controlling.

single rate a compensation plan under which everyone who performs the same job is paid the same wage, regardless of level of performance.

single-use plans plans that are developed to accomplish a specific purpose and then discarded after use, including *programs, projects,* and *budgets.*

Situational Leadership® Model a leadership model devised by Paul Hersey and Kenneth Blanchard that shows the relationship between the maturity of followers and the leadership style in terms of the leader's *task behaviors* and *relationship behaviors.*

social *or* **belonging needs** the third level in Maslow's *hierarchy of needs,* including needs for belonging, association, acceptance by colleagues, friendship, and love.

space signals nonverbal messages sent by actions such as huddling close, being distant, or sitting beside someone.

span of control principle a management principle which states that there is a limit to the number of people a person can supervise effectively.

span of management or **span of control** the number of immediate employees a manager can supervise effectively.

staff personnel employees who have the expertise to assist line people and aid top management in various areas of business activities.

staffing the process of recruiting, selecting, training and developing, promoting, and paying and rewarding people to do the organization's work; includes laying off and terminating employees.

standard a unit of measurement that can serve as a reference point for evaluating results.

standing plans or repeat-use plans plans that are used repeatedly over a period of time, including *policies, rules,* and *procedures.*

status the "pecking order" of a group, which is dependent on factors such as seniority, expertise, job classification, and job location.

stereotyping the tendency to put similar things in the same categories to make them easier to deal with.

strategic control point a performance-measurement point located sufficiently early in an activity to allow any necessary corrective action to be taken to accomplish the objective.

strategic planning a management planning system that has longer time horizons, affects the entire organization, and deals with the organization's interface with its external environment.

stress any external stimulus that causes wear and tear on one's psychological or physical well-being.

strike a situation that occurs when employees withhold their services from an employer in order to get something.

structured interviews employment interviews that are standardized and controlled with regard to questions asked, sequence of questions, interpretation of replies, and weight given to factors considered in making the value judgment as to whether or not to hire the applicant.

structuring and telling style in the Hersey-Blanchard *Situational Leadership Model,* a high-task and low-relationship leadership style, used with individuals or groups that are relatively less mature for a given task.

summarizing pausing in the coaching conversation to summarize key points.

superleadership a leadership style based on leading others to lead themselves.

supervisory management the management level that has control over the operations of smaller organizational units (such as a production line, operating unit, office, or laboratory); supervisory managers are in charge of other managers, supervisors, and nonmanagerial, or rank-and-file, employees.

T

tangible standards standards that are quite clear, concrete, specific, and generally measurable.

task behaviors leadership behaviors such as clarifying the job, telling people what to do and how and when to do it, providing follow-up, and taking corrective action.

team a collection of people who must rely on group cooperation if the group is to experience the most success possible and to achieve its goals.

team advisors supervisors who share responsibility with the team for maintaining cost, quality, and prompt and effective delivery of products.

team leaders leaders who strive to empower and develop employees.

team management a participative leadership style based on high concern for both people and production; position 9,9 on the *Leadership Grid.*

technical skills managerial skills that include understanding and being able to supervise effectively the specific processes, practices, or techniques required of specific jobs in the company.

technological unemployment a situation in which employees can no longer perform their jobs because educational or skill demands have increased beyond their capacity.

termination-at-will rule the legal standard that states that an employer has a right to dismiss an employee for any reason, or without giving a reason, unless there is an explicit contractual provision preventing it.

Theory X a leadership theory based on the assumptions that the average human being (a) has an inherent dislike of work; (b) must be coerced, controlled, directed, or threatened to work toward achieving organizational objectives; and (c) prefers to be directed, wishes to avoid responsibility, has relatively little ambition, and above all, seeks security.

Theory Y a leadership theory based on the assumptions that (a) work is as natural as play or rest, (b) the human being will exercise self-direction and self-control when committed to objectives, (c) the average person learns to accept and also seeks responsibility, (d) the capacity for imagination, ingenuity, and creativity is widely found in the population, and (e) the intellectual potential of the average person is only partially utilized in modern industrial life.

thinking decision process a decision style that focuses predominantly on analysis, logic, rationalization, and objectivity to solve problems.

time signals nonverbal messages sent by such actions as being on time or tardy, being available, or saving time.

time standards standards expressed in terms of time, such as printing deadlines, scheduled project completion dates, and rates of production (including the speed with which the job should be done).

time wages or day work a compensation method in which an employee is paid for the amount of time spent on the job, regardless of output during that period of time.

top management the management level responsible for a major segment of the organization or a basic organizational activity.

total quality approach (TQM) an approach to managing quality that reflects a major reorganization that strives to achieve customer satisfaction through continuous improvement of the organization's products and/or services and processes.

traditional quality approach an approach to managing quality that emphasizes quality assurance, quality control, or statistical quality control techniques based on random sampling.

training needs survey a survey in which supervisors state their needs on a prepared form or in interviews.

transactional leadership a traditional leadership approach similar to an exchange process whereby leaders identify desired performance standards and recognize what types of rewards employees want from their work.

transferring moving employees to a different job at the same organizational level, involving a change in duties and responsibilities, with or without a change in pay.

transformational leadership a visionary and empowering leadership style, which "converts followers into leaders and may convert leaders into moral agents;" characterized by charismatic leadership, individualized consideration, and intellectual stimulation.

tutoring the coaching situation that helps a team member gain knowledge, skill, and competency.

Type A behavior a behavior pattern characterized by (a) trying to accomplish too much in a short time and (b) lacking patience and struggling against time and other people to accomplish one's ends.

Type B behavior a behavior pattern characterized by (a) tending to be calmer than someone with *Type A behavior*, (b) devoting more time to exercise, and (c) being more realistic in estimating the time it takes to complete an assignment.

U

unfair labor practices specific acts that management may not commit against the workers and the union, as defined by the National Labor Relations Act (Wagner Act).

unified planning the coordination of plans at various management levels and for different departments or work units at the same level to ensure harmony rather than conflict or competition.

union authorization card a card to be signed by an employee, authorizing a particular union to be his or her collective bargaining representative.

union shop an agreement under which all employees must join the union within a specified period—usually 30 days—or be fired; compare to *agency shop, closed shop*.

union steward a union member elected by other members to represent their interests in relations with management.

unity of command principle a management principle which states that everyone in an organization should report to and be accountable to only one boss for performance of a given activity.

unprogrammed decisions decisions that occur infrequently and, because different variables are involved, require a separate and different response each time.

unstructured interviews employment interviews in which the pattern of questions asked, the conditions under which they are asked, and the bases for evaluating results are not standardized.

upgrading retraining unskilled or semiskilled workers to meet the changing demands of their present positions.

upward communication communication flows from lower to upper organizational levels.

V

validity a high positive correlation between the applicant's test scores and some identifiable, objective measure of performance on the job.

vocational interest tests employment tests designed to determine the applicant's areas of major work interest.

vocational rehabilitation programs programs that provide counseling, medical care, and vocational training for physically and mentally handicapped individuals.

vocational-technical education programs programs in which vocational-technical schools, business schools,

and junior colleges conduct regular or special training classes.

voice signals nonverbal messages characterized by the emphasis placed on certain words, pauses, or the tone of voice used.

W

wage surveys surveys that determine the "going rate" for jobs in the local labor market and in the industry.

wagon wheel an organization form in which figuratively there is a hub, a series of spokes radiating from the hub, and the outer rim.

work sampling or work preview a form of achievement or proficiency test in which the prospective employee must perform a task that is representative of the work usually done on the job.

ACKNOWLEDGMENTS

For permission to reproduce the photographs in the pages indicated, acknowledgment is made to the following:

0 © Greg Pease/Tony Stone Images
4 Photography by Alan Brown
15 © Todd Buchanan 1994
21 © 1995 Paul F. Gero
30 © 95 William Taufic/The Stock Market
36 © 1994 Mark M. Lawrence
41 © Kip Brundate/Woodfin Camp and Associates
50 © Andy Freeberg
60 © Charles Thatcher/Tony Stone Images
63 © PhotoDisc
67 © 1993 Greg Girard/Contact Press Images
81 © PhotoDisc
94 © David Joel/Tony Stone Images
98 © James Schnepf Photography 1995
104 © Michael L. Abramson
122 © Andy Sacks/Tony Stone Images

131 © PhotoDisc
138 Courtesy AT&T Archives
160 © Index Stock
166 Photography by Alan Brown/Photonics
182 © Roger Tully/Tony Stone Images
188 © PhotoDisc
193 Courtesy Toyota
200 © Nancy Pierce
214 © Andy Sacks/Tony Stone Images
219 © 1996 Ken Touchton
227 © 1996 Roark Johnson
242 © Steve Kahn 1990/FPG International
247 © Rick Friedman/Black Star
255 © Nation's Business/T. Michael Keza
264 © Howard Grey/Tony Stone Images
269 © 1996 Ed Kashi
284 © Paul F. Gero
292 © Michael Rosenfeld
299 © 1996 Ben Van Hook

308   © 1996 Sal DiMarco Jr./Black Star
314   © 94 John Madere/The Stock Market
320   © PhotoDisc
337   © Eli Reichman, 1995
346   © Andy Sacks/Tony Stone Images
352   Photography by Erick VonFischer/Photonics Graphics
356   © Stewart Cohen/Index Stock Photography
370   © Index Stock
377   © 1996 Robert Holmgren
392   Courtesy Philips Electronics
400   © 1995 Brownie Harris/The Stock Market

409   © PhotoDisc
420   © Andrew Garn
434   © Bruce Ayers/Tony Stone Images
442   © 1996 John Harding
466   © 1996 Michael L. Abramson
472   © Charles Thatcher/Tony Stone Images
481   © 1996 Robert Holmgren
485   © PhotoDisc
504   © Robert Kusel/Tony Stone Images
510   © PhotoDisc
523   © Jim Levitt/Impact Visuals